The most amazing places on Britain's coast

Published by
The Reader's Digest Association Limited
London • New York • Sydney • Montreal

The most amazing places on Britain's coast

Contents

Introduction

Britain boasts more miles of coast than Italy, France or Spain can muster. No shores are more amazing, from perfect beaches, dizzying cliffs and countless other wonders of nature to the manufactured genius of castles, piers and lighthouses.

Wherever you go along Britain's coast you will discover a multitude of places to thrill and fascinate you. Discover areas of outstanding natural beauty, such as the extraordinary 18-mile spit of ever-shifting shingle at Chesil Beach in Dorset; wonders crafted by man, such as the technically perfect medieval castle of Beaumaris guarding the approaches to Anglesey; or even fanciful follies, such as the water tank disguised as a weatherboarded house and named 'The House in the Clouds' at Thorpeness, Suffolk. Witness too the industrial heritage of the coast in the kipper smokehouses of Craster in Northumberland and gaunt remains of the once-thriving tin mining industry on the coast around Chapel Porth in Cornwall. This book will help you make the most of every moment spent by the sea.

Using the maps

Each of the 7 chapters in this book is introduced by a regional map (see below) that details major roads and towns, county boundaries and national parks. The coastline of this map is divided into colour-coded stretches. By each coloured strip, page numbers refer you to the relevant pages in the chapter. At the beginning of each stretch of coastline is a map (see left) that details places of interest on that stretch. Each place is numbered and follows a rough geographical progression along the coast. The numbers relate to keys that appear by each entry.

Finding your way

The Most Amazing Places on Britain's Coast starts at the Severn estuary near Bristol and proceeds in an anti-clockwise direction around the entire coast of England, Scotland and Wales, and the main offshore islands. It divides Britain's coastline into 7 regions: West Country, Southeast, East Anglia, Northeast, Scotland, Northwest and Wales. The regions are then divided into stretches of coast, each with their own map.

You can use the regional maps to find the stretch you want to visit. For example, if you are looking at the regional map for the West Country (pages 8-9) and want to explore around the Cornish resort of Rock, go to the section on Woolacombe to Rock (pages 16-23). On page 16 you will find a section map with numbered entries along that stretch. Rock is entry 31 and you will find it on page 23. Alternatively, if you're browsing the book, you can find the location of any numbered entry by consulting the map covering that particular stretch of coast and then turning to the regional map at the start of the chapter.

Scattered throughout the chapters are special features that introduce you to fascinating aspects of the seaside in each region, from beach huts in East Anglia to fishy tales from Scotland.

Planning your trip

Most of the historic buildings and other attractions included are open to the public, unless otherwise indicated, but check for opening times and seasonal closures with local tourist offices. Their telephone numbers are given in a box at the end of each stretch of coastline under 'Visitor information'.

A number of places you want to visit, such as nature reserves or historic sites, may be managed by one of the following organisations, indicated in the text by their abbreviation. Contacting them in advance can help you get the most from your visit.

EH English Heritage
www.english-heritage.org.uk
NT National Trust
www.nationaltrust.org.uk
LT Landmark Trust
www.landmarktrust.org.uk
Cadw Welsh Historic Monuments
www.cadw.wales.gov.uk
HS Historic Scotland
www.historic-scotland.gov.uk
NTS National Trust for Scotland
www.nts.org.uk
RSPB Royal Society for the Protection of Birds
www.rspb.org.uk

West Country

Lofty cliffs, broken by rocky coves, sandy bays and sheltered inlets, line the southwest peninsula of England. Long beaches of golden sand, perfect for swimming, sunbathing and watersports, attract crowds to the region in summer.

Ilfracombe

Barnstaple

Bideford

Woolacombe to Rock p16–23

Bude

Okehampton

Launceston

Dartmoor National Park

Bodmin Moor

Padstow

Bodmin

Tavistock

St Mawes to Salcombe p42–49

Newquay

Padstow to Penzance p26–33

Liskeard

St Austell

Plymouth

Truro

St Ives

Marazion to St Just in Roseland p36–41

Falmouth

Penzance

Helston

Isles of Scilly p34–35

Tresco

St Mary's

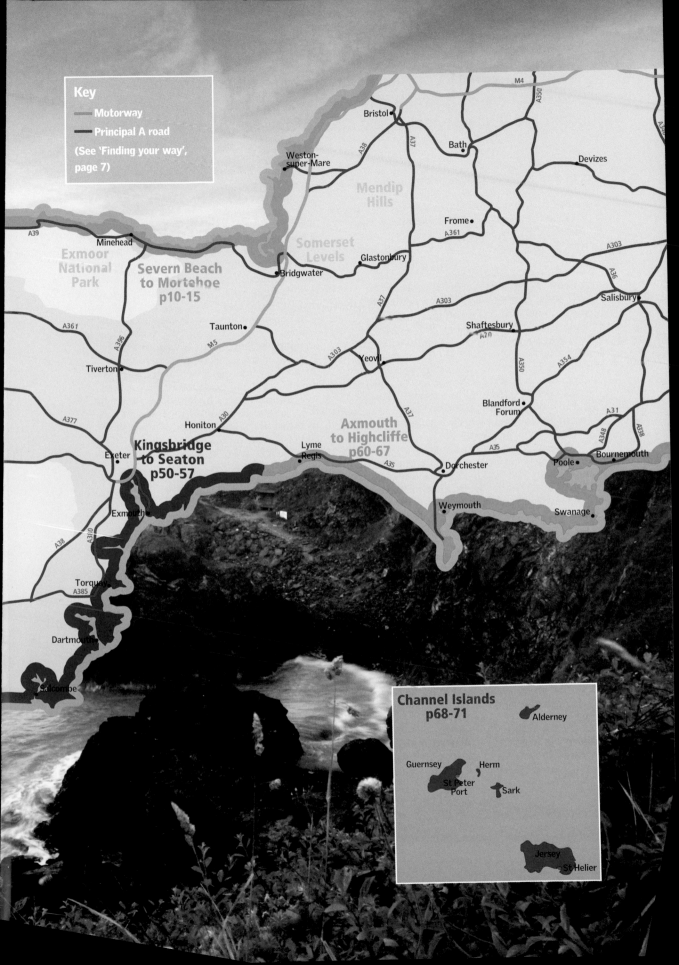

Key
— Motorway
— Principal A road
(See 'Finding your way',
page 7)

A4
M4
A350
Bristol
A38
A37
Bath
Devizes
Weston-super-Mare
A39
Mendip Hills
Frome
A361
A303
Minehead
Severn Beach to Mortehoe
p10-15
Exmoor National Park
Somerset Levels
Glastonbury
A36
A303
Bridgwater
Salisbury
A361
A37
Shaftesbury
A396
Taunton
A303
M5
A420
A350
A354
Tiverton
Yeovil
A37
A377
A30
Blandford Forum
A31
Honiton
Axmouth to Highcliffe
p60-67
A348
A338
Kingsbridge to Seaton
p50-57
Exeter
Lyme Regis
A35
Poole
Bournemouth
A35
Dorchester
Exmouth
A38
A3110
Weymouth
Swanage
Torquay
A385
Dartmouth
Salcombe

Channel Islands
p68-71
Alderney
Guernsey
Herm
St Peter Port
Sark
Jersey
St Helier

SEVERN BEACH TO MORTEHOE

Unusual landmarks, from a unique lighthouse on stilts to the steep inclines of 'Little Switzerland', catch the eye on a stretch of coastline that also marks the start of the South West Coast Path

❶ Severn Beach

Low tide at Severn Beach reveals the English Stones reef. Deep beneath, the Severn Tunnel has provided a rail link between the two banks of the river since 1885. The road bridge south of the tunnel opened in 1996, 30 years after the first Severn Bridge, 3½ miles upriver.

❷ Clevedon

A wealth of Georgian and Victorian buildings, and an elegant pier and seafront with bandstand and bowling greens, give the sedate seaside town its charm. Poet's Walk, whose name recalls Clevedon's links with literary figures such as Tennyson and Coleridge, follows the clifftops past the 12th-century St Andrew's Church. Lovers' Walk leads northeast to the rocky cove of Ladye Bay. In summer the rocks and low-tide mud of Clevedon's beaches can be exchanged for an invigorating paddle-steamer boat trip from the pier.

Clevedon Court (NT), a 14th-century manor, is where William Thackeray wrote much of his novel *Vanity Fair*. The house has a fine collection of glass made in the nearby town of Nailsea, and glass engraving and wood-turning are among the crafts demonstrated at Clevedon Craft Centre.

❸ Sand Point

Panoramic views of Exmoor and the Bristol Channel are the reward for a climb up the narrow headland to Sand Point. Grassy slopes stretch north to seaweed-covered rocks and mudflats, and south to Sand Bay. The point is reached from a car park at the north end of Sand Bay, which is also the starting place for a 2 mile walk to Woodspring Priory. Founded in 1210, the building was a farmhouse for more than 400 years; it has been restored, and one of its rooms is a museum displaying finds from the site. The priory can also be reached by road from Worle.

❹ Sand Bay

Caught in a pincer by Worlebury Hill and Sand Point are wide sands with far-reaching views over the Severn Estuary. An Iron Age hill fort stands in the ancient woods that cover Worlebury Hill. Stand at the western end of the hill for views towards tiny Birnbeck Island.

❺ Weston-Super-Mare

Two miles of sand between the prominent headland of Brean Down and wooded Worlebury Hill were the making of the resort of Weston. Among its attractions are SeaQuarium, where visitors can watch sharks and rays swim close to an underwater tunnel. The North Somerset Museum includes Clara's Cottage, a 19th-century house, with rooms furnished as they would have been in 1900. Boat trips leave from the northern end of Weston Bay, and there are donkey rides along the beach. At low tide the sea is more than a mile from the promenade – danger lurks for those who walk out too far because of the mud that lies below the sand. The southern end of the bay marks the start of the 50 mile Mendip Way to Frome in Somerset.

❻ Bleadon Hill

According to gory legend, the hill was originally known as 'Bleed Down' after a bloody fight between local people and Danish raiders in about AD 800. A footpath to the top of the hill from the nearby village of Loxton offers magnificent views of the surrounding area, and a walk along the ridge brings into sight the Bristol Channel and, on a clear day, the hills of South Wales.

❼ Brean

High dunes back the wide stretch of sand at Brean, whose holiday parks attract young families. Brean Leisure Park has indoor and outdoor swimming pools, a funfair and a golf course. Cars can be driven right onto the sand at the more

0 ⸻ 5 Miles

Bristol

Clevedon

Weston-Super-Mare

Burnham-on-Sea

Minehead

Ilfracombe

Bridgwater

northerly of the two beach car parks. Brean's 13th-century St Bridget's Church is thought to have been built on the site of a 6th-century church founded by Irish monks.

⑧ Berrow
Low tide at sandy Berrow Flats, stretching north to Brean Down, reveals the remains of a Norwegian ship wrecked in 1897. East of Berrow, a small village tucked behind the dunes, is the grassy cone of Brent Knoll. A climb to its 137m (450ft) summit reveals the clear outlines of an Iron Age fort.

⑨ Burnham-on-Sea
A distinctive wooden lighthouse rises improbably on stilts from the sandy beach at Burnham. At the start of the 19th century the enterprising Reverend David Davies sank wells on the shore in an attempt to create a spa town. The spa was not a success, but the venture established Burnham as a seaside resort. Another suprise lies behind the long promenade, inside the 14th-century Church of St Andrew. There, carved figures of cherubs and angels, once part of the chapel of London's Whitehall Palace, destroyed by fire in 1698, have found their home. The Apex Leisure and Wildlife Park, at the southern end of the town, has a large lake and fishing and picnic areas. A cattle market takes place every Monday at nearby Highbridge.

⑩ Stolford
A narrow lane winds down through farmland to this isolated hamlet on the shore of Bridgwater Bay, where low tide exposes a vast expanse of glistening, treacherous mud. Park on a grassy area behind the high pebble bank that lines the shore.

The mudflats north and east of Stolford are visited by many wildfowl and waders. Ducks, including wigeon and teal, winter there, and in summer large numbers of shelduck gather to moult. The area is part of the Bridgwater Bay National Nature Reserve – park in the village of Steart, 5 miles east of Stolford, for access.

⑪ Lilstock
A haven for the fossil-hunter, the low cliffs and shingle beach at Lilstock are only a 2 minute walk from the scattered hamlet. The view along the grass-covered clifftops to the east is dominated by the squat grey buildings of Hinkley Point nuclear power station.

⑫ Kilve
The ruins of a 13th-century chantry stand beside the lane from Kilve, with its duck pond and thatched cottages, to the sea. Cars can be parked round the corner from the chapel.

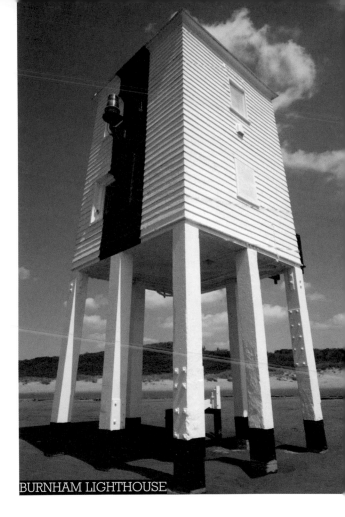

BURNHAM LIGHTHOUSE

A 5 minute walk following the stream leads to the shore, where fossils lie in the shale among the huge rocks at the bottom of the cliffs.

Southwest of Kilve, paths scale the Quantock Hills. The high moorland ridge, densely wooded on its eastern side and dotted with the remains of ancient cairns and tumuli, affords magnificent views westwards to Exmoor and northwards across the Bristol Channel to South Wales.

⑬ East Quantoxhead
Time has stood still in this village of thatched stone cottages, medieval barns and duck pond below the Quantock Hills. East Quantoxhead is dominated by Court House, the home of the Luttrells, who have owned the village since it was granted to an ancestor by William the Conqueror. The house is not open to the public. A 10 minute walk along a path behind the pond passes through fields to crumbling cliffs and a shingle shore.

⑭ St Audrie's Bay
A waterfall plunges down high, crumbling, multicoloured cliffs onto shingle and sand at St Audrie's Bay. The beach is reached by a toll road leading to a car park. There are remains of a

harbour where coal from South Wales was once landed, while above the beach a holiday park has entertained visitors for more than 70 years.

⑮ Watchet

When, as legend says, the poet Samuel Taylor Coleridge heard the tales of an old sailor in the harbour town of Watchet, the seeds for *The Rime of the Ancient Mariner* were sown. The Market House Museum tells the story of the ancient seaport, which was so important in Saxon times that it was made the site of a royal mint. A 2½ mile walk from Watchet to Washford follows the track of a railway line built in the 1850s to provide a link between iron-ore mines in the Brendon Hills and Watchet harbour.

⑯ Blue Anchor

Strikingly coloured alabaster-veined cliffs rise above a long stretch of sand and shingle at Blue Anchor. From the beach there are good views along the sweep of Blue Anchor Bay, and coast walks towards Dunster Beach to the northwest, and Watchet to the east. The Blue Anchor Railway Museum, open on summer Sundays and Bank Holidays, tells the story of the Great Western Railway. Visitors to nearby Home Farm can observe examples of old and rare breeds of pigs and sheep.

⑰ Dunster

At one end the turrets of Dunster Castle, at the other the 17th-century Yarn Market, dominate the village's broad high street lined with medieval buildings.

The castle, on a steep hill terraced with magnolias, fuchsias and rhododendrons, was remodelled in 1870 but still has plasterwork and an oak staircase from the 17th century. Two gateways and part of the walls of the original village of Dunster still stand, along with a 12th-century church, priory and gardens; nearby are an old tithe barn and monks' dovecote. By the river, and near the medieval Gallox Bridge, is a 17th-century watermill. A walk on Grabbist Hill, which rises behind Dunster, is said to have inspired the Victorian hymn writer, Mrs C.F. Alexander, to compose 'All Things Bright and Beautiful'.

The shingle-and-sand Dunster Beach is a mile from the village, and is overlooked by Conygar Hill, whose wooded summit is crowned with a folly tower. In Dunster Forest, south of the A396, waymarked walks start from Nutcombe Bottom car park.

⑱ Minehead

A long esplanade, amusement parks, nearly a mile of sandy beach and a funfair are the classic seaside features of Minehead. But a walk through Blenheim Gardens, where Sunday concerts are held in summer, leads to a quieter, older part of the town, and to the harbour, busy with ships in the 17th century and still the starting point for fishing trips and boat trips.

The eve of May Day each year marks the start of a three-day festival, in which the Sailors' Hobby Horse, shaped like a horse and draped with ribbons, dances around the streets to the accompaniment of a drum. Rising up behind the harbour are the slopes of North Hill, where there are walks and a nature trail. The South West Coast Path climbs the hill at the start of its 630 mile course to Poole in Dorset. A road leads over North Hill and on to Selworthy Beacon.

Minehead is the western end of the West Somerset Railway, whose steam trains stop at restored stations such as Blue Anchor and Watchet, on their way to Bishops Lydeard, near Taunton.

⑲ Selworthy

Clinging to a hill on the edge of Exmoor, Selworthy is a village of cream-walled and thatched cottages surrounding a green. From the largely 14th-century Church of All Saints, which overlooks the village, you can gaze on Dunkery Beacon, Somerset's highest peak at 520m (1,705ft). Behind one of the cottages, now a National Trust information centre, is a path that climbs up through woods to Selworthy Beacon, whose 309m (1,013ft) summit gives superb views northwards across the Bristol Channel and inland over Exmoor.

Thatched cottages also fill neighbouring hamlets, including Allerford, with its pack-horse bridge and museum of rural life, and the long village of Bossington, which has a bird of prey centre. Bossington is also the starting place for walks to Hurlstone Point and Porlock Bay. At nearby Lynch is a 16th-century chapel of ease, constructed for the convenience of parishioners living some distance from their parish church.

⑳ Porlock

A dizzying one-in-four gradient takes you down the wooded slopes of Exmoor to the white stone buildings of Porlock, a mile from the sea at the foot of Porlock Hill. At the east end of the village is the 15th-century Doverhay Court, which houses a small museum and information centre.

The 13th-century Church of St Dubricius takes its name from a saint who, according to legend, crowned King Arthur and married him to Guinevere.

㉑ Porlock Weir

Sea-driven shingle encloses a narrow inlet where a small port developed in the 15th century. Pleasure craft now moor in the harbour, and houses and a pub cluster on

LYNTON CLIFF RAILWAY

the tiny quayside. A crescent of shingle stretches eastwards to Hurlstone Point, although strong currents make it dangerous to swim anywhere in Porlock Bay.

22 Culbone Church

England's smallest complete parish church lies isolated in a quiet combe a 2 mile walk from Porlock Weir through dense oak woodland. St Bueno's, only 10m (34ft) long and 4m (12ft) wide, can seat about 30 people, and is still used for services. To shorten the walk, follow the coast path from a roadside parking area on the toll road that climbs up Ashley Combe.

Not far from the road are the overgrown remains of tunnels that once formed part of a house built for the daughter of the poet Lord Byron, in the style of an Italian castle.

23 Countisbury Common

The clifftop perched lighthouse at Foreland Point awaits those who walk 1½ miles across Countisbury Common. Start at the car park next to the A39. The walk passes through a churchyard to a hair-raising path cut into 302m (991ft) gorse-covered cliffs and gives a bird's-eye view of the Bristol Channel, and of Lynton to the west.

24 Lynton

High cliffs and roads resembling mountain passes led the Victorians to call the area round Lynton and Lynmouth 'Little Switzerland'. In August 1952 Lynmouth suffered a disastrous flood that swept away trees, buildings and bridges and claimed 34 lives. Boat trips can be taken from the harbour, which is dominated by a Rhenish tower, a reconstruction of a 19th-century tower used to supply a local home with seawater for baths.

Lynton, on a plateau 152m (500ft) above the harbour town, is reached by a road with a one-in-four gradient or by a two-car cliff railway, which opened in 1890. The two cars each have a counterbalancing water tank filled at the top of the hill and emptied at the foot.

The oddly delightful Lyn and Exmoor Museum, housed in a restored 17th-century cottage, has exhibitions of local history and arts and crafts. It contains everything from an otter trap to a peat plough, from a homemade barometer to a 100-year-old jar of gooseberries. You can take woodland walks from nearby Hollerday Hill or trek up a path to the Valley of Rocks.

25 Valley of Rocks

Jagged pinnacles of sandstone flank the 1½ mile long, riverless Valley of Rocks, east of Lee Bay. Castle Rock is said to be the site of an ancient castle haunted by the devil, and

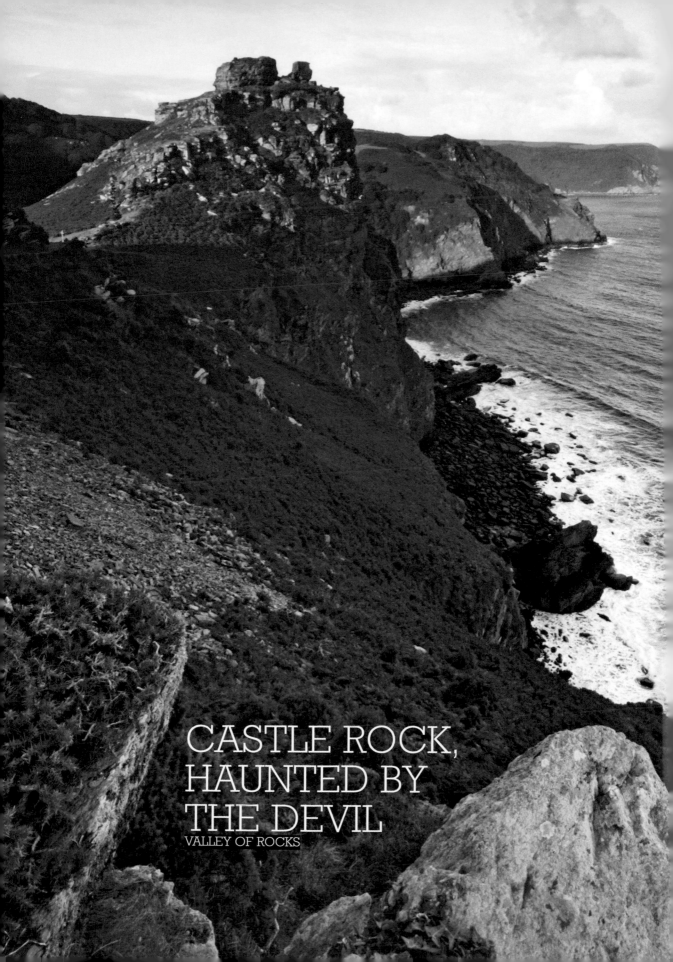

CASTLE ROCK, HAUNTED BY THE DEVIL
VALLEY OF ROCKS

Rugged Jack, the main ridge separating the valley from the sea, is topped by tors and screes. Wild Cheviot goats graze on the cliffs, where sea birds such as guillemots and razorbills nest.

26 Lee Bay

High, tree-clad slopes shelter Lee Bay's beach of sand and large boulders, where a river seeps through the rocks. The fast-flowing tides can trap walkers exploring the foreshore, and strong currents sweep past the bay's headlands. The tiny cave-like chapel on the beach is owned by a Christian community.

27 Woody Bay

A steep track zigzags down through dense oak woodland to the rocks and sand of Woody Bay. The walk takes about 25 minutes and offers the chance of spotting wood warblers and pied flycatchers.

28 Heddon's Mouth

A deep dramatic valley, the sides covered with scree, leads to Heddon's Mouth, a small shingle cove dominated by the remains of an 18th-century limekiln. The kiln was used for burning limestone brought from Wales to help neutralise Exmoor's acid soil and make it more fertile. The walk to the cove starts at a car park at Hunter's Inn; a 2½ mile path eastwards from there to Woody Bay passes the site of a Roman fort built as a defence against Welsh tribes.

29 Combe Martin

Strung out along a deep valley, Combe Martin is said to have England's longest village street. The 2 mile stretch leads down to a sand and shingle beach, with a concrete path on one side giving views of large clear rock pools. The village was formerly a centre of silver and lead mining, and a seafront museum explains its industrial and agricultural history.

A cliff walk leads eastwards past the secluded Wild Pear Beach and climbs to fine viewpoints at Little Hangman and 318m (1,043ft) Great Hangman. A narrow road from Combe Martin to Hunter's Inn skirts the 349m (1,146ft) summit of Holdstone Down, which can be reached on foot from a roadside car park.

30 Water Mouth

Small boats fill the narrow sheltered inlet of Water Mouth, where low tide reveals sand and shingle. A short walk to the headland at the mouth of the inlet starts at the yacht club; beyond the headland, the path continues for a farther 1½ miles to Hele Bay. Watermouth Castle, built in 1825, has a museum of working Victorian pier machines, a smugglers' dungeon and a theme park packed with children's amusements.

The coast from Combe Martin, just east of Water Mouth, to Croyde, is a marine reserve that includes dolphins, porpoises and basking sharks. A good way to spot them is on one of the guided shore walks.

31 Hele Bay

At low tide, rock pools are exposed around a beach of shingle and coarse sand overlooked by grassy cliffs. A path from the western end of the bay leads to Hillsborough Nature Reserve, which includes Bronze Age and Roman sites. A 16th-century watermill on the edge of the village of Hele has a restored 5m (18ft) water wheel. The mill produces flour and is open to visitors from April to October.

32 Ilfracombe

Boats have few refuges on this stretch of coast, so Ilfracombe's harbour was busy with fishing vessels long before the town became a holiday resort in Victorian times. St Nicholas's Chapel, on a crag at the harbour entrance, contains a small maritime display. Pleasure craft still use the harbour, and in summer there are boat and fishing trips along the Exmoor coast, and day cruises to Swansea and Lundy.

The town is built on steep slopes that rise from a shore of rocks and coarse grey sand. At the Tunnels Beaches are two large tide-filled pools that were built in Victorian times for single-sex bathing, now open to all. Ilfracombe Museum, on the promenade, has displays of local and natural history, as well as agricultural and military exhibits. The Torrs Walk skirts the edge of clifftops west of the town; walkers can continue to Lee, 3 miles away, along a track that was once the main route between Ilfracombe and Lee.

33 Mortehoe

A Norman barrel roof and fine Tudor bench ends and are features of Mortehoe's 13th-century St Mary Magdalene Church. The village, perched on a hill on the edge of Woolacombe, is the starting point for walks over the headland to Morte Point. From there 2 miles of coast path lead round Rockham Bay, where steps descend to a strip of rocks and a sandy beach, and on to Bull Point lighthouse.

Visitor information

Burnham-on-Sea ☎ (01278) 787852
Combe Martin ☎ (01271) 883319
Ilfracombe ☎ (01271) 863001
Lynton & Lynmouth ☎ (0845) 660 3232
Minehead ☎ (01643) 702624
Weston-Super-Mare ☎ (01934) 888800

WEST COUNTRY Severn Beach to Mortehoe

WOOLACOMBE TO ROCK

Surfers and wildlife flock to this rugged coast, still commanded by Tintagel, fabled site of King Arthur's court. Wet-suited wave-chasers head for the beaches, while dophins, seals and sharks circle Lundy Island, and birds gather to breed at Baggy Point

❶ Woolacombe
The spectacular sweep of Woolacombe Sand, backed by high dunes, draws surfers and swimmers alike. A car park runs the length of the dunes, and walkways lead across them to 2 miles of open beach. Barricane Beach, north of Woolacombe village, consists almost entirely of shells carried over by sea currents from the Caribbean. Putsborough Sand, another surfing beach, at the southern end of Morte Bay, is reached by a narrow lane from Croyde.

❷ Croyde
A stream runs through the heart of Croyde, past thatched cottages and shops selling clotted cream. The village's Gem, Rock and Shell Museum has exhibits from all over the world. Small, sandy Croyde Bay is a magnet for surfers, but swimming can be dangerous at low tide and near the rocks. For the less adventurous, the village also has a leisure pool with water rides. The National Trust car park at the northern end of Croyde Bay is the start of a mile-long clifftop walk to Baggy Point, where gulls, fulmars, shags and kestrels breed. Baggy Erratic, under the low cliff at Baggy Point, is a 50 ton boulder carried by glaciers from western Scotland during the last Ice Age.

❸ Saunton Sands
A snow-white clifftop art deco hotel peers down on the 3 mile expanse of sand, backed by the grass-tufted dunes of Braunton Burrows. It is a fine family beach, and surfing, watersports and sand-yachting are popular, but take care not to swim in the strong currents round Bideford Bar at the southern end, and avoid the rocks below Saunton Down.

❹ Braunton Burrows
A vast wilderness of sand dunes, some 30m (100ft) high, lies behind Saunton Sands. The southern part is a national nature reserve, and among the 400 species of flowering plants that grow there are purple thyme and yellow birdsfoot, as well as the rarer sand pansy and sand toadflax. Newts and frogs gather round ponds dug to ensure that water is present in summer. The dunes are occasionally used for military training; at such times access is restricted.

❺ Braunton
The wide main road of reputedly England's largest village is lined with surfing shops, contrasting with the narrow, quieter streets of the older parts. The Braunton Museum explains the life and work of local farmers and fishermen, and is close to St Brannock's Church, which dates from the 13th century. Southwest of the village is Braunton Great Field, where narrow strips of cultivated land, separated by lines of grass, are a rare surviving example of the medieval open-field system. Braunton Marsh, south of the Great Field, was drained in the early 19th century and is now grazed by cattle. The marsh has several small circular buildings, called linhays, built to provide shelter for livestock in the 19th century.

❻ Instow
Backed by dunes to the north, a wide sweep of sand reaches out in front of the peaceful village of Instow, from where there are views across the sheltered Torridge estuary to Appledore. The village is popular with waterskiers, sailors and artists.

❼ Bideford

A long quay, built in the 17th century when wool was imported from Spain, recalls the days when Bideford was one of Britain's busiest ports. Fishing and cargo boats, as well as pleasure craft, come and go from the quay, and there are day excursions to Lundy Island throughout the year. The aptly named Long Bridge is 206m (677ft) in length with 24 arches, and has spanned the Torridge since the Middle Ages. It has now been joined by a second road bridge that bypasses the town to the north.

On Tuesday and Saturday mornings local artefacts and produce are sold at Bideford's Pannier Market, continuing a tradition that dates back to 1272, when the first market charter was granted. Eight cannons in Victoria Park, known as the Armada Guns, are said to have come from a 16th-century Spanish wreck. A cycleway, forming part of the 180 mile Tarka Trail, through countryside that inspired Henry Williamson's novel *Tarka the Otter*, follows the course of a disused railway line to the north and south of the town.

❽ Appledore

Tudor buildings constructed from ships' timbers stand alongside colour-washed fishermen's cottages in Appledore, whose seafaring traditions go back more than a 1,000 years. Boat-building has been an important industry here since the 15th century, and continues at a yard on the water's edge. The quay, used by many sailing ships until the 1930s, overlooks a muddy estuary where strong currents make bathing unsafe. The North Devon Maritime Museum explains the nautical history of the area. Fishing trips for cod, bass, skate and other varieties start from the harbour; in summer, you can take a ferry across the estuary to Instow. A path from the old custom house and lifeboat station leads to Northam Burrows Country Park.

❾ Westward Ho!

Founded only in 1863, Westward Ho! is the baby in an area of old-established towns and villages. The small resort, which has holiday camps, beach huts and amusements, takes its name from Charles Kingsley's seafaring adventure story, written in 1855. Rising to the west is the bracken-covered Kipling Tor, where footpaths offer a choice of walks. The hill was named after Rudyard Kipling, who was a pupil at the United Services College in Westward Ho! from 1878 to 1882, and recalled his time there in his book *Stalky and Co.*

North of the town is a 2 mile sweep of sand backed by a huge bank of pebbles. Behind the pebble bank is Northam Burrows Country Park, an area of sand dunes, salt marsh and pasture populated in winter by a wide variety of birds, such as cormorants, eider ducks and Brent geese.

❿ Buck's Mills

A pebble-and-sand beach and the ruins of a large ivy-covered limekiln await at the end of the narrow village street. According to legend, the villagers of Buck's Mills are descendants of the survivors from a 15th-century Spanish shipwreck. The tree-clad cliffs that rise up behind the beach extend westwards as far as Clovelly, and eastwards for nearly 2 miles. To the west of the village, the coast path passes through Buck's and Keivill's Wood, part of an extensive woodland area that supports stunted mature oaks and mature sycamores.

Life on Lundy

Lundy means 'puffin island' in Norse. Today the puffin is sadly much less common, but more than 400 other species of birds have been recorded here. Grey seals, sika deer, wild goats and Soay sheep also inhabit the island, and shark or dolphin-watching is also possible.

In the 19th century the island was ruled by the Heaven family and referred to as the 'Kingdom of Heaven'. This seems an apt description, even today, for a slip of grass-topped granite that is 3½ miles long and ½ mile wide and entirely free from the hustle and bustle of everyday life. Not even dogs are allowed.

It was not always so peaceful. For years Lundy was the haunt of Vikings, Normans, pirates and outlaws. But the island fell into economic decline, and since 1969 it has belonged to the National Trust and is administered by the Landmark Trust.

All around the island there are 122m (400ft) cliffs with superb views of England, Wales and out to the Atlantic. There are also two lighthouses, both erected in 1897; above Lametry Bay stands Marisco Castle, probably built in 1243 by Henry III.

Nowadays you can visit for the day or longer to walk the 7 miles of soaring cliffs before visiting the Marisco Tavern to eat roast goat and drink Old Light Bitter. The island's own boat, the *Oldenburg*, sails fron Bideford, and the paddle-steamer *Waverley* makes occasional trips from Ilfracombe in summer. You can also travel to the island by helicopter.

▶ Bideford ❼

A HARBOUR BUILT ON HERRING
CLOVELLY

⓫ Clovelly
Donkeys and sledges are the only form of transport in Clovelly's steep, cobbled main street, flanked by whitewashed cottages. At the foot of the street is a small harbour, built in Tudor times and once the base of a fishing fleet, which prospered in the 18th and 19th centuries on huge catches of herring. Now boats will take you on trips around the bay. The beach is shingle and pebbles, with a little sand revealed at low tide.

Cars must be left in the car park outside the village, where a visitor centre has an audiovisual display explaining Clovelly's history. In summer a Land-Rover ferries visitors between the top of the village and the harbour, avoiding the main street.

If time seems to have stood still in Clovelly, it is mainly due to Christine Hamlyn, who owned the village from 1884 to 1936 and devoted her life to protecting its buildings and beauty. Descendants of the Hamlyn family live at Clovelly Court, on the edge of the village. The house is not open to the public but the gardens can be visited.

The most attractive way to approach Clovelly is along the 3 mile wooded toll road known as the Hobby Drive, which leaves the A39 at Hobby Lodge. At The Milky Way theme park, 1½ miles south of the village, visitors can see birds of prey and falconry displays, as well as farm animals.

⓬ Hartland Point
To the Romans this craggy headland was the 'Promontory of Hercules'. Almost hidden on a plateau near the base of the cliffs is a lighthouse with a helicopter pad. From the car park, reached via a toll road, you can follow the clifftop path eastwards, passing a Ministry of Defence radar station and the pebble beach of Shipload Bay. The path continues along 6 miles of coast, accessible only on foot, to Clovelly.

⓭ Hartland Quay
Raleigh, Drake and Hawkins built the small harbour at Hartland Quay, where dark jagged cliffs slide into the sea. The harbour, intended as a safe haven for boats on this hazardous stretch of coast, was almost destroyed

by storms in the 19th century. The only buildings are a hotel converted from coastguard cottages, and a museum devoted to seafaring history and local wrecks. Go at low tide and you may see some of the vessels that came to grief along this shore.

The South West Coast Path follows high cliffs southwards to Speke's Mill Mouth, where a waterfall tumbles in stages down to a pebble beach. Walkers should keep to marked paths, as the unstable cliffs can be dangerous.

The road to Hartland Quay passes through the hamlet of Stoke, where the 14th-century St Nectan's Church has a 40m (130ft) tower, built as a landmark for sailors. In the churchyard is Stranger's Hill, where some of the victims of local shipwrecks were buried.

Nearby Hartland Abbey, which has been a family home since the 16th century, was extensively rebuilt in the 18th century on the site of a monastery founded soon after 1157. The house, open to the public in summer, contains a large collection of Victorian and Edwardian photographs, and has a woodland walk through the grounds to the coast.

⑭ Welcombe Mouth

On a bright summer's day, with the sea washing gently over the rocks, it is hard to imagine the cove as it was in the 19th century – a graveyard for ships and a haunt of wreckers. In the days of sail, any vessel coming too close to this coast with an onshore wind was almost certain to founder on the jagged rocks.

A steep lane, narrowing to a bumpy track, leads to a slate-grey shingle beach framed by cliffs. Set back from the shore is the small nature reserve of Welcombe and Marsland Valleys, whose forested slopes are alive with butterflies in summer. A footpath runs southwards from Welcombe Mouth to the rock-and-pebble beach at Marsland Mouth, where a stream marks the boundary between Devon and Cornwall. The coast path between here and Bude, some 9 miles away, offers superb views over Bude Bay.

⑮ Morwenstow

A colourful 19th-century churchman, Robert Stephen Hawker, dominates the history of this isolated hamlet. Hawker was vicar of Morwenstow for 40 years, and achieved some success as a poet. He built the vicarage, whose curious chimneys represent the towers of churches he had known. The sturdy wooden hut in which Hawker wrote some of his poems can be reached down 17 steps from the top of the precipitous Vicarage Cliff.

The fine Norman Church of St Morwenna, notable for its stone carvings and 16th-century carved bench ends, is dedicated to a 9th-century Celtic saint. More than 40 seamen are buried in its churchyard, and the figurehead of the *Caledonia*, wrecked in September 1843, is a memorial to some of them. The land between the church and the cliffs is National Trust property dedicated to Hawker's memory.

⑯ Duckpool

Fresh water from a Coombe Valley stream, contained within a natural dam of pebbles, is the 'pool' that gives this sheltered cove its name. A National Trust car park overlooks a sandy, shingle-backed beach littered with rock falls from the crumbling cliffs. The rock-pooling is good but swimming can be unsafe.

A mile inland is the enchanting village of Coombe, a huddle of thatched cottages reached across a ford. The woodlands of Coombe Valley support a rich variety of plants, birds and small mammals. Walks start from the car park at the east end of the valley. Nearby is Stowe Barton Farm (NT), built in 1793 using materials from the 17th-century mansion of Stowe, which stood on this site; it is not open to the public.

⑰ Bude

Dolphins can sometimes be seen off Bude's sandy Summerleaze and Crooklets beaches. Between the two beaches is a natural seawater pool washed daily by the tides – go at low tide for exhilarating walks along the shore. Although best known as a beach and surfing resort, Bude itself is a quiet town, separated from the sea by a wide band of springy turf. Bude Castle, designed by the 19th-century Cornish scientist and inventor Sir Goldsworthy Gurney, is thought to have been the first building in Britain constructed on sand, using a concrete raft. Gurney's achievements are explained in the Heritage Centre at the castle.

⑱ Bude Canal

The sea lock marking the entrance to Bude Canal is one of the last working locks of its kind in Britain. It is also the only working lock on this remarkable waterway, which ran for 35 miles from Bude to Launceston and rose to a height of 107m (350ft) in 6 miles. The change in levels was achieved by inclined planes, or ramps, between each level, and wheeled tub-boats, which were pulled up the ramps on metal rails.

Opened in 1823, Bude Canal was the longest tub-boat canal ever built. It carried lime-rich sea sand for fertilising inland farmlands, and on the return trips brought oats and slate to the trading vessels in Bude harbour. Today the waterway is used by rowing boats, canoes and small pleasure craft and is undergoing a major facelift. It is navigable only as far as Helebridge, whose picnic area and old wharf buildings can be reached by a 2 mile walk from Bude, which leads past the Bude Marshes Nature Reserve.

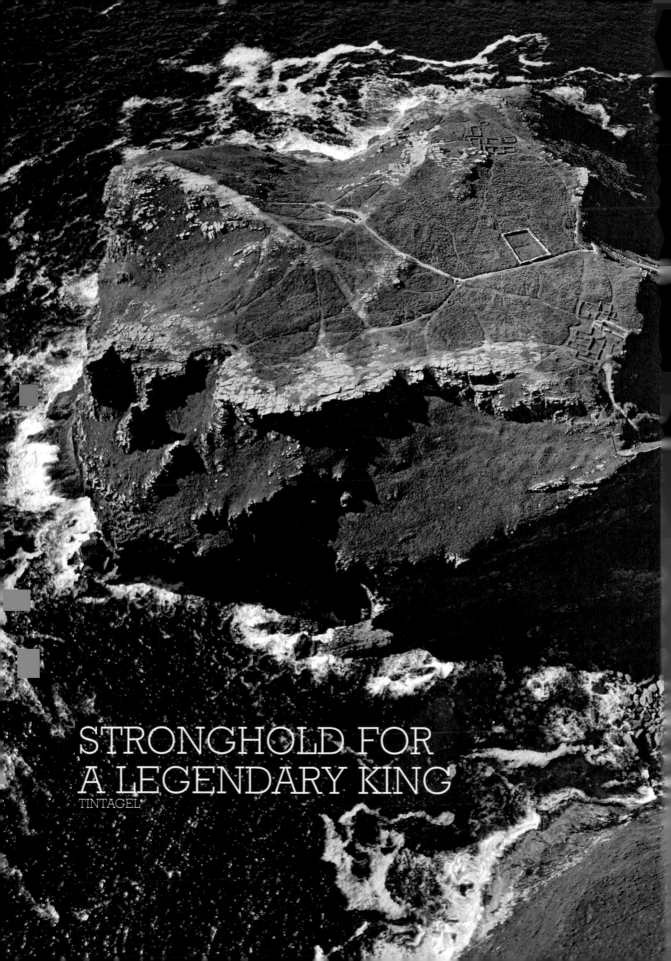

STRONGHOLD FOR
A LEGENDARY KING
TINTAGEL

⑲ Crackington Haven
A peaceful, unspoiled shingle-and-sand beach lies at the foot of towering, unstable cliffs. Set back from the bay, at the end of a no-through road, with views of the sea across well-wooded countryside, stands the Church of St Gennys, whose tower has been a landmark for centuries. The graveyard has memorials to some of the seamen who lost their lives in the tempestuous waters below, including the crew of the Swedish brigantine *William*, wrecked in the haven in 1894, and seven others drowned six years later when storms claimed the steamer *City of Vienna* and the barque *Capricornia*.

The clifftop path from Crackington Haven to Cambeak provides some of the most majestic coastal scenery in Britain, but keep away from the crumbling cliff edge.

⑳ The Strangles
The sinister name is well deserved – in the 1820s more than 20 sailing ships perished in one year on this rocky shore. The path to the remote beach winds steeply down 137m (450ft) of rocky hillside, zigzagging in the last stages. Low tide in the bay reveals large patches of sand between mounds of rocks, but swift currents and undertows make swimming unsafe.

The 15 minute walk to the beach starts opposite a parking area just south of solitary Trevigue Farm. For some spectacular views, take the alternative walk following the clifftop southwards for about a mile to High Cliff, Cornwall's highest cliff at 223m (731ft).

㉑ Boscastle
The narrow, winding inlet of Boscastle harbour provides rare shelter for boats on this intimidating stretch of coast. Tourism is the main activity today, but in the 19th century Boscastle was a busy commercial port, importing coal and timber and exporting slate and china clay. Ships had to be towed in by eight-man rowing boats because of the dangerous harbour entrance. A blowhole in the outer harbour sometimes sends out plumes of spray.

A mile walk eastwards along the South West Coast Path leads to Pentargon, a small bay where a waterfall cascades over sheer black cliffs.

㉒ Tintagel
Arthurian myth envelops Tintagel, which fully exploits the legends made popular by Lord Tennyson. His mid 19th-century *Idylls of the King* made much of the village's supposed links with King Arthur and his Knights of the Round Table. Nothing, though, can trivialise the awesome impact of the reputed site of Arthur's court – a craggy headland, called The Island, but in fact connected to the mainland by a strip of wave-lashed land.

A winding wooden stairway of some 300 steps, which can be treacherous when wet, clings to the sheer rockface as it climbs to the top of The Island. Ruins rising from the steep slopes are those of the 13th-century Tintagel Castle (EH). There is no evidence that Arthur actually lived there, but the 'island' fortress had been a stronghold of Cornish kings for centuries before the castle was built, and in even earlier times may have been the site of a Roman signal station and a Christian monastery. There is a good view of The Island from the clifftop to the south, where the Norman Church of St Materiana stands apart from the rest of the village of Tintagel. In the church is an inscribed Roman milestone.

The weather-beaten Old Post Office (NT), a manor-in-miniature on the village's main street, dates from the 14th century and was first used as a post office during the 19th century. King Arthur's Great Halls nearby were built in the 1930s from 52 different types of Cornish granite, and have more than 70 stained-glass windows telling the story of Arthur and his knights.

㉓ Trebarwith Strand

Slate was once quarried from the crumbling cliffs that back the sweeping sands of Trebarwith Strand. Two large car parks on the approach road testify to the popularity of its long beach. The sand lies beyond a scattering of large, lumpy rocks; signs warn of the potential danger to swimmers, and of the risk of being swept off the rocks by giant waves.

Nearly 2 miles inland, near the hamlet of Trewarmett, is a picnic area from where a short nature trail leads through a disused slate quarry.

㉔ Delabole

The vast crater at Delabole, 152m (500ft) deep and half a mile wide, is a slate quarry that dates back to the 11th century and has been worked continuously since the early 17th century. A pool of vivid blue-green, the colour created by natural minerals, lies at the bottom of the crater, and a fenced walk runs for 1½ miles round the quarry. Until the railway arrived in the 1890s, slate was shipped out from Port Gaverne and Boscastle; now it is moved by road.

To the northeast of the quarry are the ten tall wind turbines of Delabole Wind Farm, which produces enough electricity to power 3,000 homes.

㉕ Tregardock Beach

Great slabs of shining grey rock rear from low-tide sand on secluded Tregardock Beach. It can be reached only on foot, from a path that starts on a lane at Tregardock, where roadside parking is very limited, and descends

a gentle, gorse-covered valley that becomes rocky and is slippery in wet weather. A notice warns of hazardous swimming conditions and unstable cliffs.

To the south, the path along the top of the cliffs to Portgaverne passes a collapsed tunnel known as Barrett's Zawn, through which slate was once hauled.

㉖ Portgaverne

Long arms of rocky land protect a natural harbour close to Portgaverne. In the 19th century the village was a thriving fishing port, and its fish cellars, referred to as 'pilchard palaces', processed up to 1,000 tons of pilchards in a season. The stone buildings still stand behind the pebbled beach. A hundred ships a year used to call at Portgaverne to pick up slate from the Delabole quarry.

Tourism is now the village's main business, and most of the pilchard cellars have been converted into visitor accommodation. Parking is limited, so it may be best to use the car park on top of the hill at nearby Port Isaac.

㉗ Port Isaac

There are few working fishing villages on the north Cornwall coast, but Port Isaac is one of them, with fish sold in the cellars and restaurants beside the small, 18m (60ft) wide slipway. Cars can be parked on the beach at low tide, but the best approach to Port Isaac is on foot from a car park above the village, taking the route that overlooks the sea and the headland to the west. Boat trips and fishing trips for mackerel, cod and other fish start from the harbour.

Flower-filled hanging baskets decorate the cottages in Port Isaac's maze of narrow alleyways. Among these is Squeeze-ee-belly Alley, which is perhaps a warning about the dangers of consuming too many cream-ladened Cornish delicacies.

㉘ Port Quin

Deserted in the 19th century, the tiny former pilchard-fishing hamlet by a small shingle cove has been brough back to life. The little cottages are now holiday homes owned by the National Trust. On Doyden Point, a short walk to the west, stands a squat 19th-century castellated folly known as Doyden Castle, now also renovated as a holiday house. A 2 mile clifftop walk to the east ends in a descent of 80 steps to Port Isaac.

About 2 miles southeast of Port Quin, outside the village of Trelights, are a large maze and a 'secret garden' at Long Cross Victorian Gardens. A 6th-century Christian burial stone stands at the crossroads outside the grounds.

㉙ Lundy Bay

A winding path leads through a grassy valley to meet the cliffs at Lundy Bay. It starts from a National Trust car park about 1½ miles northeast of Polzeath. On the beach, at the bottom of a short flight of steps, are large flat boulders forming comfortable seats from which to view the rocky bay. In the cliffs above the beach, a collapsed sea cave known as Lundy Hole gives glimpses of the sea churning between splintered rocks below at high tide. The coast path continues eastwards across a narrow stream towards the secluded cove of Ebbhaven.

㉚ Polzeath

Surfers and other holidaymakers flock to Polzeath and the vast, flat sands of Hayle Bay. The coast path north of Polzeath leads to the cliffs and farmland of the Pentire peninsula and Rumps Point (NT), where there are traces of the banks and ditches of an Iron Age fort.

South of Polzeath at Trebetherick is the long sandy beach of Daymer Bay, with views across the Camel estuary to Stepper Point. The simple Church of St Enodoc, surrounded by a golf course, is the burial place of the poet Sir John Betjeman, who loved Cornwall, often celebrating it in verse. The church was almost completely buried by sand in the 19th century, but it was restored in the 1860s and is now used for regular worship.

㉛ Rock

With a sailing club and schools for sailing and waterskiing, the large village of Rock is nautical through and through. Nearby Porthilly Cove is packed with pleasure craft in summer. The sandy beach, just north of the cove, is the departure point for a passenger ferry to Padstow. During winter, the ferry can be summoned from Padstow by waving a flag left for the purpose at the ferry point.

Visitor information

Barnstaple ☎ (01271) 375000
Bideford ☎ (01237) 477676
Bude ☎ (01288) 354240
Camelford ☎ (01840) 212954
Holsworthy ☎ (01409) 254185
Ilfracombe ☎ (01271) 863001
Woolacombe ☎ (01271) 870553

PORT ISAAC

Nightwalking gentlemen

The lonely beaches, rocky coves and quiet creeks of the West Country were ideal for smuggling contraband in days of old

From the early Middle Ages until the 19th century smuggling was a way of life along the coast of the West Country. Every port had boats that combined fishing or legitimate trade with smuggling; in lonely rocky coves barrels of spirits were secretly brought ashore and hidden in caves or loaded onto carts.

Tales of the smugglers of the 18th and 19th centuries, such as Rudyard Kipling's 'A Smuggler's Song', imbue them with a sort of rough glamour, that of basically good-natured locals to whom smuggling was as much a jolly game of hide and seek as it was a means of earning a living:

'Five and twenty ponies
Trotting through the dark –
Brandy for the Parson,
'Baccy for the Clerk;
Laces for a lady, letters for a spy,
And watch the wall, my darling, while
    the Gentlemen go by!'

Yet the smuggling gangs ruled their neighbourhoods with a rod of iron, enforced their will with beatings and intimidation and did not scruple to maim and kill the Customs officers who were set to stop their activities. It's curious that these merciless thugs enjoy today a rose-tinted reputation as romantic figures that would have amazed most citizens of their day.

A prosperous trade in contraband

During the 18th century, war with France had made it almost impossible to get hold of those little luxuries – fine wine, decent tobacco, French lace – that made the lives of gentlemen and ladies so agreeable. Those goods that did make their way legally to England were very heavily taxed. The business opportunities for ruthless and determined men, natural organisers who were cool enough to flout the law and take big risks, were obvious. All they needed was a reliable supplier across the Channel, and plenty of willing hands who could be counted on to turn up for duty when required and to keep their mouths shut. In the impoverished, isolated coastal communities of the West Country, such willing hands were not hard to find. Life for labouring folk – fishermen, farmhands, quarrymen, tin miners – was exceptionally hard and the chance to earn good money by humping a barrel up the beach or hiding a bale of lace in your barn was difficult to resist.

The legal penalties for smuggling were very severe, including transportation for life to the penal colonies of Australia, or being hanged in public. Yet the chances of being caught were slim, if you held your tongue and relied on the security of gang membership. And many winked an eye at the activities of the Nightwalking Gentlemen, either because they were clients or because they did not dare to do otherwise.

Secret places for hiding loot

The beaches of the West Country were perfect for landing the goods, with nests of caves for hiding gear and remote cottages and farms inland where 'little barrels, roped and tarred' could be concealed before delivery to the customers. One such Dorset hiding-place was Spyway Barn in the Isle of Purbeck, where the sympathetic farmer kept a savage bull to deter nosey parkers.

Another popular method of discouragement was to spread rumours of ghosts and hauntings. No credulous local would go near the church at Fleet near Chesil Beach by night, after the local smugglers declared that a spirit haunted the crypt they were using to store their goods. John Meade Falkner used the tale to great effect in his classic 1898 smuggling story *Moonfleet*.

The authorities did what they could, establishing their 'preventive officers' at well-known smuggling spots in dwellings such as the Watch House below Dunscombe Cliff near Sidmouth in Devon, or the coastguard cottages at Port Isaac on the North Cornwall coast. They paid good wages to recruit officers and offered rewards for information. But they were up against a very effective conspiracy of silence.

Legendary smugglers

Two of the West Country's most famous smugglers were the 'King of Prussia', John Carter of Prussia Cove in Mount's Bay, Cornwall, and the 'Rob Roy of the West', Jack Rattenbury of Beer in East Devon. Both enjoyed their heyday around the turn of the 19th century, the Golden Age of smuggling. Carter had his story immortalised in prose by his brother Henry (who in the course of one fight had his nose cut in two and lumps chopped out of his skull); Rattenbury wrote his own, bathing it not unnaturally in the rosiest of glows. Mention of his having cut up an offending Exciseman for crab bait, a deed often ascribed to him, is absent from his book.

In the end it was economics, rather than the forces of law and order, that saw the end of the smugglers. War with France came to an end, trade resumed, taxes became less punitive, and the whole violent scene faded more or less quietly away.

SMUGGLERS' CART TRACKS CUT INTO THE ROCKS

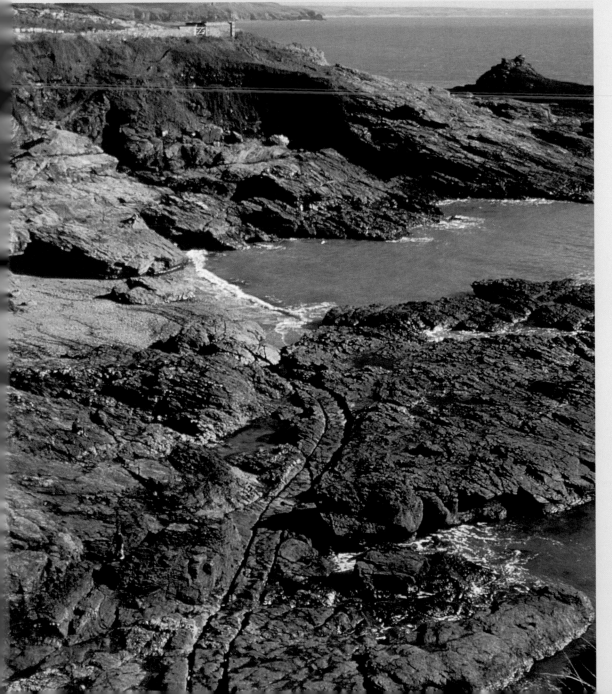

PADSTOW TO PENZANCE

Past and present meet on a coast where mining was once the lifeblood of many locals, but which now tempts families with golden-yellow sands and traditional seaside holiday trappings, and draws surfers to its mighty waves

❶ Padstow

Put on the map by TV chef Rick Stein and his seafood restaurant, this popular holiday resort retains the character of a working fishing port. The 15th-century Church of St Petroc stands amid Padstow's network of narrow streets, which converge on the harbour, a pleasing clutter of boats, lobster pots and ropes. The town was well known by Elizabethan sea captains – Sir Walter Raleigh spent much time there when Warden of Cornwall in the late 16th century – and it was a thriving commercial port in the 19th century. The Doom Bar sandbank at the mouth of the Camel prevented the passage of larger modern vessels, and the harbour is now the embarkation point for fishing trips and pleasure cruises. The port's history is illustrated in a little museum above the library; the Shipwreck Museum on South Quay displays items recovered from wrecks around the Cornish coast.

Also on the quayside are the tanks of the National Lobster Hatchery where visitors can learn about marine conservation and the local fishing industry. The town is at its most traditional during the May Day festival, when a figure in black tarpaulin and a grotesque mask, dubbed the 'Obby 'Oss, parades through the town followed by dancers and musicians, before being ritually 'done to death'.

On the northern edge of Padstow is 16th-century Prideaux Place, whose mansion, dairy, formal gardens and woodland are open to visitors during summer. South of the town is the starting point for the Saints' Way, an ancient route used by travellers making their way from

Brittany to Ireland. The path climbs up Dennis Hill and passes a monument to Queen Victoria before carrying on to Fowey, 25 miles away.

❷ Hawker's Cove

Low tide exposes wide stretches of sands at Hawker's Cove, on the western side of the Camel estuary. It is a popular place from which to watch pleasure craft negotiating their way past the Doom Bar sandbank. The coast path from Padstow heads north to Stepper Point, a lofty promontory crowned with a tower built as a landmark for sailors.

❸ Trevone

A large beach of flat, firm sand is the focal point of this quiet village, bordered to the west by Newtrain Bay, where rock pools form at low tide. One of the pools, some 457m (500yd) west of the car park beside Trevone beach, is about 1.8m (6ft) deep and its still water makes it popular with swimmers, although strong tides can make sea bathing risky. A clifftop walk leads past Round Hole, a collapsed sea cave.

❹ Harlyn Bay

The half-mile sandy crescent of Harlyn Bay, on the sheltered, eastern side of Trevose Head, is backed by dunes and fields, with low cliffs stretching towards Trevone. Harlyn Bay was the site of an Iron Age cemetery, relics of which can be seen at the Royal Cornwall Museum in Truro.

❺ Trevose Head
At the tip of Trevose Head, on sheer granite cliffs, stands the round white tower of a lighthouse, its lantern 62m (204ft) above the sea. A toll road leads to the jagged headland, where grassy picnic areas provide magnificent views northeast to Pentire Point and south to Newquay.

Padstow's lifeboat is based in rocky Mother Ivey's Bay, on the eastern side of the headland. The station was moved here in 1967, after Padstow had lost three lifeboats on the treacherous sandbars of the Camel estuary.

❻ Constantine Bay
Marram grass and tamarisk shrubs cloak Constantine Bay's sand dunes, and long, flat, dark-grey rocks edge the sandy beach, creating numerous pools at low tide. Bathers and surfers should beware of strong currents. The South West Coast Path skirts the popular bay and heads northwards over low cliffs towards the quieter beach at Booby's Bay before continuing to Trevose Head.

❼ Treyarnon Bay
At low tide a large natural pool emerges in the rocks on the northern side of the broad and shallow bay enclosed by high headlands. This and the sandy beach lined by slabs of dark rock make this a popular place for families. Conditions are often ideal for surfing, but watch out for the strong currents that can make swimming hazardous.

❽ Porthcothan
The dunes backing the sandy beach at Porthcothan are perfect places for families on summer days. But it also pays to respect the currents sweeping past the headlands at each end of the beach that make it dangerous to swim at low water. A short walk over the low southern headland leads to Porth Mear, a secluded cove made up of rock and low-tide shingle; beyond the cove is the low plateau of Park Head, whose defensive banks and ditch are believed to date from the 1st century BC.

❾ Bedruthan
The massive slate rocks on the beach, called Bedruthan Steps after a legendary Cornish giant, are one of the most dramatic features on the Cornish coast. One rock, Samaritan Island, is named after a brig that was wrecked there in 1846; her cargo of silks and satins was 'rescued' by local people, who used the luxurious materials for dresses and quilts. Another has been

christened Queen Bess Rock, but its supposed likeness to the profile of Queen Elizabeth I has been lost through erosion. The best view of the rocks is from the clifftop above the beach. A steep flight of steps leads down to the shore, where an expanse of sand is exposed at low tide.

❿ Mawgan Porth
The stream flowing down the deep Vale of Mawgan ends its course in the horseshoe-shaped sandy bay at Mawgan Porth. The surfing school on the beach is ideal for beginners, or you can enjoy the soft sand and rock pools. St Mawgan village, 2 miles upstream from the bay, provides an oasis of calm. Its 13th-century church has an early 15th-century lantern cross in the churchyard and some fine 15th and 16th-century brasses of the local Arundell family.

⓫ Whipsiderry
A reassuringly substantial iron handrail helps with the steep descent down 134 rocky steps to a sandy cove fringed by tall, dark cliffs. To the north is Watergate Beach, a 2 mile sweep of sand popular with surfers.

A 10 minute walk to the west is Trevelgue Head, whose ramparts and ditches are the remains of large Iron Age fortifications; a burial mound there dates from the Bronze Age.

⓬ Newquay
Something for everyone are the watchwords of Cornwall's biggest resort. Around Fistral Beach is Surf City, the scene of international surfing championships, while the sandy beaches to the east of Towan Head are busy in summer with hundreds of families enjoying a traditional seaside holiday.

In the harbour, where lobster pots are stacked up high, fishermen continue Newquay's traditional occupation: long before the first holidaymakers arrived the town was a thriving fishing community. It also exported metal ores.

Just above the harbour is the Huer's House, where a lookout man scanned the sea for shoals of pilchards, netted in vast quantities in the 18th and 19th centuries. The cliff path to the west of the Huer's House provides good views of the Tea Caverns, which were excavated by miners quarrying the cliffs for metal ores, and later the haunt of smugglers who used to hide contraband tea there.

Newquay's wide range of holiday attractions includes a zoo, a boating lake among the lushly subtropical vegetation of Trenance Gardens, the Blue Reef Aquarium with an underwater see-through tunnel, and pools at the Blue Lagoon Leisure Centre. You can take a fishing trip for mackerel, bass and pollock, or fish from the shore in winter.

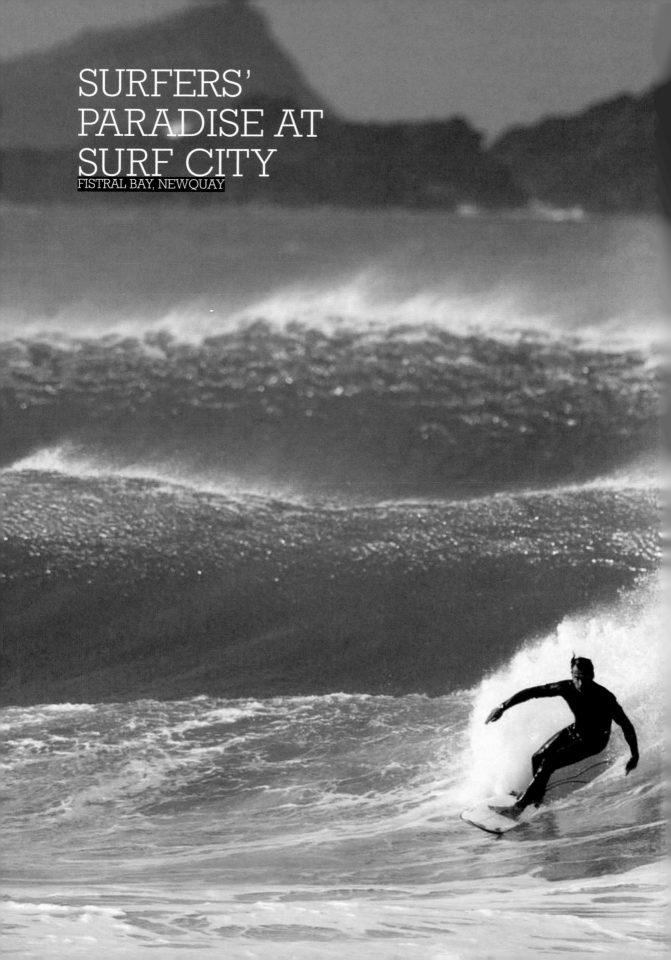

SURFERS' PARADISE AT SURF CITY

FISTRAL BAY, NEWQUAY

Porth, which has become an extension of Newquay, once had its own separate identity, with shipbuilding yards and pilchard cellars – buildings in which the fish were salted to preserve them. The main attraction of the village today is its wide sandy beach – avoid swimming on the north side of the sands, though, as a river takes a course past Trevelgue Head into the sea.

⓭ Crantock Beach

Held between the East and West Pentire headlands the broad stretch of sand is backed by high dunes and an undulating grassy plateau known as Rushy Green. The beach can be reached from the National Trust car park at the lower, older part of Crantock village. Swimming is banned at the northern end of the beach, which is the mouth of the River Gannel. At low tide, the river estuary can be crossed by two bridges that are exposed as the sea retreats; in summer a rowing-boat ferry operates at high tide.

⓮ Porth Joke

This 'joke' is no laughing matter. The name comes from the same source as the word chough, the red-legged crow that was thought to be extinct in the wild in Cornwall but is now re-establishing small breeding colonies. The unspoiled sandy cove, known locally as Polly Joke, can be reached only on foot, but the route from West Pentire requires a mere 5 minute stroll beside a field ablaze with poppies in early summer. To the west Kelsey Head offers wonderful views along the coast and across the sea to the rocky islet called The Chick.

⓯ Holywell Bay

Keep your eyes trained on the two Gull Rocks in the bay and you may get to see dolphins. A stream crossed by a wooden bridge meanders past steep sand dunes, and a slithering scramble over the dunes is rewarded with a view of nearly a mile of golden sand. The location of the holy well that gave the bay its name is not clear – it may have been within a cave, which can be visited at low tide, on the northern side of the bay. A golf course and a family fun park add to the resort's lively summer attractions.

⓰ Gear Sands

A simple stone marks the place where the 6th-century St Piran's Oratory lies buried in Gear Sands, an eerie area of steep, grass-covered sandhills. The small church was founded by St Piran, patron saint of tinners, who arrived in Cornwall from Ireland in the 6th century. Shifting sands have alternately buried and revealed the oratory over the centuries, but it has remained engulfed since 1980. A 15 minute walk to the oratory site starts from the Perranporth to Mount road, and is marked by white stones. A large holiday camp lies within the dunes.

⓱ Perranporth

Old mine workings stretch beneath this former fishing and mining community. It is now a popular resort with two miles of sand, backed by dunes, sweeping northwards. Swimmers should keep away from the southern end of the beach, where streams running into the sea past Chapel Rock create treacherous currents. Chapel Rock has a natural tidal swimming pool, reached by a scramble over the rocks. For those who like fishing, bass, pollock and mackerel can be caught on trips from Perranporth, and there is coarse fishing at nearby Bolingey. For birdwatchers, sedge warblers, reed buntings and others can be spotted in the reed beds of the Nansmellyn Marsh Nature Reserve.

⓲ Trevellas Porth
Take the road from Trevellas village, signed Cross Coombe, and wind down a shaded, leafy, narrow tunnel of a road to the disused Blue Hills Mine. In the 19th century the whole of this quiet coombe, known locally as Jericho Valley, was thick with the dust and noise of tin mining; today the shingle cove is silent apart from the noise of the waves. Erosion makes the cliffs treacherous, and bathing is dangerous because of strong currents.

⓳ Trevaunance Cove
A few granite blocks are all that remain of Treavaunance Cove harbour, torn apart by a fierce storm in 1915. It was the main harbour for the mines of St Agnes, and coal and other imports were winched up the hill using horses, and outward cargoes of ores were poured down chutes to the quay. You approach the cove from a road at the northern end of St Agnes village and descend to a car park above the beach – a wide expanse of sand at low tide. To the east is a jumble of craggy outcrops. The beach is popular with surfers, and fishing from the shore yields mackerel, pollack and bass.

⓴ St Agnes
It may be sleepy and calm today, but the gaunt outlines of former mine buildings rising above the streets of St Agnes are evidence of the days when up to a 1,000 people were employed in local tin and copper mines. The museum's displays and films illustrate the mining history of the village, as well as its associations with the sea. A path beside the Church of Our Lady, Star of the Sea, leads to the engine house of Wheal Friendly Mine, now used as holiday accommodation, and Trevaunance Cove.

At the bottom of the village is a stepped terrace of cottages, some dating from the 18th century, called Stippy Stappy. A path winds its way up to the extensive buildings of Wheal Kitty, an important copper and tin mine until it closed in 1930. Wheal Kitty gives views of several former mine buildings; one, the Polberro Mine, was once Cornwall's richest source of tin.

㉑ St Agnes Beacon
From the top of St Agnes Beacon, 192m (629ft) above the sea, you can see 30 parish churches, both coasts of Cornwall and, at night, the beams of 12 lighthouses. A footpath that starts opposite a car park on the seaward side of the Beacon climbs through gorse and heather to the exhilarating open landscape around the summit. It is claimed that in 1588 fires blazed there to warn of the approach of the Spanish Armada; more fires were lit in 1977 to celebrate the Silver Jubilee of Queen Elizabeth II.

㉒ Chapel Porth
As you approach Chapel Porth it appears as a blue wedge of sea between heather-covered hills. The lane ends in a National Trust car park at the head of a sandy, shingle-backed beach flanked by rocks that provide many sun traps. Swimmers and surfers should beware of currents and undertows.

In a steep valley southeast of the cove, the ruined engine house and chimney of the Charlotte United mine are a reminder of the tin and copper mines that flourished round Chapel Porth in the 19th century. To the north are the buildings of Wheal Coates tin mine, which was worked from at least the 17th century until its

TATE ST IVES

closure in 1889. Dramatically positioned on the edge of a cliff is the Towanroath engine house, constructed in 1872 to house the pumping engine that was needed to keep Wheal Coates free of water.

㉓ Porthtowan
A long, steep hill winds down to the sea at the holiday resort of Porthtowan, where a small cluster of shops and cafes and an amusement arcade overlook a sandy, gently shelving beach. The 19th-century engine house of a copper mine is now a private dwelling. More dramatic evidence of local mining can be seen just over a mile inland, at Tywarnhale, where there are the remains of copper-mine buildings.

㉔ Portreath
Today's cheerful holiday bustle around Portreath's harbour and sandy beach, popular with surfers, makes it hard to imagine that in the 19th century the village was a busy port, exporting 100,000 tons of copper a year and importing vast amounts of South Wales coal to feed mining engines. Even in the 1960s, the present beach car park was a coal depot. The remains of the ramp used to transport cargoes up and down the hill can be seen from the harbour.

㉕ Basset's Cove
The stretch of coast between Portreath and Navax Point is a place of stimulating views and bracing walks along the flat-topped cliffs. A series of coves at the foot of the cliffs, inaccessible from the coast path, includes the chillingly named Deadman's Cove and Hell's Mouth. Basset's Cove, littered with fearsome, steep-sided rocks, is overlooked by a car park, which can be reached by following an unsignposted rough track opposite an entrance to Tehidy Country Park. The park provides woodland walks, a lake and nature trails.

㉖ Godrevy Point
Low cliffs rise above the flat rocks, dappled with low-tide pools, which flank the dangerous channel between Godrevy Point and Godrevy Island. Although popular, Godrevy Point does not become overcrowded because visitors disperse to the headland's many paths and picnic spots, or to the long, sandy beach to the south. The lighthouse on the island – which is a useful navigational guide for motorists as well as for sailors – is thought to be the one referred to in Virginia Woolf's novel *To The Lighthouse*.

㉗ The Towans
Part of a 3 mile stretch of sand between Hayle and Godrevy Point, The Towans means, aptly, 'sand dunes' in Cornish. The sand is wide and flat, and there are plenty of rocky pools to investigate at low tide. Cars can be parked close to the beach, the route to which lies through a village of holiday chalets.

㉘ Hayle
Stunning sandy beaches draw people to this former industrial town and harbour. Machines for the Cornish mining industry, including the engine at the Levant Mine near Pendeen, were made in the foundries of Harvey & Co until the early 20th century. Paradise Park, in the western part of the town, is devoted to the conservation of rare and endangered species, including the Cornish chough, a red-legged crow. Peregrines, kingfishers and great northern divers are among the rare species that bring birdwatchers to the Saltings, at the head of the Hayle estuary.

㉙ St Ives
The town has been an artists' colony since the 1880s, attracting talents as diverse as James McNeill Whistler, Patrick Heron and Walter Sickert. Trewyn Studio, where the sculptor Barbara Hepworth used to work until her death in 1975, is now a memorial museum to her. Among some 30 art galleries, Tate St Ives, on a hillside above the surfing beach of Porthmeor, displays the work of 20th-century painters and sculptors, and offers wide views of the Atlantic.

Its narrow, winding streets and sandy beaches have made St Ives popular with tourists, but fishermen still use the harbour. Visitors can arrange their own fishing trips from the quayside. Although cars are restricted from entering the town in high summer, there is extensive parking overlooking the bay. An unusual and attractive way to approach St Ives is to park at Lelant and go by train, from which there are spectacular views of the coast on the way to Porthminster's golden beach.

㉚ Zennor
Granite 'hedges' up to 2m (7ft) thick separate the small fields that surround the village of Zennor. Some date back to the Bronze Age. The serene 12th-century Church of St Senara has a chair from the 4th century with carvings of a mermaid illustrating a local legend of tragic love between a man and a mermaid. The Wayside Museum, in a former mill beside a stream with a turning water wheel, tells the village's history and includes exhibits on tin mining, milling and fishing. Outside is a plague stone, which during outbreaks of cholera was filled with vinegar to disinfect the money passed between outsiders and villagers.

D.H. Lawrence and his German wife Frieda lived in Zennor during the Second World War. He worked on *Women in Love* there until the couple were ordered to leave because of suspected pro-German sympathies. This incident was later recalled in his semi-autobiographical novel *Kangaroo*.

An hour's walk along a track southeast of the village leads across moorland to the largest surviving chambered tomb in Britain, dramatic Zennor Quoit. Dating from the early Bronze Age, it measures 5m by 3m (18ft by 9½ft).

③① Pendeen Watch
The lighthouse standing on a slate promontory above a sandy cove has guided ships for almost a century. From the eastern end of the car park near the lighthouse, a 15 minute walk leads to Portheras Cove, where a perfect semicircle of sand is revealed at low tide.

A mile inland in the village of Pendeen, Geevor Tin Mine, which ceased production in 1990, is now a museum. Displays include a dazzling collection of iridescent minerals found in the mines. Underground tours are available.

③② Trewellard
Cornwall's oldest steam engine, built in 1840, has been restored and housed in the engine house of the old Levant tin mine. It is part of the Cornish Mining World Heritage Site, designated as such in 2006. The mine was the scene of a disaster in 1919 when the 'man engine', which carried the miners, collapsed and 31 men died. Botallack Mine, where old engine houses crouch on a ledge close to the sea, lies to the south. Among the buildings is a 1908 'calciner' used to refine tin ore and to produce arsenic – the smell of which still hangs in the old flues.

③③ Cape Cornwall
The narrow road from St Just to Cape Cornwall passes a tall chimney, all that remains of what was Britain's most westerly tin mine when it was worked in the 1870s. From the headland – the only one in England and Wales to bear the name 'Cape' – there are views of Land's End, which extends 914m (1,000yd) farther westwards than Cape Cornwall, and of the Longships lighthouse.

On the southern side of the headland, a short walk from the car park descends to the boulder-strewn Priest's Cove. The South West Coast Path continues southwards past Ballowall Barrow (EH), an unusually elaborate Bronze Age burial chamber. The cove can also be reached by road from St Just, England's westernmost town, which was a thriving Victorian tin-mining centre. At its centre is a natural grass-covered amphitheatre where medieval miracle plays were performed until the 17th century. The much-restored Church of St Just includes two medieval wall paintings and a 5th-century burial stone.

Graveyard of shipping
Off the coast of Cornwall and around the Isles of Scilly, scattered reefs and rocky islets have for centuries taken a grim toll of shipping. Sailing ships blown off course or running for shelter from Atlantic gales and steamships lost in fog have had their hulls ripped open, often with huge loss of life.

Modern navigational aids have lessened the threat in recent years. In 1967, however, the oil tanker *Torrey Canyon* went aground on Seven Stones, northeast of Scilly, carrying 120,000 tons of crude oil. It was eventually bombed to burn off the flow of oil polluting the beaches of Cornwall and Devon. And in 1995 three people died when the 137-year-old *Maria Assumpta* was wrecked off Padstow.

③④ Sennen Cove
The great sweep of Whitesand Bay, a surfing beach more than a mile long and backed by steep grassy cliffs, is the focus of Sennen Cove. South of the beach is a huddle of cottages, a lifeboat station, two slipways and a harbour with a huge granite breakwater.

Land's End can be reached by a half-hour walk starting near the harbour car park. The coast path climbs to the headland of Pedn-mên-du, and continues south past a Bronze Age barrow and the remains of Britain's earliest known cliff castle, dating from before 300 BC.

③⑤ Land's End
Known to the Romans as Belevian, or 'Seat of Storms', the wave-lashed granite headland of Land's End is the most southwesterly point on the British mainland. From Land's End, there are views to the Longships reef and its lighthouse, a mile offshore; on the horizon lie the Isles of Scilly and in between, according to legend, is the lost land of Lyonesse. Visitors pay to enter the area, where there are restaurants, craft shops and displays of Cornish history and legends using special sound and lighting effects. In summer, RSPB staff are on duty at birdwatching sites.

③⑥ Porthgwarra
A steep cobbled slipway runs down to a snug cove with a beach of sand and bladderwrack flanked by sheer cliffs. The cliff

on the eastern side is pierced by a tunnel, beyond which are dark granite rocks with low-tide pools. A huge hole in the headland just west of Porthgwarra drops the full height of the cliff, and the sea can be seen rushing in at the bottom. No roads touch the remote, unspoilt coastline between the cove and Land's End, and the rugged terrain poses a challenge to walkers.

37 Porthcurno

The tiny triangle of Porthcurno's beach, made up of ground-down shells, was once known as the 'centre of the universe', for the cove was the landing place for undersea cables that linked Britain to the world telegraph network. The first cable was laid in 1870.

Just south of the cove is the open-air Minack Theatre, an amphitheatre cut into the high cliffs. Completed in 1932, the theatre stages performances in summer, and has an exhibition centre explaining its history. Half a mile west of Porthcurno is 13th-century St Levan's Church, which dominates the tiny scattered village of St Levan. Across the road from the church, a short path to Porth Chapel ends with a difficult climb down to a small sandy beach, sheltered by cliffs.

A mile walk along the coast path eastwards from Porthcurno leads to the headland of Treryn Dinas, where a huge earth-and-stone rampart is all that remains of one of Cornwall's most substantial Iron Age promontory forts. Nearby Logan Rock is a granite boulder estimated to weigh more than 60 tons and once balanced in such a way that it could be made to rock or 'log'. In the 1820s a group of high-spirited sailors dislodged the stone, but were unable to restore it. Treryn Dinas can also be reached by a 15 minute walk across fields from Treen.

38 Penberth Cove

A stone slipway serves the small fishing fleet based at the tiny, rocky Penberth Cove, which is described by the National Trust, as 'the most perfect of Cornish fishing coves'. There is parking for a few cars in the leafy lane that follows a stream down to the cove, past rose-covered cottages and a scattering of stone houses.

39 Lamorna Cove

In the 19th century ships loaded with high-quality granite from nearby quarries plied this tiny harbour, at the end of a steep, narrow lane. From about 1880 to 1910, the village and the surrounding area attracted many artists. Now the seaweed-covered rocks and small area of sand are used as a base for divers exploring local reefs and wrecks. The cove is privately owned, and there is a charge to enter and park. A mile west of Lamorna are standing stones known as the Merry Maidens, and along the coast path to the west of the cove is the Tater-du lighthouse.

40 Mousehole

The little port, pronounced 'Mowzull', was described by Dylan Thomas as 'the loveliest village in England'. Houses crowd around a harbour with curving stone quays, where a small area of sand is revealed at low tide. Mousehole was a major pilchard port until nearby Newlyn developed in the 19th century; now pleasure craft and fishing boats use the harbour, and shark and deep-sea fishing trips start there. Dolly Pentreath, a Mousehole fishwife who died in 1777, was thought to be the last woman to speak Cornish as her native tongue.

Steep Raginnis Hill, south of the harbour, leads to the Wild Bird Hospital and Sanctuary, which is open to visitors; this is also the starting point for an exhilarating 2 mile walk to Lamorna.

41 Newlyn

Narrow streets of stone cottages wind down to the harbour, the base of a 120-strong fishing fleet. It is overlooked by a fish market, and large crowds are drawn here for the Newlyn Fish Festival held around the August Bank Holiday weekend. A beach north of the harbour consists of shingle leading down to sand and scattered rocky outcrops. Artists started going to Newlyn in the 1880s, attracted by the special quality of light. The Newlyn Art Gallery, opened in 1895 and recently refurbished, exhibits both international and local contemporary artworks.

42 Penzance

Nearly half of Cornwall's tin was shipped from Penzance in the 19th century. Though it has long ceased to be a major port, the town has a harbour used by fishing boats, pleasure craft, and summer passenger ferries to the Isles of Scilly. A town trail begins at the granite Market House, in front of which is a statue of Sir Humphry Davy, inventor of the miner's safety lamp, who was born here in 1778. The Penlee House Gallery and Museum is best known for works by artists of the 'Newlyn School'. In Chapel Street is the arresting Egyptian House, built in 1835 and now used as holiday accommodation. Morrab Gardens contains palms, camellias, magnolias and other sub-tropical plants, and a large Victorian house, which is now a private library.

Visitor information

Newquay ☎ (01637) 854020
Padstow ☎ (01841) 533449
Penzance ☎ (01736) 362207
St Ives ☎ (01736) 796297
Truro ☎ (01872) 274555

ISLES OF SCILLY

Lying about 28 miles southwest of Land's End, the Scilly Isles have a mild, sunny climate and miles of sandy beaches. The islands, part of the Duchy of Cornwall, are a treat for birdwatchers

Map labels: Higher Town, The Town, New Grimsby, Maypole, Hugh Town, Old Town, St Agnes, 0 1 Mile

❶ St Mary's

Nearly three-quarters of Scilly's population of more than 2,000 lives on St Mary's, the largest of the Isles, just 2½ miles across at its widest point. Gently undulating fields and low, bracken-clad headlands are surrounded by an easily explored coastline with several sandy beaches and many rocky coves. Pelistry Bay on the east coast becomes dangerous at high tide when currents sweep over the sand bar between St Mary's and Toll's Island.

The 'capital' of Scilly, Hugh Town, stands on a narrow strip of land between the sands of Town Beach and Porth Cressa beach. The main street leads to a harbour where trawlers and visiting yachts mingle with private craft, and with the sturdy passenger launches that take about 20 minutes to reach the outlying islands of St Agnes, Bryher, Tresco or St Martin's. The launches provide opportunities to observe grey seals and a great variety of sea birds at close quarters. Hugh Town developed under the protection of Star Castle, an eight-pointed fortress completed in 1593 when a second Spanish Armada was feared. Now a hotel, the fort forms part of The Garrison. The beams of eight lighthouses – the Bishop Rock, Round Island, Peninnis, Wolf Rock, Longships, Pendeen, Tater-du and Lizard – are visible from The Garrison on a clear night.

The history and natural history of the islands are illustrated in Hugh Town's museum by exhibits spanning more than 6,000 years. The museum's outstanding features include the pilot gig *Klondyke* built in 1873, and a superb bronze gun recovered from the wreck of the 90 gun *Association*, the flagship of Rear-Admiral Sir Cloudesley Shovell, which sank in 1707 after striking the Gilstone reef, in the Western Rocks. Old Town is an attractive cluster of stone cottages; its sandy, rock-studded bay curves round to the Old Church, shaded by palm trees and with the date 1662 carved above its door. Many victims of the *Schiller* disaster of 1875 are buried in the graveyard.

Porth Hellick, a very sheltered bay of sand framed by seaweed-draped rocks, is the starting point for one of two way-marked nature trails. The other runs from Old Town Bay to the A3111 near Sandy Banks Farm.

The turf-topped Porth Hellick Down Burial Chamber (EH) dates from the Bronze Age and is one of Scilly's many links with prehistory. Another burial place, Bant's Carn (EH), is on the northwestern rim of St Mary's and overlooks the granite hut circles of a Romano-British village inhabited almost 2,000 years ago.

❷ Gugh

The little island – its name pronounced to rhyme with 'Hugh' – has only two houses and is linked to St Agnes by a sand bar that is covered at high tide. There are sandy beaches on either side of the bar at low water, but the incoming tide creates dangerous currents as it sweeps over the barrier. The Old Man of Gugh, a 2.7m (9ft) standing stone, was erected by the island's Bronze Age inhabitants.

❸ St Agnes

The disused 17th-century lighthouse, whose portly white tower dominates the little island, overlooks a patchwork of tiny fields, sheltered by lofty hedges. A road just wide enough for a single vehicle runs from the quay at Porth Conger to the sand and shingle beach at Lower Town, half a mile away on the opposite side of the island, whose population numbers fewer than 100. The east window of St Agnes Church is dedicated to crews who manned the lifeboat based nearby from 1891 to 1920.

Troy Town Maze, on the west of the island, measures 9m (30ft) across and consists of ankle-high stones set into the ground. Who laid out the maze is a mystery; one theory is that it was made by a lighthouse keeper, another that it dates from Celtic times.

Annet, just over half a mile off St Agnes, is a bird reserve where puffins and Manx shearwaters breed. Boat trips from St Mary's take visitors near the island, but do not land there.

The Bishop Rock lighthouse stands sentinel over the southwest tip of the Isles of Scilly, 4½ miles from St Agnes. Its light has a range of nearly 30 miles.

④ Samson

Small and humpbacked, Samson has been uninhabited since 1855 and is now a breeding ground for lesser black-backed gulls. Boat trips from St Mary's land on Samson between April and October; ruins of islanders' cottages can still be seen.

⑤ Bryher

Battered into weird shapes by the power of Atlantic storms, Bryher's western coast contrasts with the sheltered beach that faces Tresco and the tranquillity of Rushy Bay, at the southern end of the island. The bay's sands are overlooked by Bronze Age cairns on Samson Hill. About 90 people live on the island.

⑥ Tresco

Scilly's second largest island, with a population of 180, Tresco is a private estate leased to the Dorrien Smith family by the Duchy of Cornwall since 1834. The first of the line, Augustus Smith, built Tresco Abbey near the site of the island's medieval priory and created its luxuriant subtropical gardens, which are open to visitors. Tresco's beauty is enhanced by two lakes, Great Pool and Abbey Pool, where coots, moorhens, mute swans and other birds nest.

A fort known as Cromwell's Castle (EH) was built in 1651 when the Royalist islands finally capitulated. From the fort it is only a short walk to the ruined King Charles's Castle (EH), which, despite its name, was built 100 years earlier than Cromwell's Castle. The island has many other superb walks, as well as an art gallery, and excellent beaches for visitors seeking nothing more than relaxation.

TRESCO

⑦ St Martin's

Just 2 miles long with a population of 120, St Martin's 'capital', Higher Town, is overlooked from the east by a steep little hill whose striped Daymark Tower has been a landmark for sailors since the 17th century. The island has several beautiful beaches.

Visitor information
Hugh Town ☎ (01720) 422536

MARAZION
TO ST JUST
IN ROSELAND

The beaches and quiet coves that dot the most southerly part of
Britain belie the shipwrecks once common on this wild stretch of
coast; the South West Coast Path continues on its 630 mile journey

❶ Marazion
**Granted a charter by Henry III in 1257, the
narrow streets of Cornwall's oldest town
snake down to the sea.** Tin and copper were
exported from here until the late 19th century
and the museum in the old fire station relates
some of the town's history.

The quiet waters of Marazion's sandy bay
make for good sailing and wind-surfing. On the
northwestern outskirts of the town is Marazion
Marsh RSPB reserve, where breeding colonies
include grey herons, and aquatic warblers visit.

❷ St Michael's Mount
**Rising from the waters facing Marazion, the
massive granite crag bears a spectacular
battlemented castle,** built in the 14th century
on the site of an earlier monastic shrine. The
island and its buildings are now in the care of
the National Trust, and much of the castle is
open to the public. At low tide a half-mile
causeway joins the mount with Marazion; small
boats provide a link with the mainland when the
causeway is covered.

❸ Perran Sands
**A steep flight of stairs leads down from a
small village to Perran Sands,** part of a long
stretch of sandy beach that is a popular location
for surfing, body-boarding and kite-surfing. To
the southeast the cliffs wind their way to jagged
Cudden Point (NT), on whose rocks many ships
have foundered.

❹ Prussia Cove
**Named after John Carter, a notorious
18th-century smuggler who styled himself
the 'King of Prussia',** the clifftop settlement
of Prussia Cove is part of a private estate,
reached by a narrow winding lane from
Rosudgeon. From the car park it is a 10 minute
walk to a group of old cottages and houses
standing on the top of a dark rockface that slides
ominously into the sea. The path runs behind
the cottages to a slipway that crosses the small
shingle beach.

To the east, above Kenneggy Sands, the cliff
path passes the dumps of a disused tin and
copper mine.

5 Praa Sands

A mile-long crescent of sand is enclosed by two headlands and high dunes. The western end of the beach is sheltered from westerly winds by the cliffs of Hoe Point. The coast path leads eastwards towards rugged Lesceave Cliff (NT). Gaze over the bay and you may spot terns, auks and gannets and passing dolphin or porpoise.

6 Rinsey Head

Fulmars nest on the rockface near the bracken-clad headland where waves pound the granite cliffs. Just to the east is Wheal Prosper (NT), the restored 19th-century engine house of a disused tin and copper mine. Half a mile farther east along the coast path are the ruins of Wheal Trewavas copper mine. Both are part of the Cornish Mining World Heritage Site. The head is reached via a lane from Aston which peters out into a rough track.

7 Porthleven

The deep harbour at the base of Porthleven's steep streets was built by London industrialists in 1811 primarily to export tin and import mining machinery. Boats can be launched at high tide, but the harbour dries out at low tide. Sunken wrecks and a local reef make the area popular with divers. A memorial to the many sailors who have lost their lives in the bay stands on the western cliff.

8 The Loe

A large freshwater lake, separated from the sea by the large shingle barrier of Loe Bar, it has been formed over centuries by winter gales and fierce undercurrents at the mouth of the Cober Estuary. A network of footpaths includes a 5 mile circuit of The Loe and Carminowe Creek. The marshes and tangle of water-tolerant trees at the northern end of the lake are a winter refuge for wildfowl such as teal and coots, and cormorants and herons can also be seen. Strong currents and freak waves make the coast dangerous for swimmers and shipping. Many ships have come to grief there, including the frigate *Anson*; a memorial marks the spot where more than a 100 men died in 1807.

9 Church Cove

A small stream cuts through a sand-and-shingle beach backed by the rounded cliffs of Castle Mound. At the foot of the mound is the predominantly 15th-century Church of St Winwaloe, whose detached bell tower is built right into the rock; the bell was given by a grateful shipwreck survivor. Ancient Winnianton Farm is the only evidence of the large settlement that existed here from the 9th to the 11th centuries and is mentioned in the Domesday Book. The soft rock of the mound is severely eroded, and granite has been deposited to try to prevent the sea from isolating the church.

ST MICHAEL'S MOUNT

⑩ Poldhu Cove

This popular square of sandy beach, almost entirely edged by a low stone wall, is backed by grassy dunes. An attractive clifftop walk leads southwards to the Marconi Memorial, erected near the spot from which the first radio message across the Atlantic was sent in 1901. The Marconi Centre Museum tells the story.

⑪ Mullion Cove

Giant greenstone rocks face the walls of the old harbour, still a working harbour, and a few ancient buildings. Most of the shore around the cove is owned by the National Trust, as is Mullion Island, a nesting site for guillemots and kittiwakes that is closed to the public. The town of Mullion is the largest on the Lizard and has a 15th-century church with bench carvings depicting Jonah and the whale A 1½ mile circular walk climbs south over Mullion Cliff before joining a valley lane back to the harbour.

⑫ Kynance Cove

Huge outcrops of serpentine rock shelter the popular beauty spot, where the pale golden sands are completely covered at high tide. The cove is best visited within 2½ hours of low tide, when it is possible to explore the caves to the west, including the Devil's Bellows, which is transformed into a spectacular blowhole by the surging sea. One of the giant mounds of rock on the beach is known as Albert Rock, after a visit in 1846 by Prince Albert and the royal children. Nearby Asparagus Island is so named because wild asparagus used to grow on its slopes. The South West Coast Path leads southwards past Lion Rock, and slopes down to tiny Caerthillian Cove before rounding Lizard Point. Cornish heath, unique to Cornwall, is among the wild flowers that flourish in the Lizard National Nature Reserve. Britain's rarest breeding bird, the Cornish chough, has recently returned here.

⑬ Lizard

A scattered village on a lonely plateau, Lizard is a centre for polishing and fashioning the local serpentine rock into ornaments. The richly coloured stone became very popular in the 19th century, after Queen Victoria visited Cornwall and ordered items for Osborne, her new house on the Isle of Wight.

A narrow lane from the village leads southwards through farmland for half a mile to the tip of the flat-topped Lizard peninsula which is lashed on three sides by waters that have been the cause of many shipwrecks. Near the end of the road is a lighthouse dating from 1751. At tiny, rocky Church Cove, to the east of Lizard village, there is just room for a slipway and an old boathouse. The cove was once the site of a pilchard fishery, and fish cellars built around a courtyard beside a stream can still be seen. A footpath south from Church Cove leads past the lifeboat station at Kilcobben Cove to the slopes of Bass Point, with good views of the cliffs.

⑭ Cadgwith

With thatched stone cottages sitting in a narrow valley, and small boats, used by fishermen to catch lobsters and crabs on the shingle beach, tiny Cadgwith is a prime example of an 'ideal' Cornish fishing village.

A turf-topped mushroom of land, known as The Todden, separates the main cove from Little Cove, to the south. A steep 5 minute walk up the southern slopes of Little Cove you will pass rare dwarf elms to reach the Devil's Frying-pan, where at high tide waves foam through a natural rock archway and into a collapsed cave.

⑮ Carleon Cove

It is hard to imagine the deserted cove as it was in the 19th century, humming with industry. A pilchard fishery operated in Carleon Cove until the mid 19th century, when the building became a factory for working serpentine rock. The pilchard cellar buildings were extended to accommodate a steam engine, used to power machinery for cutting and polishing the stone, and a stream was deepened to allow flat-bottomed barges to ferry the products out to waiting ships. All that remains of the works is the shell of the warehouse. Finished items included shop fronts, which were made for businesses in London and Paris. The coast path follows a section of track along which rock used to be taken to the serpentine works at the cove.

⑯ Kennack Sands

The wide sandy beach at Kennack is the largest and one of the most popular on the Lizard peninsula's east coast. From the beach and the heather-topped cliffs, visitors may see seals, basking sharks and dolphins offshore, while the mild climate and spring flower display are a treat earlier in the year.

⑰ Porthallow

Porthallow's north-facing gravelly beach looks across Falmouth Bay to the lighthouse on St Anthony Head. The hamlet's inn displays relics of the *Bay of Panama*, wrecked in 1891 at Nare Point, about a mile north of Porthallow.

⑱ Flushing

Not to be confused with Flushing on the River Fal, the hamlet lies on a hillside that slopes down to Gillan Creek. A lane leads to a beach of shingle and sand. Similar beaches to the east, at Mênaver and Gillan, can be reached on foot – the best way of travelling round this peaceful and unspoiled area.

⑲ St Anthony-in-Meneage

According to tradition, the Church of St Anthony-in-Meneage (pronounced 'meneeg'), at the centre of the tiny village, was founded by shipwrecked Normans grateful to have reached dry land. There may be some truth in the legend, for the church tower is built of granite found in Normandy but not in Cornwall. It overlooks a small beach of sand and shingle, where sailing boats and sailboards can be hired. Behind the church a path leads to the promontory of Dennis Head, which was fortified as a defence against Spanish attack in Elizabethan times.

⑳ Helford

Hugging an inlet on the Helford estuary, the peaceful village has thatched cottages and gardens that blaze with colour in summer – in spring the nearby woodlands have swathes of daffodils and primroses. In former times trading ships brought French rum, tobacco and lace from Europe and duty was collected at the old custom house. Today the former port is much quieter. You can take a ferry across the banks of the Helford or explore its many creeks and inlets under your own steam.

㉑ Frenchman's Creek

Perhaps best known as the subject of Daphne du Maurier's novel of the same name, the isolated inlet with its overhanging trees is more reminiscent of an Amazonian backwater than a Cornish creek. Local people insist that its waters are haunted, and even in high summer the creek can be deserted. Herons, cormorants and kingfishers are among the birds seen there.

Frenchman's Creek can be reached on foot from Helford, or by a 10 minute walk from nearby Kestle.

㉒ Gweek

In Roman times traders called at Gweek, and from the 14th century it was a busy port, where timber, coal, lime and other cargoes were exchanged for tin and local produce. Standing on a creek at the head of the Helford estuary, today pleasure boats are overwintered and maintained in the village. Gweek's National Seal Sanctuary, the largest in the UK, cares for sick, injured and starving seals before returning them to the wild. Visitors can watch the animals being fed, and there is an underwater observatory.

KYNANCE COVE

㉓ Helford Passage

Houses stand by the sand-and-shingle beach at Helford Passage, a hamlet that looks across the estuary towards the village of Helford and its frame of green hills. A ferry runs across the estuary in summer. The north and south banks of the Helford River have been linked by ferry since the Middle Ages. Until around 1910 a cart would have been carried across by boat while the horse, tied to a rope, swam alongside. Helford Passage is one of many popular mooring spots on the river. Sailing boats and motor boats can be hired, and river trips arranged. 'Trigging', or digging for cockles, takes place on the foreshore on Good Friday.

㉔ Durgan

For centuries the daily catch of fish was transported from Durgan to Falmouth in donkey panniers. Tin was also once exported from Durgan, now a peaceful waterside hamlet, much of which is owned by the National Trust. Visitors must park at the top of the hill, from where a 10 minute walk leads to cottages beside a sand-and-shingle shore. Sailing and motor boats can be hired.

To the west, the superb, subtropical Glendurgan Garden (NT) straddles a valley running down to the Helford River. Planted at the beginning of the 19th century, the garden includes tulip trees as well as a beautifully planned cherry laurel maze and arrays of azaleas, camellias and hydrangeas.

Nearby is Trebah Garden, planted in a ravine as a 26 acre pleasure garden by the Quaker polymath Charles Fox. The garden slopes descend steeply to a private sandy beach, which may be used by visitors to the garden. Palms and 100-year-old tree ferns flourish, along with exotic water plants, giant Brazilian rhubarb and rhododendrons towering to 18m (60ft). A path zigzags through a rare and beautiful collection of Mediterranean plants.

㉕ Mawnan

The 13th-century church of St Mawnan, near the tiny hamlet of Mawnan, stands on high ground. Its tower has been a

landmark for sailors for centuries, and in times of war lookouts have been placed there to watch for the coming of invaders. The coast path leads westwards through fields and along oak-covered cliffs to Toll Point, from where there are magnificent views across the mouth of the Helford River. Eastwards, the path cuts through the shade of steeply sloping woodland, and continues to Rosemullion Head. There is limited parking space by the church.

㉖ Swanpool Beach

A popular sandy beach with a cluster of brightly coloured beach huts, it is safe for swimming and taking part in a range of watersports Swan Pool, bordering the Falmouth road, is encircled with reeds and, true to its name, patrolled by swans. The local nature reserve contains a number of rare species, including the uniquely local trembling sea mat.

㉗ Falmouth

Near the colourful ranks of pleasure craft in Falmouth's harbour, tall cranes rise from the docks, where ocean-going vessels ride at anchor. Narrow, crowded streets run behind the busy port, which faces the sheltered waters of Carrick Roads, the estuary of the River Fal. On one of these streets is Falmouth's oldest surviving domestic building, the 16th-century Arwenack House. To the south, stately hotels line the cliff walk, overlooking the popular, spacious sandy beaches.

Falmouth's National Maritime Museum, housed in an award-winning building, has a wealth of displays explaining the activities of the fast Post Office packet ships that carried mail and expensive cargo to and from places as far afield as the East Indies and Spain and brought prosperity to the town during the 18th and 19th centuries. At Custom House Quay is the 'Queen's Pipe', a freestanding, brick-built incinerator in which seized contraband tobacco was burned. Pendennis Castle (EH) was one of the many castles erected by Henry VIII against the French. During the First World War a garrison was stationed here and in the

GWEEK SEAL SANCTUARY

Second, it housed a secret underground base. Today, it remains a brooding presence on the headland, a half-hour walk east from the town centre. There are passenger ferries from Falmouth to Flushing and St Mawes, and summer cruises up the River Fal to Truro and to the Helford River, to the southwest.

28 Flushing
A sign in the small village of Flushing warns of swans crossing the road. Otherwise, it comes to life with the arrival of the passenger ferry from Falmouth. Tourism, boat-building and fishing are the principal sources of income today, though it was a prosperous port in the 17th and 18th centuries. Elegant houses, once the homes of naval officers and captains of packet boats, line the waterfront. Riverside walks lead west to Penryn and north to Mylor Churchtown.

29 Mylor Bridge
Two villages blend into each other on the south side of Mylor Creek. From Mylor Bridge, a lane leads along the southern shore of the creek to the busier harbour of Mylor Churchtown and the Norman Church of St Mylor. In the churchyard is a fine Celtic cross. A footpath follows the north shore of the creek and continues along Carrick Roads to the narrow channel at Restronguet Passage, a quiet hamlet with an old riverside inn.

30 Loe Beach
With a name derived from the Cornish word for rock and harbour, Loe Beach is reached by a steep road from Feock village that ends at a small bay. Here a sand-and-shingle beach is exposed at low tide. The beach faces due south, giving good views down Carrick Roads towards Falmouth. From Feock, a lane leads through fields to the rocky tip of Restronguet Point.

31 Trelissick
Encompassing rolling parkland, landscaped gardens studded with subtropical shrubs, and woodland plantations, the estate of Trelissick (NT) is bounded on three sides by the River Fal and two of its many creeks. The 18th-century mansion is open to visitors on a few days each year. There are 5 miles of paths around the estate, including a riverside woodland walk that passes the embarkation point for the King Harry Ferry, a car ferry pulled across the Fal by a diesel-powered chain drive. Neither side of the river has parking for traffic not using the ferry.

32 Truro
The tall towers and spires of Truro Cathedral, completed in 1910, rise above the handsome market town. In the 14th century Truro became one of Cornwall's 'stannary'

towns, where tin had to be brought for testing and stamping, and the town developed as a port until the 17th century, when much of its shipping trade was lost to Falmouth. There is still some commercial activity on the Truro river, but it is now used mainly by pleasure craft. Mining continued to bring prosperity to the town, however, as reflected in its many fine Georgian buildings. There are summer cruises to Falmouth.

33 St Clement
The 14th-century Church of St Clement in a sleepy hamlet by the Tresillian is a favourite subject for photographers and painters. It is reached via a 1 mile footpath north from Malpas. St Clement's unusual lich gate has an upper room said once to have served as the village school. Near the church porch is a stone dedicated to Isniocus Vitalis, a 3rd-century Roman, and bearing inscriptions in the ancient Celtic Ogham alphabet. A similar stone, dedicated to the father of Isniocus, can be found in the churchyard at Yealmpton, Devon.

34 Turnaware Point
A secluded National Trust headland with splendid views towards the mansion and landscaped parkland of Trelissick to the north and the rolling fields edging Carrick Roads to the south. From the B3289 north of St Just in Roseland, a lane leads past privately owned Commerrans Farm to Turnaware Point. It is an ideal area for picnics, but parking space is very limited. The remains of a concrete dock are evidence that the spot was used by Allied troops in the run-up to the D-Day landings of 1944, which are commemorated by an obelisk.

35 St Just In Roseland
The evocative name of the hilltop hamlet comes from the Cornish word ros, or roos, meaning promontory. The 13th-century Church of St Just, whose lich gate stands level with the top of its tower, overlooks the pleasure craft in St Just Pool and the big ships in Falmouth harbour. The path to the church is flanked by granite tablets carved with verses, and subtropical plants such as Chilean myrtle and Chinese fan palms tumble down to the waterside. Most of the land surrounding the coastal path south to St Mawes is owned by the National Trust.

> **Visitor information**
> **Falmouth** ☎ (01326) 312300
> **Truro** ☎ (01872) 274555

ST MAWES TO SALCOMBE

Fishing boats and pleasure craft mingle on these waters; close to the busy market town of St Austell, the Eden Project delights visitors with its unique perspective on plants and the environment

① St Mawes

Set on steep slopes at the end of a peninsula flanked by Carrick Roads and the Percuil river, St Mawes clusters around a harbour busy with fishing boats and pleasure craft, where in summer many day visitors arrive by the ferry from Falmouth. The narrow winding road that forms a triangle around the town passes St Mawes Castle (EH), built in the mid 16th century to a clover-leaf design of three bastions around a low tower. The castle faces Falmouth's Pendennis Castle on the opposite side of Carrick Roads, and its grounds provide a splendid vantage point from which to watch big ships ease into the waterway. Nearby are the Lamorran House Gardens, where subtropical plants and water gardens cover precipitous hills. The gardens open two days a week from spring to early autumn. Seals are occasionally seen close to St Mawes harbour in the early morning.

② St Anthony Head

The squat headland affords superb views of Falmouth Bay and the surrounding countryside. At low tide, stretches of sand appear along the shore between St Anthony Head and Carricknath Point to the north. At the foot of the headland a lighthouse marks the entrance to Carrick Roads and on the cliff behind are concrete remains of the St Anthony Battery, in military use until the 1950s.

③ Towan Beach

The beach is a sweeping half-circle of sand, but although towan is the Cornish word for sand dune, there are no dunes here today. They may have disappeared through erosion, or because the sand was removed by farmers and mixed with seaweed to enrich agricultural soil, once a common practice. Today it is very popular with surfers and can get crowded at peak times. The peaceful sandy beach of Porthbeor, a mile to the south, can be reached by the coast path or by an unmarked track from Bohortha, where there is limited parking.

④ Portscatho

Sturdy stone-built houses are gathered around Portscatho's small harbour. The coast path leads south to secluded rocky coves. To the north is the sandy beach of Porthcurnick. The trim, brightly painted Methodist and United Reform chapel overlooking Portscatho harbour was built by a local fisherman in 1822.

⑤ Pendower Beach

At low tide Pendower Beach (NT) and Carne Beach fuse to become one long stretch of sand. At its western end Pendower Beach is crossed by a stream that flows down the wooded Pendower Valley. By a lane to the northeast is Carne Beacon, one of the largest Bronze Age barrows in Britain and reputed to be the grave of a Cornish king. Inland is the village of Veryan, distinguished by its thatched round houses, designed by a 19th-century vicar to stop the Devil from lurking in corners.

⑥ Nare Head

Wide-ranging sea views from Nare take in Gull Rock, a nesting site for sea birds such as kittiwakes and guillemots, about half a mile offshore. Although the headland rises to more than 91m (300ft), the 15 minute walk from a National Trust car park above Kiberick Cove to jagged Nare Head is a gentle stroll through open fields.

❼ Portloe
In stormy weather the narrow gap in the towering rockface that encloses the unspoiled village's tiny harbour is impossible for boats to negotiate. At other times it is picturesquely packed with fishing boats, winches, lines and lobster pots. There are memorable walks along the cliffs southwest to Nare Head and east to Porthluney Cove.

❽ Porthluney Cove
Caerhays Castle and its grounds, dating from the early 19th century, can be seen from the sandy beach at Porthluney Cove. It was designed by architect John Nash, whose works include Brighton's Royal Pavilion and London's Marble Arch. The gardens are open to visitors from March to May, and part of the castle is often open during this period. You can take a very pleasant 1 mile stroll west along the coast path towards the twin villages of East and West Portholland.

❾ Hemmick Beach
Narrow, sunken lanes are part of Cornwall's charm, and they do not come much narrower or steeper than those approaching Hemmick Beach (NT), a quiet sandy cove with many rock pools. Though vehicle access to the beach is difficult, ample parking is available at Penare, a 10 minute walk away.

❿ Dodman Point
The 20 minute walk from Penare to this striking headland follows the course of a massive Iron Age earthwork. The tree-lined track then joins the coast path, which continues south to a granite cross built in 1896 as a navigational aid. The view inland includes the white 'lunar' landscape of the china clay workings near St Austell, 10 miles to the north.

⓫ Gorran Haven
Formerly a fishing village, at Gorran Haven today, boats housed in the old pilchard-curing cellars offer cruises and angling trips. There is a fine sandy beach that at low tide connects with the longer and sheltered Great Perhaver Beach to the north. Half a mile to the southwest, a very steep path descends to Bow or Vault Beach, a sweep of sand and shingle at the foot of bracken-clad cliffs.

⓬ Mevagissey
The heart of Megavissey is its large harbour where fishing boats and pleasure craft mingle. Its attractions include an aquarium, a small museum and the nearby World of Model Railways. Restaurants, bars, pubs and shops line the village's only through street, reflecting its popularity with holidaymakers. The steep, narrow streets of Mevagissey are unsuitable for cars, and visitors are directed to car parks at the edge of the village.

MEVAGISSEY HARBOUR

To the south is the former fishing and boat-building village of Portmellon. Seen on a sunny day in summer, the cove has a serene quality, but high tides and strong easterly winds sometimes lash the shore, sending spray into the streets. As a defence against the sea, the houses are protected by stout shutters and fronted by concrete walls 1m (3ft) thick. From Portmellon, paths head inland along a stream that flows through a quiet narrow valley.

About 2 miles northwest of Mevagissey are the Lost Gardens of Heligan, where a long-neglected 19th-century garden has been carefully restored to feature summerhouses, a crystal grotto, rockeries and a jungle-like ravine.

⑬ Pentewan

The harbour at Pentewan has been silted up for decades but it was once the centre of a thriving port. The St Austell river reaches the sea here, crossing the northern end of a long sandy beach. Local stone was quarried in the 18th century, and later the harbour was used for shipping coal, timber and clay. A 2 mile stretch of strenuous coast path leads east to the promontory of Black Head.

⑭ Porthpean

A narrow lane drops steeply from the neat little village of Higher Porthpean to the sheltered sandy beach, with fine views across St Austell Bay. The village was once a fishing community, and the old fish cellars are now used by the local sailing club.

⑮ St Austell

The busy market town owes its development to the discovery in the mid 18th century of kaolin, or china clay, used in the making of paper and porcelain. To the north of St Austell, near the white 'moonscape' formed by the quarry spoil-heaps, is the Wheal Martyn China Clay Heritage Centre, a restored 19th-century site with a 5m (18ft) water wheel, historic and nature trails, and two working clay pits.

In the town centre, narrow streets spread out from the Italianate market hall, built in the 1840s. The nearby Holy Trinity Church has a carved 15th-century tower, and its central aisle was constructed in a sharp curve. Guided tours are available of the St Austell Brewery.

⑯ Eden Project

This triumph of architecture and engineering contains the world's biggest greenhouse, the Humid Tropics Biome. Built on a disused claypit at Bodelva, near St Blazey, 2½ miles northeast of St Austell, the whole enterprise is the idea of Tim Smit – the man behind the Lost Gardens of Heligan. The domes rise up like alien life-forms and are as exciting on the inside as they are on the outside. These vast spaces – the biggest dome is 110m (361ft) across and 55m (180ft) high – contain a botanical wonderland. The educational centre, known as The Core, has been designed to reflect the principles of plant growth.

⑰ Charlestown

Named after Charles Rashleigh, a local mine-owner who built the harbour in the late 18th century, Charlestown's main export was initally copper, but the town grew prosperous from the export of St Austell's china clay. Better port facilities at Fowey, Par and Plymouth led to the decline of Charlestown's docks at the close of the 19th century, and tourism has largely replaced shipping.

On the edge of the dock area is the Shipwreck and Heritage Centre, which houses an extensive collection of shipwreck artefacts and traces the history of deep-sea diving with audiovisual displays; the centre's square-rigged tall ships, in the inner harbour, can be visited. On either side of the harbour are two small pebbly beaches.

⑱ Par Sands

Sand dunes line a large, flat beach that extends seawards for half a mile at low tide. To the west are the slender chimneys of Par's clay-processing plant, and to the east is an opening in a low rocky cliff, called Little Hell Cove, accessible when the tide is out.

⑲ Polkerris

A narrow lane leads to a quiet harbour, where a curving breakwater shelters a sandy, west-facing beach hemmed in by rocky cliffs. The large fish cellar here was known as the fish palace. It is now the Rashleigh Arms.

⑳ Gribbin Head

At the tip of this craggy headland stands a red and white landmark for sailors, 26m (84ft) high. It is a 20 minute walk south from the privately owned Menabilly Barton farm. The footpath skirts the private grounds of Menabilly, which was Daphne du Maurier's home for many years and the 'Manderley' of her novel Rebecca.

㉑ Fowey

The estuary of the River Fowey is a busy waterway, used by ferries, water taxis and pleasure craft, as well as by huge ships making their way to the china clay docks north of Fowey. On the waterfront, shops, restaurants and pubs trade under the shadow of the Church of St Fimbarrus, rebuilt in 1460 after a fire, and houses cover the steep hills behind the ancient port. A small museum has displays on the china clay industry and local shipbuilding. To the south of the town is sandy Readymoney Cove, from which a wooded path climbs up to the remains of 16th-century St Catherine's Castle (EH). Parking is severely restricted in Fowey, but there are large car parks on hills above the town.

The coast path leads southwest to Gribbin Head, and sea and moorland views can be had from the Saints' Way, which runs for 26 miles to Padstow. About 2 miles northwest of Fowey are the Iron Age earthworks of Castle Dore.

㉒ Polruan
You'll get a fine view of Polruan's cottages, stacked high above the village's waterfront from the passenger ferry from Fowey. By Town Quay is a 15th-century blockhouse from which a heavy chain was connected to Fowey to seal off the river mouth; deep grooves carved by the chain can be seen in the rock. Cars can be parked in the large car park above the village.

㉓ Pencarrow Head
A track heads south to the broad headland crisscrossed with trails, reached from a National Trust car park about 1½ miles east of Polruan. West of Pencarrow Head is Lantic Bay, a sandy cove lashed by powerful currents, which is reached by a steep path. In the more sheltered Lantivet Bay to the east is the small shingle beach of Lansallos Cove. From the village of Lansallos, a half-mile track, which starts beside 14th-century St Ildierna's Church, follows a tree-lined stream that falls to the shore as a small waterfall.

㉔ Polperro
Picturesque, improbable narrow streets of whitewashed fishermen's cottages lead down to a little harbour, which swarms with holidaymakers in summer. Non-resident traffic is banned in Polperro; but visitors can ride in a shuttle minibus or a horse-drawn carriage from the car park to the harbour. To the west of the harbour, a climb of some 40 steps leads to Chapel Hill, with its wide-ranging views. In the village is the Heritage Centre, to the east of which is a 2 mile clifftop walk to Talland Bay.

㉕ Talland Bay
A sheltered shingle cove is overlooked by the 13th-century Church of St Tallan. The coast path leads east to the headland of Hore Point (NT), passing large black and white panels used for offshore speed trials by the Royal Navy.

㉖ Looe
A narrow estuary separates residential West Looe from the popular waterfront and sandy beach at East Looe. The small streets around the Old Guildhall, built in 1500 and now housing the local museum, converge

on Banjo Pier, where there is a fish market most mornings. Boat trips include a visit to privately owned Looe Island that lies half a mile offshore, a haven for sea birds. The train station in East Looe is a terminus for the scenic 8 mile Looe Valley Line to Liskeard.

㉗ Seaton
At the mouth of the River Seaton lies a wide sandy beach where you can dive, sail and windsurf. A major local attraction, set on a hillside bordering Looe Bay, is the Monkey Sanctuary; here several generations of Amazon woolly monkeys, all of which have been bred in Cornwall, roam free in gardens or in outdoor enclosures. There are talks and exhibitions on the life of the monkeys.

㉘ Downderry
A large, sprawling village, sandwiched between steep slopes and the sea, backs a beach of fine shingle, where low tide exposes a network of rock pools, ideal for dabblers, especially as the south-facing beach is sheltered from northerly winds by a towering sea wall.

㉙ Whitsand Bay
East of the hamlet of Portwrinkle, 4 miles of sands fringe a gently curving bay that is one of east Cornwalls best beaches. Access is via steep paths that zigzag down slate cliffs more than 76m (250ft) high in places. Along some stretches of the beach, high rocks create tiny sheltered coves, and large seawater pools form at low tide. The area west of Tregantle Cliff forms part of a military firing range and is sometimes closed to the public.

㉚ Rame Head
On the tip of Rame Head 14th-century St Michael's Chapel had a beacon that was kept blazing to guide ships into Plymouth. This, the southernmost point of Mount Edgcumbe Country Park is a headland of exhilarating beauty. You can reach the now-ruined chapel by a 10 minute walk from the coastguard station. The lane to the headland passes through the hamlet of Rame, whose Church of St Germanus is still lit by candles.

㉛ Kingsand and Cawsand
Cawsand Bay was a magnet for smugglers from Tudor times until the 18th century, and the twin villages of Kingsand and Cawsand, with their narrow streets and colour-washed buildings, retain the character of smuggling haunts. Parking is restricted in both. Their tiny sand and shingle beaches, sheltered from the prevailing winds by Rame Head, are good places from which to watch ships sailing in and out of Plymouth.

❸❷ Mount Edgcumbe Country Park

Combining woodland and rugged coastline with formal gardens and open grassy slopes that rise to 115m (377ft) above sea level, the park runs along the coast from Cremyll to Tregonhawke. Its centrepiece is Mount Edgcumbe House, rebuilt in its original Tudor style after being destroyed by bombs in 1941. Exotic plants that thrive in the gardens include 600 different species of camellia. The country park can be reached from Plymouth by passenger ferry to Cremyll or by car ferry to Torpoint.

❸❸ Torpoint

The busy little town of Torpoint could be described as the gateway to Cornwall, with a ferry connecting it to Plymouth across the river Tamar; a service of some kind has run since 1791. To the south is St John's Lake, an inlet of tidal marshes and saltings. A mile northwest is Antony House (NT), an 18th-century mansion with grounds by Humphry Repton. Antony Woodland Garden is crisscrossed by walks.

❸❹ Saltash

A former fishing port, with narrow streets rising steeply from the riverbank, Saltash offers spectacular views of the Tamar's two mighty bridges. The Royal Albert Bridge, which carries the railway, was designed by Isambard Kingdom Brunel, and completed in 1859. It runs alongside the slender toll-bridge for vehicles, built 102 years later.

❸❺ Plymouth

At the Hoe, the grassy expanse overlooking Plymouth Sound, Sir Francis Drake reputedly finished his game of bowls before sailing to meet the Spanish Armada in 1588. An unusual modern landmark, the Armada sundial, now stands at the heart of Plymouth city centre, completely rebuilt after its devastation by air raids during the Second World War. A much older landmark, Smeaton's Tower, dominates the Hoe. Built in 1759 by John Smeaton, the red and white tower was the third lighthouse to stand on the treacherous Eddystone rocks, 14 miles offshore, before it was moved stone by stone to its present site in 1882. Energetic visitors can climb the 93 steps to the top.

Nearby is the imposing Royal Citadel, a 17th-century fortress that can be explored by guided tour. The citadel watches over Sutton Harbour, with its busy fish market, and the largely pedestrianised Barbican area, with its narrow cobbled streets and the Elizabethan House. The Plymouth Gin distillery, where gin has been made to a special recipe for more than 200 years, offers guided tours. Island House is where the Pilgrim Fathers are believed to have lodged before sailing to North America in 1620. Their voyage is commemorated by the Mayflower Stone and Steps. On the east side of the harbour is the National Marine Aquarium.

The Barbican includes an array of small art galleries, but the city's main Museum and Art Gallery is to the north, at Drake Circus.

Boat tours of the warships and dockyards of Devonport naval base depart regularly from the Mayflower Steps, and occasional cruises venture up the Tamar as far as Calstock and Morwellham Quay. Morwellham, where visitors can walk around a reconstructed Victorian copper-mining village, may also be reached by train from Plymouth along the Tamar Valley Line.

36 Jennycliff Bay
The cliffs above Jennycliff Bay offer wide views of Plymouth and Plymouth Sound. Steps cut into the chalk cliff lead to a small beach of shingle and rocks where the ebbing tide leaves many pools.

37 Wembury Bay
Part of a voluntary marine conservation area stretching from Fort Bovisand to Gara Point, at Wembury Beach wardens from the Marine Centre conduct 'rock-pool rambles' in summer. The car park next to the Church of St Werburgh is the starting point for two walks. The westward route gives good views over the mouth of Plymouth Sound and the Great Mew Stone. The eastward route leads to the Yealm estuary, which can be crossed in high summer by ferry to Newton Ferrers and Noss Mayo.

38 Newton Ferrers
Tucked away in the sheltered estuary of the Yealm, pronounced 'Yam', Newton Ferrers is a small sailing centre set on the edge of a creek and overlooked by the attractive village of Noss Mayo. From the mouth of the estuary there is a fine 6 mile walk eastwards over the cliffs to Erme Mouth and Mothecombe.

39 Mothecombe
A short walk from this isolated hamlet leads to a long stretch of low-tide sands at the mouth of the Erme, which runs inland between wooded banks. Wonwell Beach, on the other side of the estuary, can be reached by wading across the river from Mothecombe an hour either side of low tide.

40 Bigbury-on-Sea
A small resort, set on low cliffs, with wide views over a sandy beach curling round to the mouth of the Avon, 2 miles seaward of the village of Bigbury. Burgh Island is joined to the mainland by sand at low tide, but can be reached at other times by sea tractor; the island's 14th-century inn was once a smugglers' haunt. At low tide walkers can follow a 'tidal lane', marked by a line of poles, for 4 miles along the west bank of the Avon from Bigbury to Aveton Gifford. West of Bigbury-on-Sea is a beach of sand and fine shingle backed by the holiday village of Challaborough.

41 Thurlestone
A long, curving main street, lined by thatched cottages, leads to the 13th-century All Saints' Church and a clifftop golf course fringed by sandy coves. Beyond is the sweep of South Milton Sands, favoured by surfers. Thurlestone Rock, a pinnacle holed or 'thirled' by the waves, lies just offshore.

PILCHARD INN

A NOVEL METHOD OF TRANSPORT
SEA TRACTOR, BIGBURY-ON-SEA

ONE OF BRITAIN'S YACHTING MECCAS

SALCOMBE

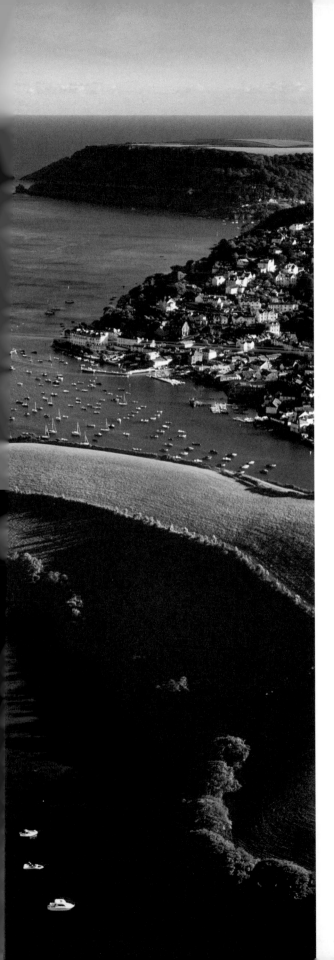

42 Bolberry Down

This exhilarating expanse of turf, gorse and bracken is part of a strip of National Trust land that runs all the way from Bolt Tail to Bolt Head and on towards Salcombe. It offers superb views along the coast to the mouth of the English Channel. There are clifftop walks to Hope Cove and Soar Mill Cove.

43 Soar Mill Cove

A steep 10 minute walk from Soar Village leads to a sheltered cove of sand and rock pools. The Ham Stone, a few hundred yards offshore, claimed the Finnish barque *Herzogen Cecilie* in 1936. She was one of the last sailing ships to be wrecked on Britain's coast.

44 South Sands

The popular beach at the end of a wooded valley on the outskirts of Salcombe is backed by a hotel and leisure complex. A passenger ferry runs to Salcombe in summer. On the headland overlooking the beach is Overbeck's Museum and Gardens (NT) at Sharpitor, where palm trees, magnolias and other subtropical plants flourish in the mild climate. The museum explains the area's history, and has special attractions for children, including a secret room and a ghost hunt. The lane from South Sands to Salcombe passes North Sands, another popular beach framed by wooded cliffs.

45 Salcombe

With one of the West Country's finest natural harbours, Salcombe is the gateway to nearly 2,000 acres of tidal creeks and a long-established haven for yachtsmen. Small boats can explore the tranquil waters as far inland as Kingsbridge. The town's narrow streets are packed with visitors in summer, when the estuary becomes a forest of masts and billowing sails. The Island Cruising Club, based in a converted Mersey ferry, is a sailing school open to day visitors. A maritime museum illustrates Salcombe's history as a sailing port, and as a US base during the Second World War.

> **Visitor information**
>
> **Falmouth** ☎ (01326) 312300
> **Fowey** ☎ (01726) 833616
> **Looe** ☎ (01503) 262072
> **Mevagissey** ☎ (0870) 443 2928
> **Modbury** ☎ (01548) 830159
> **Plymouth** ☎ (01752) 306330
> **Salcombe** ☎ (01548) 843927

Map labels:

Ottery St Mary
Lyme Regis
Exeter
40 Seaton
31 36 Sidmouth 37 38 39
Exmouth 34 35
30
29 32 33
28
27
26
Newton Abbot 25 24 Teignmouth
23
Buckfastleigh Torquay 22
19 21
20
Paignton
Totnes 18
10 17 16 14 13
Brixham 15
9 12
8 11
Dartmouth 7
6
Kingsbridge
1
5
4
3
2

0   5 Miles

KINGSBRIDGE TO SEATON

Although rightly famous for the palm-fringed seafronts of the English Riviera, this stretch of the Devon coast has much more to offer, from scenery rich in contrasting colours to abundant wildlife and many secluded coves

❶ Kingsbridge

The hub of the South Hams district, Kingsbridge is a lively old town with steep streets leading down to the head of the estuary, where small boats anchor by the quays. Cookworthy Museum of Rural Life has a reconstructed Victorian kitchen and an Edwardian pharmacy.

❷ Prawle Point

Devon's southernmost tip is reached via a sunken lane that zigzags down from East Prawle. The point is a sanctuary for birds including buzzards, ravens and hawks and a refuge for the rare cirl bunting. From Salcombe you can take a ferry to East Portlemouth and follow the coast path along the southern edge of the Prawle peninsula. At Mill Bay, trees shelter a sandy beach with fine views across the estuary to Salcombe. Between here and Prawle Point is rugged terrain for walkers, but breaks can be taken at secluded coves.

❸ Start Point

The lighthouse at the tip of the promontory warns of Black Stone rock, where five ships were wrecked during a single night In 1891. Today, a 15 minute walk along narrow, bracken-clad promontory will take you to Start Point but swirling currents still make for dangerous swimming. Deserted ruins at the foot of a low cliff 1½ miles northwest of Start Point are the remains of the once-thriving fishing village of Hallsands, nearly all of which was destroyed by storms in 1917. The village was left highly vulnerable to the sea and wind when some 650,000 tons of shingle were taken to Plymouth at the end of the 19th century to make concrete for new docks at Devonport.

The shingle beach, popular with fishermen whatever the weather, slopes steeply down to the sea, and there is a wild-flower meadow at the northern end. You can also reach Beesands by car along steep, narrow roads.

❹ Torcross

Sandwiched between Slapton Ley and Start Bay is the small resort and former fishing village of Torcross. Its proximity to Slapton Ley makes it a draw for birdwatchers and nature lovers. The Sherman tank behind the Start Bay Inn stands as a memorial to the US servicemen who lost their lives in the bay in April 1944.

❺ Slapton Sands

During the Second World War, US troops used Slapton Sands, and nearby villages, to rehearse for the 1944 D-Day landings. A granite monument records the US Army's gratitude to the local people. In April 1944, 749 US servicemen died when two of their craft were sunk by German E-boats during a practice exercise off Portland Bill in Dorset.

A busy road hugs the beach and for part of its length runs along the top of a narrow shingle bar, behind which is Slapton Ley, a shallow freshwater lake. The lake and the neighbouring reed beds are a national nature reserve and the haunt of many birds, including great crested grebes and Cetti's warblers and, in winter, huge flocks of migrating wildfowl. The reserve's rich plant life includes the rare strapwort, and fungi found only there; Slapton Ley Field Centre organises guided walks.

❻ Blackpool Sands

High wooded cliffs shelter the crescent of golden sand and fine shingle at the northern end of Start Bay, which attracts many visitors in summer. The village of Stoke Fleming perches 91m (300ft) up on the cliffs above the beach. The tall tower of its 14th-century Church of St Peter was for centuries a landmark for shipping.

❼ Dartmouth Castle

Standing guard at the mouth of the Dart estuary, Dartmouth Castle (EH) dates largely from the late 15th century but has been added to and altered over the centuries. It was one of the first castles in Britain designed to take cannon, and you can enjoy splendid views across the harbour from its roof. To defend Dartmouth harbour against invaders, a 229m (750ft) chain could be stretched across the river to Kingswear on the opposite bank; the chain was used at the time of the Spanish Armada and during the Civil War. Artillery was concealed at Dartmouth Castle during the Second World War, and the harbour mouth was protected by an anti-submarine boom, which supported steel mesh reaching right down to the seabed.

You can reach the castle by boat from Dartmouth Harbour, as well as by road, though parking is very limited. The 17th-century Church of St Petrox, next to the castle, contains some fine brasses.

❽ Dartmouth

Dartmouth's narrow streets are steeply sloped or stepped, and many are overhung by the upper floors of medieval houses. In the 12th century, Crusaders set sail from here for the Holy Land. In Elizabethan times 12 ships sailed from the town's fine natural harbour to join the English fleet opposing the Spanish

DARTMOUTH

Armada. Down the centuries, Dartmouth grew prosperous as a trading port, with merchants exchanging English wool for French wine and, later, venturing farther afield to Newfoundland. On June 4, 1944, more than 480 ships left Dartmouth to take part in the D-Day landings.

Grapes carved on Dartmouth's buildings reflect the town's days as a wine port. Elegant 17th-century houses face the waterfront at the cobbled Bayard's Cove, where the Pilgrim Fathers called on their way to America in 1620. The Butterwalk is a row of merchants' trading houses built in the 1630s; the upper floors, supported on columns, sheltered the traders as they went about their business below. One of the houses is now a museum, which traces the town's nautical past and has a collection of model ships.

Thomas Newcomen, inventor of the atmospheric steam engine, was born in Dartmouth in 1663; a late 18th-century model, very similar to his first engine of 1712, has been reconstructed at the Newcomen Engine House.

Riverboat cruises along the Dart give fine views of the Britannia Royal Naval College, which dominates the hill overlooking the harbour. The college, which replaced the training ships moored on the Dart, was completed in 1905. George V, George VI and the Prince of Wales all trained there.

9 Dittisham

Pronounced 'Dit'sum' by local people, the village sits high above the broadest part of the Dart, its skyline is dominated by the tower of the medieval Church of St George. Lanes run steeply down to the tidal shore, where a passenger ferry crosses to the jetty at Greenway Quay. Above the quay is Greenway House (NT), the home of the crime writer Agatha Christie from just before the Second World War until her death in 1976. Now restored by the National Trust, you can visit both house and gardens.

10 Stoke Gabriel

A former port whose upper reaches have been dammed to form a tranquil pool, Stoke Gabriel stands on sloping river banks above a narrow creek. A magnificent yew tree flourishes in St Gabriel's churchyard; local legend says that if you walk backwards round the tree three times and make a wish it will be granted.

11 Kingswear

Facing Dartmouth across the Dart, Kingswear is the southern terminus of the Paignton and Dartmouth Steam Railway, whose trains run beside Tor Bay and along the Dart estuary. The line was originally opened in 1864 as part of the Great Western Railway. Ferries for foot passengers and cars link Kingswear and Dartmouth, sharing the river

with pleasure craft and fishing boats landing crabs. At Coleton Fishacre Garden (NT), 2 miles east of Kingswear, tree ferns and bamboos flourish in the mild, humid climate, along with plants from many parts of the world including South America and China.

12 Southdown Cliff

You can explore Southdown Cliff by following the South West Coast Path from Sharkham Point. The cliff is 107m (350ft) high and some sections of the path are steep, including the descent from Southdown Cliff to the shingle beach at Man Sands but the spectacular views from the top are worth the effort. To the north, steep slopes enclose the sand and shingle beach of St Mary's Bay.

13 Berry Head

Berry Head lighthouse is said to be both the lowest and the highest in Britain – the building is only 4.5m (15ft) tall, but because of the height of the cliffs on which it stands the light is 61m (200ft) above sea level. Massive 19th-century fortifications on the headland, which gives superb views across Tor Bay, were built to defend the coast against Napoleonic forces. Berry Head is a country park and nature reserve, and has a large breeding colony of guillemots, known locally as Brixham penguins.

14 Shoalstone Beach

A small pebbly beach lies to the east of Brixham's long breakwater, and a few hundred metres along is the shingle and rock Shoalstone Beach, a favourite place for rock-pool dabblers at low tide. Or try the open-air seawater swimming pool here.

15 Brixham

Narrow streets and attractive old buildings cling to the steep slopes that almost encircle Brixham's harbour, home of a large fishing fleet and the oldest town in Tor Bay. Pleasure trips start at the harbour, where yachts and cruisers are moored around a life-size replica of the *Golden Hind*, looking too small to sail round the world as it did under the command of Sir Francis Drake from 1577 to 1580.

The Old Market House, beside the harbour, houses an innovative museum called The Deep, where you can explore a sunken pirate ship, look into a mermaid's underwater cavern and descend towards the seabed in a bathysphere – a spherical deep-diving chamber.

Brixham Museum, housed in a former police station in the town centre, has exhibits on the fishing industry, the coastguard and the boat-building industry. You can also view a collection of pictures embroidered by seamen on their long voyages.

⑯ Fishcombe Beach
Wooded red sandstone cliffs back pretty Fishcombe Beach and the neighbouring shingle beach of Churston Cove. A steep path zigzags up from the beach through mature woodland.

⑰ Broad Sands
Steam trains chug along a viaduct behind popular Broad Sands, whose wide sandy beach slopes very gently to the sea's edge. The beach has a cafe and you can hire loungers and deckchairs. A short walk over the cliffs will lead you to the relative seclusion of Elberry Cove, which has a shingle beach.

⑱ Paignton
Paignton was a small fishing village until well into the 19th century. Its early patrons included Isaac Singer, manufacturer of the sewing machine, who in the 1870s built Oldway Mansion; parts of its interior were inspired by the Palace of Versailles, and some rooms and the formal gardens are open to the public.

The less grand neighbour of Torquay, Paignton has a long sandy beach, lined with brightly coloured beach huts. Boat trips and fishing trips start at the harbour, a reminder of the town's fishing history. The town includes the northern terminus of the Paignton and Dartmouth Steam Railway, which runs along the coast and on to Kingswear. Paignton Zoo, founded in 1923 and set in botanical gardens, has an extensive collection of more than 1,300 animals.

⑲ Torquay
Described by the poet Lord Tennyson as 'the loveliest sea village in England', Torquay is a town of genteel Victorian terraces, manicured gardens and wide promenades. It became a fashionable resort in the early years of the 19th century, when war in Europe prevented wealthy people taking their holidays abroad.

The Mediterranean atmosphere of Torquay's spacious harbour, palm-fringed and choked with yachts and cabin cruisers, led to comparisons between the town and the French Riviera, and by the 1920s the trio of Tor Bay resorts – Torquay, Paignton and Brixham – were being dubbed 'the English Riviera'.

Torquay's first small harbour was established at the end of the 12th century by the monks of Torre Abbey, whose foundation dates from 1196, making it the town's oldest building. In the 18th century the abbey's remains were incorporated into a Georgian mansion, with furnished period rooms and collections of glass, silver and porcelain. Within the Abbey Gardens is the Spanish Barn, which is so named because it was used to hold Spanish captives at the time of the Armada in 1588. Sandy beaches lie to the west of Torquay's harbour and shingle coves to the

east. At the harbour, where recreational boat trips around the local shores start, is Living Coasts, a marine wildlife centre.

A mile inland, and a sharp contrast to Torquay's elegant ambiance, is the village of Cockington, with its leafy lanes, thatched cottages and pretty gardens. Cockington Court, the village manor house, is set in an expanse of parkland and has a Norman church, a craft centre and organic and walled rose gardens.

⑳ Hope's Nose
Just off Hope's Nose is Ore Stone, which has Devon's largest breeding colony of kittiwakes. A grassy slope dotted with pine trees sweeps down from the elegant Ilsham Marine Drive to the Nose, a rocky headland marking the northern end of Tor Bay.

On the Torquay side of the headland is Meadfoot Beach, whose sands completely disappear at high tide.

㉑ Babbacombe
The town grew up as a winter resort in the early 19th century, and Bygones, a museum at nearby St Marychurch, contains a full-scale replica of a Victorian street, which includes shops, a pub and a forge; it has even re-created the smells of the time. A dauntingly steep 10 minute walk from St Marychurch leads to the shingle Petit Tor Beach. Kents Cavern, a large cave system to the south of Babbacombe, has beautiful rock formations; finds from the caves, which were inhabited in prehistoric times, are displayed in Torquay Museum.

Below Babbacombe Downs are the sandy Babbacombe and Oddicombe beaches. A steep path leads down to the beaches, or you can reach Oddicombe Beach by cable car. At Babbacombe Model Village there is a chance to explore a thatched village, a modern town, an industrial area and a rural landscape – but all scaled down to just one-twelfth life size.

㉒ Watcombe Beach
High red sandstone cliffs protect the small, secluded beach at Watcombe, which is 5 minutes walk down a very steep tarmac lane. A terrace with a shop and cafe overlooks the sand and shingle shore. If you enjoy angling there is good fishing from the rocks, in particular for dogfish and mackerel.

㉓ Maidencombe
The small, secluded sandy beach here, framed by high red cliffs and fallen boulders, is reached by a precipitous path and a long flight of steps leading down from Maidencombe village. Visitors are warned not to climb at the foot of the cliffs because of the danger of rock falls.

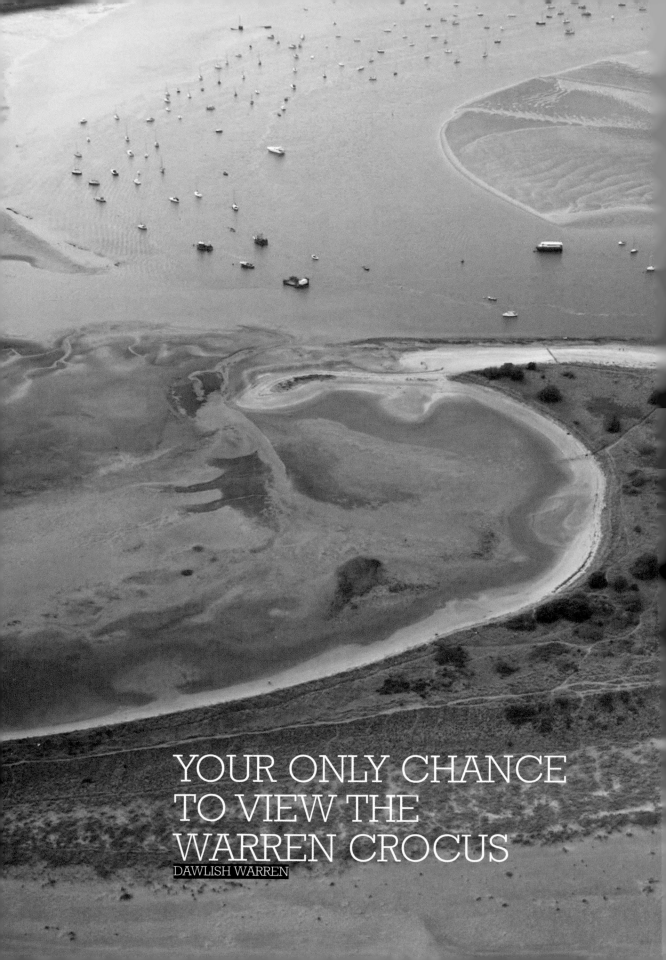

YOUR ONLY CHANCE
TO VIEW THE
WARREN CROCUS
DAWLISH WARREN

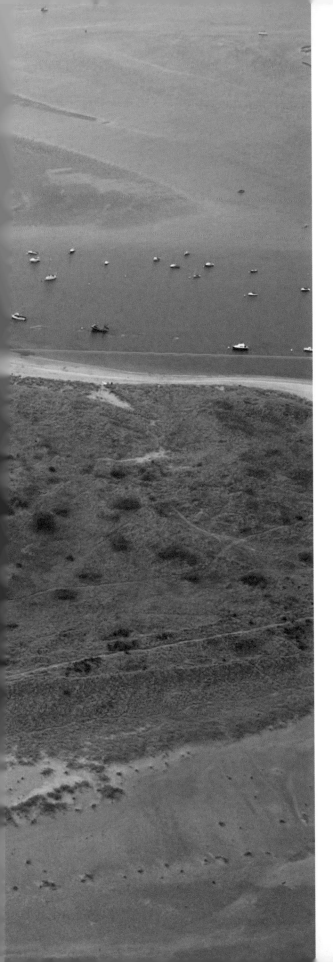

㉔ Shaldon
Georgian cottages, shops and pubs surround the carefully tended bowling green in Shaldon, which overlooks the Teign estuary and connects with Teignmouth by passenger ferry. Fast currents here make bathing dangerous. A well-lit smugglers' tunnel through The Ness headland leads to Ness Cove, a popular sandy beach at the foot of high cliffs. At the landward end of the tunnel is the Shaldon Wildlife Trust.

㉕ Coombe Cellars
Hidden away at the end of a narrow lane leading to the Teign estuary is an inn once notorious for smugglers, who were reputed to have eluded capture by using a secret passage leading under the estuary to the far shore. The name 'Cellars' is a corruption of *solaria*, Latin for salt; the Romans once panned for salt from the nearby marshland. From the shore there are good views of the granite outcrops of Hay Tor on Dartmoor. At lonely Arch Brook Bridge, half a mile to the east, waders flock onto the mudflats at low tide, and there is a breeding colony of herons at Netherton, a mile southwest.

㉖ Teignmouth
Dartmoor granite was shipped from Teignmouth in the early 19th century for the building of the former London Bridge, now in the USA, and the British Museum. Teignmouth harbour exports ball clay from nearby quarries; the clay is used to make crockery and bathroom fittings.

Today a long beach of dark red sand is backed by a promenade with a bowling green, playgrounds and a miniature golf course. At the southern end of the beach, near the mouth of the Teign estuary, the shore shelves steeply and there can be treacherous currents.

㉗ Dawlish
Charles Dickens was a regular visitor to Dawlish and set part of his novel *Nicholas Nickleby* there. At the centre of this family resort is The Lawn, an ornamental garden through which Dawlish Water flows over a series of small weirs, and black swans can often be seen here. A railway line runs right along the seafront, and a tunnel under the track will lead you to a long beach of deep red shingle and sand, typical of this part of Devon's coast.

㉘ Dawlish Warren
Langstone Rock, a huge block of sandstone with a wave-carved arch dominates the view to the south of Dawlish Warren. The landward end of this 1½ mile sandspit, which juts out across the mouth of the Exe estuary, is a popular holiday resort, although there are fast-flowing currents to be found at the tip of the

BEER

spit. A lane under the railway line leads to a
funfair, and there is a long sandy beach with
abundant shells.

If you enjoy birdwatching, Dawlish Warren
National Nature Reserve, which embraces an
extensive area of mudflats and salt marsh, as well
as dunes and sandy shore, attracts large numbers
of waders and wildfowl, including dunlins, black-
tailed godwits and Brent geese. Among the
hundreds of flowering plants growing here is the
highly localised Warren crocus, whose delicate
lilac-blue flowers can be seen nowhere else in
mainland Britain.

㉙ Starcross
**The tall building overlooking the jetty where
the ferry starts was one of the pump
houses built in the 1840s** to serve the
'atmospheric' section of Isambard Kingdom
Brunel's Great Western Railway between Exeter
and Newton Abbot. In summer, a passenger
ferry links the quiet village of Starcross with
Exmouth, across the estuary.

㉚ Powderham Castle
**The battlemented Powderham Castle stands
in a deer park beside the Exe.** Built between
1390 and 1420, it was altered and renovated in
the 17th and 18th centuries after it suffered
damage in the Civil War; it has fine state rooms.

㉛ Topsham
**Attractive houses, with Dutch gables and
bow windows, date from the 17th century.**
Topsham was then a busy port, where merchants
came from Holland to trade in Devon wool. The
town was also a shipbuilding centre until the late
19th century. Topsham Museum explores the
area's maritime history and wildlife.

㉜ Exmouth
**Stylish and spacious, the resort of Exmouth
has immaculate gardens and parks,** and
attractions such as a putting green and boating
pond. The cliffs dominating the East Devon
coastline give way at the town to 2 miles of flat,
sandy beach, and from the old dock area there
are magnificent views upriver towards Exeter.
A summer foot ferry sails to Starcross on the
opposite bank of the Exe estuary. Exmouth
Nature Reserve encompasses Cockle Sand and
the surrounding mudflats; from the footpath or
'drive-in' path near the railway station you may
see redshanks, dunlins, and even sanderlings and
grey plovers. Farther east an area of sand dunes
and grassland forms Maer Nature Reserve, where
around 400 species of plant grow.

On the northern edge of Exmouth you will
find A la Ronde (NT), a unique 16-sided
house built in 1796, whose interior is encrusted
with shells.

③③ Budleigh Salterton

Budleigh's sea wall was the setting for Sir John Millais's painting *The Boyhood of Raleigh*. Behind part of the wall stands the house, marked by a plaque, where the painter lived. One of the pews in All Saints' Church at nearby East Budleigh bears the coat of arms of the Raleigh family.

The River Otter reaches the sea at Budleigh Salterton, whose broad sweep of pink, pebbled beach is guarded to the west by 152m (500ft) red sandstone cliffs. You can follow the coast path with little interruption for 6 miles southwest to Exmouth and 6 miles northeast to Sidmouth.

③④ Otterton

A shimmering stream passes thatched houses in Otterton's main street, and a signpost points the way to Otterton Mill. This restored watermill continues a tradition going back to the 11th century, when the original mill was built. There is a delightful 3 mile walk south through riverside meadows to Budleigh Salterton, and Bicton Park, to the north-west, has a woodland railway and themed gardens.

③⑤ Ladram Bay

Fulmars fly above the spectacular red cliffs here, parts of which have been eroded by the sea into isolated columns, and cormorants hunt in the waters below. It is a good beach for fishing, particularly for mackerel. The small bay can be reached only from the large parking area at the caravan park near Otterton village.

③⑥ Sidmouth

When the weather is rough, the sea at Sidmouth is streaked with red from the sand of the crumbling, ruddy-coloured cliffs that rise on each side of the bay. The half-mile shingle beach is popular for sunbathing, sailing and fishing. Handsome hotels, many of them Regency or Victorian, line the esplanade, and a fine indoor swimming pool lies at the eastern end. Peaceful gardens and clipped lawns stretch along the western end of the seafront. On Salcombe Hill is the Norman Lockyer Observatory, which has a planetarium and two telescopes from the late 19th century.

③⑦ Weston Mouth

There can be an almost eerie sense of isolation on the small, pebbly beach at Weston Mouth. Inaccessible by car, it is the most secluded bay in this area. A walk of about 15 minutes leads you from a tiny, grass-covered parking area in the hamlet of Weston through woodlands and open fields; from there you descend to the beach by means of a flight of steps cut into the red hillside flanking Weston Combe.

③⑧ Branscombe Mouth

The road from Beer to Branscombe passes through varied scenery of dramatic sea views and gentle green valleys, and narrows as it approaches the beach. At a thatched cafe on the sheltered, shingle shore; from here you can take in views to the east of the awesome columns of Hooken Cliffs, scene of a massive landslip in 1790. Branscombe itself is a pretty village with a thatched smithy, dating from Norman times, and a 12th-century church. St Winifred's has a triple-decker pulpit, one of only two in Devon, and the remains of a 15th-century mural.

③⑨ Beer

Highly prized white stone is quarried a mile west of Beer, and used in such buildings as Westminster Abbey and Exeter Cathedral. Opposite the present quarry are the old workings of Beer Quarry Caves, where you can take a conducted tour of the immense halls and galleried passages that were first worked in Roman times. A grassy headland west of the beach provides spectacular views towards Lyme Regis. Similar fine views add to the pleasures of a trip on the miniature railway at the Pecorama Pleasure Gardens.

④⓪ Seaton

Seaton's most popular attraction is its Electric Tramway, which has a fleet of 13 trams, some open-top, and travels for 3 miles inland from Harbour Road to Colyton. The route is excellent for birdwatching as it runs beside the mudflats and marshes of the River Axe, where many waders and ducks feed and breed. The sedate resort itself has a mile-long beach of shingle and pebbles that curves east from the bulk of White Cliff to Haven Cliff.

Visitor information

Budleigh Salterton ☎ (01395) 445275
Dartmouth ☎ (01803) 834224
English Riviera (Brixham, Paignton and Torquay) ☎ (0906) 6801268
Exeter ☎ (01392) 265700
Exmouth ☎ (01395) 222299
Kingsbridge ☎ (01548) 853195
Newton Abbot ☎ (01626) 215667
Seaton ☎ (01297) 21660
Sidmouth ☎ (01395) 516441
Teignmouth ☎ (01626) 215666
Totnes ☎ (01803) 863168

Dudes and divers

Bucket-and-spade holidaymakers have long enjoyed the tranquility of the West Country. Now there are noisy new kids on the block

The West Country coast is the sort of wild place where any kind of adventure seems possible. Its beaches and seas have become the coolest of the cool among surfers, divers, extreme kite-sporters, shark fishermen, wreck explorers and other salt-water sporting dudes.

Kite-powered sports have taken off like a Flexifoil in a Force 10: everything from kite-buggying through kitesurfing, kiteboarding and ... well, flying a kite. Sail-powered sports ditto – windsurfing, landsailing, blokarting and ... simply going sailing. Coasteering gets you running, scrambling, climbing, swimming and jumping into the sea from a great height. Wakeboarding is to water-skiing as snowboarding is to skiing; lots of bumps, lots of tricks. Sea kayaking is big. Zapcatting is bigger – racing inflatable catamarans that can reach 50mph and corner on a sixpence. It's to the West Country that these divers and dudes look to get their kicks.

Cornish encounters with the sea

Cornwall is recognised as the best when it comes to extreme sea sports – particularly the rugged north coast with its exposure to the full force of waves coming in off the open Atlantic. Surfing can be wonderful at Summerleaze Beach in the far north resort of Bude, on South Fistral bay round the corner from Newquay, on the long, deep beach at Polzeath where the enclosing cliffs trap the rollers, and out at the 'far end' at Gwenvor near Sennen Cove. Daymer Bay in the mouth of the Camel Estuary downriver of Rock is excellent on its day for windsurfing.

Slapton Sands is great for kitesurfing, while Bigbury and Burgh Island are magnets for surfers, windsurfers, kitesurfers and kite-buggy riders. Devon's north coast holds a famous surf paradise just north of Barnstaple - Croyde Bay, whose west-facing location between the headlands of Saunton Down and Baggy Point produces steep and powerful surfing waves.

On the south-facing Dorset coast, diving is good in the wide expanse of Lyme Bay, especially off Chesil Beach where experienced divers enjoy wreck sites and marine life. Sailors and windsurfers of all abilities flock to the sheltered waters inside Portland Harbour, and cliff climbers take advantage of several bolted routes up the freestone flanks of the adjacent Isle of Portland. Poole Harbour, another broad expanse of tidal but sheltered water, caters for all kinds of power-kiting. The Zapcat freaks here display to each other like peacocks on speed.

Britain's tidal wave

In contrast to the coasts of Devon and Cornwall, the estuarine shore of Somerset is scarcely renowned for its ruggedness. Windsurfing and kitesurfing can both be good when the tide's in at Minehead, though, and also further up the Severn Estuary at Weston-super-Mare (there's landsailing and mountain-boarding on wheels here, too), while Berrow on the south side of the Brean Down promontory is popular with high-tide windsurfers.

Keen water-sporting dudes wouldn't miss the spectacle of the renowned Severn Bore, swollen to 3m (10ft) or more above normal river level on some spring tides, as it sweeps majestically up the river with an entourage of surfers and canoeists.

Perhaps the best all-round West Country venue for seaside sporting adventures is the most often overlooked – the Channel Islands. Jersey measures only 45 square miles at high tide. But at low water the island swells to twice that size as reefs, sands and rocks are exposed in a vast skirt around the island. There are nearly 30 beaches to choose from, including west-facing St Ouen's Bay for blokarting, kite-surfing and wakeboarding; south-facing Beauport and Portelet for swimming; and the gold sands of St Brelade's for little children.

Scuba diving is superb in some of the most unpolluted waters around the British Isles – see pearly-shelled ormers, stripy cuttlefish, John Dory with spines like punk mohicans, black-faced blennies doing their courtship dances. Sea kayakers make adventurous forays to the isolated reefs of Les Écréhous and Les Minquiers, each with a handful of houses perched precariously amid the waves – edge-of-the-world places for the most daring of dudes and divers.

South coast divers find heaven off the sheltered east side of the Lizard peninsula where the 1898 wreck of SS *Mohegan* lies 30m (100ft) down in the clutches of the deadly Manacles reef. West Cornwall is popular among more daring divers, too, with seals, basking sharks and spectacular reefs among the strong currents off Pendeen near Land's End. Those who are just looking for a swim or a go at surfing enjoy the three main beaches of the artists' haven of St Ives – the sheltered family strand of Porthminster, the tiny and toddler-friendly Porthgwidden, and wide Porthmeor where surfers and swimmers find bigger waves.

Devon also boasts a sheltered south coast and a more vigorous northern aspect. A vast east-facing scoop of coast encloses the deceptively calm-looking breadth of Start Bay. The sea bed rises to within a few feet of the surface; at some states of tide it's said that a man can stand a mile out to sea with his feet on the sea floor and his head in the air. Hundreds of ships have come to grief here down the years; the wrecks are fished by anglers and explored by divers.

AXMOUTH TO HIGHCLIFFE

This geologically fascinating area, with crumbling, fossil-rich cliffs at Lyme Regis and a natural amphitheatre at Lulworth Cove, was once a haven for smugglers

❶ Axmouth
Now a somnolent village of thatched cottages lying beside a marshy estuary, Axmouth was one of Roman Britain's busiest ports. Described in the 16th century by historian John Leland as 'an olde and bigge fischar toune'; it was also a centre for the export of West Country wool and iron. Over the centuries landslips have choked the mouth of the Axe, stranding the former port a mile from the sea, but the resulting estuary attracts curlews, redshanks, common sandpipers and many other birds. Stepps Lane winds up to Hawkesdown Hill, where there is an Iron Age fort and a path to the Undercliffs nature reserve.

❷ Undercliffs National Nature Reserve
Stretching for 6 miles through some of southern England's wildest, most unspoiled countryside, the area now occupied by Undercliffs National Nature Reserve, was created in 1839 by a massive landslide. Around 20 acres of chalkland between Axmouth and Lyme Regis slid seawards, creating what became known locally as Goat Island.

A narrow footpath, part of the coast path, runs through the reserve, but it is rough and slippery in wet weather. There are no points of access from the path to the beach, or to the land on either side of the path, and only experienced walkers should attempt the full journey. But it is possible to walk for a couple of miles and enjoy the tranquillity of this undisturbed countryside, where deer and badgers roam and 120 species

of birds have been recorded. From Lyme the reserve is reached by a footpath from Holmbush car park at the top of Pound Street. Energetic walkers may enjoy the challenge of the climb to the car park from Monmouth Beach, where the grey, glutinous nature of the slips can be seen at close quarters.

❸ Lyme Regis
A dashing, heroic past involving sea battles, smugglers and sieges lies behind Lyme's present appearance as a quiet and charming resort. Many of these adventures centred on The Cobb, the 183m (600ft) long stone breakwater protecting the harbour. The Cobb remains the focal point of the town, with visitors enjoying the salty atmosphere of yachts and fishing boats. Lyme's attractions include a marine aquarium on The Cobb, and a Dinosaurland exhibition. The Philpot Museum has samples of local fossils. Narrow streets lined with colour-washed houses climb steeply from the seafront, and there are several vantage points with fine views towards Golden Cap over Black Ven, the fossil-bearing cliffs between Lyme and Charmouth. These cliffs continue to slip, and the coast path over them is closed. The beach area can be subject to cliff falls, tides and mud flows.

❹ Charmouth
World famous for its abundance of fossils, exposed during centuries of cliff erosion, Charmouth is a popular resort, with a beach of shingle and low-tide sands. The first complete fossil of an ichthyosaurus, a meat-eating reptile

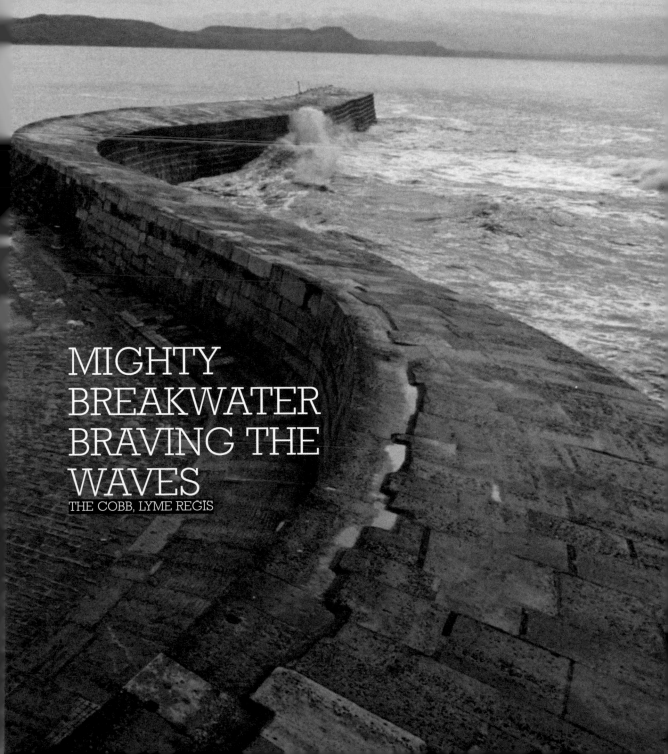

resembling a giant porpoise, was discovered at Black Ven in 1810 by 11-year-old Mary Anning. Some 95 miles of Dorset and East Devon coast have been designated as the Jurassic Coast World Heritage Site. A heritage coast centre on the seafront gives information about the fossils, including where they can be found, preferably with the help of an expert guide. The cliffs and the tides can be treacherous, and fossil-hunters should take great care.

5 Golden Cap

Soaring to 189m (619ft) above sea level, the golden-orange sandstone peak of Golden Cap is the tallest cliff in southern England. Dramatic views from the top stretch out as far as Portland Bill to the east and Start Point to the west. The cliff is part of a National Trust estate that embraces most of the coastal land between Charmouth and Seatown, and includes 18 miles of walks over terrain ranging

MIGHTY BREAKWATER BRAVING THE WAVES
THE COBB, LYME REGIS

from steep cliffs to undulating meadows and clumps of ancient woodland. You can take a number of different paths to reach the summit of Golden Cap, but the shortest route is from the car park at Langdon Hill to the northeast. Stonebarrow Hill, found to the west, has a car park and information centre.

⑥ Seatown

A village of thatched cottages of honey-coloured stone with an open shingle beach that shelves steeply above low-tide sands, Seatown is reached by a lane from Chideock. Golden Cap can be seen a mile to the west and along the coast path to the east Thorncombe Beacon rises to more than 152m (500ft).

⑦ Eype Mouth

A narrow lane winds steeply through the tiny village of Eype, pronounced 'eep', to a car park, from which steps descend to a small, secluded shingle beach backed by crumbling clay and sandstone cliffs. West Bay is a mile-long walk over the cliffs, or 3 miles by road.

⑧ Bridport

Ropes and nets have been made in Bridport since the 13th century, with craftsmen adapting to changing social conditions. During the age of sail the town was so closely associated with rope-making that the hangman's noose was known as 'the Bridport dagger'. Modern workers, by contrast, use their skills to provide nets for snooker-table pockets. Bridport is now a busy shopping centre, with markets on Wednesdays and Saturdays. Buildings of note include the Georgian town hall, and Britain's only thatched brewery, established in the late 18th century. The town's museum explores Bridport's local history. On the northern side of the town is Mangerton Mill, a 17th-century working watermill and rural museum.

⑨ West Bay

Bridport's former harbour, where ships were built until 1879, is a mile from the centre of the town. West Bay, which marks the westernmost point of Chesil Beach, is now visited mainly by sunbathers, walkers and fishermen. The River Brit reaches the sea here, but silting has always been a problem at the manmade harbour.

⑩ Burton Beach

The expanse of fine shingle and sand overlooked by the village of Burton Bradstock, though officially called Burton Beach (NT), is known locally as Hive Beach, and is signposted as such from the village. From the car park at the end of Beach Road, there is a grassy picnic area and a track leading to the

A HAVEN FOR BREEDING WILDFOWL AND WADERS

CHESIL BEACH

beach, where the erosion of soft layers in the cliffs creates the impression of an end-view of stacks of timber.

A rough track, for walkers only, leads down from a parking area next to the B3157 to the shingle bank of Cogden Beach (NT). The Old Farming Collection, on the road between Burton Bradstock and Litton Cheney, is a working farm on the River Bride, with displays of old farming equipment.

⑪ West Bexington
The road through the small village ends by a steeply shelving shingle beach backed by a few beach huts and a car park used mainly by sea anglers. From the top of Wears Hill, a few miles to the east on the road to Abbotsbury, there are superb views of Chesil Beach and the Isle of Portland.

⑫ Abbotsbury
A village of honey-coloured houses with a thatched stone barn, buit in about 1400 to store the riches of the Abbey of St Peter nearby. A wall and an archway of the Abbey still remain. The Tithe Barn and the Abbotsbury Swannery are within easy walking distance of available car parking. The Swannery, which was founded by the abbey monks as a source of food, now gives sanctuary to hundreds of mute swans, which breed in the lagoon that lies behind the shingle beach.

On a hill overlooking Abbotsbury is the 14th-century St Catherine's Chapel (EH), once used to store thatchers' reeds, but now in a state of disrepair. St Nicholas's Church has a pulpit pockmarked with shots fired during the Civil War, when the village fell to Cromwell's Parliamentarians.

Just west of the village are the subtropical Abbotsbury Gardens, set in a valley where a very mild microclimate allows exotic trees and shrubs to flourish outdoors all year round. The gardens include streams and ponds.

⑬ Chesil Beach
The billions of pebbles that make up Chesil Beach are now naturally graded from west to east. The fine gravel found at West Bay increases gradually in size to large cobbles at Portland, 17 miles away. Chesil Bank, part of the beach east of Abbotsbury, rises to a height of 12m (40ft) and protects a lagoon known as The Fleet. The lagoon forms a nature reserve that attracts swans, waders such as curlew and dunlin, and many wintering wildfowl. The Bank can be reached from either end of the reserve, at Abbotsbury and Portland but there is no pedestrian access along the beach between May and August to prevent the disturbance of breeding birds.

14 Isle of Portland

Stories of smugglers and shipwrecks abound in this dramatic rocky peninsula, which author Thomas Hardy called 'the Gibraltar of Wessex'. Steep on its northern side and gently sloping to the south, the isle is pitted with quarries, several still producing the pale Portland stone from which both St Paul's Cathedral and Buckingham Palace were built.

At the southernmost tip, the fast-flowing currents known as 'Portland Race' have been responsible for many shipping disasters. Portland Bill lighthouse looms above the rocky foreshore, and a short distance inland a white Trinity House tower is now an RSPB observatory.

Portland Castle (EH), built by Henry VIII, has an interior little changed since Tudor times. From the shattered walls of the 11th-century Rufus Castle, named after the ruddy-faced William II, steep steps lead down to Church Ope Cove, a small beach lined with fishermen's huts. Nearby Portland Museum explores the island's history. Tout Quarry Sculpture Park uses a former quarry as a natural gallery for modern sculptures, many carved from the living rock. The wildlife information centre at Chesil Bank and The Fleet Nature Reserve is the starting point for two nature trails.

15 Weymouth

A long, wide, sandy beach is backed by an elegant curve of small hotels and boarding-houses, many dating from the late 18th or early 19th centuries. George III began to visit Weymouth for his health in 1789, and established it as a fashionable resort. The pinnacled clock tower was built in 1887 for Queen Victoria's Golden Jubilee. During 1869–70 Thomas Hardy worked for a Weymouth architect, and the town features in some of his writings as Budmouth Regis.

At Brewers Quay, just south of the harbour, an 18th-century brewery now combines a period shopping village with attractions such as the Timewalk, illustrating six centuries of Weymouth's maritime past. Deep Sea Adventure tells the story of global underwater exploration. Nothe Fort, built in 1860–72 as a bulwark against the threat of French invasion, has been converted into a museum of coastal defence. Radipole Lake is an RSPB reserve in the heart of the town, while Lodmoor Country Park includes another bird reserve and a Sea Life Park.

16 Bowleaze Cove

The cove, with a beach of sand, shingle and seaweed-covered rocks, is overlooked by Furzy Cliff, a favourite spot for picnics and kite-flying. From the cliff there are exhilarating views over Weymouth Bay to the Isle of Portland. A short track from the road leads to the foundations of Jordan Hill Roman Temple (EH), a small shrine dating from the 4th century AD.

17 Osmington Mills

The 13th-century Smugglers Inn recalls a favourite landing spot for 'gentlemen of the night'. North of Osmington village is a huge figure of George III on horseback, that was cut into the chalk slope in 1808.

⑱ Ringstead Beach

Follow the narrow lane through the hamlet of Upton to a sloping shingle beach with imposing views of Weymouth and Portland. When the tide goes out, plenty of sand and an offshore reef are revealed. Above Ringstead village, the South West Coast Path takes walkers along the cliff to the imposing chalk headland of White Nothe, a mile to the east. Burning Cliff nearby consists largely of oil-rich shales. When these ignited in the 1820s, the resulting fires smouldered on for several years.

⑲ Durdle Door

A spectacular limestone doorway, carved out by the sea, is reached by a steep track from the clifftop. On either side of the arch, flights of steps lead down to shingle coves. Both beaches are popular with swimmers and subaqua divers. Another, smaller hole pierced through the rock can be seen at Bat's Head.

⑳ Lulworth Cove

High cliffs of crumbling chalk form a natural amphitheatre round a beautiful, oyster-shaped bay. Stair Hole, west of Lulworth, is a similar cove in the making. Lulworth Heritage Centre explains the area's geology.

㉑ Lulworth Range

The coast from the east side of Lulworth Cove round to Kimmeridge Bay forms part of a Royal Armoured Corps tank and gunnery range, but the roads and paths are open to the public most weekends, and during the week in certain holiday periods. A narrow lane runs east for 3 miles across the range from East Lulworth. The picnic area on Povington Hill has fine views and several waymarked footpaths, including the South West Coast Path, cross the range.

㉒ Lulworth Castle

Designed as a hunting lodge in the 17th century, the restored castle is set back from the road on the edge of East Lulworth. There are superb views from one of the 30m (100ft) towers. In the park behind is the Rotunda, built in 1786; it was the first Roman Catholic church built in England after the Reformation.

㉓ Tyneham

Quietly tucked away in a valley, the village has been deserted since 1943, when the inhabitants had to quit their homes to make room for a wartime firing range. It is still used by the army, but is open to the public most weekends. The story of the valley is movingly told by displays in the church and school.

㉔ Kimmeridge Bay

On the beach at Kimmeridge, a 'nodding donkey' oil pump bobs on the unstable cliff. It produces about a million gallons of oil a year. A tower, still visible across the bay, was built in about 1820 by an amateur astronomer, the Rev John Clavell. His family home, Smedmore House, dates from the 1630s, and is open a few days each year. At the east end of the bay is Purbeck Marine Wildlife Reserve and visitors can wander along natural ledges to explore marine creatures.

㉕ St Aldhelm's Head

A primitive 12th-century chapel stands on top of 91m (300ft) cliffs at St Aldhelm's Head, at the southern tip of the Isle of Purbeck, reached only on foot. Between Corfe Castle and the coast, the village of Kingston perches on a high slope. St James's Church, a landmark for miles around, was completed in 1880 with pillars of Purbeck marble, the term for the topmost layer of Purbeck stone.

㉖ Durlston Country Park

The activities of a colony of guillemots are beamed back to the Park Centre, and an underwater microphone near Durlston Head enables visitors to hear the echolocation signals of bottle-nosed dolphins. A 10ft Portland stone globe, made in 1887, stands by the cliffs of the country park. The globe was the idea of George Burt, a stone merchant and amateur astronomer.

㉗ Swanage

Sheltered within its wide bay, Swanage is a popular resort with a sandy beach and colourful gardens. Boats can be hired, and there are boat trips, fishing trips and a diving school. The lifeboat station is open to visitors.

PORTLAND BILL

An area rich in fossils

The coast east of Lyme Regis is a fertile hunting ground for amateur fossil collectors. For thousands of years the cliffs have been crumbling, and this has helped reveal the great wealth of fossils for which the area is famous. It also means that climbing the cliffs is dangerous, and care must be taken at the cliff base, especially during stormy weather. Among the stones on the beach below are the remains of animals that lived 200 million years ago and the rock pools are also worth investigating.

The most common fossils are those of extinct molluscs, such as the spiral-shaped ammonite – distant ancestor of the squid – the bullet-shaped belemnite, and bivalves. Brachiopods and crinoids can also be found. Some lucky collectors have even come across bone fragments from ichthyosaurs and plesiosaurs, but finds such as these are extremely rare.

▶ Lyme Regis ❸ ; Charmouth ❹ , page 60

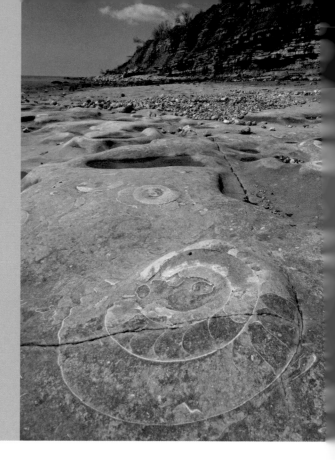

Near the pier is the Wellington Clock Tower, which once stood at the southern approach to London Bridge and was moved to Swanage in 1867. The carved stone facade of the Town Hall was formerly the front of the Mercers' Hall in the City of London. Steam trains on the Swanage Railway run to Corfe.

㉘ Studland
The village is home to St Nicholas Church, an exceptionally well-preserved Norman building. To the west is Studland Heath National Nature Reserve, an area of heath, woods, mudflats and open water with two waymarked trails. Lizards and snakes, including adders, can be found on the heath, and roe deer live in the woods. Paths from Studland and Knoll lead to the Agglestone, a 5m (17ft) high boulder of resistant sandstone.

The South West Coast Path starts at the northern end of Shell Bay and follows the coast to Minehead. A mile's walk along the path east of Studland leads to The Foreland, overlooking Old Harry Rocks. Walkers can continue onto Ballard Cliff for a magnificent panorama of Swanage Bay.

㉙ Brownsea Island
The patchwork of woods, grassland and heath on Brownsea Island (NT) is the home of many animals and birds, including sika deer, semi-wild peacocks and the last southern refuge of the red squirrel. The northern half of the island is a nature reserve with a large heronry. Lord Baden-Powell held an experimental Scout camp on Brownsea Island in 1907. You can get here by ferry from Poole Quay and Sandbanks.

㉚ Poole Harbour
One of Europe's largest natural harbours with more than 90 miles of coastline and 14sq miles of tidal water. Sailing clubs, marinas and boatyards are scattered along the northeast shore. Oil is extracted on Furzey Island, but trees mask the installations from the rest of the harbour.

㉛ Arne
China dolls, tin toys, musical boxes and games and puzzles can be seen at *A World of Toys*, a museum in the tiny hamlet of Arne. To the north lies Arne RSPB reserve. A trail leads through heathland, where you may catch a glimpse of the rare Dartford warbler.

㉜ Poole
Tugs, fishing vessels and pleasure boats moor at Poole Quay, the departure point for boat trips to Brownsea Island and round Poole Harbour. The quayside is lined with Georgian buildings. At Poole Pottery Studio visitors can watch craftsmen at work. Poole Museum has wide harbour views from the terrace. Nearby is

Scaplen's Court Museum, built in the 15th century as a merchant's house. The Lighthouse Centre for Performing Arts is now the home base for the Bournemouth Symphony Orchestra.

Poole's long, sandy beaches lie some 3 miles southeast of the town centre. Strong currents make swimming dangerous near the entrance to Poole Harbour. A vehicle ferry from Sandbanks crosses the harbour mouth. Car ferries to France depart from the docks, south of Poole Quay.

Just inland from the beaches are Italian and Japanese gardens at Compton Acres. Close by is Branksome Dene Chine, a wooded valley with pine trees, rhododendrons and strawberry trees. On the west side of Poole, Upton Country Park has gardens round a 19th-century house.

㉝ Bournemouth
A popular destination since Victorian times, with two piers, classic seaside amusements and a long promenade bordering part of a 7 mile sandy beach. The 'Chines', natural pine-clad valleys once used by smugglers, cut through the sheltering cliffs to the shore. The Lower Gardens, complete with aviary, lie behind the seafront and follow the Bourne Stream to Central Gardens and Upper Gardens. From there it is a short walk to Meyrick Park, a large pine-covered estate with walks and a golf course.

In the town centre, the Russell-Cotes Art Gallery and Museum is an Italianate villa housing Victorian and Edwardian paintings, and Oriental and Victorian artefacts. The 1929 Pavilion includes a theatre and ballroom. Explore the undersea world at the Oceanarium or go up in the Bournemouth Eye, a tethered hot-air balloon, with views for 25 miles. In summer there are day cruises to the Isle of Wight.

㉞ Hengistbury Head
A narrow, hooked finger of land, comprised of 2 miles of heath, woods, marsh and meadow, almost completely encloses Christchurch Harbour. From its southern side paths run to the 36m (118ft) summit of Warren Hill, an important archaeological site, with its traces of Stone Age settlement. There are superb views from the hill across the Solent to the Isle of Wight. Mudeford Sandbank is a strip of dunes at the head's tip; it can be reached either by ferry from Mudeford Quay, on the other side of the harbour mouth, or by 'land train', a small mock train that runs on a path from Double Dykes, two defensive ditches built in Viking times. The head is an important wildlife conservation area.

㉟ Christchurch
Known in Saxon times as Twynham, 'the place between two waters', Christchurch lies at the meeting point of the Avon and Stour, which made it an ideal centre for smuggling in the 17th century. The town's most notable feature is the imposing 11th-century Priory Church. At 95m (312ft), it is the longest church in England, longer even than most cathedrals.

The Priory Gardens in front of the church stand on the site of a Norman castle, of which only the ruined walls of the keep and the Constable's House remain. A short heritage trail takes in the church and the Georgian Red House Museum, which chronicles the borough's history from its earliest settlement. The trail leads down to the yacht-filled quay from where ferries leave in summer for Hengistbury Head and Mudeford. The trail continues to Place Mill, an Anglo-Saxon watermill built in one of the town's few remaining monastery buildings. The Priory also marks one end of the Avon Valley Path, which can be followed for 34 miles northwards to Salisbury. On the harbour's northern shore is the small Stanpit Marsh Nature Reserve.

㊱ Mudeford
A narrow stretch of water known as the Run separates Mudeford Quay from the tip of Hengistbury Head. The quay is the centre of the local fishing industry, whose salmon-netting methods have changed little over 200 years. In spite of residential development, a few old fishermen's cottages remain, along with the original Haven House Inn, the site of a battle between smugglers and the Royal Navy in the 17th century. Mudeford is linked to Hengistbury Head in summer by a passenger ferry.

㊲ Highcliffe
Just over a century old and originally known as Newtown, Highcliffe has expanded to become an attractive residential area. Highcliffe Castle, built around 1830 by Lord Stuart de Rothesay, replaced an earlier house constructed by his grandfather, the Earl of Bute, prime minister during the reign of George III. The dilapidated castle is undergoing long-term restoration and is being opened to the public in stages. From the car park near the castle, steps zigzag down to a sandy beach, hemmed in by green slopes. Farther east is a natural glen, known as Chewton Bunny, through which a stream flows.

> **Visitor information**
>
> **Bridport** ☎ (01308) 424901
> **Lyme Regis** ☎ (01297) 442138
> **Poole** ☎ (01202) 253253
> **Swanage** ☎ (01929) 422885
> **Wareham** ☎ (01929) 552740
> **Weymouth** ☎ (01305) 785747

CHANNEL ISLANDS

Each Channel Island has its own way of life. While the capitals of Jersey and Guernsey, the two largest islands, offer Continental flair, sedate Sark is a place without cars still run along feudal lines

❶ St Helier

Pavement cafes and tree-lined squares give Jersey's capital a French flavour, but the island's mainland neighbour was not always friendly. Looming above the harbour is Fort Regent, built between 1806 and 1814 when Napoleonic France seemed poised to invade. The fort now contains a leisure complex, and nearby you will find Jersey Museum, which includes a renovated 19th-century merchant's house.

The Maritime Trail takes in the Maritime Museum and the Occupation Tapestry which is kept in a converted warehouse on the quayside. The tapestry, made by islanders, depicts Jersey life under German occupation in World War II.

On an islet in the bay, and reached by a low-tide causeway, stand a 12th-century hermitage and the 16th-century Elizabeth Castle.

❷ St Aubin

Linked today to St Helier by a seafront road, promenade and cycle track, St Aubin was Jersey's original port. In the narrow streets above the small 17th-century harbour are houses built by merchants who used the port.

Just north of Beaumont, on the road skirting St Aubin's Bay, a mile of corridor was hewn from solid rock by forced labour during the German occupation to create an underground hospital; it is now part of the Jersey War Tunnels complex.

❸ Portelet Bay

Just offshore is an islet, Ile au Guerdain, crowned by an 18th-century Martello tower, one of many built in the Channel Islands during the Napoleonic Wars. At Noirmont Point, a bluff headland on the eastern side of the bay, is a World War II German command bunker, which you can visit during the summer.

❹ St Brelade's Bay

One of Jersey's most popular beaches, with a mile of firm, golden sand at low tide, is backed by an attractive promenade, gardens and fountains. Just to the south-west is Beauport, a small sandy beach sheltered by rocky headlands.

❺ Corbiere Point

The barren peninsula's jagged, needle-sharp rocks are frighteningly impressive here, and a low-water causeway at the tip of the headland leads to Britain's earliest concrete lighthouse, built in 1874. A siren sounds 15 minutes before the fast incoming tide covers the causeway.

❻ St Ouen's Bay

Jersey's finest beach stretches almost the full length of the island's western coast. When the tide is out, the water's edge almost disappears from view; when it comes in, it can be in spectacular fashion. St Ouen's Bay is very popular with surfers, and competitions are held here. Strong currents make bathing dangerous in places, but there are designated swimming areas.

Behind the coast road, dunes stretching inland incorporate the Les Mielles conservation area, one of the most important dune systems in northern Europe. It supports hundreds of plant species.

❼ Greve de Lecq

From the visitor centre, a coast walk leads east to Sorel Point, along the top of rugged rockfaces falling sheer to the water. The path leads past the Devil's Hole, where the sea has cut through a huge rock; at high tide it boils and booms in a rocky cauldron. The hole can be reached by car from a lane off the B33.

The B40 to the Grève de Lecq beach runs through a wooded valley, passing an old watermill, now an inn. The small sandy bay exposes flat rocks at low tide and is sheltered by grassy cliffs.

❽ Bouley Bay

At the bottom of a winding road is a small pier used by lobster boats. Skin-diving lessons and equipment are available, but bathing in this mostly shingle bay is safe only for strong

MONT ORGUEIL CASTLE, GOREY

swimmers. To the east is the sandier Rozel Bay, a little fishing harbour by a wooded valley.

Inland from Bouley Bay, on the B31, is a zoo created by the naturalist Gerald Durrell in the 1960s, officially titled the Durrell Wildlife Conservation Trust. Rare animals bred in the zoo include Brazilian tamarins, a species of small monkey, and Mauritian pink pigeons.

9 Gorey

Overlooking the harbour at Gorey is Mont Orgueil Castle, with its magnificent 13th-century keep, Elizabethan tower and rambling outworks. The shingle Archirondel beach to the north offers a good view of the mile-long breakwater protecting St Catherine's Bay. To the south, the sandy beach of Royal Bay of Grouville sweeps down to La Rocque Point, which is the winter home of large numbers of migrating waders, including turnstones and sanderlings.

About 2 miles west of Gorey, next to the archaeological and geological museums at the inland hamlet of La Hougue Bie, a medieval abbey crowns a Stone Age passage grave.

10 St Clement's Bay

The long sandy beach is easily reached from St Helier, 2 miles to the west. Nearby Green Island can be reached at low tide, when the surrounding rocks offer a vast area to explore.

11 Alderney

St Anne, Alderney's only town, resembles a Normandy village with its tiny squares, pastel-shaded cottages and granite-cobbled streets. There are few roads on the island, and the best way to get about is on foot or by bicycle. Rough tracks lead to magnificent viewpoints such as Giffoine, Telegraph Bay, and Essex Hill, with its spectacular outcrop known as Hanging Rock. Sandy beaches include Corblets Bay, Arch Bay and Save Bay.

Dotted around the coast are fortifications built during the German occupation. Pleasure cruises around the island are available.

12 St Peter Port

Guernsey's capital is a town of narrow, cobbled streets and solid grey-granite buildings clambering up a steep hillside above the harbour. The town has a Continental flavour, although the architecture is largely English, from the Georgian, Victorian and Edwardian periods. Within the 18th-century Royal Court sits Guernsey's parliament, the States of Deliberation, for although the islands are Crown Possessions they are not part of the United Kingdom, and Guernsey's laws of government date back to Norman times.

In the harbour are three marinas, docks for car and passenger ferries, and three piers from which launches cross to Herm and Sark. At the harbour entrance stands the 13th-century Castle Cornet, whose massive walls embrace three museums and an art gallery. South of the harbour is the town beach, in Havelet Bay. The foreshore is shingle, with sand at low tide. The house in which the French novelist Victor Hugo lived from 1855 until 1870 is now a museum displaying rooms and objects as he left them.

The cliff path from St Peter Port, joined at La Valette just south of the town, leads you to Fermain Bay, where trees tumble almost to the water's edge. The beach, which has stretches of firm sand at low tide, can also be reached by a lane leading from the main coast road.

13 Moulin Huet Bay

Three sandy beaches are sheltered within rocky headlands linked by a coastal path. From the coast road, a lane leads you to Moulin Huet beach, painted by Auguste Renoir in 1883. Rocks are exposed at low tide, and there are caves in the cliffs. Although Petit Port is harder to reach, the final approach being down a long flight of steps, you can reach Saint's Bay by a lane that runs through a wooded vale.

14 Icart Point

One of many such rocky headlands on Guernsey's south coast, Icart Point has perhaps the finest views on the island. Westward lie La Bette Bay, Le Jaonnet Bay, Petit Bot Bay and Portelet Bay, with La Moye Point a craggy finger on the skyline to the west. Petit Bot is one of the few bays on the south coast that can be reached by road, and it is served by bus. The beach there has a pebbly foreshore with sand and rocks exposed at low tide, and a cliff path runs along the length of the south coast.

At Les Vauxbelets, north of Icart Point, stands the Little Chapel. This tiny church, encrusted with seashells and pieces of broken china, was built in the 1920s by a monk, who based it on the grotto at Lourdes in France.

15 Rocquaine Bay

The high cliffs of Guernsey's southern coast give way abruptly on the western side of the island to wide, flat bays of rock, sand and shingle. At Pleinmont Point, the south-westerly tip of the island, the cliffs overlook the large sandy beach of Rocquaine Bay. A small rocky peninsula, Pezeries Point, juts into the southern end of the bay, giving a good view of Hanois lighthouse about a mile offshore. Within the bay is the tiny fishing harbour of Portelet (one of two places so named on the island), which has a small sandy beach, while at the end of a causeway is Fort Grey, a 19th-century fortification in which a shipwreck museum chronicles the many wrecks that occurred on this treacherous coast.

⑯ Perelle Bay

A World War II lookout tower dominating this small rocky bay is one of many reminders of the German occupation. Below the tower a low-water causeway leads to Lihou Island and the ruined 12th-century priory of Notre Dame de la Roche. East of the lookout tower is Le Trepied, one of Guernsey's many dolmens, or prehistoric stone tombs.

⑰ Vazon Bay

The wide crescent of sand and shingle is popular with surfers, although they are restricted to the centre of the bay. The water here is generally safe for bathing but you should check on the state of the tide.

⑱ Cobo Bay

Rust-coloured rocks are exposed at low tide on this sand-and-shingle beach. About a mile to the north, high rocks flank the sandy cove of Port Soif, where the tide hurtles in fast and furiously. The Guernsey Folk Museum, run by the National Trust of Guernsey, is about half a mile south-east of Cobo Bay.

⑲ Grand Havre

The coast road north from Cobo skirts the sand-and-pebble beaches of Port-infer and Pequeries before turning eastwards to follow the curve of Grand Havre, a fishing harbour set in a wide, irregular, sandy bay, where there are boat moorings and three slipways.

A short distance to the east across the narrow headland is L'Ancresse Bay, a broad horseshoe of jagged rocks and shimmering sands, considered to be one of Guernsey's finest bathing beaches. Half a mile farther east you will find Beaucette Marina, a tiny haven flanked by high rocks.

⑳ St Sampson

Tall cranes line the dockside of the small commercial port of St Sampson. By contrast, a mile north of the docks, the fishing village of Bordeaux sits prettily by its harbour. At first the coast road south from St Sampson is lined with warehouses and oil storage tanks, but then the wide beaches of Belle Grève Bay and the harbour walls of St Peter Port come into view.

㉑ Herm

Within this compact island, 1½ miles long and half a mile wide, lie towering cliffs, wooded valleys, sandy beaches and enough pastureland to support some 40 Guernsey cows. The island, which is a 20 minute boat trip from Guernsey, is leased from the States of Guernsey,

and the Tenants live in the 15th-century granite-built Manor House. By the small harbour are a few pastel-coloured cottages, a hotel, a pub and a shopping square. There are no cars or roads.

North of the harbour are the sandy Fisherman's Beach and Bears Beach, beyond which a path cuts across heathland to the island's showpiece, Shell Beach. On a golden strand, millions of tiny shells have been washed up, from as far away as the Gulf of Mexico. About 10 minutes' walk away is Belvoir Bay, small and secluded, then the going gets tough as the path climbs along the cliffs and valleys of Herm's southern half. Another walk, from Belvoir or from the harbour, leads you to the tiny St Tugual Chapel, which dates from Norman times.

Half a mile off Herm's southern tip stands the island of Jethou, a desolate rocky cone that was divided from Herm around AD 700 by a storm. It is privately owned and is not open to visitors.

㉒ Sark

The island of Sark is still run along feudal lines, governed by a seigneur whose feudal rights date back to 1565, when they were granted by Elizabeth I. You can visit the gardens of La Seigneurie in summer.

No cars are allowed on Sark. Instead, tractor-drawn trailers take visitors up the steep hill from the harbour; horse-drawn carriages can be hired for a drive around the island; and bicycles are available. But you are advised to explore the island on foot, as the paths that lead down to the bays and beaches are often too steep for bicycles.

The island is about 3 miles long and 1½ miles across, and at the southern end it is almost cut in two. The southern section, called Little Sark, is reached by a natural causeway of rock, 76m (250ft) above sea level, called La Coupée. Though some of Sark's bays can be reached easily the island's glory is in the views from its headlands. From Havre Gosselin, on the west coast, the view extends across to the lonely, privately owned Brecqhou Island. Below the cliffs the sea licks around jagged rocks and probes the dark caverns of the Gouliot caves.

Almost half of Sark's eastern side can be seen from Banquette, including the lighthouse at Point Robert to the south. On a clear day it is possible to see France, some 20 miles away.

Visitor information

Alderney: St Anne ☎ (01481) 822994
Guernsey: St Peter Port ☎ (01481) 723552
Herm ☎ (01481) 722377
Jersey: St Helier ☎ (01534) 448800
Sark ☎ (01481) 832345

Southeast

Here is defiance writ large: the great chalk bastion of the Kentish and Sussex coast, facing down would-be invaders from the Norman Conquest until the present day. In among the jolly resorts from Margate round to Brighton stand forts, towers and castles, ancient sentinels along the cliffs and low marshy shores.

Marlborough

Newbury

M4

A339

A33

Basingstoke

A338

A34

A303

Andover

Winchester

A36

M27

New Forest National Park

Southampton

M27

A3(M)

A31

Portsmouth

Lymington

Newport

Isle of Wight

Hurst Castle to Freshwater Bay
p74-79

St Margeret's Bay
to Gravsend
p98-103

The North Downs

Warsash to
Newhaven
p80-87

Seaford to
Dover
p90-97

The South Downs

Key

— Motorway
— Principal A road

(See 'Finding your way',
page 7)

Gravesend
Rochester
Chatham
Margate
Woking
Canterbury
Maidstone
Dorking
Reigate
Guildford
Royal
Tunbridge
Wells
Ashford
Dover
Haslemere
Folkestone
Crawley
Haywards
Heath
Crowborough
Rye
Lewes
Bexhill-
on-Sea
Chichester
Worthing
Brighton
Hastings
Bognor
Regis
Eastbourne

A322
M3
A3
A31
A3
A272
A27
A24
A264
A23
A24
A26
A27
A22
A26
A259
A259
A21
A229
A228
A26
A21
M23
M25
M26
A21
M20
A2
A20
A28
A2070
A259
A256
A2
M2
A299

HURST CASTLE TO FRESHWATER BAY

This dramatic coastline is a haven for yachtsmen and women, drawn to Cowes, the renowned sailing hub, on the Isle of Wight. But the golden sands, sunny climate and many nature reserves make this a favourite spot for many holidaymakers

❶ Hurst Castle
Built by Henry VIII between 1538 and 1540 Hurst Castle (EH) crouches at the end of a lonely spit, a mile from Cliff End on the Isle of Wight. You can reach it by a strenuous 2 mile walk across a pebble causeway that starts just outside Milford, or by ferry in summer from Keyhaven. The castle has a 12-sided central tower, and on display are two Victorian 38 ton guns; an exhibition relates the castle's history.

❷ Keyhaven
The marshes of this quiet, sheltered inlet were once used for salt production, but they now form part of the Lymington-Keyhaven Nature Reserve, which is visited by redshanks, dunlins, oystercatchers and curlews. There is a sailing club here, with numerous yachts in the small harbour, and summer ferries leave from the quay for Hurst Castle and the Isle of Wight. A sea-wall footpath from the harbour winds along the marshes for 4 miles to Lymington.

❸ Lymington
Historically a market town, granted a charter between 1184 and 1216, Lymington still hosts a Saturday market in its Georgian high street. Cobbled Quay Hill winds down from the bottom of the high street to a yacht-filled harbour from where there is a ferry service to Yarmouth on the Isle of Wight. The Royal Lymington Yacht Club marks the start of a 7 mile walk to Bucklers Hard; the path forms part of the Solent Way.

❹ Needs Ore Point
A haven for birdwatchers, the eastern tip of the North Solent National Nature Reserve covers most of the Beaulieu River's western shoreline. The reserve includes Gull Island and boasts the country's largest population of black-headed gulls. You can reach Needs Ore Point along a private gravel road, signposted Warren Lane; it begins 2 miles south of Bucklers Hard near the ruins of St Leonard's, a grange that once served Beaulieu Abbey. Entry to the reserve is by permit from the Beaulieu estate office, at the National Motor Museum.

❺ Bucklers Hard
Two rows of 18th-century cottages and a grassy 'high street' sloping gently down to the Beaulieu River make up this beautifully restored, tree-lined village. Between 1698 and 1827 it was a busy shipbuilding centre, and two warships for Nelson's fleet were built there – *Agamemnon* in 1781, and *Euryalus* in 1803. The fee paid to enter the village includes admission to the Maritime Museum, where tableaux re-create the 18th-century life that was once found here. There are river cruises from the jetty, and a 2½ mile riverside walk from the boatyard to Beaulieu.

❻ Lepe Country Park
The small park that covers a narrow stretch of the Solent coast is within an Area of Outstanding Natural Beauty. You will find clifftop walks, picnic spots and an information centre next to the car park.

A shingle spit, where swimming is dangerous, is revealed at low tide. In winter Brent geese and many wading birds feed on the mudflats.

❼ Calshot
Built by Henry VIII in 1539 Calshot Castle (EH) stands tucked away behind three giant hangars, the remains of one of Britain's most important seaplane stations. A pebbly beach lined with bathing huts leads you to a bleak spit overlooked by the 198m (650ft) chimney of Fawley power station. The coastline of Calshot Marshes forms a nature reserve, where you find black-tailed godwits and other migratory birds.

❽ Hythe
Between 1930 and 1940, flying boats were designed and built at this industrial and residential suburb of Southampton. Pointing out across Southampton Water is the long, thin finger of Hythe's 100-year-old pier, whose narrow-gauge railway carries passengers to the ferry that crosses to Southampton.

❾ Southampton
Britain's major passenger port has a nautical heritage stretching back more than a thousand years. The Museum of Archaeology shows its growth from separate Roman, Saxon and medieval settlements, while the Maritime Museum has an exhibition on the *Titanic*, which set sail on its fateful voyage from the port in 1912. Although Southampton was heavily bombed during the Second World War, the towers of the 14th-century town walls remain, along with the 12th-century Bargate building and the 15th-century Tudor House.

Ocean Village, at the southern end of Southampton, is a modern waterfront development where luxury yachts moor alongside wooden schooners dating from the 1920s. The last working coastal passenger and cargo steamer, SS *Shieldhall*, built in 1955, is permanently docked in the harbour, and is open to visitors. A passenger ferry operates to both Hythe and Town Quay, another harbour development, which has a Sunday market where traders from France sometimes set up their stalls.

The Lower Test Nature Reserve, on Southampton's western outskirts, has a nationally important population of rare Cetti's warblers.

❿ Netley
The remains of the country's first purpose-built military hospital, opened in 1856 by Queen Victoria to care for Crimean War casualties dominates the Royal Victoria Country Park. All that is left of the hospital is a chapel, housing a museum of the hospital's history, and a tower, which you can climb for

BUCKLERS HARD

A LINK, ONCE, BETWEEN THE ISLE OF WIGHT AND THE MAINLAND

THE NEEDLES

panoramic views of the area. The park was once part of the grounds of nearby Netley Abbey (EH), built by the monks of Beaulieu in the 13th century. A mile long walk follows the western shoreline of the park, and a narrow-gauge railway runs through it on a line formerly used to transport wounded soldiers to the hospital. Westwood Park, north-west of Netley, is an area of ancient woodland with grassland and stream-side walks.

⑪ Hamble le Rice

Known for many years as simply Hamble, meaning 'crooked river', the village has now reverted to its original name, le Rice meaning 'in the brushwood'. It is predominantly a yachting centre, with five marinas, and a pebble beach that looks over Southampton Water to Fawley oil refinery and power station; you can take a foot ferry to Warsash across the Hamble.

Hamble Common, south-east of the village, is an area of heath, salt marsh and woods that has variety of wildlife, including nesting stonechats and linnets. Hamble Point, where a Second World War anti-aircraft battery stands, is also the site of an Iron Age fort.

⑫ The Needles

The three towering 30m (100ft) pinnacles are the remnants of a chalk ridge that used to join the Isle of Wight to the mainland. A pleasure park with funfair amusements and picnic areas stands on The Needles peninsula near a vast parking area. From here a walk of almost a mile across the headland leads you past the Old Battery (NT), a restored Victorian fort, to a closer, even more spectacular view of The Needles.

Tranquillity can be found east of the peninsula on the grassy chalk ridge of Tennyson Down, named after the poet Lord Tennyson, who lived at nearby Farringford House. He walked on the down regularly, and declared the air there to be worth 'sixpence a pint'. A monument to him was erected on the summit in 1897.

⑬ Alum Bay
The pebbly bay is backed by steep cliffs of coloured sands formed of white quartz, red iron oxide and yellow limonite. You can reach Alum Bay by chairlift from the pleasure park, or by a footpath and steep steps. Boat trips round The Needles leave from the beach.

⑭ Fort Victoria
Built as part of 19th-century defensive measures against a French invasion, Fort Victoria now houses a marine aquarium, a planetarium and a maritime heritage exhibition. Sconce Point, on which the fort stands, is an ideal place from which to watch shipping in the Solent. There is good offshore fishing from the sandy beach, while Fort Victoria Country Park, which surrounds the fort, has a nature trail.

⑮ Yarmouth
The home of the Royal Solent Yacht Club, Yarmouth is a charming village of stone quays and attractive, narrow lanes. There are two small beaches, one shingle, the other sand and shingle, and the pier, built in 1876, is popular for fishing and for its views across the Solent. Boat trips round offshore Hurst Castle (EH) and The Needles are available in summer, and a car ferry sails to Lymington, on the mainland. Behind the ferry port stands Yarmouth Castle (EH), built by Henry VIII in 1547.

⑯ Cowes
Regattas take place at East Cowes every summer, making the most of the long promenade which allows superb views of yacht racing outside the harbour. A chain ferry across the River Medina links the town to the world sailing centre of West Cowes, where yachts ride at anchor in the bay below the headquarters of the Royal Yacht Squadron. A maritime museum is housed in the town's library. You can cross to Southampton by ferry from East Cowes or by passenger hydrofoil from West Cowes.

⑰ Osborne House
Queen Victoria's country retreat, Osborne House (EH) provides an intimate glimpse of the monarch's family life, as it has been left almost unchanged since her death there in 1901. A grove of cork trees in nearby Barton Manor Gardens and Vineyards was planted by her husband, Prince Albert. He also designed the flamboyantly Gothic Church of St Mildred at Whippingham, a mile to the southwest.

⑱ Fishbourne
The pretty green and small, shingle beach at Fishbourne faces Wootton Creek, a lively centre for watersports. Visitors to the town can take a car ferry service to Portsmouth.

Approaching Fishbourne from the sea you will notice the redbrick spire of Quarr Abbey, built in 1912. A path from its driveway, signposted on the A3054, leads you to the ruins of a 12th-century Cistercian abbey.

⑲ Ryde
A broad esplanade between the sea and the Victorian hillside town gives the busy resort of Ryde a rather grand air. Golden sands stretch out on each side of the mile long pier, which was built in 1813 and is thought to be the oldest in Britain. There are boating lakes, an ice-skating arena and a miniature train on the seafront, and to the east, in the landscaped gardens behind Appley Beach, is a heated swimming pool. Regularly departing catamarans and ferries carry foot passengers to Portsmouth.

Shire horses, miniature ponies, a children's farm and a collection of horse-drawn carriages are among the many attractions at Brickfields Horse Country in Binstead, west of Ryde.

⑳ Seaview
The sailing village of predominantly blue and white houses is aptly named. Its long, sandy beach gives broad views of the Spithead area of the Solent, and of the four forts built at sea in the 1860s to protect mainland harbours from the feared invasion from France. A sea-wall walk of about a mile leads to Ryde. Seaview Wildlife Encounter, northwest of Seaview, has many species of waterfowl, as well as water-garden displays.

㉑ Bembridge
Houseboats line the village's wooded harbour, where yachts sail sedately in and out. On the northern side of the harbour is St Helens Duver (NT), an area of gorse and open grassland on a narrow, sandy spit that attracts migrant birds. There are also fine views of boats in the Yar estuary, while on the outskirts of the village is Bembridge Windmill (NT), the island's only surviving windmill. Built in the early 18th century, it was the subject of a sketch made by the artist J.M.W. Turner in 1775.

㉒ Culver Down
The stone needle on Culver Down is a memorial to the Earl of Yarborough, first commodore of the Royal Yacht Squadron. From this point you can pause to take in the spectacular views of the long, golden sands of Sandown to the west and Whitecliff Bay to the north. Bembridge Down, which has an orientation table identifying features of the surrounding view, merges with Culver Down to give a wide area for exhilarating walks. Added interest comes from watching light aircraft flying in and out of Bembridge airport.

㉓ Sandown
The 5 mile long sandy beach here, stretching from Shanklin to Sandown and beyond, is the longest on the island. At the northern end of the beach, a 19th-century fort is home to the Isle of Wight Zoo, which specialises in breeding endangered species.

㉔ Shanklin
A largely Victorian seaside town blends into the scattering of thatched houses to the south that make up Old Shanklin. The old village overlooks Shanklin Chine, a deep, wooded ravine with a roaring waterfall; a walk through the chine passes a Victorian brine tub, in which heated seawater baths could be taken. It also passes part of the PLUTO pipeline used in the Second World War to carry fuel under the Channel. Shanklin's other main attraction is a long, inviting, sandy beach at the foot of honey-coloured cliffs, which can be reached by a lift from Keats Green, named after the poet John Keats, who stayed in the town in 1819.

㉕ Bonchurch
A fishing and quarrying hamlet during the 19th century, Bonchurch is home to the ancient Church of St Boniface, said to have been built in 1040 by monks from Normandy. A path runs from the church to the former home of the 19th-century poet Algernon Swinburne, above Monk's Bay, where there has been extensive work to protect Bonchurch from the erosions caused by The Landslip. The slip was caused in the early 19th century when 30 acres, and later 50 acres, of land slid into the sea. A further 25 acres of earth has since fallen away.

㉖ Ventnor
The town is built on a series of steep terraces that rise above a sandy, sheltered beach lined with hotels, restaurants and shops. In the battle against cliff erosion, 30,000 tons of Mendip limestone has been deposited on the shore to the west, and a mile long sea wall has been built to the east, extending as far as Bonchurch. St Boniface Down, the highest point on the island, has good all-round views of the coast and inland hills.

The island's benign climate enables many subtropical plants to thrive in the Botanic Garden to the west of the town. Farther west, the 12th-century church at St Lawrence is one of the smallest churches in Britain, measuring just 14m x 5m (45ft x 15ft).

㉗ St Catherine's Point
Until the lighthouse was built in 1840, the sea around St Catherine's Point was a graveyard for ships: between 1748 and 1808 an average of ten ships a year came to grief here.

Visitors to the lighthouse should park in Niton village to the north, and make the 5 minute walk from there. The open headland of Knowles Farm (NT), with its bracing winds, lies to the west of the lighthouse.

㉘ Blackgang Chine
Landslips are common along this stretch of coast, and Blackgang has suffered many over the years. The viewpoint over Blackgang Chine gives an almost aerial vista of the contrasting chalk and clay cliffs of the southwest of the island. On a clear day it is possible to pick out the Isle of Purbeck, 28 miles away, and even Portland Bill, 50 miles distant. The area's main attraction is a fantasy theme park, while a 14th-century lighthouse base, known as the pepperpot, stands on the summit of St Catherine's Hill.

㉙ Whale Chine
The long, deep chine got its name from an incident in 1758, when a 19m (63ft) whale was stranded there. You can reach the chine's secluded rock and shingle beach down a footpath, which descends to a wooden staircase through Whale Chine's dark, damp walls. In the event of a landslip the path may be closed.

㉚ Brook
The hamlet of Brook marks the southern end of the Hamstead Trail, an 8 mile walk from Hamstead Ledge on the northern shore of the island. On the seaward side of the village is Brook Chine (NT), where a path from the car park leads to a sand and shingle beach, flanked by crumbling clay cliffs. Compton Bay, north-west of Brook, is a sandy beach; behind the 61m (200ft) cliffs that back it soars Compton Down, popular with hang-gliders.

㉛ Freshwater Bay
Two chalk stacks, smaller versions of The Needles, stand in the bay here, and another is being carved out of the cliff face by the relentless sea. Badly eroded chalk cliffs rise beside a curving sea wall and a steeply shelving pebble beach. Farringford House, on the western edge of Freshwater, was the home of the poet Lord Tennyson between 1853 and 1864; it is now a hotel.

Visitor information

Bournemouth ☎ 0845 051 1700
Christchurch ☎ (01202) 471780
Lymington ☎ (01590) 689000
Lyndhurst ☎ 023 8028 2269
Southampton ☎ 023 8083 3333
Isle of Wight ☎ (01983) 813813

WARSASH TO NEWHAVEN

This strategically important stretch of coastline contains Portsmouth, England's most important naval base, as well as the lively town of Brighton, one of the country's major seaside resorts

❶ Warsash

The yachting village of Warsash marks the start of a 4 mile coastal path leading to Hill Head and passing Hook Nature Reserve. The reserve is visited by oystercatchers, shelducks, linnets and meadow pipits.

From the western end of Warsash a passenger ferry sails to the village of Hamble le Rice, while east of Warsash are the superb ruins of 13th-century Titchfield Abbey (EH), comprising the original priory buildings and a four-storey Tudor gatehouse.

❷ Hill Head

A promenade and large grassy area back the shingle beach of this old smugglers' haunt. Strong currents restrict swimming, but there is good fishing to be had at the western end. Coast walks lead to Lee-on-the-Solent, a mile to the east, and to the Hamble estuary, 4 miles to the west. You will have to pay to enter the Titchfield Haven National Nature Reserve, where hides give views of waders and wildfowl, especially wigeon.

❸ Lee-on-the-Solent

The Hovercraft Museum at Lee houses a collection of rare examples of the craft, including the largest and earliest. The promenade runs behind a shingle beach, at the eastern end of which are sailing and angling clubs.

❹ Gosport

The history of this former fishing village is explained in the Gosport Discovery Centre, while to the south of the town is the Royal Navy Submarine Museum, where you can board HMS *Alliance*, as well as *Holland I*, the navy's first 'submarine boat'. A ferry service to Portsmouth, which has run since the reign of Edward I, operates from the Ferry Gardens at the end of the high street.

To the north is Fort Brockhurst (EH), built as a defence against invasion by Napoleon III, and used by the navy until the Second World War. Stokes Bay, to the south, has been well defended since Tudor times, and you can still see an early 19th-century battery, or gun emplacement, at the western end of the 3 mile beach. The bay is now a popular centre for watersports.

'Little Woodham', on the western outskirts of the town, is a reconstruction of a 17th-century hamlet with timber-framed houses, which recalls life in the area before the Civil War.

❺ Portchester Castle

The ancient outer walls of Portchester Castle (EH) are those of Europe's most complete surviving Roman fortress. The castle's Norman keep houses an exhibition of its history, and a path from the Water Gate leads to the shore and offers good views of Portsmouth Harbour. A coastal path close by heads west towards Fareham.

The chalk escarpment of Portsdown Hill, a mile northeast of Portchester, has footpaths and outstanding views across Portsmouth and the Solent. Fort Nelson, built by Lord Palmerston in the 1860s, houses the Royal Armouries Museum of Artillery.

❻ Portsmouth

A fortress town since the 15th century, Portsmouth is England's most important naval base and the home of the Royal Dockyard founded by Henry VIII in 1540. Among the dockyard's Georgian storehouses is the Royal Naval Museum, together with Henry VIII's warship *Mary Rose* and Lord Nelson's flagship, HMS *Victory*. Here you can also board HMS *Warrior*, which was the world's most advanced warship when it was launched in 1860, and is permanently docked in the harbour. Soaring above the retail and entertainment complex at Gunwharf Quays is the 170m (558ft) Spinnaker Tower, which offers spectacular views along the coast.

Old Portsmouth is the site of the City Museum and Art Gallery, and the 12th-century Cathedral of St Thomas of Canterbury. The Camber, in the western part of Old Portsmouth, where Sir Walter Raleigh landed with England's first supplies of potatoes and tobacco in 1585, was the city's original harbour.

Although still a working dockyard, with the 15th-century Round Tower guarding the harbour entrance, fishing is now its principal activity. On the northern side of the city is the Continental Ferry Port, while the nearby house where the novelist Charles Dickens was born in 1812 is now a museum containing memorabilia and effects including the couch on which he died in 1870.

❼ Southsea

Though part of the City of Portsmouth, Southsea still has the character of a traditional seaside resort. It has a long shingle beach with patches of low-tide sand, two piers, and a string of seaside attractions, including a fairground, a D-Day Museum and the Pyramids leisure centre.

Southsea Castle was built by Henry VIII around 1544 to defend the Royal Dockyard. Its battlements offer good views of the Solent and of Spitbank Fort, a coastal defence that you can visit by ferry from Portsmouth's naval base. South Parade Pier, popular for fishing, marks the start of Southsea's esplanade, which is backed by the Rose Gardens and a boating lake. At Eastney, at the east end of the beach, is the Royal Marines Museum, which is housed in Eastney Barracks.

PORTCHESTER CASTLE

8 Langstone

At the end of the high street is a small salt-marsh inlet where the Old Mill, once a smugglers' hideout, is said to be linked by tunnels to two waterside inns. Langstone Harbour is now a Site of Special Scientific Interest that includes an RSPB reserve and also Farlington Marshes Nature Reserve, where many species of waders and wildfowl can be seen from a public footpath.

Behind the Old Mill, now a private residence, a path leads eastwards to the village of Warblington and the ruins of its 17th-century castle. The nearby Church of St Thomas a Becket has a Saxon tower and two 18th-century gravewatchers' huts, whose occupants once guarded against body-snatching.

9 Hayling Island

Linked to the mainland by a bridge, the island is fringed by marshes except on its southern shore, where there is a long stretch of sand and shingle. There are funfairs and amusement arcades along the seafront, as well as three yachting clubs, and a golf course on Sinah Common. The Hayling Billy Leisure Trail is a 3 mile coast walk from West Town, tracing the route of a former railway line, and is the best place from which to view birds such as bar-tailed godwits and dunlins on the Kench Nature Reserve, which adjoins Langstone.

10 Emsworth

There are two old tide mills on the harbour of this former fishing port at the mouth of the River Ems. One houses the sailing club and sits at the head of the harbour in front of a tidal pond. The harbour wall, a delightful promenade, is the start of two long-distance trails – the 60 mile Solent Way west to Milford on Sea and the 90 mile Wayfarer's Walk inland to Newbury.

11 Thorney Island

The westernmost of three peninsulas that jut into Chichester Harbour, Thorney Island is largely flat and featureless. The island is mostly the property of the Ministry of Defence, and the road south to the village of West Thorney is closed by a barrier.

Although access is restricted in some parts, you can explore the island using an 8 mile footpath that skirts the foreshore. There are good views of the harbour from the path, and Longmere Point, at Thorney's southern tip, overlooks the RSPB reserve of Pilsey Island.

12 Prinsted

A lane from the village of cottages that overlook tidal flats runs down to a shingle beach at the head of Thorney Channel. The small car park here is a good starting point for walks in both directions round Chichester Harbour. Small boats can be launched near high water.

13 Bosham

One of the south coast's most renowned beauty spots, the harbour village of Bosham, pronounced 'Bozzam', sits on a small wedge of land between two tidal creeks. Its sailing club is housed in an old quayside watermill in the marina, while Quay Meadow (NT) is a grassy picnic area, beyond which rises the steeple of the Saxon Holy Trinity Church.

14 Fishbourne Roman Palace

Seven years of excavation during the 1960s unearthed the remains of a magnificent palace on this early Roman site. The palace, built around AD 75, is thought to be that of the British King Cogidubnus, who had supported the Romans' invasion of AD 43, enjoyed their patronage and been allowed to rule on their behalf. The detailed floor mosaics and the remains of luxurious chambers and corridors are protected beneath a modern building. At the Collections Discovery Centre you are allowed to handle Roman artefacts.

15 Dell Quay

In the 18th century Dell Quay was the seventh most important port in England, along with neighbouring Apuldram. Today it is no more than a quiet sailing hamlet. Cottages are dotted along the narrow lane that leads down to the quayside and the yacht anchorages, where parking is very limited. Walks in both directions along the shore give wide views over Chichester Channel, where wildfowl and waders abound.

16 Birdham

With neat bungalows and cottages scattered about St James's Church and a green with its water pump, Birdham retains a village character. Close by lies the entrance to the Chichester Canal, which separates two huge marinas, Chichester Yacht Basin and Birdham Pool. Each has its own sailing club, boatyards and chandlers.

The Sussex Falconry Centre, east of Birdham, breeds and displays owls, kestrels, sparrowhawks and buzzards.

17 West Itchenor

Formerly a busy commercial port, West Itchenor is now a pretty sailing centre. The main road through the village leads to a shingle beach and a public jetty, from which boat tours of the harbour operate. In summer you can take a ferry across Chichester Channel to Bosham.

Bosham's historic church

The little village of Bosham contains one of the most famous Saxon churches in Sussex. The church is even featured on the Bayeux Tapestry, which depicts in detail the story of the Norman Conquest over its 70m (230ft) length.

Harold, Earl of Wessex, who was soon to become King of England, set out from Bosham on his fateful voyage to Normandy, stopping en route in Bosham Church for prayer. His oath of loyalty to Duke William triggered a chain of events that eventually led to William invading and conquering England.

The church is also the burial place of King Canute's young daughter, who is thought to have drowned nearby.

▶ Bosham **13**, page 82

18 West Wittering

A popular holiday village, West Wittering has a mile long sandy beach fringed with dunes, reached by a signposted drive from the main street. The road ends at a large car park and picnic area.

West of the village, the shingle spit of East Head (NT) attracts birdwatchers and naturalists, who may spot ringed plovers, little terns and several species of butterfly on the tidal lagoon and among the dunes.

19 East Wittering

You can reach the beach at East Wittering, where a large expanse of sand is revealed at low tide, either from Shore Road, which has no nearby parking, or from a car park where the B2198 ends at Bracklesham.

A maze of 17 themed gardens, including a Scented Garden and a Seaside Garden, has been laid out at Earnley Gardens, northeast of Bracklesham. Tropical butterflies, exotic birds and farm animals can also be seen there.

20 Selsey

From Selsey Bill there are fine views across to the Isle of Wight and eastwards along the coast. The low-lying headland, along either side of which stretch sandy beaches, is built up with holiday homes and residential properties. Fast currents can make bathing hazardous here. Extensive parking that is found behind the sea wall attracts most holidaymakers to East Beach,

located near to the lifeboat station, where you can buy many types of fish and shellfish that have been caught locally.

21 Pagham Harbour

Now a nature reserve, dunlins, grey plovers, curlews and Brent geese are among the many species that gather on the mudflats of this former port, while much of the surrounding land is a haven for small mammals, insects and butterflies. The reserve is reached along a path from a visitor centre at Sidlesham, 2 miles north of Selsey.

The village of Pagham is centred on the seafront, and the mainly 13th-century Church of St Thomas a Becket is one of the few indications that an earlier settlement existed. Pagham's sandy beach, backed by pebbles, has a car park and plenty of cafes and amusements.

Two paths in the village lead you to the harbour; one starts near the church, the other at Harbour Road behind the seafront. There is also a path along the harbour's southern edge that leads across Church Norton churchyard, which has a chapel dedicated to St Wilfrid, who introduced Christianity to the South Saxons in the 7th century.

22 Bognor Regis

One of the most popular resorts on the south coast, Bognor Regis has sandy beaches, funfairs, holiday camps and bandstands as well as a pier with amusement arcades, cafes and a nightclub. The museum explains the history of the town and includes a wireless exhibition.

23 Middleton-on-Sea

The site of a seaplane base during the First World War; the present village of Middleton developed mainly between the wars. Houses now line the seafront in this predominantly residential area situated on the edge of Bognor Regis, and several footpaths lead to the shingle and sand beach.

24 Climping Sands

A large parking and picnic area behind the sea wall at Climping Sands is the start of foreshore walks in both directions along 2½ miles of undeveloped coastline. The walk eastwards, to the mouth of the River Arun, gives good views of the castle and cathedral at Arundel, and passes shingle colonised by sea kale and the yellow-horned poppy.

A few houses on the road to the shingle beach are all that remains of the village of Atherington, the rest of which was washed away in the 16th century.

The tower of St Mary's Church, almost 2 miles inland in the village of Climping, was built around 1170 and has a finely carved doorway. The rest of the church was built 60 years later and its structure is little changed since then.

25 Littlehampton

Sandy beaches have drawn visitors to Littlehampton since the late 18th century, and in the early 20th century the resort was promoted as 'the children's paradise'. The East Beach is backed by a wide green, and there is an amusement park on the western promenade. A footbridge and, in summer, a ferry cross from the town to the west bank of the Arun, where there are boatyards, marinas and a sailing club, as well as the West Beach, backed by dunes. It can be dangerous to bathe near the river mouth.

26 Rustington

Old flint-walled cottages and the medieval Church of St Peter and St Paul at Rustington have been engulfed by housing estates, although steps from the promenade lead to a beach of pebbles and low-tide sand.

Angmering-on-Sea, to the east, is a village of mostly private estates. You can walk to the beach along paths between some of the houses.

27 Ferring

Fishing boats can often be seen drawn up on the shingle above the sandy beach at Ferring, which is separated from Worthing by fields and woods. Highdown Chalk Gardens, on the South Downs 2 miles inland from Ferring, has plants from all over the world, including Chinese maples and Indian chestnuts. The garden was established in 1910 by Sir Frederick and Lady Stern, who worked for 50 years to prove that plants would grow on chalk.

28 Goring-by-Sea

The modern English Martyrs Church at Goring has a copy of Michelangelo's ceiling in the Vatican's Sistine Chapel; it was completed in 1993. A residential suburb of Worthing, the town has a shingle beach, with low-tide sand that hosts a variety of watersports, including kitesurfing.

29 Worthing

After 1798, when Princess Amelia, the Prince Regent's delicate younger sister, visited for her health, Worthing developed from a fishing hamlet into a fashionable resort and some buildings from the town's early years survive. The museum and art gallery has a costume collection from 1700 to the present day.

Five miles of seafront, a wide promenade, colourful gardens, and a pier with amusements and good fishing still attract many holidaymakers to this large resort. The beach at Worthing is shingle with low-tide sand; signs warn swimmers of the danger of submerged storm water outfalls.

On Worthing's northern edge is High Salvington Windmill, a black post mill completed in 1720 and now restored and producing flour; it is open on two Sundays a month in summer. St Mary's Church at Sompting Abbotts, 2 miles northeast of the town centre, has a Saxon tower unique in Britain.

30 South Lancing

Lancing College chapel, 2 miles from the sea and founded in 1868, is a landmark along the coast. A narrow strip of grass stands between the coast road and a beach of sand backed by shingle.

WORTHING PIER

③① Shoreham-by-Sea

The busy port of Shoreham lies astride the River Adur, where the river turns sharply eastwards before meeting the sea. The Church of St Nicholas at Old Shoreham, the original village and port, dates from Saxon times, but by 1100 the Adur was silting up and the Normans chose a site farther south for their town of New Shoreham, with its 12th-century Church of St Mary de Haura, meaning 'of the harbour'. The Marlipins Museum, housed in an early 12th-century building, contains paintings and ship models.

A footbridge over the Adur from the town centre leads you to Shoreham Beach, built on a shingle bank between the Adur and the sea. At Widewater, a landlocked lagoon at the west end of Shoreham Beach, you can view herons, swans and ducks. Shoreham Airport, the oldest airport in Britain, has an art deco terminal building; pleasure flights and flying lessons are available here.

③② Southwick

Traditional flint-walled houses cluster round a spacious green in Southwick, an old village now engulfed by later development. To the south, a narrow inlet that runs to Hove contains Shoreham's marina, and forms the commercial, eastern arm of Shoreham harbour, flanked by Portslade-by-Sea. Facing the harbour entrance, Kingston Beach is a crescent of shingle with a disused lighthouse built in 1846, and the Shoreham lifeboat station. All that remains of the power station, which once dominated the harbour, is a tall chimney.

③③ Hove

Wide expanses of lawn along the seafront give an open feeling to Hove, Brighton's sister resort and more sedate neighbour. The beach here consists of a broad bank of pebbles with a narrow strip of sand at low tide. Among the town's many elegant crescents and terraces is the monumental Brunswick Square, which dates from the 1820s and opens onto the seafront. Number 13 is being restored as a town house of the period and is open to the public by appointment.

A Victorian villa houses Hove Museum and Art Gallery, which has paintings by British artists, together with ceramics, toys and clocks; there is also a section on early 20th-century commercial film-making in Hove.

Nearby, West Blatchington, a downland village swallowed up by the expansion of Hove, is crowned by an early 19th-century smock windmill, containing a milling museum; it is open on summer Sundays and Bank Holidays.

High above the northern outskirts of Hove is Foredown Tower Countryside Centre, where a camera obscura focuses wide-ranging views extending over the South Downs and the English Channel onto its white concave surface.

③④ Brighton

The onion-domed Royal Pavilion forms an extraordinary centrepiece to the queen of British seaside resorts. Brighton's oriental fantasy, its interior as whimsical as its exterior, was the early 19th-century creation of the Prince Regent, who later became George IV. Fashionable society followed the prince to Brighton, and the town expanded steadily, its elegant terraces and squares surrounding the old fishing village of Brighthelmstone. Brighton Museum and Art Gallery, housed in the former stables of the Royal Pavilion, traces the town's development into a major resort.

The narrow streets of the old village are now a pedestrianised shopping area known as The Lanes, which has many antiques, clothes and jewellery shops, while the beach consists of pebbles leading down to a narrow strip of low-tide sand. The Palace Pier, renowned for its amusements and funfair, looks out over the old West Pier, which is awaiting restoration after fire damage.

Volk's Electric Railway, the first such railway in Britain when it was opened in 1883 by Magnus Volk, rattles along the seafront from Madeira Drive. The Sea Life Centre and the Fishing Museum are both on the seafront.

③⑤ Rottingdean

Rudyard Kipling lived in the village from 1897 to 1902, and the Grange Museum, housed in an 18th-century vicarage, has a collection of items relating to the writer. The road between Brighton and Rottingdean skirts the cliff edge, giving views over the Channel.

③⑥ Newhaven

Ferries to and from Dieppe, in Normandy, inch their way along the narrow River Ouse and berth on its eastern bank. The town centre and a marina are on the west bank, where there is also a small shingle beach.

Newhaven Fort, high above the western side of the river mouth, is one of a chain of 72 coastal defences built in the 1860s to withstand French attack. The fort has displays on army life, the Royal Observer Corps and the 'Home Front' during the Second World War. On the ramparts, guns point menacingly out to sea.

Visitor information

Bognor Regis ☎ (01243) 823140
Brighton & Hove ☎ 0906 711 2255
Gosport ☎ 023 9252 2944
Hayling Island ☎ 023 9246 7111
Littlehampton ☎ (01903) 721866
Portsmouth ☎ 023 9282 6722
Worthing ☎ (01903) 221307

BRIGHTON'S
ORIENTAL
FANTASY
BRIGHTON PAVILION

Guardians of the coast

An extraordinary chain of military strongholds stand in a grand parade on the south coast, the defenders of fortress England

With its famous white chalk cliffs and its many military fortifications, the 200 miles of coast that run from the Thames Estuary south and west to the Isle of Wight form Britain's most iconic shore. Strength and defiance seem the chief characteristics for this coast, which has been defended many times down the centuries against invasion, or the threat of it. The roll-call of successful invaders incorporates Celtic adventurers of the last millennium BC, Roman legions in 43AD, Anglo-Saxon warriors in the 5th century, Danish sea-wolves some 300 years later, and Norman knights in 1066. The list of failed would-be conquerors, or of invaders whose plans existed more in British minds, number many more.

Whatever the substance of each successive invasion scare, the English responded to the threat with a flurry of defensive construction. Given its proximity to mainland Europe, it is not surprising that this coastal span of southern England is the most heavily fortified region in Britain. A tour by boat along the coasts of Kent, Sussex and Hampshire reveals an extraordinary string of defensive strongpoints: castles built on promontories, tunnels burrowed in cliffs, gun emplacements sited on headlands, towers rising from marshes and shingle, forts planted on sandbanks in the sea.

These are a sobering reminder of just how much money, ingenuity and sheer sweated labour were poured out on defending this short piece of coast before modern air power and nuclear missiles rendered them redundant.

Under attack through the ages

The period following the Norman Conquest was one of great uncertainty within England, epitomised by the development and strengthening of Dover Castle over the centuries into the mighty fortress that dominates the harbour today. But it was with Britain's expansion into a world power in the 16th century that the threat of invasion, real or imagined, really began to bite on the minds of public, politicians and Crown.

In the 1530s and 40s King Henry VIII feared attack by Catholic France and Spain, either separately or together, after his split with Rome and establishment of the breakaway Protestant Church of England. His response was to build the rosette-shaped castles at Walmer and Deal on the Kentish Coast and out on the end of Hurst Point shingle spit in the Solent, their bulgy flanks intended to give a wide field of fire while remaining less vulnerable to mining.

The 19th century dawned with Napoleon Bonaparte's French army rampant across Europe and a huge flotilla of military barges assembling in the ports of the northern French coast. Britannia still ruled the waves, but attack and invasion across the insignificant little waterway of the English Channel seemed inevitable.

Between 1805 and 1810 a total of 74 stumpy, oval-shaped Martello towers were built along the south coast. This defensive chain, stretching from Folkestone in Kent round to Seaford in east Sussex and soon extended northwards along the East Anglian coast, was commissioned by the Government quite as much for its morale-boosting effect on the British public as for any military purpose – invading soldiers would simply have bypassed the towers and their roof-mounted guns. Twenty-five Martello towers still stand, some converted into dwellings or museums, others gently crumbling.

Fanciful fears of invasion

The shadow of Napoleon proved a long one in the British imagination. Forty years after the Little Emperor's death, the threat of invasion by his great-nephew Emperor Louis Napoleon III became a huge source of apprehension in Britain, even though it was largely groundless. In the 1860s and 70s Prime Minister Lord Henry Palmerston ordered the reinforcement of many existing forts and the construction of a whole string of new ones – these latter gaining the telling nickname of 'Palmerston's Follies'. Many of the biggest and most bizarre were sited in, around and off the Hampshire coast, with the aim of defending Portsmouth.

These new forts included the huge complexes of Fort Nelson and Fort Brockhurst; smaller but no less wondrous to behold are the circular forts of Spitbank, Horse Sands, No Man's Land and St Helen's, founded on sandbanks out in the Solent as a deterrent to the French navy. Examples further east include the Hoo and Darnet forts, built to guard Chatham Dockyard and still squatting low on their muddy islets in the throat of the Medway estuary.

Rumours were rife at the turn of the 20th century concerning a possible invasion of Britain's east coast by a newly resurgent and aggressive Germany. These proved insubstantial. But in the summer of 1940 the threat of invasion across the English Channel by the seemingly unstoppable army and air force of Nazi Germany was all too real. Fortified bunkers, gun emplacements, pillboxes and searchlight batteries dotted the south coast; the beaches were wired and mined, and concrete anti-tank blocks lined cliffs and shores. Many are still in situ – ugly, awkward-looking structures that stand as mute reminders of the vigilance and defiance that have so often been the saviours of this island nation.

A FORT BUILT TO EASE A PRIME MINISTER'S FEARS
FORT BROCKHURST, HAMPSHIRE

SEAFORD TO DOVER

From Dover's distinctive white cliffs to the flat and windswept landscape of Dungeness, this is an area with a history just as dramatic as its scenery

❶ Seaford

The shingle beach bordering the quiet, mainly residential seaside town shelves steeply, and at high tide the sea is suitable for strong swimmers only. A small local history museum is housed in a seafront Martello tower – the westernmost of the chain of circular, early 19th-century fortress towers that extends round England's east and southeast coasts. Another attraction is The Crypt, a restored 13th-century stone undercroft with an art gallery, or you can take a 15-minute walk along the shingle to the massive foundations of Bishop stone tide mill, which once harnessed tidal power to grind corn.

❷ Seaford Head Nature Reserve

Behind the 86m (282ft) cliffs of Seaford Head is a nature reserve where migrant birds, including willow warblers, chiffchaffs, whitethroats and redstarts, stop to feed while heading south in autumn. Ring ouzels and pied flycatchers may also be seen, and nightingales are heard in spring. A clifftop path from Seaford to the headland gives spectacular views along the coast, while the path from the car park to Hope Gap gives a splendid view of the scalloped white wall of cliff known as the Seven Sisters.

❸ Cuckmere Haven

At a gap in the chalk cliffs, 18th-century smugglers found an ideal place to land cargoes of brandy, lace and other French contraband. The tranquil River Cuckmere, whose name is pronounced 'Cookmere', makes a series of enormous loops through water meadows before reaching Cuckmere Haven. The main road is a mile inland, and the stone-scattered beach is reached only by footpath along the valley. There is a large car park near the start of the walk, at Exceat, pronounced 'Ex-seet'.

The eastern side of the Cuckmere valley and the western end of the Seven Sisters cliffs make up a country park that includes meadows, downland, chalk cliffs, salt marsh and shingle, and supports a variety of wildlife. Barns by the Seaford to Eastbourne road at Exceat house a visitor centre, with exhibitions including The Living World, where you can see stick insects, scorpions and butterflies, plus a display of seashore life.

❹ Seven Sisters

Between Cuckmere Haven and Birling Gap the striking vertical chalk cliffs rise and fall like the waves in the sea far below. Despite its name, there are in fact eight summits in the range, the highest of which is 77m (253ft).

❺ Friston Forest

Dense forest, mostly of broad-leaved trees, sprawls across the downs and can be explored by a 2¾ mile waymarked walk that starts at the car park at the west end of the forest. South of the coast road, a lane beside Friston's St Mary the Virgin Church leads down to Crowlink, which has fine views.

❻ Birling Gap

Like Cuckmere Haven, this narrow gap in the cliffs was once the haunt of smugglers, who used the flint-built village of East Dean, a mile inland, as their headquarters. Birling Gap's shingle beach is reached by steep steps down the 9m (30ft) cliff, which is wearing away.

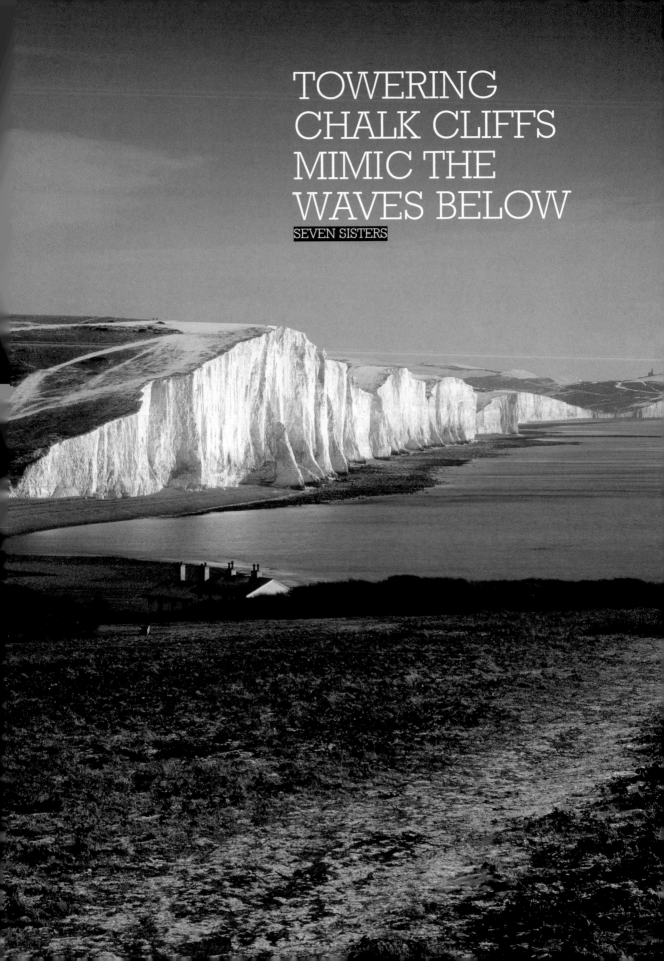

TOWERING CHALK CLIFFS MIMIC THE WAVES BELOW

SEVEN SISTERS

DE LA WARR PAVILION, BEXHILL

At the nearby Seven Sisters Sheep Centre you can watch sheep-shearing and milking and see 30 breeds of sheep, including now rare, older breeds not seen on modern farms. To the east of Birling Gap, the former Belle Tout lighthouse perches close to the cliff edge; built in 1834, it is now a private house. In 1999 it was raised onto tracks and moved 17m (55ft) inland.

❼ Beachy Head
The Normans called it Beau Chef, meaning 'Beautiful Headland', but over the centuries the name of this colossal chalk rampart has been corrupted to 'Beachy'. The 163m (534ft) cliff rises sheer from the rocky foreshore, and from its grassy summit the view on a clear day takes in the English Channel from Dungeness in the east to the Isle of Wight in the west.

A breezy path from the main car park leads you past clumps of sea lavender and samphire to the cliff edge; from here there are good views of the red-and-white lighthouse far below. Exhibits in the Beachy Head Countryside Centre include a rock pool with tides.

❽ Eastbourne
A lively pier and a turquoise-roofed bandstand, where military bands play in summer, stand at the centre of 3 miles of seafront in Eastbourne, which has plenty of

stuccoed Victorian buildings. Colourful public gardens that line the seafront include the Carpet Gardens, where flowerbeds are laid out in the patterns of Persian carpets. The beach is mainly shingle, with sand at low tide; fishing trips are available, and boat trips take visitors past Beachy Head and the Seven Sisters cliffs.

On the seafront is Wish Tower, a restored Martello tower, while the neighbouring Lifeboat Museum is housed in a former lifeboat station. Eastbourne's heritage centre, a few minutes' walk inland, traces the town's growth since the 17th century, and the nearby 'How We Lived Then' museum of shops illustrates how people shopped and lived from 1850 to 1950. Farther east along the seafront is the Redoubt, a restored Napoleonic fortress housing military exhibitions.

Polegate Windmill, on Eastbourne's northern outskirts, is a restored tower mill built in 1817 and open to the public on various summer days and Bank Holidays. Between Eastbourne and Pevensey Bay is Sovereign Harbour, a large marina and leisure area.

❾ Pevensey Bay
In 1066 William the Conqueror landed somewhere along this stretch of coast, although the precise spot is not actually known because the coastline has changed to a great degree over the centuries. Today, the shingle

beach is fringed with holiday chalets and small houses, which continue along the coast towards Norman's Bay.

The old village of Pevensey, a mile inland, is dominated by the mighty Pevensey Castle (EH), whose outer walls were built by the Romans as a defence against Saxon raiders. Within are the remains of a castle dating from soon after the Norman Conquest. From Pevensey, a minor road meanders across the flat grazing land of Pevensey Levels towards Bexhill. Part of the level is marshland and forms a national nature reserve. No paths cross it, but from the roadside you can get good views of its birdlife – yellow wagtails and reed and sedge warblers in summer, golden plovers and lapwings in winter.

⑩ Bexhill
This quiet resort is dominated by the long, low lines and great sweeps of glass of the De La Warr Pavilion, which was built in 1935 and extensively restored as an arts venue in 2005. Bexhill's shingle beach with a broad expanse of sand was the first in Britain to allow mixed bathing in 1901. Half a mile inland, a small group of weatherboarded houses and St Peter's Church, founded in 772, make up the old town of Bexhill. The former stable block of the old manor house is now a museum.

⑪ Bulverhythe
The long stretch of stone and shingle at Bulverhythe was once a favourite landing place for smugglers. A pub by the main road, the Bo-Peep, takes its name from the nursery rhyme, which is said to have been written in the 18th century for the landlord's daughter. The sheep in the rhyme are supposed to have been smugglers, and their tails casks of smuggled French brandy. At very low tides the timbers of the *Amsterdam*, a Dutch merchantman wrecked in 1748, can sometimes be seen offshore.

⑫ St Leonards
A planned seaside resort of villas and gardens, rising along the sides of a valley behind the seafront, St Leonards was built between 1827 and 1837 by the architect James Burton and his son Decimus for wealthy visitors. Buildings dating from this period include the assembly rooms, now a Masonic hall, and the Royal Victoria Hotel, which is dwarfed by the huge white bulk of Marine Court, flats built in the 1930s to resemble an ocean liner. St Leonards long ago coalesced with Hastings.

⑬ Hastings
Although Hastings gave its name to the battle that took place in 1066, Duke William of Normandy actually defeated King Harold and his Saxon army 6 miles inland, at Battle.

Hastings was already a flourishing harbour town when the Normans landed at Pevensey to the west, and in the Middle Ages the town was one of the Cinque Ports, along with Dover, Hythe, Romney and Sandwich. The Old Town's long, narrow High Street slants inland from the harbour between East Hill and West Hill, and is lined with half-timbered and weatherboarded houses. Tiny lanes and stepped paths climb the steep hillsides of the Old Town, and cliff railways climb to the summits of both hills.

Hastings Castle, of which only fragments survive, on West Hill, was the first castle built by William after the Conquest; a daily audiovisual show in the grounds re-creates the Battle of Hastings. St Clement's Caves burrow far into West Hill, and at Smugglers Adventure tableaux depict smugglers and their activities.

At the harbour, known as the Stade, fishermen winch boats ashore on the shingle. A few yards away are tall, black-painted wooden sheds, known as 'net shops', built for drying nets but now used for storage. Early-morning fish auctions take place at the fish market above the shingle. Nearby are the Shipwreck and Coastal Heritage Centre, the Fishermen's Museum and Underwater World, with an 'ocean tunnel' that allows you a close look at rays, sharks and other marine creatures. West of the Stade are a traditional pier, and the Hastings and St Leonards beach, a continuous expanse that consists of shingle with low-tide sand and rock pools.

⑭ Hastings Country Park
A superb open space of woods, grassland and heath, cut through by deep glens, extends along the clifftop from East Hill, in Hastings, and eastwards to Fairlight. Here you can see woodpeckers, linnets, greenfinches and redpolls. A lane by Fairlight's tall-towered St Andrew's Church leads to the main car park, below which is heathland known, perhaps from its yellow-flowered gorse, as the Firehills. A small rocky cove at the cliff foot is a naturist beach.

From Fairlight, a narrow road twists down to Cliff End, where the shingle beach is lined with groynes and rows of wooden stakes, which protect the coast from erosion. Notices warn of mud-holes, rockfalls, underwater obstructions and treacherous tides.

⑮ Pett Level
An expanse of flat land, crisscrossed by watercourses and with reedy ponds that are a haven for herons and other water birds, Pett Level lies between the sea and the western end of the Royal Military Canal. The canal was dug in the early 19th century as part of the defensive system against Napoleon. The beach is shingle, with muddy sand uncovered at low tide; steps lead down to the beach from the road.

SHARPLY SCULPTED DUNES AND RAPID INCOMING TIDES

CAMBER SANDS

⑯ Winchelsea

Weatherboarded cottages and tile-hung houses face each other across streets laid out on a grid pattern in this sleepy little town. Winchelsea now stands more than a mile inland, but during the Middle Ages it was one of the principal harbours on the south coast. From the 15th century the build-up of shingle along the shore gradually cut the town off from the sea. Winchelsea was repeatedly attacked by the French, who destroyed most of the Church of St Thomas the Martyr; only the choir and side chapels remain intact. Three medieval gateways survive, however, as does the Court Hall.

At Winchelsea Beach, south of the town, there are chalets, caravans and camp sites, lying above a beach of shingle with low-tide sand.

⑰ Camber Castle

Crouching low amid farmland about a mile from the sea, Camber Castle (EH) is a solitary and impressive ruin, surviving virtually in its original form. It was one of a defensive chain built in the 1530s, at a time when Henry VIII feared invasion from the Continent, to a clover-leaf plan with rounded walls to deflect cannonballs. It is open at weekends in summer, and access is by a level walk of more than a mile across fields.

⑱ Rye

This gem of a medieval hilltop town is entered through an imposing stone gateway; its narrow streets, many of them cobbled, rise to the fine Norman Church of St Mary, distinctive for its 'quarterboys', gilded cherubs that strike the bells on the tower clock. Rye is surrounded by water on three sides: the Rother to the east; the Tillingham to the west; and the Royal Military Canal to the south. It has a small fishing fleet, and there are usually fishing boats moored in the Rother.

Lamb House (NT), built in the 18th century, was the home of the American novelist Henry James from 1897 to 1914, while steep, cobbled Mermaid Street, with its half-timbered Mermaid Inn, was once a haunt of smugglers. The 13th-century Ypres Tower, all that remains of Rye Castle, has a museum with exhibits that include one of the world's oldest fire engines; the tower overlooks the Gun Garden, where cannon still point out to sea. Rye Heritage Centre, on Strand Quay, houses the Town Model, showing Rye as it was in the late 19th century.

⑲ Rye Harbour

Set at the mouth of the River Rother, Rye Harbour consists of a Martello tower, a cluster of cottages and the prominent Victorian Church of the Holy Spirit. From the car park by the tower, a path leads to Rye Harbour Nature Reserve, an area of salt marsh and farmland that has some of the most varied coastal shingle vegetation in the south of England. Many wader species can be seen from the hides including little and common terns, oystercatchers and ringed plovers.

⑳ Camber

The vast sand dunes that loom over Camber have been replanted with marram grass and shrubs to prevent erosion, and fenced footpaths lead across the dunes to Camber Sands, where the sea goes out for half a mile at low tide. The coast road from Rye zigzags past gravel pits and across golf links and walkers should beware as there is a danger of being cut off by fast, incoming tides. East of Camber the dunes gradually give way to the shingle of Dungeness, where the currents become progressively more dangerous.

㉑ Lydd

All Saints' Church, built in the 1440s, dominates the village and is known as the 'Cathedral of Romney Marsh'. It is 61m (200ft) long and has a tower 40m (132ft) high. Lydd gave its name to the explosive lyddite, first tested there around 1890. Lydd (London Ashford) airport has daily flights to Le Touquet, and offers flying instruction. You can reach the Dungeness foreshore from Dengemarsh Road, which runs for 3 miles across the shingle, passing Herons Park leisure complex.

㉒ Dungeness

The windswept shingle promontory, where thick fog can roll in suddenly, and whose coastline is forever changing, has been a constant danger to shipping, and two lighthouses stand on the foreshore. The graceful structure of Dungeness lighthouse throws a beam for 17 miles, and the tall, brick tower of the disused 1904 lighthouse has spectacular views round the coast from its parapet. The base of Samuel Wyatt's lighthouse of 1792 has been converted into houses and flats. Scattered about the shingle are fishermen's huts, where you can buy fresh fish.

Behind the lighthouses loom the massive square blocks of Dungeness nuclear power station. The late film director, Derek Jarman created a wild garden in its shadow which is still there today. Dungeness is also the southern terminus of the Romney, Hythe and Dymchurch Railway, whose miniature steam trains puff north along the coast to Hythe, nearly 14 miles away.

Dungeness RSPB Reserve, down a track off the Lydd-Dungeness road, has an information centre and waymarked walk. The reserve is a wintering ground for many migratory birds, and more than 300 species have been recorded there, including firecrests, little terns and stone curlews.

㉓ Greatstone-on-Sea
Low tide here exposes a sunken section of a Mulberry artificial harbour, which was towed across the English Channel for use during the Normandy invasion of 1944. The resort forms part of a straggling stretch of seaside development that runs for 3 miles from Lydd-on-Sea, past Greatstone to Littlestone, where tall Victorian houses face a stretch of grass above the sea. The beach is shingle, leading down at low tide to a broad expanse of sand.

㉔ New Romney
Until storms at the end of the 13th century diverted the mouth of the Rother to Rye, the river flowed into the sea here, and boats used to moor below the churchyard wall. As the shingle built up, Romney, the 'capital' of Romney Marsh and an original Cinque Port, became stranded a mile from the sea. The superb St Nicholas Church here is Norman in origin but was greatly enlarged in the 14th century. Also worth a look is the station of the Romney, Hythe and Dymchurch Railway, which has a museum with a fully operational model railway.

㉕ Dymchurch
Lying more than 2m (7ft) below high-tide level, Dymchurch crouches behind the massive, possibly Roman, embankment known as Dymchurch Wall. This old Romney Marsh township is full of amusement arcades and funfairs, forming a lively contrast behind the sand and shingle beach with the dignified main street and imposing Martello towers. Tower Number 24 (EH), which has a cannon on its roof, has been restored and has displays about the defences against Napoleon.

From as early as the 13th century to 1930 the complex Romney Marsh drainage system was run from Dymchurch by the grandly named 'Lords of the Level'. They operated from the Court Room in New Hall at the northern end of Dymchurch, where the present drainage board have their offices. The original court room is still on view in the museum at New Hall, along with relics from the town's past.

㉖ Hythe
The town centre is now half a mile inland, yet in medieval times Hythe was right on the sea and one of the Cinque Ports – the confederation of southeast coastal towns that supplied ships and crew for the defence of the realm in return for special charters and privileges. The older part of Hythe is separated from the largely Victorian resort area by the Royal Military Canal, which was dug during the early 19th century as part of the defensive system against Napoleon and is now used by small pleasure boats.

In the old part of town, on a steep slope above the canal, streets of mainly 18th-century houses run parallel to each other below the medieval Church of St Leonard. The church's crypt contains 1000 skulls and 8000 thighbones from inhabitants of the period 1200 to 1400; they were probably placed there when the graveyard was cleared to make room for fresh burials.

Seaside Hythe has a long promenade above a shingle and sand beach protected by massive groynes. Fishing boats line the shingle below a Martello tower – a circular, early 19th-century fortress tower – that marks the eastern end of a 2 mile long military firing range.

Hythe is the northern terminus of the Romney, Hythe and Dymchurch Railway, a miniature steam railway that runs for nearly 14 miles to Dungeness. Brockhill Country Park, in hills northwest of the town, is the starting point for three waymarked country walks.

㉗ Sandgate
Rows of old fishermen's cottages are squeezed between the road and the sea at Sandgate. On the small esplanade are the battered remains of Sandgate Castle, which you can visit by appointment. The castle was one of a chain built by Henry VIII in the 1530s at a time of threatened invasion.

㉘ Kent Battle of Britain Museum
In 1940, fighter aircraft that took off from Hawkinge Airfield played a crucial role in the Battle of Britain. The now-disused airfield is the base for a museum with a large collection of German and British aircraft remains and reconstructions, as well as wartime uniforms, weapons and photographs.

㉙ Folkestone
A superb clifftop promenade, called the Leas, with wide lawns and colourful flowerbeds stretches westwards from the town centre for more than a mile. It is flanked on the landward side by tall stucco Victorian houses and a few large hotels, and on the seaward side by steeply sloping cliffs crossed by paths.

Folkestone's old High Street slopes down to the harbour, where fishing boats lie stranded on the mud at low tide. You can reach the main beach, East Cliff Sands, from The Stade, the fish-market area by the harbour. One of the three Martello towers houses a visitor centre; guided walks start at the tower, and at the harbour.

㉚ The Warren
A wilderness of cliffs, scrub, grassland and woodland, The Warren is a favourite place for walkers, who can follow a waymarked trail that starts at the Martello tower visitor centre. More than 200 species of birds have been

Derek Jarman's Dungeness

Derek Jarman's garden at Prospect Cottage, Dungeness, has become a landmark in this enticingly strange area. Notable for its bleak, eerie beauty, the shingle garden serves as a memorial to the iconic and controversial British film director and artist, who died in 1994. Jarman spent his last years here in this flat, windswept landscape, creating his garden, which stands in the shadow of Dungeness power station, from local materials, driftwood and debris he found on the beach. It contains plants chosen for their ability to survive the wind and salt spray of this remote and inhospitable environment.

▶ See Dungeness ㉒, page 95

recorded at The Warren; chaffinches and yellow-hammers may be seen all year, and migrating birds, including blackcaps, chiffchaffs and nightingales, arrive in spring and autumn.

The hummocky land beneath the chalk cliffs has been created by landslips. A major slip, in 1915, sent blocks of chalk into the sea and buried the railway line that crosses The Warren.

㉛ Capel-le-Ferne

Just west of the village, the RAF flag flutters above the clifftop Battle of Britain Memorial. The shape of a huge aircraft propeller, with blades 37m (120ft) long, has been cut into the chalk; on the central boss of the propeller is a sculpture of a seated Battle of Britain fighter pilot, gazing at the sky. From Capel-le-Ferne's clifftop road a steep footpath leads down over the railway line to the beach, where a concrete apron has been constructed above the shingle to prevent landslips.

㉜ Shakespeare Cliff

The most monumental of the white cliffs that guard Dover on both sides, this massive headland towers 91m (300ft) above the sea. Its name comes from a scene in Shakespeare's *King Lear*, in which Edgar describes the cliff to his blind father Gloucester. Near the cliff, the chalk spoil from the Channel Tunnel workings has been used to create a huge flat skirt called Samphire Ho, its name taken from the same speech in *King Lear*, in which Edgar describes the 'dreadful trade' of gathering the fleshy-leaved samphire plant from the cliffs.

㉝ Dover

The naval significance of the town dates back through many centuries; the Romans made Dover the headquarters of their northern fleet; in the Middle Ages Dover was one of the Cinque Ports; and during both World Wars it was shelled and bombed from across the English Channel. Today, cross-Channel ferries and cargo ships come and go from the giant harbour.

On a hill above the eastern side of the town is the huge fortress of Dover Castle (EH). The castle's square keep was started in the 1180s; outer walls were added and remodelled in later centuries, and a labyrinth of underground tunnels was dug in Napoleonic times. During the Second World War some of the tunnels were used as an operations centre, where the evacuation of troops from Dunkirk was planned, and others were adapted as a hospital. Guided tours of the tunnels are available.

On a grassy mound next to the castle are the 12m (40ft) high remains of a Roman *pharos*, or lighthouse, built soon after the Romans arrived in the 1st century AD, and beside which stands the Saxon Church of St Mary-in-Castro. In a clearing behind the castle, the granite outline of an aircraft sunk into the turf commemorates Louis Bleriot, who landed there after making the first cross-Channel flight in 1909.

The town's museum, housed in the Dover Discovery Centre, tells the story of Dover since prehistoric times and has the Bronze Age Boat, the world's oldest known seagoing vessel. Nearby are the remains of a Roman town house with wall paintings and a hypocaust (heating system).

A minor road from Dover to St Margaret's at Cliffe passes Langdon Cliffs, from where you can get a bird's-eye view of Dover's Eastern Docks. A 45 minute walk from Langdon Cliffs leads you along the top of the white cliffs to South Foreland Lighthouse (NT), which can be visited but is no longer working.

Crabble Corn Mill, 2 miles northwest of the town centre, was built in 1812 to produce flour for the troops guarding Dover against Napoleon's threat of invasion. The mill has been restored to working order.

Visitor information

Dover ☎ (01304) 205108
Eastbourne ☎ 0871 663 0031
Folkestone ☎ (01303) 258594
Hastings ☎ (01424) 781111
Hythe ☎ (01303) 266421 (summer)
New Romney ☎ (01797) 362353
Rye ☎ (01797) 226696
Seaford ☎ (01323) 897426

SOUTHEAST
Seaford to Dover

ST MARGARET'S BAY TO GRAVESEND

This stretch of coastline, which includes the much-loved holiday resorts of Margate, Broadstairs and Whitstable, provided inspiration for Charles Dickens, who spent much of his life here

❶ St Margaret's Bay
A cove of shingle and rocks, with towering chalk cliffs on either side, the bay is the English mainland's nearest point to France, 21 miles away, and is the traditional starting or finishing point for cross-Channel swimmers.

The bay can be reached by a narrow road that zigzags down from the town of St Margaret's at Cliffe, but the town suffers from heavy traffic during the holiday season. The climate in St Margaret's is so mild that subtropical plants flourish; one public garden, The Pines, has a 3m (9ft) bronze sculpture of Sir Winston Churchill. Above the cliffs to the north, the tall, granite obelisk of the Dover Patrol Memorial commemorates naval personnel of two world wars who died patrolling the Channel. Towards Kingsdown, a clifftop path, part of the long-distance Saxon Shore Way, will take you across The Leas (NT), an area of rolling heathland.

❷ Kingsdown
Holiday homes and fishermen's cottages overlook a broad shingle beach dotted with boats and small huts. A range of high white cliffs begins at Kingsdown, and extends past Dover as far as Folkestone. Paths lead along the foreshore and up onto the cliffs.

❸ Walmer Castle
Like Deal Castle, Walmer Castle (EH) was built by Henry VIII in 1540, when the sea came right up to its walls. The castle is now the official residence of the Lord Warden of the Cinque Ports. Its interior is elegantly panelled, with portraits and relics of the Duke of Wellington, who died there in 1852.

❹ Deal
In the days of sail, naval fleets and merchantmen anchored in The Downs – the stretch of water between Deal and the treacherous Goodwin Sands – waiting for favourable winds to help them on their journey. That era is recalled by the Timeball Tower, whose time-keeping mechanism was used by sailors in The Downs to check their chronometers. The tower now houses a museum, while the Deal Museum explores the town's maritime history. A quiet town with a steeply sloping shingle beach,

Deal today remains much as it was in the 18th century. In the west of the town is the Tides Leisure Pool complex.

Deal Castle (EH) was built by Henry VIII in the shape of a Tudor rose, and a roadside plaque just south of the castle makes the doubtful claim that Julius Caesar first landed here in 55 BC.

⑤ Sandwich Bay
The wide expanse of dunes between Sandwich and the sea provides the setting for three championship golf links – Royal Cinque Ports, Royal St George's (featured in the James Bond film *Goldfinger*) and Prince's.

A toll road from Sandwich leads through the opulent Sandwich Bay Estate to the disused Prince's clubhouse. From here a walk along the shingle foreshore leads you to Pegwell Bay and Sandwich Bay National Nature Reserve, Kent's last untouched complex of beach and foreshore, dunes and salt marsh. It supports ducks, geese and large numbers of waders, and its salt-tolerant plants include sea holly and marsh orchids.

⑥ Sandwich
The northernmost of the Cinque Ports, Sandwich is a delightful old town with a complex network of streets and three medieval churches. Though the town is now almost 2 miles inland, it can be reached from Pegwell Bay by the winding 5 mile navigable channel of the River Stour. Boats can be launched from the quay at Sandwich, but only for 2 hours on either side of high tide.

The entrance to the town is guarded by the twin-turreted Barbican Gate, built in 1539 and facing north across a narrow bridge over the Stour, while the stone Fisher Gate was built in 1384 at a time of savage raids by the French. You can see Cinque Port treasures and other historic exhibits at the Guildhall Museum.

Between the town and the river are the ponds and dykes of Gazen Salts, a small nature reserve.

⑦ Richborough Castle
In Roman times, the Isle of Thanet was a true island, separated from Kent by a mile wide channel. Richborough Castle (EH), at the southern end of the channel, was one of the Forts of the Saxon Shore, built about AD 285 to deter Norse raiders. Much of the outer wall survives, as do the foundations of a triumphal arch built soon after the Romans invaded in AD 43.

⑧ Pegwell Bay
A bay of sand and mudflats at the mouth of the Stour is fringed to the north by low chalk cliffs. To the west is the northern section of Pegwell Bay and Sandwich Bay National Nature Reserve. Paths lead onto the reserve from a car park by the main road, with fine views

across the bay, while a short way to the north, a grassy picnic area offers a peaceful setting for the war-like *Hugin*, a replica of a dragon-prowed Viking longship. St Augustine landed in the bay in AD 597 on a mission to convert the pagans of Kent, and is commemorated by a stone cross outside the village of Cliffs End.

⑨ Ramsgate
Graceful early 19th-century terraces line a busy harbour, served by a ferry service to Ostend. Known as the Royal Harbour since George IV embarked there on a voyage in 1821, it has a crowded marina, and a Maritime Museum based in the 19th-century Clock House, whose attractions include the steam tug *Cervia*. The 19th-century architect Augustus Pugin lived and designed here – Ramsgate Town Trail takes in some of his architectural highlights, and his Grade I listed Grange has tours on Wednesdays by appointment. The main bathing beach is at Ramsgate Sands, a wide strip of sand stretching north of the harbour.

⑩ Broadstairs
There are reminders of Charles Dickens at almost every corner of the narrow, twisting streets of the sedate town of Broadstairs, where the novelist spent many summer holidays. Now a private house, the battlemented Bleak House is where Dickens wrote *David Copperfield*. A house on the seafront was once the home of Miss Mary Strong, the model for the character Betsey Trotwood in the book; it is now the Dickens House Museum. In June each year, Broadstairs holds a week-long Dickens Festival, when people dress up in Dickensian costume.

Viking Bay has a sandy beach, sheltered by the curving pier, where fishing boats land their catch.

⑪ Kingsgate
On the cliff edge half a mile round the coast is the vast battlemented Kingsgate Castle, built about 1860; it once belonged to Lord Avebury, the politician who introduced Bank Holidays in 1871. The sandy beach at Botany Bay is reached by steps from the end of Kingsgate Avenue, while below the castle, another flight of steps leads down to the sheltered sands of Kingsgate Bay.

Inland from the promontory south of Joss Bay is the 30m (85ft) North Foreland Lighthouse, built to warn ships of the treacherous Goodwin Sands, 7 miles offshore. On clear nights, its beam is visible for 20 miles.

⑫ Cliftonville
Set well back from the cliffs behind a grassy expanse, Cliftonville is a suburb of Margate with many hotels, and has at its centre a wide garden and bandstand known as

The Oval. At Cliftonville's Palm Bay, the wide, sandy beach is backed by a promenade. The clifftop Princes Walk leads east round Foreness Point, an important site for migrating birds; footpaths continue along the coast to Kingsgate.

⑬ Margate
The superb crescent of gently sloping sand has lured Londoners to the town since 1753, when Benjamin Beale, a Margate glovemaker, invented the covered bathing machine. Before the arrival of the railway, visitors came from London by sea, in special boats called Margate hoys, which docked at the curving stone jetty known as Margate Pier. Confusingly, Margate's traditional seaside pier was known as the Jetty; unfortunately most of it was destroyed by a storm in 1978, and the wreck of the pier was subsequently demolished.

The underground Shell Grotto is made up of winding passages decorated from floor to ceiling with intricate shell designs. In the old quarter of the town, centred on the Market Place, you will find the Old Town Hall, where a local history museum charts Margate's development as a major seaside resort. Visitors to the museum can also see Victorian prison cells.

Drapers Windmill, on the southern outskirts of Margate, is a restored black smock mill, built about 1850. It is open to the public on various Saturday and Sunday afternoons during summer.

⑭ Westgate on Sea
The sedate western suburb of Margate is characterised by streets of red-brick Victorian and Edwardian houses, green open spaces, and two sandy bays, divided by a promontory laid out with landscaped gardens. At Westgate Bay, the cliffs dip sharply on either side of a gently sloping beach, while lively St Mildred's Bay is popular and lined with beach huts.

A wide, grass-covered clifftop separates Westgate from Margate; in the middle is a sheltered sunken garden that attracts many migrant birds in spring and autumn.

⑮ Birchington
Victorian artist and poet Dante Gabriel Rossetti died at Birchington in 1882 and is buried in the churchyard of the medieval Church of All Saints. The Rossetti Memorial Garden in Sandles Lane commemorates his links with the town.

Though it forms part of Margate, Birchington is still recognisable as a separate village, grouped round the church. The most westerly of its four bays is Minnis Bay, whose wide sweep of sand was once a landing place for smugglers. Grenham Bay, below a clifftop expanse of grass, has a wide undercliff promenade. Beresford Gap

is a designated area for powerboats and water-skiing, and Epple Bay is a sandy cove surrounded by steep chalk cliffs.

The Powell-Cotton Museum, in the park of Quex House, has dioramas showing African animals in their natural habitats, and collections of antique firearms and Chinese porcelain. A tall bell tower in the park contains a peal of 12 bells and is crowned by a graceful wrought-iron spire.

⑯ Reculver
Sharply etched against the sky, the twin towers of Reculver's ruined St Mary's Church are the main landmark along the 10 mile stretch of coast between Herne Bay and Margate. The grassy area round the towers is the site of the Roman fortress of Regulbium, built in the 3rd century AD to guard the northern end of the Wantsum Channel, which once separated the Isle of Thanet from the mainland of Kent. In AD 669 King Egbert of Kent founded a monastery and church inside the fort; the towers on the site today date from a rebuilding in the 12th century.

Most of the church was demolished in the early 19th century, when the sea threatened to undermine it, but the towers were regarded as such an important navigational aid that they were restored by Trinity House. They now overlook a small resort of caravan parks and amusement arcades.

Alexanders, a plant about 1ft high with sprays of yellow flowers, grows at the base of the towers; it was introduced by the Romans, who ate the celery-flavoured stems.

⑰ Bishopstone Glen
A small overgrown ravine cuts through the yellow-brown clay of Bishopstone Cliffs to a shingle beach where fossils may be found. A footpath to the glen starts at a small car park at the end of Bishopstone Lane; wooden steps descend to the beach.

Bishopstone Glen is at the western end of Reculver Country Park, whose clifftop grassland is ideal for walking, picnicking and birdwatching; skuas, terns and sandpipers are among the birds you can see here. There is an also an interpretation centre by the car park at Reculver.

⑱ Herne Bay
A 24m (80ft) clock tower dating from 1837 forms the seafront centrepiece of Herne Bay, a quiet seaside town laid out as a resort in the 1830s. The town's long pier was destroyed by storms in 1978, but the seaward end survives as a forlorn 'island' three-quarters of a mile offshore. The Pier Pavilion, at the landward end, is a leisure centre.

A curving harbour arm to the east of the Pier Pavilion shelters a sand and shingle beach,

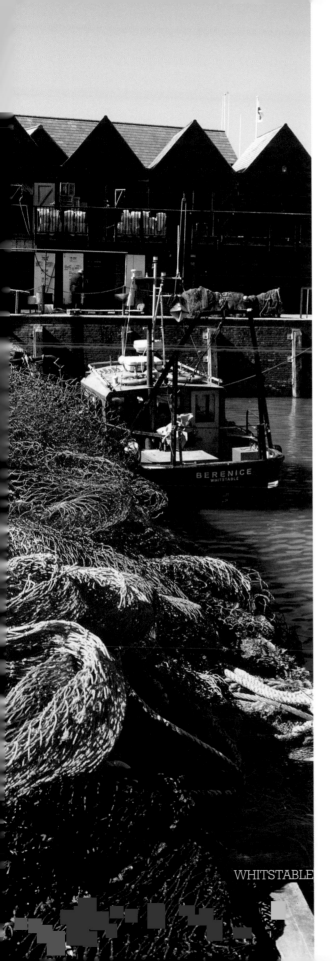

WHITSTABLE

backed by neat gardens along the promenade. The beach to the west of the pavilion is shingle, with sand and some mud holes at low tide.

The village of Herne, 1½ miles inland, has the fine medieval Church of St Martin, and a black smock windmill built in the 1780s. The mill has been restored and is open in summer on Sundays and Bank Holidays, and some afternoons.

⑲ Whitstable

There is a strong flavour of the sea in Whitstable, with its rows of weatherboarded fishermen's cottages, black-tarred boat sheds and sailing dinghies, and whose pebbled beach is flanked by a sea wall. The busy harbour, once the port for Canterbury, has an active fishing fleet, and is lined with sheds where you can buy fresh fish. For centuries Whitstable was famous for the quality of its oysters, and although the oyster trade gradually declined due to changes in climate and sea conditions, in the 1960s it was revived and began to flourish again. At the far end of the harbour, the Oyster Fishery Exhibition tells the story of the industry, and Whitstable-grown oysters can be sampled there. In July the town holds an oyster festival.

The quiet resort of Tankerton is separated from Whitstable by a tree-covered hill topped by a ship's mast and a pair of cannons, marking its highest point. A wide grass bank slopes down from the village to the beach, from which a shingle finger, known as The Street, protrudes. It is dangerous to swim near The Street, but at low tide it is a favourite place for shell collectors.

⑳ Graveney Marshes

Three miles of sea wall and foreshore extending from Faversham Creek to the Sportsman Inn, a mile north of Graveney, make up the South Swale Nature Reserve. In winter, the mudflats attract large numbers of waders and wildfowl, and the grassland beside the sea wall, part of the Saxon Shore Way, is abundant in flowering plants.

㉑ Faversham

The town, at the head of a wide creek, has a harmonious blend of architectural styles. The main landmark is the carved stone steeple of St Mary of Charity Church, but other notable buildings include the painted Guildhall and the large working brewery. Once a busy port, until the creek silted up, Faversham regained its prosperity through its gunpowder industry, whose heyday is vividly recalled at the restored Chart Gunpowder Mills. The mills, dating from the late 18th century, remained in use until the 1930s; the town's history is recalled at the Fleur-de-Lis Heritage Centre. Standard Quay, at the northern end of Abbey Street, provides moorings for an array of colourful Thames barges.

In the southern suburb of Ospringe is Maison Dieu (EH), an unusual combination of hospital and pilgrims' hostel, little changed since the 16th century, which is open to visitors at weekends and Bank Holidays. To the north of Faversham is Oare Marshes Nature Reserve. A car park just outside Oare village gives access to the Saxon Shore Way, a 160 mile footpath.

22 Elmley Marshes
Owned by the RSPB, wigeon, teal and white-fronted geese, winter on the marshes, while breeding birds include redshanks, lapwings and shovelers. The reserve is reached by a 2 mile track, a mile north of the Kingsferry Bridge and Sheppey Crossing.

23 Leysdown-on-Sea
Warden Point, just north of Leysdown, is an ideal spot from which to view shipping in the Thames estuary. From Leysdown a road, which soon becomes a potholed track, leads to Shell Ness. Footpaths from there lead across Swale National Nature Reserve. From the hides you can watch lapwings, warblers, marsh harriers and many other birds.

24 Minster
The village clusters round the 7th-century Church of St Mary and St Sexburga, one of the oldest places of worship in England. The imposing Abbey Gatehouse next to the church has a museum explaining Sheppey's history. The broad sand and mud beach between Minster and Leysdown is noted for its fossils, including gigantic sharks' teeth, but visitors should beware of fast incoming tides.

25 Sheerness
The north-west tip of Sheppey is largely concealed behind the high wall of Sheerness dockyard, constructed in Charles II's time. Much of the town consists of Victorian houses built for dockyard workers. A promenade, with wide views across the Thames to the Essex coast, backs the sand and shingle beach. Barton's Point, on the eastern outskirts of the town, is a recreational and picnic area.

26 Sittingbourne
Muddy Milton Creek winds its way into Sittingbourne, which was once a busy harbour town. Nearby is the southern terminus of the Sittingbourne and Kemsley Light Railway, whose steam trains carry passengers for 1½ miles on certain summer days and Bank Holidays. East of the town, the coast road to Faversham runs through some of Kent's finest orchards.

27 Lower Halstow
Sailing dinghies moor in the village's small dock at Halstow Creek, and the tiny, partly Saxon, Church of St Mary of Antioch stands on a low mound above it. The coast road north of Lower Halstow joins the A249 just south of the Sheppey Crossing and the monumental Kingsferry Bridge, which cross The Swale.

28 Chatham
In 1547, when Henry VIII first maintained a storehouse to service his fleet at anchor in the River Medway, the town's long history as a naval dockyard began. Drake, Hawkins and Nelson sailed from Chatham, and Nelson's flagship HMS *Victory* was one of 400 ships built

there. The working dockyard closed down in 1984, but the site has been given a new lease of life as The Historic Dockyard museum.

Among the many 18th and early 19th-century buildings in the dockyard is the Ropery, where you can watch ropes being made. Another exhibition re-creates a day in 1758, and demonstrates how craftsmen built the wooden warship HMS *Valiant*. Cruises along the Medway can be taken on the paddle steamer *Kingswear Castle*, based at the dockyard, while Dickens World, beside the Medway, has themed attractions based on life in the 19th century. Fort Amherst was built in its present form to defend the naval dockyard from attack by Napoleon's armies and has more than a mile of tunnels.

29 Rochester

For the last 12 years of his life, Charles Dickens lived at Gads Hill Place, 2 miles northwest of Rochester and now a school. He made the small cathedral city on the Medway the background for many scenes in *Great Expectations*, *Pickwick Papers* and other novels.

Rochester Cathedral, begun in 1077, has massive Norman pillars and a Norman crypt. Close by is the tall keep of Rochester Castle, while the Guildhall Museum, in the high street, traces Rochester's history from pre-Roman times. Farther along the high street is Watts Charity, built in 1579 to house poor travellers.

Among Rochester's other historic buildings is Restoration House, where Charles II stayed in 1660 on the eve of his restoration to the throne. Dickens used the house, which is closed to visitors, as the model for Miss Havisham's house in *Great Expectations*.

30 Upper Upnor

The wedge-shaped defensive platform of Upnor Castle juts into the muddy waters of the Medway. The neat little castle was built in 1559 to guard the approaches to the naval dockyard at Chatham. Sharp wooden stakes protrude from the castle's battlements, and exhibits inside show the extent of the Medway's defences. The only time this defensive system was really put to the test was in 1667. It then failed completely, and the Dutch navy burned ten ships of the British fleet at Chatham.

31 Gravesend

In the 14th century, Gravesend ferrymen were granted the sole right to ferry passengers into London. Today, the town is the headquarters of the Port of London Authority's Thames Navigation Service, and tugs put out from the Royal Terrace Pier to guide ships into Tilbury docks. St George's Church, rebuilt in the 18th century after one of the many fires that destroyed much of the old town, is a striking feature of the waterfront. In the churchyard is a bronze statue of Pocahontas, who married John Rolfe, an early Virginia colonist, and accompanied him to England in 1616, only to die the following year from fever.

There are superb views of shipping on the Thames from the wide grassy expanse of Gordon Promenade, named after General Gordon. In the late 1860s, Gordon supervised the construction of forts to defend the Thames against the threat of a French invasion, and also worked with the poor in Gravesend.

The town marks the northern end of the Saxon Shore Way.

Visitor information

Broadstairs ☎ 0870 264 6111
Deal ☎ (01304) 369576
Dover ☎ (01304) 205108
Faversham ☎ (01795) 534542
Gravesend ☎ (01474) 337600
Herne Bay ☎ (01227) 361911
Margate ☎ 0870 264 6111
Medway Visitor Centre (Rochester, Chatham, Gillingham) ☎ (01634) 843666
Ramsgate ☎ 0870 264 6111
Sandwich ☎ (01304) 613565 (summer)
Whitstable ☎ (01227) 275482

ELMLEY MARSHES

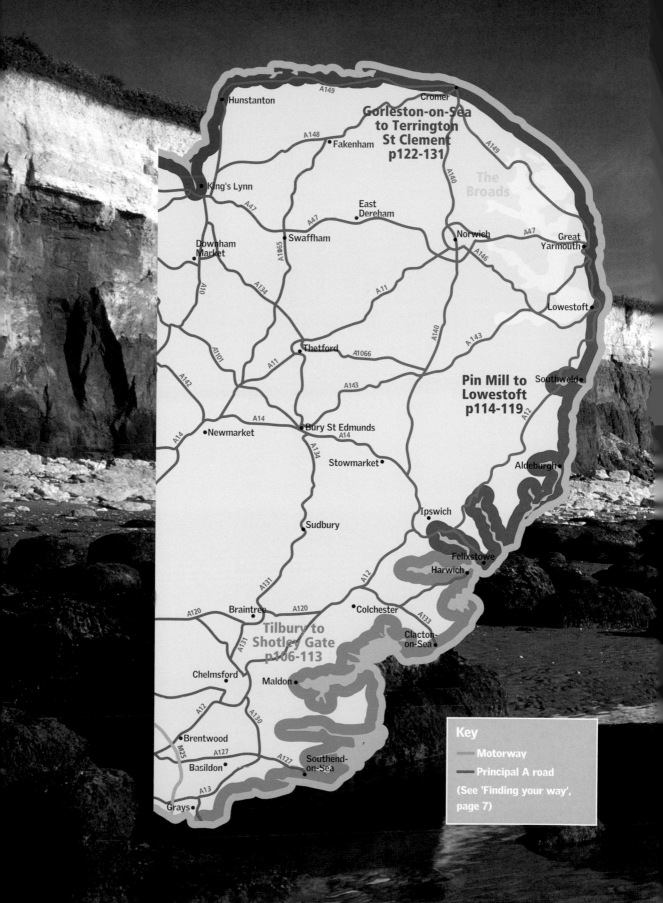

Hunstanton

A149

Cromer

Gorleston-on-Sea to Terrington St Clement p122-131

A148

Fakenham

A149

A140

The Broads

King's Lynn

A47

East Dereham

A47

A47

Great Yarmouth

Swaffham

Norwich

Downham Market

A1065

A146

A10

A134

A11

Lowestoft

A140

A142

A1101

A11

Thetford

A1066

A143

A143

Southweld

Pin Mill to Lowestoft p114-119

A14

A12

Newmarket

A14

Bury St Edmunds

A134

A14

Aldeburgh

Stowmarket

Sudbury

Ipswich

Felixstowe

Harwich

A12

A131

Braintree

A120

A120

Colchester

A133

Clacton-on-Sea

Tilbury to Shotley Gate p106-113

A131

Chelmsford

Maldon

A12

A130

Brentwood

M25

A127

Southend-on-Sea

Basildon

A127

A13

Grays

Key

Motorway

Principal A road

(See 'Finding your way', page 7)

East Anglia

A great fractured maze of muddy creeks and forgotten islands in eastern Essex gives way to the heaped shingle banks of the lonely Suffolk coast. The tottering cliffs of Norfolk pay their tribute of clay to the North Sea before subsiding into vast salt marshes, the winter haunt of wildfowl.

TILBURY TO SHOTLEY GATE

While Southend dazzles with bright lights and the world's longest pier, peace can be found elsewhere in the many sheltered estuaries and nature reserves

❶ Tilbury
Tilbury Fort (EH) was built in 1682 to defend the Thames against the Dutch and the French. A moat surrounds the fort on the inland side, and on the river side is an elaborate triumphal arch; displays inside show how London was defended against attack from the sea. Tilbury can be reached from Gravesend by a passenger ferry across the Thames; from the ferry terminus a 10 minute walk takes you to the fort.

The town's modern port is largely hidden behind a high wall, with only the tops of its cranes visible from outside. Large cruise ships still leave from the port, which also handles timber, grain and other cargo.

❷ Wat Tyler Country Park
Covering a large area of tidal creeks, grassland, marshes and scrub, which attracts more than 160 species of bird, the park offers waymarked walks and several hides. At its southern end is a 100-berth marina; from here a narrow-gauge railway runs to the National Motorboat Museum, where more than 30 boats are on display.

❸ Canvey Island
Created from reclaimed land, Canvey is protected by a massive sea wall, built after floods swept across the island in 1953, drowning 58 people. From the top of the wall there are wide views across the Thames to the Kent shore. On its seaward side is a beach of muddy sand and shingle.

❹ Hadleigh Castle Country Park
The park is a patchwork of pasture, woodland, marsh and coast. To the east are the ruins of Hadleigh Castle, built for Edward III in the 1360s; the area between the towers and outer walls offers sweeping coastal views. Two 3 mile walks between Leigh and Benfleet stations cross the park – one follows the sea wall; the other takes an inland route past the castle.

❺ Two Tree Island
An island of grassland and scrub is bisected by a narrow road from Leigh station. The western half of the island forms part of Hadleigh Castle Country Park, while to the east is a nature reserve with large areas of salt marsh and mudflats. In autumn you can see thousands of migrating Brent geese, which gather on the salt marsh to feed on eel-grass.

❻ Leigh-on-Sea
A narrow street of cottages and shops, cut off on the landward side by the railway, retains an old-fashioned air, with stalls selling jellied eels and Maplin Sands cockles. The small sandy beach at the eastern end of the street is the start of a 7 mile seafront walk to Shoeburyness.

❼ Southend-on-Sea
Originally a village at the 'south end' of medieval Prittlewell Priory, Southend developed as a seaside resort in the early 19th century, and boomed during Victorian

SOUTHEND-ON-SEA

times, spreading to embrace surrounding villages. Southend's pier – at 1.3 miles the longest pleasure pier in the world – has regained some of its former glory after fires in 1976 and 2005. An electric railway runs alongside the walkway, and the pier museum is open in summer. A tree-lined esplanade with a Victorian bandstand overlooks the resort's sand and shingle beach, which becomes muddy towards low-water mark. Seafront entertainments include a fairground known as Adventure Island, a water theme park, and an aquarium, where visitors can walk underwater through a glass tunnel, and enter a shark exhibition through a model of the jaws of a great white shark. Also within Adventure Island is a half-size replica of Drake's *Golden Hind*.

Foremost among Southend's extensive parks and gardens is Priory Park in the north of the town, where you can follow a 'tree trail'. The park, with its lakes, bowling greens and tennis courts, surrounds the remains of Prittlewell Priory, which is now a local history museum with a section tracing the development of communications from the early days of printing to the invention of the pocket television. Horse riders and golf enthusiasts flock to nearby Garons Leisure Park.

Among Southend's annual events are an air show, a carnival and a race to Greenwich contested by 20 or more magnificent Thames sailing barges.

8 Shoeburyness
Round the Ness from Southend is the sand and shingle of the popular East Beach, one of two Blue Flag beaches near the town, while Rampart Terrace, running behind the beach, has fine views of the Thames estuary. At the eastern end of Southend, beyond Thorpe Bay, spiked railings extending into the sea mark the boundaries of a Ministry of Defence artillery range, which takes up the whole tip of Shoebury's 'ness', or promontory. The railings enclose about 1½ miles of beach.

9 Wakering Stairs
Beyond Samuel's Corner, a narrow road leads across Ministry of Defence land to Wakering Stairs. The road is usually closed, but when the barriers are open you can drive to the shoreline, and from there walk out onto the wide expanse of Maplin Sands. A track known as The Broomway, uncovered at low tide, is named after the wooden 'brooms' or poles that used to mark the route, which runs parallel to the shore for 5 miles to Foulness Island. Walkers are advised not to follow the track, as it can be very treacherous.

10 Paglesham Eastend
The hamlet offers the only proper access by land to the estuary of the Roach. At the end of the unpaved road is a boatyard and a

EAST ANGLIA Tilbury to Shotley Gate

sailing centre, whose slipway is defended by a metal floodgate. There are walks along the sea wall towards Rochford and Wallasea Island.

⑪ Canewdon
The tower of St Nicholas's Church, once a landmark for Thames shipping, at 26m (85ft), dominates the surrounding countryside. Beacon Hill, on which it stands, is said to have been the Danes' command post before the Battle of Ashingdon in 1016, when the Danish King Canute defeated the English Edmund Ironside.

⑫ North Fambridge
The Fambridges, two small settlements, face each other across the Crouch. At North Fambridge a scattering of old cottages and a 15th-century inn overlook a boatyard where a boardwalk leads 46m (50yd) into the river. From South Fambridge, on the opposite bank, paths upstream and downstream skirt the river wall.

⑬ Mangapps Railway Museum
A working farm is the setting for a fine collection of vintage engines, rolling stock and railway memorabilia of all kinds. A restored country station is the starting point for short rides in trains pulled by various engines, including an 1878 colliery steam engine; the exhibit resembling Thomas the Tank Engine is popular with children.

⑭ Burnham-on-Crouch
A major yachting centre for more than a century, Burnham has an elegant Georgian high street and a neat, pedestrianised quayside whose buildings include the headquarters of two yacht clubs; the yacht harbour has berths for 350 boats. The town hosts the annual South-East Boat Show in June, and at the end of August several hundred boats compete in Burnham Week. Burnham Country Park, west of the harbour, offers several riverside walks.

⑮ Dengie Flat
The sweep of low-tide mudflats between the Blackwater and the Crouch is a national nature reserve, with ideal breeding grounds for wading birds. At the northern end is Bradwell Shell Bank, a large area of sand, shingle and compacted cockleshells, protected by a line of sunken barges, while the coastline itself is lined by a low sea wall, along which runs part of the St Peter's Way footpath. The path starts from St Peter's Chapel and runs for 45 miles inland to Chipping Ongar.

⑯ St Peter's Chapel
One of Britain's oldest churches is set on an isolated and beautiful spot on the site of the Roman fortress of Othona. St Cedd, who arrived there in AD 653 as a Northumbrian missionary to the East Anglians, later used stones from the fortress to build the chapel, whose full

TOLLESBURY BOATHOUSES

name is St Peter's-on-the-Wall. It stands on open grassland, and the last half mile has to be walked from Bradwell-on-Sea. Footpaths lead along the sea wall in both directions.

⑰ Bradwell-on-Sea

A small village surrounded by marshes and reclaimed farmland, Bradwell is the start of a 6½ mile circular walk taking in part of the long sea wall. The walk starts beside Westwick Farm, northwest of the village, and leads past the former Bradwell Power Station as far as St Peter's Chapel before turning inland. Bradwell's Church of St Thomas has a fine 18th-century brick tower, and a 14th-century porch, which was transported in 1957 from Shapland, near Southend, to save it from demolition.

⑱ Bradwell Waterside

The village is the base of Bradwell Outdoors, an environmental and education centre run by Essex County Council. A salt marsh protected by a sea wall stretches northwards to the former Bradwell Power Station, which dominates this part of the coast. A large marina and a group of houses overlook the narrow, sheltered creek separating the mainland from Pewet Island, which is covered by water at high tide.

⑲ Northey Island

Surrounded by creeks and marshes, and screened by mature hedgerows, Northey Island (NT) resembles a secret garden. You can reach the secluded spot along a private road through South House Farm and over a causeway that is covered at high tide; you will need a warden's permit to visit the island, which is part farm, part nature reserve. A nature trail leads over fields to a hide from where herons, shelducks, pintails and curlews can be seen.

Stone Age flint scrapers have been found here, and the causeway is probably Roman. In AD 991 an army of Danes crossed the causeway to defeat the Saxons, the story of which is recounted in the epic poem *The Battle of Maldon*.

⑳ Maldon

One of the oldest recorded settlements in Essex, Maldon's ancient seafaring traditions live on at the Hythe, where restored Thames barges loom over the quayside. The quay itelf leads onto a promenade, where a sweep of sloping grass gives you good views of pleasure craft thronging the Blackwater. The high street rises from the harbour to the Church of All Saints, with its triangular tower, and to the 15th-century Moot Hall, which can be visited on Saturday afternoons in summer.

The 13m (42ft) Maldon Embroidery, created in 1991 to mark the 1000th anniversary of the Battle of Maldon, is displayed in the Maeldune Centre, which was formerly St Peter's Church. The Plume Library on the first floor of the building contains some 6000 antiquarian books, while in the grounds of the church, of which only a tower remains, the Millennium Garden has an array of plants used in the 10th century for medicinal and culinary purposes.

㉑ Heybridge Basin

The moorings above the lock are packed with a huge range of sailing boats, from small dinghies to much larger yachts. The banks of the basin, reached by a narrow road that leads south from the B1026, lie at the end of the Chelmer and Blackwater Navigation, which stretches inland for 11 miles towards Chelmsford. Running east along the sea wall is the 12 mile North Blackwater Trail, which leads to Tollesbury. Especially in winter, you should get a good view of the many waders and wildfowl that overwinter in the estuary.

㉒ Tollesbury

From the centre of the village, with its large market square and Norman Church of St Mary the Virgin, a narrow lane leads down past boathouses to a 250-berth marina. The nearby saltings, which are crisscrossed by boardwalks, include moorings for several hundred more craft. A 5 mile circular footpath, starting from the marina, skirts Tollesbury Wick Nature Reserve, a large area of former farmland and marshes. Part of the path follows the North Blackwater Trail.

To the north is the remote RSPB reserve of Old Hall Marshes. You will need a special permit to enter the reserve, whose birdlife includes Brent geese, wigeon, shelduck, teal and short-eared owls. A public footpath runs round the edge of the peninsula.

㉓ West Mersea

Evidence of human habitation from about 10,000 BC has been found at West Mersea. There are two yacht clubs on the seafront of this popular boating centre, which includes a sweeping curve of densely packed boatyards, backed by a large residential area, as well as a scattering of sailmakers, chandlers and oyster huts. The oysters themselves, once plentiful in the area, are now mostly brought in as oyster spat from elsewhere to be raised locally. A small museum specialises in local history. A causeway liable to flooding at high tide carries the B1025 across salt marshes to the town.

Every August, during Mersea Week a round-the-island yacht race takes place here as well as a host of other events, including sailing, rowing and other watersports. The regatta has been running since 1838.

24 East Mersea

Knots, plovers, dunlins and oystercatchers flourish on the the salt marsh and mudflats protected by brushwood fences at the foot of low eroded cliffs. Compared with the bustle of West Mersea, the thinly populated farmland of East Mersea, seems part of a different age. A narrow road leads to Cudmore Grove Country Park, which borders the Colne Estuary National Nature Reserve.

25 Fingringhoe

By St Andrew's Church stands a huge gnarled oak tree that is believed to be 500 years old. The village itself is centred round a village pond, while a walk down Ferry Road will lead you to the banks of the Colne, from where there are views of a tidal barrier, and of Wivenhoe across the river.

A woodland lane south of the village winds up to Fingringhoe Wick Nature Reserve, which stands on a rise overlooking the Colne and the flat sweep of Geedon Saltings.

From the conservation centre there are two trails that pass through a large area of reclaimed gravel pits, woodland, heath, reed beds, tidal mud and salt marsh. Eight hides allow visitors to see some of the 40 species of birds and 20 species of butterflies that have been recorded there.

26 Colchester See box on page 112.

27 Wivenhoe

A lane leads through a maze of old streets to a waterfront of 18th and 19th-century houses and disused boatyards. Once a fishing and boat–building centre, the village is now largely residential, with an immense concrete barrier, closed at very high tides, ¼ mile downriver. A passenger ferry runs to Rowhedge and Fingringhoe on summer weekends and bank holidays, tides permitting.

Three miles northeast, at Elmstead Market, are the Beth Chatto Gardens, with a thousand different species of plants and a special interest in 'ecological' gardening techniques.

A BROAD PIER FLANKED BY SANDY BEACHES
CLACTON-ON-SEA PIER

28 Brightlingsea

In medieval times Brightlingsea was an important port and the only associate member of the Cinque Ports outside Kent and Sussex, though it retains few vestiges of its historic past apart from some fine old Essex fishing smacks.

Today, with a broad, firm beach, overlooked by a hotel, yacht club and shops, Brightlingsea is a popular boating centre. The beach-side road is cut off from the water by a sea wall, which is pierced by a launching ramp.

29 Point Clear

The salt marshes and mudflats of Colne Point Nature Reserve, where many wildfowl and waders feed in winter lie to the south of Point Clear. You will need a permit to visit the reserve. A holiday village spreads across this small peninsula at the mouth of the River Colne; the beach is sand and shingle, with mudflats exposed at low tide.

30 St Osyth

Named after the daughter of a 7th century East Anglian king, beheaded by Danish invaders, because she would not worship their idols, St Osyth has old weatherboarded houses at its well-preserved centre. The Priory (now a private house) was built in her honour. West of the village is Howlands Marsh Nature Reserve, an area of low-lying, grassland grazed by sheep.

The road to Point Clear crosses St Osyth Creek, which has been dammed to form a lake for waterskiing and windsurfing. Two miles to the south, holiday parks back St Osyth Beach, a sand and pebble expanse partly used by naturists. Several Martello towers – circular, early 19th-century fortifications – stand on the coast to the west and east of Jaywick.

31 Clacton-on-Sea

A lively, old-fashioned seaside resort, Clacton has a broad pier flanked by long sandy beaches, and well-tended flower gardens backing a wide promenade.

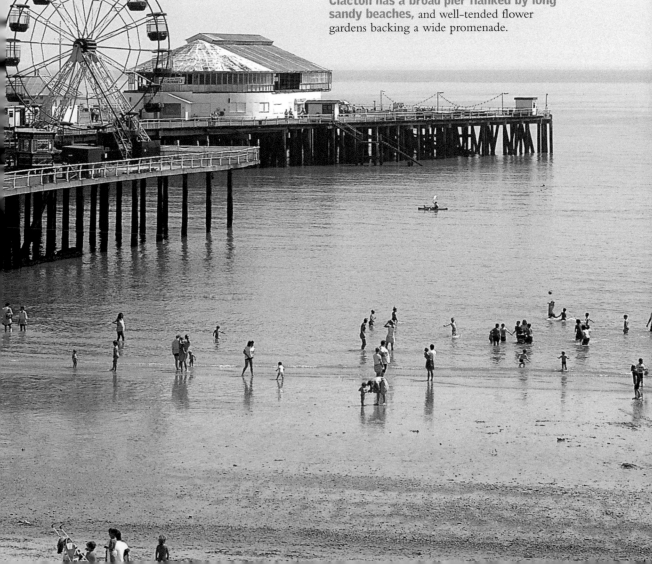

Amusements on the pier include an aquarium, while fishing from the end of the pier yields bass, eel, whiting and cod. A nearby pavilion offers fairground rides, or you can enjoy the panoramas of the surrounding countryside and nearby coastal resorts on a pleasure flight from Clacton Airfield.

Until the 1860s the name of Clacton applied to two inland villages, Great Clacton and Little Clacton. The first pier, built in 1877 for goods and passengers, was rebuilt in the early 1890s, after which the town flourished as a resort.

The long beach and seafront continue north-eastwards past Holland-on-Sea, a residential area. Beyond is Holland Haven Country Park, a quiet expanse of marshland and grassland that is crisscrossed by a network of footpaths.

32 Frinton-on-Sea
First developed in the 1890s, Frinton retains the air of a genteel Victorian resort and is relatively free of conventional seaside entertainments. Redbrick houses flank wide tree-lined roads that lead to a long esplanade and a broad stretch of clifftop grassland known as The Greensward. Below the cliffs, a fine sandy beach runs the full length of the town, making this a popular area for swimming, sailing and windsurfing enthusiasts.

A 1½ mile walk along the promenade, lined with colourful beach huts, leads to Walton-on-the-Naze.

33 Walton-on-the Naze
A family resort, it has sandy beaches that are almost covered at high tide, and a pleasure pier that is the second longest in Britain after that at Southend at ¾ mile. From the pier there is fishing for codling, skate and conger eel. The town developed as a resort from about 1830 onward, and was once renowned for its sea holly, whose candied roots were prized for their supposed aphrodisiac qualities. The former lifeboat house here is next to the coastguard station and is now a maritime museum.

North of Walton is The Naze, a wide clifftop area crowned by a brick tower built in 1720 as a navigational aid, and which is now an art gallery. The headland gives views of shipping going to and from Harwich and Felixstowe. A 1¼ mile nature trail leads to the tip of the headland, where a small area comprising blackthorn and bramble thickets, rough grassland and ponds forms a nature reserve. It attracts migrant birds, including chats and warblers, during spring and autumn. Visitors are warned to keep away from the eroding cliff edge.

Roman legacy at Colchester

A great Roman city was built at Colchester by the Emperor Claudius in about AD 50, just a few miles inland from Manningtree, and many fine artefacts from the Roman period have been found in and around this area. Some are housed in Colchester's Castle Museum, and it is worth making a detour to see them.

The Romans introduced their gods into Britain, which some Britons accepted. Aspects of the religion and myth are in evidence in artistic creations such as statues and intricately patterned floor mosaics that still survive. Even before the invasion of AD 43, close links had been forged between Rome and the British tribes, as witnessed by the discovery of coins and medallions dating from the reign of the Emperor Augustus (29 BC–AD 14).

▶ Colchester 26

34 Kirby-le-Soken Quay
Until the early 20th century, flat-bottomed Thames barges transported coal and horse manure from London to Kirby, and carried away grain and hay. A lane from the village of Kirby-le-Soken leads to the Quay, a small inlet and a footpath along the sea wall gives good views over the solitary Walton Backwaters. On rising winter tides you may see avocets.

35 Beaumont Quay
Fragments of a wall built of stone from Old London Bridge, demolished in 1831, are all that remains of Beaumont Quay. The lonely spot can be reached on foot by a lane, marked 'Private', to Quay Farm. From the quay are views across Hamford Water, a national nature reserve, mudflats and inaccessible marshy islands.

36 Harwich
The port's long maritime history dates from 1340, when Edward III's fleet assembled at Harwich before departing to defeat the French at Sluys, in the first major sea battle of the Hundred Years' War. Queen Elizabeth I, who stayed in Harwich in 1561, said it was a 'pretty place and wants for nothing'.

The quayside in the old town is an ideal spot from which to watch shipping. By the quay itself you will find pleasure craft and small fishing boats. Continental ferries go to and from Parkeston Quay, and large container ships berth at Felixstowe, on the opposite side of the Orwell and Stour estuaries.

The Harwich Maritime Heritage Trail winds through the old town, where Georgian and Victorian houses line the narrow streets and passageways. The trail starts at the Low Lighthouse, now a Maritime Museum, while the 1818 High Lighthouse nearby is now a private house. Near the Low Lighthouse is a 17th-century treadmill, designed to lift ammunition and stores; it was worked by two men walking inside twin wooden treadwheels. St Nicholas Church, near the High Lighthouse, was rebuilt in the 1820s with cast-iron pillars, some of the first ever to be used; the church contains a display of 17th-century Dutch tiles.

Ha'penny Pier, named when its toll was a halfpenny, was the original departure point for steamships bound for the Continent. A ferry to Felixstowe and Shotley operates from the pier, along with summer pleasure cruises along the Stour and Orwell rivers.

Dovercourt, to the south of Harwich, has a sandy beach backed by a sea wall. On the beach is a pair of disused lighthouses on stilts. The lighthouses, built in 1863, were fitted with gas lamps and were in use until 1917.

③⑦ Wrabness
All Saints' Church at Wrabness has a detached belfry – the single bell is housed in a wooden cage in the graveyard. From the rear of the church, on the village's north side, there is a fine view across the river to the Royal Hospital School, while a narrow lane leads to one of the few sandy stretches on the Stour.

East of Wrabness you will find the Stour Estuary RSPB Reserve, an area of woodland and mudflats. Wildfowl are present all year round, but winter is an especially good time to see black-tailed godwits and Brent geese. The observation hides are reached along a path from the car park.

③⑧ Mistley
In the 18th-century, attempts were made to turn Mistley into a spa and the Swan Basin fountain is a symbol of those efforts. The town is now a small but flourishing commercial port at the head of the Stour, with a Victorian malt-house and a resident population of mute swans. You can arrange a visit to Mistley Quay Workshops, where craftsmen make pottery and musical instruments, and a showroom and teashop offer panoramic views of the river.

On the road to Manningtree, the twin Mistley Towers (EH), situated in the middle of a graveyard, are the remains of a church built by the architect Robert Adam as part of the unrealised scheme to turn Mistley into a fashionable spa resort.

③⑨ Manningtree
During the 17th century, Manningtree was the headquarters of Matthew Hopkins, who terrorised East Anglia in his role of 'Witch Finder General'. He was himself eventually accused of witchcraft, and later hanged.

A busy port and cloth-trading centre in Tudor times, Manningtree gradually lost its trade to neighbouring Mistley, but the town retains some attractive Georgian and Victorian buildings. Every June or July, Manningtree holds a punt regatta with displays of flat-bottomed boats, and dinghy and yacht racing.

④⓪ East Bergholt
The landscape painter John Constable was born in the charming village of East Bergholt in 1776. The house where he lived no longer exists, but a plaque near the Church of St Mary the Virgin marks the site. Constable's parents and his friend Willy Lott are buried in the churchyard, which has a free-standing, timber bell cage, whose bells are rung by hand.

Flatford Mill, south of the village, was owned by Constable's father. Both the watermill and nearby Lott's cottage are little changed since the artist's day; they are not open to the public. The National Trust property of Bridge Cottage includes a restored dry dock and a John Constable Exhibition. The willow-lined river and its surroundings make up the true heart of 'Constable Country', and guided walks round the sites depicted in the artist's paintings depart from the cottage in summer.

④① Shotley Gate
At the end of Shotley Gate peninsula, which separates the Orwell from the Stour, a towering ship's mast marks what used to be the naval training base HMS *Ganges*, and which is now a museum housing shipping memorabilia and information about life in Shotley, including a large collection of photographs.

At the end of the road by Shotley quay there are fine views of shipping entering and leaving the docks at Harwich and Parkeston.

Visitor information
Clacton-on-Sea ☎ (01255) 686633
Colchester ☎ (01206) 282920
Harwich ☎ (01255) 506139
Southend ☎ (01702) 215620

EAST ANGLIA Tilbury to Shotley Gate

0 [____] 5 Miles

PIN MILL TO LOWESTOFT

Birdlife, classical music and sailing can all be enjoyed on Suffolk's colourful coastline, which takes in the bustling port of Felixstowe, the final resting place of composer Benjamin Britten and the delightful, old-fashioned charm of Southwold

❶ Pin Mill

The name Pin Mill is said to be derived from the wooden pegs or 'pins' that were made there and used in boat-bulding. This riverside beauty spot lies at the end of a narrow lane from Chelmondiston. High spring tides on the Orwell allow sailors to moor close to the walls of the Butt and Oyster Inn and order drinks without stepping ashore, and the Pin Mill Barge Match, a dazzling display of ornately painted barges, is held annually in late June or early July. The Cliff Plantation (NT), reached only from a short footpath east of Pin Mill, is an attractive area of pine woodland and open heath stretching along the bank of the river.

❷ Woolverstone Marina

An extensive marina and sailing centre at Cat House, home of the Royal Harwich Yacht Club, is reached by private road. In the 18th century a stuffed cat, placed at night in a lighted window, was the signal to smugglers that the coast was clear. A path along the foreshore leads a mile downstream to Pin Mill, and 2 miles upstream to Freston Tower.

❸ Ipswich

Suffolk's county town was one of the most prosperous ports of the Middle Ages, exporting wool and trading in skins, leather and fish. The docks still thrive on the products of industries such as agriculture and brewing and some parts of the waterfront are being redeveloped with bars and restaurants. A Wet Dock Maritime Trail explores a large area of the historic docks and the surrounding streets.

Cardinal Wolsey was born in Ipswich in 1475; a few fine half-timbered buildings from the Tudor period survive, notably the Ancient House, once a merchant's house, which has fine pargetting, or moulded exterior plasterwork. Displays at the Ipswich Museum include replicas of treasures from the Anglo-Saxon burial site at Sutton Hoo near Woodbridge, northeast of Ipswich, while a self-guided walk takes you on a tour of Ipswich's 17 historic churches.

Near the town centre is Christchurch Mansion, built in 1548. Furnished in period styles from the 16th to 19th centuries, the mansion contains paintings by Constable and Gainsborough.

❹ Nacton

In the 17th and 18th centuries Orwell Park, now a school, was the home of Admiral Sir Edward Vernon, nicknamed 'Old Grog' because of his suit of grogram cloth. It was he who introduced to the navy the daily rum ration known as 'grog'. Orwell Park School is reached through Nacton; nearby is a domed 19th-century observatory, which is closed to the public. The medieval Church of St Martin is on the other side of the lane.

❺ Suffolk Yacht Harbour

A huge marina with launching and berthing facilities lies on the foreshore southeast of the village of Levington. It can be reached along a road marked 'Private', and you need to declare your arrival at the marina office. A 3 mile coastal path crosses the tranquil Trimley Marshes downstream to Felixstowe.

❻ Felixstowe

A sedate Edwardian resort, stretching round a long, gently curving bay, is combined with one of Europe's busiest container ports. In the resort part of the town a paved promenade is backed by a series of well-tended seafront gardens, and beyond the Spa Pavilion is a sand and shingle shore with old-fashioned beach huts. Bathing is not safe a mile north of the pier, where the remains of a fort lie close to the waterline, although it is possible to fish from the pier and the beach.

At the southern end of town a road leads to Landguard Fort (EH), originally built in 1540 to guard the harbour entrance, and rebuilt in 1718. The chapel overlooking the Fort's gateway was the scene of a notorious scandal in 1763, when the acting governor held a dance there and used the altar as a bar. The fort has a museum explaining its history, and a nearby viewing area is a good place to watch ships in Harwich Harbour.

To the north is Landguard Nature Reserve, whose less common visitors include barred warblers and black redstarts. You can arrange visits in advance with the wardens. West of the headland of Landguard Point is the huge port.

❼ Felixstowe Ferry

Huddled round one of the Martello towers that dot this stretch of coast, the village can be reached by road, or on foot across Felixstowe golf course. A passenger ferry to Bawdsey Quay operates at certain times during summer. Swift-running currents can make swimming unsafe here.

❽ Waldringfield

A busy sailing centre on the Deben with a waterfront of muddy shingle, and a sandy beach, firm enough for launching boats. Chandlers and boatyards are scattered along a lane that skirts the edge of the foreshore, where teal, wigeon and shelduck can be seen. You can arrange river trips along the estuary from the boatyard in summer, and walks of about a mile lead both upstream and downstream.

Parking at the waterfront is severely restricted, but there is a large car park behind the Maybush Inn up the hill.

❾ Woodbridge

Sailmaking, rope-making and boat-building made Woodbridge prosperous between the 14th and 15th centuries. It is now one of the most attractive towns in East Anglia, with timber-framed and Georgian houses, and steep streets running down to the quayside.

WOODBRIDGE

Dominating the centre of the triangular market place are the magnificent 15th-century Church of St Mary and the Dutch-gabled Shire Hall, built in the 16th century by Thomas Seckford, a wealthy courtier of Queen Elizabeth I. The hall contains the Suffolk Horse Museum, which illustrates the history of the world's oldest breed of working horse. Nearby Buttrum's Mill is a restored six-storey tower mill built in 1835. Four pairs of original millstones are on display. On the quayside, amid the boatyards, chandleries and yachts, is the white, weather-boarded Tide Mill. Built in the 1790s and operating until 1957 the mill is today in full working order.

Sutton Hoo, east of the town, is a group of grassy burial mounds on a heath where a Saxon king's treasure was excavated in 1939. The site is managed by the National Trust; an exhibition tells the story of early English history. Woodbridge Museum has an exhibition of archaeological findings from Sutton Hoo.

South of Woodbridge is Kyson Hill (NT), a finger of land projecting into the Deben, with panoramic views from the southern slopes across the river. A footpath leads you to the muddy foreshore and follows the river bank northwards to Woodbridge quay a mile away.

⑩ Ramsholt Quay

Fine views towards the Deben estuary can be had from the top of the hill above this pretty boating haven. However, parking on the shingle foreshore is limited, and the last part of the road down to the quayside is private. Nearby is a small, sandy beach known as The Rocks. The isolated All Saints' Church, which has a distinctive Norman round tower, can be reached by a half mile walk along a footpath north of the quay.

⑪ Bawdsey Quay

North of Bawdsey Quay you will find a small, shingle beach, and although it is private property, the quay, which has a small parking area, is open to the public. A passenger boat to Felixstowe Ferry, on the opposite bank of the Deben, operates daily between April and September, and at weekends only in October.

⑫ Bawdsey

A track leads down East Lane to a red shingle beach, and a foreshore footpath, part of the 50 mile Suffolk Coast and Heaths Path, runs for 2½ miles northwards past a row of Martello towers to Shingle Street. Bawdsey College, beside the Bawdsey Quay road, is the former base of RAF Bawdsey, where radar was developed before the Second World War.

⑬ Shingle Street

Little more than a row of cottages built along a wide stretch of shingle thrown up by the sea into a high bank, Shingle Street is reached down a twisting, narrow road from Hollesley. A footpath leads to the mouth of the Ore, opposite North Weir Point, which lies at the end of the 10 mile shingle bank that forms Orford Beach.

⑭ Havergate Island

Britain's oldest and largest breeding colony of avocets returned to breed here in 1947 after an absence of 100 years. This RSPB bird sanctuary is a marshy island, lying in the long Ore channel that runs downstream from Orford to the sea. The water levels in the muddy lagoons are artificially maintained to provide the correct depth of water for the avocets. Gulls, terns, redshanks and shelduck are also present.

ALDEBURGH

The island can be reached only by boat from Orford Quay, and you need to request a permit in advance from the warden.

⑮ Orford
A prosperous port in the 12th century, Orford was cut off from the sea by the gradual growth of Orford Ness, a spit of shingle measuring some 10 miles. The village's past importance is symbolised by the imposing St Bartholomew's Church, parts of which date from Norman times, and by its large 12th-century castle keep (EH). A small museum tells the history of the village.

Waymarked paths include an hour's circular walk that starts at the quay. You can also take boat trips up the River Alde or across to Havergate Island RSPB Reserve and Orford Ness.

⑯ Iken
Once a thriving fishing village, Iken is now a scattered hamlet set on high ground above the marshes of the Aide. Good views of the river can be had from beside the thatched Church of St Botolph, reached through a gate at the end of a narrow cul-de-sac.

At Ikencliff, a mile to the west, is a picnic site with wide views across the reeds and mudflats. Birdlife includes shelduck, redshanks and herons.

⑰ Snape Maltings
A group of magnificent Victorian buildings, formerly used to process barley for brewing, was converted in 1967 by various commercial businesses and the organisers of the annual Aldeburgh Festival into an international centre of music. The complex includes a craft centre, an art gallery, shops, bars and a teashop, and a School for Advanced Musical Studies dedicated to Benjamin Britten and Peter Pears, the founders of the festival. River trips in the Aide estuary start from the quay. The footpaths across the marshes to the village of Iken are sometimes impassable at high tide.

⑱ Aldeburgh
A main street of Georgian houses and older cottages, behind a wide shingle beach, gives elegance to this small historic town.
Mentioned in Domesday Book, Aldeburgh was a prosperous port and fishing centre by 1600. Early in the 19th century the town became a popular resort, and in 1948 the composer Benjamin Britten and the singer Peter Pears established the annual music festival, now held at nearby Snape Maltings. The shingle beach, with a lifeboat station and a line of fishing boats, stretches north to Thorpeness.

The half-timbered Tudor Moot Hall, or Town Hall, is now almost on the shore, the three roads that originally separated it from the sea having been washed away over the centuries. The Moot Hall is open to visitors in summer and has a museum of local life. Britten and Pears are buried side by side in the churchyard of largely 16th-century St Peter and St Paul. Inside the church is a bust of the poet George Crabbe, who was born in Aldeburgh in 1754. Britten used Crabbe's pen-portrait of fisherman Peter Grimes in the poem *The Borough* as the basis of his first opera.

South of the town is a sea wall, which is wide enough for cars to park on, while at Slaughden Quay boats can be launched into the River Alde. South of the Martello tower, the shingle tip known as Orford Ness is owned by the National Trust, and there is no public right of way along the shoreline. Orford Ness can be reached by ferry from Orford.

⑲ Thorpeness

A track leads from the main street to the distinctive House in the Clouds, originally a water tower served by the nearby windmill, but now a private house. The restored windmill, first built at Aldringham 2 miles to the north-west in 1804 and moved to Thorpeness in the 1920s, is open to visitors in summer.

Thorpness is a unique holiday village, centred on a shallow manmade lake called The Meare, on which small boats can be hired. Thorpeness was created by Glencairn Stuart Ogilvie when he inherited the family estate in the early 1900s. The houses vary in style and include Tudor, Jacobean and traditional 18th-century East Anglian tarred weatherboard. Shingle beaches stretch to the north and to the south, where North Warren RSPB Reserve is made up of wet meadows, woodland and heath.

⑳ Minsmere RSPB Reserve

At the mouth of the Minsmere river you may see marsh harriers, sandpipers, avocets and meadow pipits amid the reed beds, artificial lagoons and islands, heath and woodlands. The reserve shelters one of the widest varieties of breeding birds and many migrants.

㉑ Dunwich Heath

Green woodpeckers and kestrels are among the heath's resident birds, and migrants include the nocturnal nightjar. Two miles south of Dunwich, a stretch of heathland crowns the crumbling clifftops, from which a waymarked walk provides panoramic views.

㉒ Dunwich

Hidden in bushes near a shallow cliff is a fragment of a 1790 grave – the final link with All Saints' Church, which collapsed into the sea in about 1920. Saxon and Norman Dunwich flourished as a port, but in 1286, a huge storm threw tons of sand and shingle across the harbour mouth, diverting the River Blyth northwards. Trade was destroyed and Dunwich declined. By 1677 the sea had reached the market place, and the town became an estate village. Behind its Victorian Church of St James are the remains of a leper chapel, and nearby are the clifftop ruins of a 13th-century friary. The village museum chronicles the area's history from Roman times.

㉓ Blythburgh

Now a little village set on the edge of marshes, Blythburgh was once a thriving port with its own mint and jail. Sharing the fate of many other river ports, it lost its trade when ships grew in size and the Blyth silted up.

Blythburgh's imposing Church of the Holy Trinity is floodlit at night and visible for miles

THORPENESS

around. Cromwell's men desecrated the church, using the great winged angels of the ceiling for target practice and screwing tethering rings for their horses into the pillars.

24 Walberswick

Sands, marshes, river and sea make the somewhat isolated village of Walberswick a place of interest. On the western edge of this former port are the eerie ruins of the 15th-century Church of St Andrew, part of which has been rebuilt and restored.

The reed beds of Westwood Marshes form part of Walberswick National Nature Reserve, whose regular visitors include the marsh harrier and the bittern with its distinctive 'boom'.

25 Southwold

A small town that has remained remarkably unchanged for the past century, Southwold is a jewel of the Suffolk coast. Its redbrick and flint cottages and colour-washed houses are built around a series of delightful greens, created after a fire devastated the town in 1659. The promenade is lined with 250 brightly coloured beach huts, while the tallest buildings in Southwold are the brilliant white Victorian lighthouse and the great flint Church of St Edmund.

Several houses display a Dutch influence, including the little town museum, which is crammed with local memorabilia. The Sailors' Reading Room on the cliff and the Lifeboat Museum at the harbour both have mementos of tall ships and oil-skinned heroes, while six 18-pounder cannons stand sentinel on Gun Hill.

You can take walks across the common, part of which is a golf course, to Southwold harbour, where you can buy fresh fish from fishermen's huts. From the harbour there is an iron footbridge, and a small passenger ferry in summer, across the Blyth to Walberswick. Boat trips up the river are available in summer.

26 Covehithe

Lonely and dramatically sited, Covehithe's ruined Church of St Andrew is remarkable for the thatched chapel built in 1672 inside its roofless nave. The original, 15th-century church, whose fine tower survives, became too large for the parishioners to maintain, so they constructed the smaller church using materials from the old.

The road ends at a barrier a short way beyond the church; there is no public access to the beach from here because of the dangerously eroded cliffs. A footpath starting just opposite the church leads to low cliffs with a distant view of Southwold to the south – the sand and shingle beach stretches as far as the eye can see.

27 Benacre Ness

South of the Ness is Benacre National Nature Reserve, a tranquil area of heath, dunes, broads and woodland, where breeding birds include little terns and marsh harriers. Entry to the reserve is from the coast path, which can be dangerous in bad weather, while the shingle headland here may be reached only on foot, along the Suffolk Coast Path, or by a 1½ mile walk from outside the village of Benacre.

28 Pakefield

A southern suburb of Lowestoft with a sandy beach and a 14th-century church set in a large churchyard on the edge of low cliffs. Until 1748 St Margaret and All Saints was two churches in one, with two separate parishes and two rectors. Two miles inland is the East Anglian Transport Museum.

29 Oulton Broad

The southern gateway to the Broads, reed-fringed Oulton Broad is one of the finest yachting lakes in Britain, and the only place on the Broads where powerboat race meetings are held. Other attractions include Nicholas Everitt Park, on its south bank; the Lowestoft Museum; and Mutford Lock, the starting point for boat tours along the Waveney to Beccles.

30 Lowestoft

The most easterly town in Britain is a fishing port and busy resort; Lake Lothing, a narrow strip of water divides the town, whose two halves are linked by a bascule bridge.

Lowestoft's fortunes were founded on the development of the Dogger Bank as a trawling ground in the mid 19th century. The main catch was herring, most of which was smoked and sent by rail to London and the Midlands.

Today the port plays an important role in supplying off-shore oil and gas operations. Though badly damaged during the Second World War, the old town retains a unique series of parallel lanes, known as 'scores'. A Maritime Museum covers the history of the local fishing fleet, and nearby is a Royal Naval Patrol Service Museum. South of the bridge is South Beach and the East Point Pavilion, an imposing glass building in Edwardian style.

Visitor information

Aldeburgh ☎ (01728) 453637
Beccles ☎ (01502) 713196
Felixstowe ☎ (01394) 276770
Harwich ☎ (01255) 506139
Ipswich ☎ (01473) 258070
Lowestoft ☎ (01502) 533600
Southwold ☎ (01502) 724729

Seaside cheer

Hundreds of brightly painted beach huts line up on the sands in East Anglia, many of them now regarded as family heirlooms

Take a one-roomed cabin with wooden walls and a felt-roof that is scarcely big enough to serve as a garden shed. Transport it to the shore and stand it in line with a hundred others. Festoon it with tarry loops of rope, wave-worn bottle glass, fishermen's floats, crab pots, oystercatcher feathers, dried bunches of seaweed, the egg cases of whelks, or even the chalky skeletons of cuttlefish. Call it 'Curlews', or 'Here's Hoping', maintain it scrupulously and love it unreservedly through storm and shine. Savour its smells of salt, sand and pure essence of nostalgia, then pass it on to the next generation. This is the British beach hut.

Close together

Each beach hut tends to stand in close company with dozens more huts of exactly the same dimensions and shape, yet each in itself is a perfect expression of individuality. In almost every seaside location you can paint a beach hut any shade you like. You can give it curly finials, barley-sugar balustrades, a pagoda roof, even add a bargeboard fretworked with hearts and flowers. A beach hut in its colour and decorations can be both idiosyncratic and eccentric, while at the same time conform to the norm. Could anything be more representative of the British personality?

The UK coastline is home to nearly 30,000 of these characterful huts, many of them to be found in the seaside towns and villages of East Anglia. Southwold, the archetype of a quiet, family resort on the Suffolk coast, boasts hundreds of beach huts. Dozens more stand in line along the seafronts of Essex resorts, such as Dovercourt near Harwich, Frinton-on-Sea and Southend-on-Sea. On the Norfolk coast, a line of huts, separated from their parent town of Wells-next-the-Sea by nearly a mile of marsh, perches on stilts like a row of brightly coloured storks at Mardi Gras.

The distant ancestor of the modern beach hut was the Victorian bathing machine. This single-room hut on wheels gave privacy while changing, and was drawn by a horse into the shallows so that the occupant could enter the water directly from its shelter. This allowed men and women to avoid the shocking possibility of seeing one another on land in a bathing costume. When attitudes relaxed at the turn of the 20th century, rows of gaily striped changing tents made their appearance on the beaches. Soon semi-permanent changing rooms or chalets were erected along the shore, the immediate precursors of today's beach huts. The 'gabled shed' style of architecture still holds sway today.

SOME HUTS CHANGE HANDS FOR MORE THAN A HOUSE
SOUTHWOLD, SUFFOLK

The heyday of the beach hut coincided with the golden age of the British seaside resort – the 1950s, a post-war era when money was tight, foreign package trips by cheap jet were a dream of the future, and almost all Britons stayed home and took their family holiday by the sea. At this time there might have been as many as 50,000 beach huts on the shores of these islands.

From the 1960s onwards, the glamour and sunshine of the Mediterranean seduced most British holidaymakers away from the traditional domestic resorts. Local councils put up ground rents and brought in stricter planning regulations. The coast itself – especially along the geologically softer and lower east coast of Britain – retreated inland as the sea eroded its clay cliffs and marshy margins.

Beach hut numbers fell to about half what they had been. But since the start of the new millennium, thanks to a mixture of seductive television programmes about the coasts of Britain, nervousness about flying and the increasing heat that climate change is bringing to the Mediterranean, the popularity of beach huts is on the rise again. The British have begun to look with revived appreciation at their own seaside – and at the homely beach hut on the shore, a fixture so familiar and so modest as to have been taken entirely for granted.

Beach hut owners have felt the effects of this renewed fascination. Some huts have changed hands in the south and east of England for far more than a three-bedroom house of solid bricks and mortar would fetch in the north and west of the country. Yet the fact is that very many private owners would never countenance selling their beloved beach hut. They see it not as a commercial property, but as a precious and much-adored heirloom, imbued with the presence of past and current generations of family and friends, rich in bits of driftwood, curls of dried kelp, ice lolly sticks, silly drawings, cockle shells and wine corks that make up a mosaic of good times and memories. Such memories can't be transferred to a new owner, and certainly can't be either bought or replaced with money.

Simple pleasures

What beach hut owners get from their tiny dwellings is the thrill of being able to own, as an adult, the gingerbread cottage of childhood stories, with the added benefit that there is no fear of witches in this grown-up deal – just enjoyment of a seaside fairy tale, with a happy ending every sunset around the barbecue or on the verandah. The balcony of a well-sited beach hut is the perfect place to sip a sundowner and watch the world go by.

Many people love the sense of community that a row of beach huts engenders; for others there is nothing to beat shutting the door, lowering the blinds and basking in sweet solitude. Beach huts essentially represent escapism – something that will never go out of style.

GORLESTON-ON-SEA TO TERRINGTON ST CLEMENT

Birds and other wildlife flock to north-east Norfolk's flat landscape, with its host of windmills; like countless visitors, they are drawn to the many nature reserves that dot this prominent coastline

❶ Gorleston-on-Sea

Quieter than neighbouring Yarmouth, Gorleston has amusement arcades and a flat, sandy beach. The harbour mouth is a good place from which to view ships and boats sailing in and out, and to watch anglers catching a wide variety of fish. St Andrew's Church, dating from the 13th century, has one of the earliest and most interesting military brasses in England, representing a knight in chain mail.

❷ Breydon Water

In summer the main channel through Breydon Water is busy with pleasure craft. Breydon Water Nature Reserve, reached along footpaths from Great Yarmouth, is an area of mudflats that attracts many bird species. At the western end the grazing marshes and saltings of the Berney Marshes RSPB Reserve provide another haven for wildfowl. You can reach Berney Marshes by train, which stops at Berney Arms Halt, by boat from Great Yarmouth, or on foot from either end of the water.

❸ Great Yarmouth

East Anglia's biggest and brashest resort, with long sandy beaches, two piers and a lavish fairground, Great Yarmouth grew from a small fishermen's settlement on a sandbank in the estuary of three rivers. Fishing, especially for

herring, was the foundation of its wealth and prosperity from the Middle Ages until just after the First World War, when foreign competition and overfishing led to a steady decline.

The 13th-century Tolhouse, once a courthouse and prison, is one of the oldest surviving civic buildings in England. It is now a museum of local history, with a brass-rubbing centre and dungeons. At the northern end of the broad Market Place is the splendidly restored 12th-century Church of St Nicholas, and from there it is a short walk to South Quay, with its network of alleys known as The Rows.

The Elizabethan House, which dates from 1596, is a museum of domestic life, and contains panelled rooms and exhibitions of toys, games, china and civic plate. The Old Merchant's House (EH), a 17th-century town house, contains splendid plaster ceilings; nearby are the ruins of Greyfriars Cloisters. Time and Tide, a museum dedicated to Great Yarmouth's maritime history, is housed in a Victorian herring-curing works, while the Sea Life Centre re-creates a marine environment.

Set back from South Beach is Nelson's Monument, a memorial to Norfolk's greatest hero. By booking in advance, on a few days in summer, you may climb its 217 steps to a viewing platform, which looks out over Yarmouth and Breydon Water.

❹ Caister-on-Sea

Built in around AD 125 to handle trade between Norfolk and the German Rhineland, Caister was once a thriving port. The Roman Town (EH) is an excavated part of the old port that includes a defensive wall and the south gateway, while in the village a lifeboat memorial lists the nine crew who lost their lives during a rescue operation in 1901. A window in Holy Trinity Church has an inscription of a crewman's remark to King Edward VII: 'Caister men never turn back, Sir.'

Two miles west of the town is the splendid ruin of Caister Castle, built in the 1430s by Sir John Fastolf, the leader of the triumphant English archers at Agincourt in 1415. There is also a Motor Museum, with some 200 exhibits, in the grounds.

❺ Winterton-on-Sea

Norfolk is noted for its soaring church towers, and that of Holy Trinity and All Saints is one of the finest, dominating the countryside for miles around at 40m (132ft). Built between 1415 and 1430, the tower remains a landmark for sailors, and 'Fisherman's Corner' inside the church pays tribute to those who have died at sea, with a cross made from items from ships. A road leads north-east from the village to a desert of sand and shingle.

North of the beach are the high, grassy sands of Winterton Dunes National Nature Reserve, where signs warn that adders are common in the area. You may also see rare natterjack toads there, along with many species of birds, including reed and sedge warblers, whitethroats and chiffchaffs. A car park at Winterton Beach provides access to the reserve.

❻ West Somerton

The birthplace in 1820 of Robert Hales, the 'Norfolk Giant', who grew to 2.3m (7ft 8in) and weighed more than 32 stone, West Somerton lies almost 2 miles from the sea. His remains are buried in a sarcophagus in the churchyard. Peaceful Martham Broad nearby can be reached along a footpath to the west of the village. East of the village, up a steep lane, is the Church of St Mary the Virgin, whose nave has the remains of a 14th-century wall painting.

The church itself is dwarfed by tall power-generating wind turbines that lie just outside the official Broads National Park.

❼ Horsey

Little more than 1m (3ft) above sea level, the former smuggling village of Horsey has fought a constant battle with the sea. The Saxon All Saints' Church, hidden beneath trees, has a thatched roof, and its round tower is one of

HORSEY WINDPUMP

EAST ANGLIA'S OLDEST WORKING LIGHTHOUSE

HAPPISBURGH LIGHTHOUSE

119 such towers in Norfolk. A 2 mile circular walk that takes in the church starts at Horsey Windpump (NT), built in 1912 to drain surplus water from agricultural land. The gallery at the top offers views towards the sea, and inland across a wild, watery landscape.

Horsey Mere (NT), an offshoot of the Norfolk Broads, is a breeding ground for geese and many species of wildfowl and waders, which compete for space here with small boats. A path leads round the northern edge of the mere.

8 Waxham

The longest thatched barn in Norfolk stands just west of the partly ruined, weather-beaten Church of St John and is 54m (176ft) long. Cars can be parked in the lane near the church, and from there it is a short walk to a seemingly endless beach of soft sand, backed by imposing dunes.

The village's farmhouse, known as Waxham Hall, has an encircling wall adorned with corner turrets and a splendid 15th-century gatehouse.

9 Eccles on Sea

The sea claimed the old village and its church in 1895, and boulders of flint masonry still lie strewn on the beach. Today, holiday bungalows and beach chalets are strung out along a road that runs behind dunes planted with marram grass, while a narrow lane leads from Whimpwell Green to the sandy beach at Cart Gap.

10 Happisburgh

Soaring above the thatched roofs of Happisburgh, pronounced 'Hazeborough', are a red-and-white striped lighthouse and the 30m (100ft) tower of the Church of St Mary the Virgin. The lighthouse warns mariners of the dangerous Hazeborough Sands, about 7 miles offshore. For centuries bodies of shipwrecked sailors, including 119 crew of HMS *Invincible*, wrecked on the sands in 1801, have been buried in St Mary's churchyard. Inside the church is a fine 15th-century font, carved with figures of lions and satyrs. In October 1940 German bombs fell in the churchyard, blowing out most of the windows and destroying a statue above the porch door. Shrapnel from the bombs is still embedded in pillars along the aisle.

A car park gives access to the village's sandy beach, where deep pools sometimes form as the tide comes in.

11 Bacton

At the village's southern end, tucked away off the coast road, is the ruined gateway of Bromholm Priory, a 12th-century place of pilgrimage, now a private farm. Bromholm was famous for its supposed possession of a piece of

the 'True Cross' used in the Crucifixion, which was recorded as having raised people from the dead and restoring sight. In Chaucer's 'Reeve's Tale', the miller's wife appeals for help to the 'holy cross of Bromholm'. The relic was lost after the Dissolution of the Monasteries, and Bromholm fell into decay. The considerable remains of the priory are in a private field, but you can see them from the perimeter hedge.

The sandy beach at Bacton is protected by groynes and a sloping sea wall. Straddling the coast road is the vast complex of gasholders, pylons and pipes of the Bacton Gas Terminal, where gas from North Sea wells up to 65 miles away is piped ashore.

12 Paston

The farming community of Paston entered literary history in the early 20th century with the publication of a remarkable series of letters providing graphic pictures of 15th-century English life. Most of the 'Paston Letters' were written by Margaret Paston, who came to live at Paston Hall in 1440. The hall she knew is long gone, but St Margaret's Church, where she worshipped, has a number of family monuments. West of the church is a magnificent thatched barn some 49m (160ft) long, built by Sir William Paston in 1581; it can be seen from the road.

13 Mundesley

A tranquil resort of wide sands backed by low cliffs, Mundesley, pronounced Munsley, is mentioned in Domesday Book. The poet William Cowper (1731-1800) lived in the high street during his boyhood and towards the end of his life. He is said to have been inspired to write the hymn 'God Moves in a Mysterious Way' by the sight of a storm breaking over Happisburgh, 5 miles down the coast. Mundesley's historical connections with the sea are explored at the maritime museum, which includes a coastguard lookout tower.

South of Mundesley, past a millpond and water wheel, is the four-storey brick tower of Stow Mill, built in 1827.

14 Overstrand

The former clifftop crab-fishing village is now a popular little holiday resort. You can reach the wide sandy beach either by steps or a slipway, both of which are very steep. Because of the dangerous state of the cliffs to the east of the village, there is no access to the sea or seafront between Overstrand and Mundesley.

15 Cromer

The self-styled 'gem of the Norfolk coast', popular as a resort since the end of the 18th century, stands on a low, crumbling cliff facing the North Sea. The long sandy beach,

A STRANGE AND LONELY SAND SPIT

BLAKENEY POINT

which turns to shingle at East Runton Gap, a mile to the west, is reached by a slipway from the promenade. The long pier has a tranquil air and a large theatre which hosts a classic seaside variety show in high season. Old flint cottages and winding streets surround the 14th-century Church of St Peter and St Paul, a grand structure even by Norfolk standards, with towers soaring to 49m (160ft). Behind the church, several cottages have been restored to create a museum that evokes the changing character of the town over the past 100 years.

Cromer is known for two things apart from its beach: the quality of its crabs and the brave deeds of its lifeboatmen. The most famous of all lifeboatmen is Henry Blogg, who was coxswain for the Cromer lifeboat from 1909 to 1947 and who, during his years of service, along with his crew saved 873 people. At the end of Cromer's promenade, the RNLI Henry Blogg Museum illustrates the history of Cromer lifeboats and Blogg's most famous rescues.

Cromer lies at the eastern end of the Norfolk Coast Path to Hunstanton, and at the northern end of the Weavers' Way footpath, which travels inland through the Broads to Great Yarmouth, 56 miles to the southeast.

16 West Runton

The Norfolk Shire Horse Centre, which has a museum of horse-drawn farm equipment and a collection of horses is found south of the A149 at the village of West Runton. Farther south is the so-called 'Roman Camp' on Beacon Hill – the highest point in Norfolk, at 100m (329ft). Heathland around the camp, much of it owned by the National Trust, is dotted with early medieval iron workings.

Half a mile west of the village, a track running beside a caravan park and over a level crossing leads to the solitary All Saints' Church. The church has a fine hammerbeam roof, and its tower dates from the 11th century.

17 Sheringham

A cluster of old cottages in the centre of the town dates from the time before the coming of the railway in 1887, which turned Sheringham into a popular resort. The busy high street comes to an end at a promenade, which overlooks a sand and shingle beach. A small fleet of fishing boats still goes out for crabs and lobsters from here, and when not at sea the boats are drawn up on the beach.

The local history museum, housed in three converted fishermen's cottages, contains fossils found in the area, while the station is the headquarters of the North Norfolk Railway, called 'the Poppy Line' after the plant that thrives in this part of Norfolk. During summer, steam and vintage diesel trains travel back and forth

along the 5 mile line southwest to Holt, and there are displays of old locomotives and carriages here. Sheringham also has a golf course along the cliffs.

About a mile to the southwest is Sheringham Park (NT), designed by the landscape gardener Humphry Repton in 1812. A tower lookout gives panoramic views of the coast and surrounding countryside.

18 Weybourne

During the Second World War, Weybourne Camp was an important anti-aircraft firing range and training camp. It is now the site of the Muckleburgh Collection, a museum of military equipment that includes a display of tanks, armoured cars and artillery. East of Weybourne, the shingle shore and marshland give way gradually to higher cliffs.

Just west of the village's Church of All Saints, a lane leads north to a car park by a stretch of shingle known as Weybourne Hope. The steeply shelving beach allows ships to anchor close inshore, and it was heavily defended at the time of the Spanish Armada.

19 Salthouse

Like nearby Blakeney and Cley, the attractive village of flint cottages is a former port cut off from the sea. Lanes lead across the bird sanctuary of Salthouse Marshes to the long-distance Norfolk Coast Path. Salthouse's Church of St Nicholas is a fine example of the late 15th-century style. About a mile inland, at Gallow Hill, are some impressive Bronze Age barrows.

20 Cley next the Sea

A former port left stranded by the receding sea, Cley, pronounced 'Cly', is on the edge of one of Britain's foremost nature reserves. Breeding species in Cley Marsh, a great bed of reeds dotted with brackish and freshwater lagoons, include bearded tits and bitterns, and you can see many other wildfowl in winter. There is a visitor centre and a large car park on the coast road east of the village.

In Cley itself, traces of the old quay remain along the narrow Cley Channel, dominated by an 18th-century tower windmill. This is now a guesthouse, but visitors can usually climb to the top for a view of the coast and the surrounding countryside. South of the village is ancient St Margaret's Church, rebuilt on a grand scale in the 14th century.

21 Blakeney Point

A strange and lonely shingle spit stretches northwest for about 4 miles from Cley Eye to Blakeney Point, forming the centrepiece of Blakeney National Nature Reserve. Most visitors reach the point by boat from Blakeney or Morston; there is also a footpath from Cley. Blakeney Point is home to nesting colonies of terns, ringed plovers and shelduck, and common and grey seals can often be seen from the boats, both in the water and on the beach. Plants on the marshes and dunes on the point's landward side include sea lavender and prickly sea-wort.

㉒ Blakeney
A thriving port until the 16th century, its vessels travelling as far as Iceland, gradual silting has left Blakeney's sea access as just a narrow channel that is accessible only to small craft at high tide. Nowadays Blakeney is a resort popular with pleasure boaters, birdwatchers and naturalists.

The high street runs steeply down to the harbour between cottages of brick and flint, behind some of which lie large and unsuspected gardens, while the old Guildhall (EH) has a well-preserved 14th-century undercroft with an arched and vaulted brick ceiling.

South of the village is the vast Church of St Nicholas, dubbed the 'Cathedral of the Coast'. Its western tower, rising to more than 30m (100ft), is a landmark for miles around; a smaller tower at the eastern end of the church was possibly built as a beacon to guide ships into Blakeney harbour.

From the village quay, a popular 3 mile walk follows the sea embankment to Blakeney Eye and continues back up the western side of Cley Channel to Cley next the Sea. Blakeney harbour is the departure point for boat trips to Blakeney Point.

㉓ Morston
North of the village, paths will take you on an exploration of Morston Marshes, part of Blakeney National Nature Reserve (NT). The saltwater marshes are home to large numbers of redshanks, shelduck and Brent geese. From a quay near the car park, a ferry crosses to the bird sanctuary at Blakeney Point and beyond to sandbanks where you can see basking seals.

㉔ Stiffkey
The expression 'raking in the blues' is used to refer to the practice of striding out to the beach here with rakes and buckets to gather the local delicacy – the prized cockles known as 'Stewkey blues' – when the tide goes out. The pronunciation 'Stewkey' for Stiffkey has died out, but is still used to describe the cockles.

A track opposite the Church of St John and St Mary leads down to Stiffkey Marshes, skirted by the Norfolk Coast Path. The marsh, forming part of Blakeney and Holkham national nature reserves, is one of the largest ungrazed salt marshes in western Europe.

㉕ Wells-next-the-Sea
The old port has three distinctive parts – the quayside, the old streets behind it, and the beach area a mile to the north. The quay has cafes, shops and amusement arcades, while narrow streets lead up to The Buttlands, a tree-shaded green surrounded by dignified Georgian houses. The sandy beach is almost a mile deep at low tide, and can be reached by road, on foot along the sea wall or from Holkham Gap, or by miniature railway. On reclaimed marshland behind the sea wall there is a boating lake, while to the east are the largely inaccessible salt marshes that form part of the Holkham National Nature Reserve.

On the Stiffkey road is the terminus of the Wells and Walsingham Light Railway, whose narrow-gauge steam trains run for 4 miles inland as far as the town of Little Walsingham.

㉖ Holkham Hall
The austere Palladian mansion was built for Thomas Coke (pronounced 'Cook') Earl of Leicester, in the 18th century, based on his vision of an Italian villa. Among the many paintings on display here are works by Rubens, Gainsborough, and Van Dyck, and there are also a number of fine tapestries throughout the house, including works by the great Flemish weaver Albert Auwercx.

The Bygones Museum, housed in an old stable block, contains an exhibition of antique tools, tractors, cars, steam engines, domestic items and farm machinery. The surrounding parkland, landscaped partly by Capability Brown, has a 37m (120ft) monument to a later Coke, known as 'Coke of Norfolk', who revolutionised farming with his experiments in animal breeding, manuring and crop rotation. There is a walled garden, too, and visitors can wander through woodlands and a deer park.

㉗ Holkham Gap
Holkham National Nature Reserve includes dunes and salt marshes, and a vast expanse of low-tide sands and mudflats that attracts many waders. It is one of Britain's largest coastal reserves and is reached by a road that runs seawards from the A149 to a car park, where a boardwalk leads through pines, planted to stabilise the dunes.

㉘ Burnham Overy Staithe
Black-tarred cottages overlook a creek filled with small boats and flanked by a huge area of salt marsh. A mile long path along the eastern sea wall leads to a boardwalk across dunes and to sands, and in summer a ferry runs to Scolt Head Island. To the west of the village a six-storey tower windmill and a watermill are in view from the A149.

Treasures of Sandringham

Sandringham was Queen Victoria's much-loved country estate, set in 60 acres of gardens and described as 'The most comfortable house in England'. Inside are collections of porcelain, jade, Faberge jewellery, and silver and bronze objects set amid elegant furniture. Royal portraits are by the leading contemporary painters such as Heinrich von Angeli, Franz Winterhalter and Edward Hughes. The house also contains an important collection of oriental arms and armour, brought back from the Far East and India.

A museum in the stables contains vintage cars, including children's cars, family photographs, rare ceramics and other royal mementos. It includes the first car owned by a member of the British royal family, a 1900 Daimler phaeton.

Sandringham's grounds, regarded by some to be the finest of all the royal gardens, have magnificent trees, lawns, shrubs, flowerbeds and lily-strewn lakes, and the estate includes a country park with nature trails and picnic sites.

▶ See Sandringham **37**, page 130

29 Burnham Market
Once three separate villages, which merged into a small market town following the arrival of the railway in 1866. At the centre, Georgian houses and bow-windowed shops surround a long green. To the north, Burnham Norton's solitary Church of St Margaret has a circular flint tower and a Norman font, while Burnham Thorpe, to the southeast, was Lord Nelson's birthplace; the old rectory in which he was born was demolished in 1802.

30 Scolt Head Island National Nature Reserve
Inaccessibility has contributed to the preservation of wildlife on this island reserve, which comprises continually changing sand dunes, salt marsh, intertidal sand and mudflats and shingle. Colonies of common, Sandwich, Arctic and little terns breed in a ternery at the western end, and it is also an important breeding ground for ringed plovers, oystercatchers, black-headed gulls and waders. Visitors are not allowed on the reserve between mid April and mid August.

31 Brancaster Staithe
A small harbour – a 'staithe' is a bank, or landing stage, in Old English – stands on a channel almost choked with sand and mud. Small boats take visitors to the national nature reserve of Scolt Head Island when tides and breeding patterns permit.

Brancaster Staithe has been known for its shellfish since Roman times; some 250 tons of oysters and mussels grown from imported seed are now gathered each year in the creek between the staithe and the sea. Brancaster Staithe merges into Burnham Deepdale, one of the villages in the area jointly known as the 'Seven Burnhams'. Its Church of St Mary has a Norman font intricately carved with a series of 12 illustrations depicting the countryman's working year.

32 Brancaster
A field marks the site of the 4th-century Roman fortress of Branodunum, whose name lives on today in a different form as Brancaster. From the village centre, a road runs northwards for more than a mile to a beach car park, which is bordered by dunes and a golf course. A sea wall protects some of the sandy beach.

33 Titchwell Marsh RSPB Reserve
A shingle beach, a reed bed and an area of marsh, play host to birds including avocets, marsh harriers and, in October, a wide variety of migrating waders. Titchwell Marsh is one of the RSPB's most popular reserves, and hundreds of thousands of birds visit each year. In summer you may be lucky enough to see bearded tits or bitterns. The reserve is served by a large car park and visitor centre.

34 Holme next the Sea
This peaceful village, strung along narrow lanes, is where the 93 mile Peddars Way and Norfolk Coast Path meets the sea, after following a remarkably straight course from a point just over the Suffolk border, close to Thetford.

Holme's dunes and sandy beach lie beyond Hunstanton's championship golf links, while Holme Dunes National Nature Reserve has a range of habitats, including several environmentally sensitive dune systems. It is home to natterjack toads, now rare in Britain, and some 100 bird species can be seen there at peak migration times. Entrance tickets are available from the visitor centre.

The village of Thornham, a flourishing port until the late 19th century, is a starting point for walks along the Norfolk Coast Path, although it is important that you keep to the path as parking can be difficult here.

35 Hunstanton

The only coastal town in East Anglia to face west has more than half a mile of horizontally striped cliffs 18m (60ft) high, which have partly eroded into a litter of boulders on the sandy shore. On top an esplanade runs beside a broad grassy swathe, dominated by a disused lighthouse and the 13th-century ruins of St Edmund's Chapel. Old Hunstanton, half a mile north, is a village of red-roofed cottages.

36 Snettisham Coastal Park

Stretches of open water, dense reed beds, scrub and grassland lie behind the sea bank here. Resident birds include yellowhammers and reed buntings, and summer migrants include whitethroats. On the seaward side of the bank, where there is a hide, are the wildfowl, sea birds and waders for which The Wash is famous.

37 Sandringham

The royal country residence was bought by Queen Victoria for her son, Edward VII, when he was Prince of Wales. He rebuilt it in 1870, creating a cocktail of red brick, yellow stone, cupolas, turrets and gables. The house and grounds are open daily from August to October.

To the west is the Dersingham Nature Reserve, whose peaty marshland supports rare plants such as round-leaved sundew and bog asphodel. A large nesting population of shelduck occupies its heathland. Birch, chestnut and Scots pine trees shelter deer and many species of bird.

38 Castle Rising

The quiet hamlet is dominated by the ruins of a Norman fortress, which was once one of the most important fortifications in East Anglia. The ruins of Castle Rising Castle (EH) rest on massive defensive earthworks reached by a bridge over a dry moat, and the 15m (50ft) walls of the 12th-century keep remain standing. There are fine views of the surrounding countryside from the ramparts.

39 King's Lynn

'Lynn', as locals call it, was called Bishop's Lynn until Henry VIII dispossessed the bishop. The town's eight centuries of prosperity are reflected in its architecture, from the large 13th-century Chapel of St Nicholas to the spacious Tuesday Market, enclosed by elegant Jacobean and Georgian buildings. On the street known as Saturday Market is the 12th-century parish church of St Margaret.

HUNSTANTON CLIFFS

The 15th-century Holy Trinity Guildhall is used for auctions; housed in its undercroft are some of Lynn's treasures. From the same period, St George's Guildhall (NT) is the largest ancient guildhall in England to have survived intact. Its upper part is a theatre where William Shakespeare is said to have performed. Quiet Purfleet Quay has only a few old boats moored alongside, but downstream on the Great Ouse is a busy port, with a ferry crossing to West Lynn.

④⓪ Terrington St Clement

The magnificent Church of St Clement is known as 'the Cathedral of the Marshland'. Its unusual 15th-century tabernacle, or font cover, opens to reveal paintings of the baptism, fasting and temptation of Christ. The separate, massive tower has twice been a refuge for parishioners when the sea burst its banks, in 1613 and 1670.

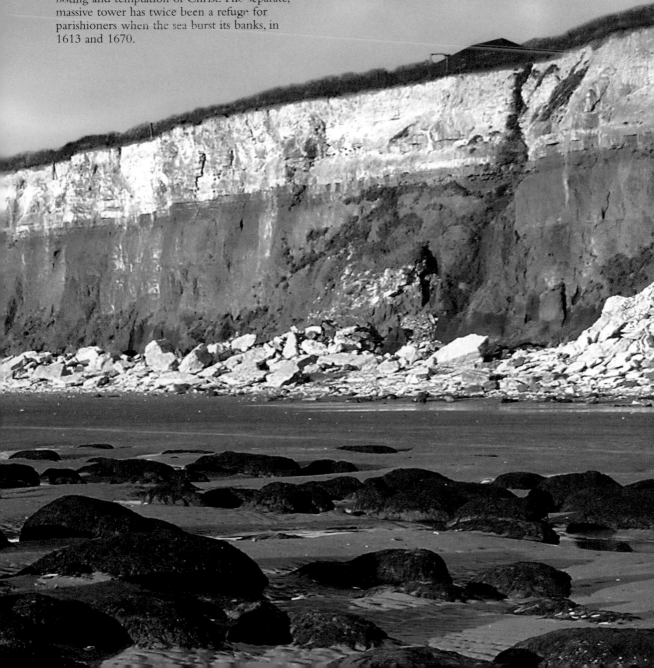

Visitor information

Cromer and Sheringham ☎ 0871 200 3071
(North Norfolk Tourist Information)
Great Yarmouth ☎ (01493) 846345
Hunstanton ☎ (01485) 532610
King's Lynn ☎ (01553) 763044
Lowestoft ☎ (01502) 533600
Mundesley ☎ (01263) 721070
Norwich ☎ (01603) 727927
Wells-next-the-Sea ☎ 0871 200 3071 (North Norfolk Tourist Information)

Berwick-
upon-Tweed

A1

A697

Bamburgh

A68

Northumberland
National
Park

A1068

Alnwick

A69

A696

Morpeth

A198

Newcastle-
upon-Tyne

Gateshead

A692

A167

Sunderland

Durham

A1(M)

Castle Eden
Dene to Berwick-
upon-Tweed
p148-153

A689

Hartlepool

A688

A66

Middlesbrough

Darlington

A172

Whitby

A66

A171

North York Moors
National Park

A1

A19

Thirsk

A170

Pickering

Scarborough

A168

A64

Yorkshire Dales
National Park

Ripon

A61

Kilnsea to
Hartlepool
p140-147

Bridlington

A166

A65

A59

Harrogate

York

A64

A1079

A1035

A56

A6068

A629

A658

Leeds

Selby

A63

Kingston-
upon-Hull

Bradford

A646

Halifax

M1

Wakefield

M62

A63

A58

M62

Huddersfield

A629

A638

A19

Scunthorpe

Grimsby

M60

A635

Barnsley

M1

A1(M)

Doncaster

M180

Peter Scott
Walk to
Spurn Head
p134-139

A628

M18

A15

Rotherham

A631

A631

A46

A16

Sheffield

A57

A156

Macclesfield

A623

A619

Chesterfield

A614

A1

Lincoln

A158

A515

A6

Mansfield

A46

A15

Skegness

A523

A52

A617

Newark
On Trent

A17

A16

A52

Stoke-on-Trent

A52

M1

A46

A1121

Boston

A50

Nottingham

A52

Grantham

A52

M6

A518

Derby

A15

Northeast

Yorkshire has a coast of two halves: the low black clay of Holderness leading into the fossil-rich cliffs of the 'Dinosaur Coast'. To the north lies the Durham Heritage Coast, now recovered from coal-mining pollution, and a 70-mile stretch of pale gold sands where the castles of Northumberland frown out at the windswept Farne Islands.

Key

— Motorway

— Principal A road

(See 'Finding your way', page 7)

PETER SCOTT WALK TO SPURN HEAD

Curving up towards and around the Humber estuary, which is spanned by the mighty Humber Bridge, this flat, often marshy stretch of coastline is still an important fishing centre; you will find much here of historical interest, including links with the Pilgrim Fathers

② Sutton Bridge
Cargo ships draw up on the west bank, where King John lost his baggage train while crossing The Wash in 1216. The small village dates from the late 19th century, when a port was established on the Nene waterway. The docks collapsed a month after opening, and it was only in 1987 that the scheme was revived.

The west bank road heads north to a car park by the sea wall near the hamlet of Gedney Drove End; from here there are wide views over The Wash, but the peace is shattered at intervals by low-flying military planes.

About 2 miles west of Sutton Bridge, Long Sutton's Butterfly and Wildlife Park stages displays by birds of prey.

③ Frampton Marsh
Miles of salt marsh, mudflats and sandbanks, incorporating an RSPB reserve, stretch from the sea wall. Sea birds and waders, buntings and finches feed on the salt-marsh plants; they in turn are fed on by hen harriers, merlins and short-eared owls, hunters best seen at dusk as they fly inland to roost. In winter migrant waders and wildfowl take over, and the incoming tide drives them off the flats towards the sea wall. There is parking by a path off the road 2 miles east of Frampton village.

④ Havenside Country Park
A stumpy granite pillar in the southeast corner of the park, the Pilgrim Fathers' Memorial marks the seizure of 13 Puritans while they were attempting to flee to Holland in 1607. After a brief spell of imprisonment, several of them eventually made it to America aboard

① Peter Scott Walk
The 10 mile walk, named after the ornithologist who studied and painted wildfowl from the east bank 'lighthouse' in the 1930s, follows the outermost sea bank from the Nene to West Lynn. To the south, the rich Fenland farmland is scored by a succession of banks marking centuries of reclamation, culminating in the outer bank of 1974.

The road north of Sutton Bridge, along the east bank of the Nene, provides views over land reclaimed in the 19th century to a picnic site and a 'lighthouse'. Together with its twin across the river, the tower was built not for navigation but to mark the opening of the Nene's new channel in 1831. Today, the buildings are private houses.

the *Mayflower* in 1620. Later migrants, who left Boston in 1630, founded Boston, Massachusetts. You can reach the memorial on foot by the coast path, or by road through Fishtoft.

A 2 mile strip along the north shore of The Haven, Boston port's link with the sea has been set aside as a wildlife haven. A variety of waders and sea birds including oystercatchers and cormorants live on the waterway. Inland, trees and shrubs shelter smaller birds such as yellowhammers and bullfinches.

5 Boston
The lantern-topped tower of St Botolph's Church was a landmark for fenland travellers and sailors on The Wash for 500 years. It shares Boston's skyline with cranes and other modern ironmongery around the busy docks. A steep climb of more than 360 steps to the top of the tower, known as the Stump, yields panoramic views of the surrounding countryside. Inside the church are misericords dating from 1390, showing intricately carved satirical scenes such as a friar preaching to geese, and memorials commemorating the town's association with early settlement in America.

South of the vast marketplace outside St Botolph's is the 15th-century St Mary's Guildhall, now a museum featuring the cells where the earliest Pilgrim Fathers were held in 1607 before their trial for an illegal attempt to reach Holland and religious freedom. Next door is Fydell House, a fine early Georgian town house now used as an adult education centre. Narrow lanes nearby follow their medieval lines, and some retain medieval buildings such as the 13th-century Blackfriars Hall, which suffered severe bomb damage during the Second World War. The building was renovated in the 1960s as Boston's arts and information centre.

North of St Botolph's, pleasure craft are moored along the shore at the Grand Sluice, built in 1766 to control flooding by the River Witham. Maud Foster Drain, a manmade waterway, runs parallel to the Witham. Beside it stands the seven-storey Maud Foster Windmill, said to be Britain's tallest mill in working order and a well-preserved example of a five-sailed Lincolnshire mill. It is open to visitors at weekends and Wednesdays throughout the year.

6 Freiston Shore
The sea wall here protects the 22 miles of shore that runs from Boston northwards to Skegness. A few houses huddle on its landward side, while on the seaward side are marshes popular with birdwatchers. You can walk the full distance of the wall, but it is inadvisable to explore the marshes without first checking the tides.

7 Wrangle
Medieval stained-glass windows grace the 14th-century Church of St Mary and St Nicholas which overlooks a tiny village green. A path from Sailor's Home, to the southeast, leads to the sea bank, a wild, marshy area that borders the mudflats of The Wash.

8 Wainfleet All Saints
The town is best known as the home of Bateman's, a British-run family brewery which has a visitor centre and runs tours. Wainfleet was once an important seaport and market town, said to be on the site of the Roman town of Vainona. The red-brick Magdalen College School was built in 1484 by William of Waynflete, Bishop of Winchester, to prepare students for his other foundation, Oxford's Magdalen College. The school now accommodates a library and museum.

9 Gibraltar Point National Nature Reserve
Visiting birds to the reserve include Brent geese, fieldfares, twites and redwings. The reserve also provides one of the few regular nesting places on the Lincolnshire coast for little terns. Gibraltar Point, comprising dunes, rough grazing, fresh and saltwater marshes, and beach and foreshore, extends for about 3 miles from the south of Skegness to the entrance to The Wash, and includes a visitor centre and a network of footpaths, leading to hides and an observation platform.

10 Skegness
A product of the railway age, familiarly known as 'Skeggy', train track was laid and opened here in 1875, to link the town with the industrial Midlands. Acres of formal gardens, line the seafront, as well as boating lakes, indoor fun centres and a model village; there is also a 6 mile stretch of firm, sandy beach, whose size is gradually increasing each year as the sea recedes.

Church Farm Museum shows how the land was farmed before tractors. The collection of faithfully reconstructed buildings includes a Lincolnshire 'mud and stud' thatched cottage, giving an insight into the living conditions of an agricultural labourer around 1790.

11 Ingoldmells
The resort was the site of Billy Butlin's first holiday camp, built there in 1936 and still open for business. One of the original chalets stands in the grounds. Nearby, the 13th-century Church of St Peter and St Paul has a 600-year-old font. Hardy's Animal Farm, north-west of Ingoldmells, is a working farm where you can see sheep, goats and ducks.

⑫ Chapel St Leonards

A centre for smuggling during the 18th and 19th centuries, Chapel St Leonards is now a bright, modern seaside village of brick villas, interspersed with chalets and caravan parks. A 4 mile sandy beach extends to the north and south, and there is an ornamental fish farm on the main Mablethorpe to Skegness road.

⑬ Sutton on Sea

During the 1953 floods the sea opened a gap 274m (900ft) wide and flooded the land for miles inland. A high, concrete promenade has been built behind the wide, firm sands to prevent another such disaster. To the south an 18-hole golf course hugs the shore.

⑭ Mablethorpe

The first parish of Mablethorpe was swept away by the sea in 1289, and occasionally at spring tides you can see the original shoreline and tree stumps. On a warm summer's day holidaymakers flock to the long, sandy beach, funfair and amusement arcades. It is a scene far removed from the 1820s, when Lord Tennyson spent his summer holidays in what was then a quiet village, roaming the sand hills and endless beaches for poetic inspiration.

The Animal Gardens and Seal Trust, in the north of the town, has two rehabilitation pools for sick and injured seals, while Ye Olde Curiosity Museum displays thousands of everyday items such as old toys, kitchen utensils and furniture.

⑮ Saltfleetby to Theddlethorpe Dunes

The sandflats, dunes and marshes of this national nature reserve support a great variety of animals and plants. In spring and summer the salt marshes are a blaze of colour, while in autumn and winter migrating birds settle here after crossing the North Sea. A trail among marsh orchids provides an easier route.

⑯ Donna Nook

A stopping-off point for 250 species of migrating birds, the breeding colonies at this national nature reserve include red-legged partridges and skylarks, while seals bask on far-off sandbanks at low tide. A sprawl of marram-covered dunes, sandflats and marshes, it extends for 6 miles from Grainthorpe Haven to Saltfleet Haven. An RAF bombing range covers part of the dunes.

⑰ Horse Shoe Point

Low tide reveals almost 2 miles of broad sandflats, though Horse Shoe Point, reached from the A1031 by a long narrow road cutting across flat fields, is no more than a spit of land above high-water mark. A 3 mile walk west leads to the Tetney Marshes RSPB Reserve.

⑱ Cleethorpes

Visitors arriving by mainline train can still step out of the station straight onto a 3 mile promenade in this holiday centre, made popular by the coming of the railway in

HUMBER BRIDGE

the late 19th century. Family amusements line the walkway north of the pier, while on Central Promenade stands Ross Castle, a 19th-century folly with a viewing platform overlooking the Humber estuary.

The sea goes out almost a mile over the sands, but walkers should take care as there are fast incoming tides. A walk along the seafront will reward you with a clear view of Bull Sand Fort and Haile Sand Fort, built during the First World War as anti-submarine defences.

At the southern end of the resort is the Lakeside leisure area, where a large lake with wildfowl is stocked with fish for anglers. The narrow-gauge Cleethorpes Coast Light Railway, which runs through the park, ends a mile to the southeast, near the Pleasure Island theme park and a plaque marking the Greenwich Meridian.

A collection of urns and cremated remains discovered in a Bronze Age barrow at Beacon Hill, Cleethorpes's cemetery, is on display at the town's library.

19 Grimsby

The *Ross Tiger*, a historic fishing trawler moored in Grimsby's docks, recalls the heyday of one of the world's greatest fising ports. Until the mid 1970s, Grimsby had a large fishing fleet with 200 trawlers sailing as far north as the Barents Sea. The deep-sea fishing fleet is now gone, but Grimsby still has a large commercial dock.

At the National Fishing Heritage Centre special effects are used to re-create the life and times of the Grimsby trawlermen. Moored outside are several fishing vessels, including the *Ross Tiger*, which fished off northern Scotland for 30 years. A marina forms part of the docks, which retain their 94m (309ft) Dock Tower, a Victorian landmark visible for miles out to sea. The dockside wholesale fish market is not open to visitors.

Grimsby's green spaces include the large riverside Freshney Parkway and the People's Park with its classic Victorian gardens and floral hall. At Waltham village, about 4 miles south of Grimsby, a windmill built in 1880 is open to visitors at weekends in summer.

20 Immingham

From a small inlet at Immingham, the Pilgrim Fathers set sail for Holland in 1608 on the first stage of their voyage to the New World, where they arrived in 1620. A 6m (20ft) monument to the pilgrims stands opposite the Church of St Andrew.

The inlet where their boat was moored has now disappeared under a huge docks and industrial complex. The docks area is not open to visitors, but in a former chapel you will find a local history museum covering their journey and development.

21 Humber Bridge

The monumental Humber Bridge was the longest single-span bridge in the world when it was completed in 1981. Built over the course of eight years, it measures 1410m

(4626ft) and its two towers stand 155m (510ft) above their supporting platforms. It took 44,120 miles of wire to make the cables, and 480,000 tonnes of concrete to build its two towers and roadway. Today, the two-lane dual carriageway over the bridge is used by some six million vehicles a year. There is a toll for motor vehicles, but the crossing is free for walkers and cyclists, and the bridge gives you magnificent views up and down the Humber estuary.

㉒ Hessle
A disused chalk-crushing mill is a reminder of hundreds of years of mineral extraction on Hessle foreshore. The foreshore of the large residential village is a popular fishing spot. Just to the west of the bridge are woodland and meadow walks in the Humber Bridge Country Park, while Hessle marks the end of the Wolds Way, a 79 mile National Trail finishing at Filey in North Yorkshire.

㉓ Kingston upon Hull
A bustling port, Hull's history is evident in its medieval old town and historic dock. Today it is a major industrial and commercial city, a modern port, and a centre of learning and research with a university but it has a history which goes back to the 12th century. Its official name, Kingston upon Hull, dates from 1299, when the port on the River Hull received a charter from Edward I. The first dock, built in the 1770s, has now been filled in, and is the site of Queen's Gardens, a large open space. Other former docks have also acquired new identities: Princes Quay shopping centre has been built on stilts above the water of the former Princes Dock, while the Humber Dock has been converted to a marina, where the restored *Spurn Lightship* is moored. The Maritime Museum, highlighting Hull's contribution to Arctic whaling in the 19th century and its involvement in North Sea fishing, is housed in the former offices of the Hull Dock Company.

Hull suffered much bomb damage during the Second World War, but some of its buildings from the 18th century and earlier survive, especially around the narrow cobbled lanes and quays of the Old Town, on the western side of the River Hull. This area is now known as the Museum Quarter and one of the houses on its

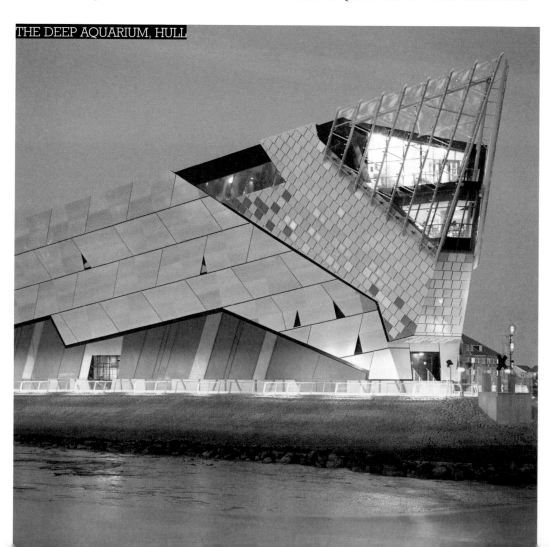
THE DEEP AQUARIUM, HULL

High Street was the birthplace in 1759 of William Wilberforce, who devoted his political life to the abolition of slavery. Wilberforce House contains a unique collection of relics of the slave trade, as well as period costumes, furniture and silver, and an oak-panelled banqueting room.

Other attractions in this area are the Streetlife Museum of Transport, the Hull and East Riding Museum and the *Arctic Corsair*, a 1960s sidewinder trawler. Elsewhere in the old town, the large Holy Trinity Church dates from the 14th century and contains some of the earliest examples of English brickwork; the nearby Ferens Art Gallery features old masters and marine paintings.

Walks along the foreshore and through the centre of the city include one route that takes in the Tidal Surge Barrier by the mouth of the Hull, near the popular riverside viewing point of Victoria Pier. On the promontory on the east side of the River Hull is the dramatically angular building of The Deep, an award-winning aquarium designed by Sir Terry Farrell. As well as housing a vast collection of sharks and other fish, it also carries out vital marine research and conservation work.

Hull's modern dockland, to the east of the city, handles fishing boats, containerised cargo ships and oil tankers, while ferries bound for Rotterdam and Zeebrugge sail from King George Dock.

24 Hedon
Boasting a 39m (129ft) high cruciform tower, St Augustine Church, known as the King of Holderness, is one of the few legacies of Hedon's former glory – many of its other medieval buildings were destroyed by a fire in 1656.

An attractive market town, founded in the 12th century, Hedon was once the most important shipping centre on the Humber's north bank. But the coming of larger ships, which could not sail up the narrow Hedon Haven, led to the port being abandoned.

25 Paull
A neat little disused lighthouse built in 1836 forms the backdrop for a good view of Hull docks and boat traffic on the Humber. From the Salt End roundabout on the A1033, the road to Paull runs between cornfields and a major BP chemical plant before continuing through farmland to the waterfront.

26 Stone Creek
An isolated beauty spot, Stone Creek lies at the end of a lane that runs through low-lying farmland. The hamlet is the base for a sailing club, although strong tidal currents can pose a challenge to sailors.

Nearby, there are nature reserves at Fisherman's Channel, which is an old creek, and at Haverfield Quarries, a large area of reed beds. Both are home to a number of wintering ducks from northern regions as well as waders such as dunlins.

27 Patrington
Known as the Queen of Holderness, the Church of St Patrick is a masterpiece of medieval English architecture. Built between 1310 and 1420, it is designed like a cathedral, with a central tower and spire soaring 58m (189ft) above the ground. Some 200 gargoyles adorn the church and there are many carvings on the capitals of the pillars. Now a quiet village, Patrington was once a busy market town that was used as a retreat by successive archbishops of York.

28 Spurn Head
The sand and shingle Spurn peninsula, 3 miles long but in places just 9m (30ft) wide, curves in a great hook into the mouth of the Humber. The peninsula, bordered by a sandy beach on the seaward side and by mudflats on the Humber side, is formed from material washed out from eroding shores to the north. Eroded and reformed over the centuries, it is held in its present precarious position and shape by sea defences that have been built up over the past 150 years.

Since 1960 the Spurn peninsula has been a nature reserve, and it is now designated as Heritage Coast. The spit is a major site from which to observe bird migration, especially in autumn when visiting birds include Brent geese and Arctic terns. You may also see seals and porpoises. There is a charge for drivers using the road to Spurn Head, at the tip of the peninsula; to prevent disturbance to wildlife, dogs are not allowed on the reserve, even in cars. The remains of military defences can also be seen near the car park.

The country's only full-time lifeboat crew and their families live at Spurn Head, and a jetty is the departure point for the pilots who accompany ships navigating the narrow and difficult shipping lanes into the Humber.

> **Visitor information**
> **Boston** ☎ (01205) 356656
> **Cleethorpes** ☎ (01472) 323111
> **Humber Bridge North Bank** ☎ (01482) 640852
> **Louth** ☎ (01507) 609289
> **Mablethorpe** ☎ (01507) 474939
> **Skegness** ☎ (01754) 899887

KILNSEA TO HARTLEPOOL

Wild cliffs offer wonderful views of this constantly evolving coastline, with land that is prone to slippage, as some of its villages have found to their cost. Centuries of mining have also affected the lay of the land here, but the crowds are still drawn to the holiday resorts and fine, sandy beaches

❶ Kilnsea
A scattered community straddles a constantly eroding spit of land that ends at Spurn. Kilnsea has two shores: the eastern shore is sandy and exposed to the North Sea; the western shore is muddy and sheltered within the Humber estuary. A plaque at the old Blue Bell inn shows that it was 488m (534yd) from the sea when it was built in 1847. Now 174m (190yd) from the sea, it has been converted to a visitor centre and tearoom by the Spurn Heritage Coast Project.

❷ Easington
Houses built from sea cobbles – large stones of various colours collected from the beach – are a feature of this attractive village. Near the medieval All Saints Church is a 15th-century thatched red-brick barn. To the north of the village is a different scene. An industrial complex includes a gas terminal to which the first North Sea gas was piped ashore in 1967, a heliport and a large gas-gathering station.

The low clay cliffs and sand and shingle beach have suffered considerable erosion since the gas terminal was built.

❸ Withernsea
Set well back from the sea, among rows of houses, is a handsome lighthouse, built in 1892. It is now a museum on the work of the RNLI and HM Coastguard, and also contains memorabilia of the 1950s actress Kay Kendall, who was born in Withernsea. This traditional resort also boasts a long sandy beach.

❹ Aldbrough
The sandy beach here is reached by steps that have to be rebuilt every year. The village is set well back from the sea, but the end of the road to the coast has been torn up by the waves and has disappeared off the cliff edge.

❺ Mappleton
Tons of rocks have been deposited at the base of Mappleton's cliffs in an effort to save the village from falling into the sea. A grassy viewing and picnic area overlooking Mappleton Sands is reached by a wide path curving down to the shore; All Saints' Church, built in the 14th and 15th centuries, has long been a landmark for shipping.

❻ Hornsea
The cobbled cottages and 15th-century Church of St Nicholas in Hornsea's main street are protected as a conservation area, which includes a folk museum housed in a 16th-century farmhouse. The old town is separated from the seafront by the golf course and Hall Garth Park. Hornsea Mere, Yorkshire's largest freshwater lake, is an RSPB reserve of international significance. A path from Hull Road traces the south side of the Mere. At the eastern side, where there is a car park, you can hire rowing and sailing boats, while Honeysuckle Farm, to the north, has farm animals and a nature walk.

Hartlepool

Redcar

Middlesbrough

Whitby

Scarborough

Pickering

Malton

Bridlington

Driffield

York

Hornsea

Beverley

Kingston upon Hull

Goole

0   5 Miles

7 Skipsea

A grassy mound near All Saints' Church is all that remains of a Norman castle belonging to Drogo de Bevrere. After the Norman Conquest, the village of Skipsea came into the possession of de Bevrere, who married a relative of William the Conqueror. The sand and shingle beach of Skipsea Sands is reached by steps down the sea-gnawed cliffs.

8 Bridlington

A bustling resort and fishing harbour, you can still see fishermen landing haddock, cod, lobsters and crabs. Originally two separate townships known as Burlington and The Quay, Bridlington is a busy resort. Burlington, now known as the Old Town, includes the Bayle Museum of local antiquities and the 12th-century priory of St Mary. The North and South Parades, each with a mile-long sandy beach, are divided by the harbour, where there is a museum explaining the harbour's history. Fishing trips can be arranged, and there are cruises round the harbour and to the bird colonies of Flamborough Head and Bempton Cliffs.

Park Rose Pottery, 2 miles southwest of Bridlington, has an owl sanctuary.

9 Sewerby

The trophies and momentos of the aviator Amy Johnson, who was born in Hull, are on show in 18th-century Sewerby Hall. The hall also houses a small art gallery and museum. A path from the east end of the high street leads behind the hall along the coast to Danes Dyke.

10 South Landing

The path leading up steep steps from the boulder-strewn shingle beach is the start of a clifftop walk east to Flamborough's lighthouse, 2 miles away. A nature trail begins at the Heritage Coast visitor centre next to the car park; there are picnic areas behind the car park and on the clifftop. To the west, Beacon Hill was used as part of a chain of beacons built in 1588 to pass news of the approach of Spanish ships during the time of the Armada.

11 Flamborough Head

The arrow-shaped headland gets its name from the Saxon 'flean', meaning dart. In Flamborough village, a street of fishermen's cottages and a market place memorial are reminders of a fishing tradition that dates back to the 9th century. The road from the village

FLAMBOROUGH HEAD

passes the Old Tower, a lighthouse built in 1674, and continues to another lighthouse built in 1806, which is open to visitors in summer.

Steep steps descend the slopes to the chalk beach of Selwicks (pronounced 'Silex') Bay, where the sea has carved inlets and sea stacks out of the face of the cliff. A mile's walk over the headland leads to North Landing.

12 Danes Dyke
The deep 2½ mile gash through Flamborough Head was created during the Bronze Age from a natural ravine; 5m (18ft) high and 18m (60ft) wide in some places, the giant incision was intended to isolate the headland from the rest of England.

The dyke's southern section forms a nature trail through woodland, while paths along the cliffs overlook a beach of smooth, white stones and lead west to Sewerby and east to South Landing.

13 North Landing
At one time as many as 80 fishing cobles used to go out for herring from the small but pretty cove. Cod and crab are still caught by a much reduced fleet, and fishing trips and excursions round the coast can be arranged in summer. A track from the car park leads to steep steps down a sand and pebble shore.

14 Thornwick Bay
Three tiny beaches, backed by icing-white cliffs topped with slabs of earth and grass, are reached from a rough track off the main North Landing road. A hazardous path zigzags over a triangular nose of land to a middle beach, blanketed by white boulders, where the chalk cliffs have slid onto the shore.

Wooden steps lead down to the chalk and sand of the western beach, while caves frame the cliffs of the easternmost beach of sand and shingle, where a short headland walk leads to North Landing.

15 Bempton Cliffs
In summer the perpendicular cliffs are home to more than 200,000 birds, including kittiwakes, gannets, razorbills and puffins. A lane from the modern village of Bempton leads through cornfields to the cliffs where an RSPB visitor centre together with viewpoint information boards give information on the birds that you can see there. As well as sea birds, corn buntings and meadow pipits breed in the grassland and fields on the clifftop.

Cruises offering the best views of the cliffs leave from North Landing and Bridlington during summer.

16 Filey
Victorian terraces and gardens look down over a promenade and 6 miles of sands, with gift shops and amusement parks at the seafront's northern end. St Oswald's Church has Norman features and an unusual 13th-century effigy of a 'boy bishop', while the Folk Museum in Queen Street has exhibits relating to sea fishing and the lifeboat service.

Reached from the beach or from the North Cliff Country Park, the slender mile-long promontory of Filey Brigg, popular with anglers, marks the ends of both the Cleveland Way and the Wolds Way, a 79 mile route from Hessle Haven near the Humber Bridge. The area has hides for birdwatching at the Brigg and at the country park. Birds such as greenshanks, pochards, ruffs, mallards and teal may also be seen from hides at Filey Dams Nature Reserve.

17 Cleveland Way
A 110 mile path traces a horseshoe-shaped route, starting inland at Helmsley and following the hills of the North York Moors before reaching the coast at Saltburn-by-the-Sea, 27 miles north of Robin Hood's Bay. The final section follows this glorious stretch of coast southwards as far as Filey Brigg.

18 Cayton Bay
Knipe Point (NT), the bay's northern headland, is reached along a footpath from the main road. The path begins behind a modern housing estate; there is very limited roadside parking. A short walk leads down to a rocky beach ribboned with sand, and Cayton Bay can also be approached along a path starting near a car park by a holiday camp. Another 3 mile walk along part of the Cleveland Way leads past the headland of White Nab to Scarborough's South Cliff.

19 Scarborough
The resort where sea bathing in Britain is said to have begun is set on slopes overlooking two wide bays. On the knob of land that divides the sands of North Bay and South Bay stands Scarborough Castle (EH), built by Henry II on the site of a Roman signal station. It retains high, buttressed walls and an impressive keep.

The 17th century saw the decline of Scarborough as a fortress town and its emergence instead as a spa resort. An ornate iron bridge, built in 1826, provides a route to the beach from elegant clifftop hotels. St Mary's Church, dating from the 12th century, contains the grave of the novelist Anne Brontë, who, after several visits, died in the town in 1849.

Cargo boats and fishing vessels berth in the inner harbour here, while the outer harbour is reserved for pleasure craft. Rowing, fishing and motor boats can be hired from the harbour slipways. The Heritage Centre, on the seafront opposite the harbour, recalls Scarborough's history from 966 to 1966.

The town's indoor attractions include the Rotunda museum of archaeology and local history, the Art Gallery, the Wood End Museum of natural history and Sitwell family memorabilia, and The Spa complex on the South Bay, with its theatre and ballroom.

On North Bay, Peasholm Park is the scene of reconstructed naval battles, using miniature craft, while the Sea Life Centre offers a window onto the life of the ocean. On the town's southern edge, a lake known as The Mere is watched over by Oliver's Mount, from where you can get good views of the resort.

20 Crook Ness

There are good views of Scarborough Castle from the rocky shore, which is reached along Rocks Lane from Burniston. From a small parking area, a path drops to a beach of rocks, backed by broken cliffs.

21 Cloughton Wyke

A 4½ mile circular walk leading from the village's former station traces part of the defunct railway, and follows the Cleveland Way to Crook Ness and a disused coastguard lookout. You can reach the rocky beach of Cloughton Wyke along an uneven path from the parking area at the end of Newlands Lane, near the village of Cloughton.

22 Hayburn Wyke

Beetles, mosses, liverworts and a variety of land and sea birds are found in the secluded valley known as Hayburn Wyke, part of which forms a nature reserve. Stone-laid paths, built in Victorian times for the day-trippers who alighted at a long-vanished railway station, form a 20 minute circular walk. The trail leads over a stream that cascades onto a boulder-strewn shore, where fossils of liverworts and ferns can be found. You may park your car, with permission, in the car park of the Hayburn Wyke Inn.

Staintondale Shire Horse Farm, to the north, offers cart rides, harnessing demonstrations and a picnic area.

23 Ravenscar

Built in 1774 as a private house, Raven Hall Hotel was visited by George III during his bouts of ill health. It crowns 183m (600ft) slopes, which plunge down to a rocky shore. The hotel's grounds, with a swimming pool, a croquet lawn and a golf course, are open to non-residents.

In the 1890s, the hotel owner planned to turn the village into a fashionable seaside resort. Streets were laid out, but the developers were deterred by the height and unstable nature of the cliffs.

A National Trust Coastal Centre marks the start of a path to the abandoned Peak Alum Works. Alum, produced here from 1650 to 1862, was used in textile manufacture and in tanning.

24 Stoupe Beck Sands

A mosaic of seaweed, sand, pebbles and rocks, the beach is reached by steps from the car park behind Stouple Brow Farm. From the crossroads by the disused windmill near Ravenscar, a road cuts precipitously downhill over moorland, revealing the curve of Robin Hood's Bay.

25 Boggle Hole

The stream-chiselled valley owned by the National Trust is named after the boggle, or goblin, who was said to haunt its slopes. A steep 5 minute walk will take you down from the car park at the top of the valley, past a youth hostel housed in a former watermill, to a small cove.

26 Robin Hood's Bay

Stone cottages with red pantiled roofs hug the steep slopes overlooking the bay with which the village shares its name. The narrow, cobbled streets and stepped paths twisting down to the sea here were once thick with smuggling activity in the 18th century. Today, visitors must park at the top of the village and walk down.

In the 19th century, 'Bay Town', as it is also known, outranked Whitby as a fishing centre. The Fisherhead Museum recalls local seafaring life and contains displays of the area's fossils and wildlife.

A waymarked walk northwards from the village follows the Cleveland Way to join a disused railway track, making a 2½ mile circuit. 'Bay Town' is also at the eastern end of the 190 mile Coast to Coast Walk from St Bees in Cumbria.

Bearing southeast, the Cleveland Way leads along exhilarating clifftops. At low tide it is possible to walk along the sandy, rock-strewn beach to Stoupe Beck Sands, 2 miles away.

27 Saltwick Bay

Steep steps lead down the cliffside, which has been hollowed out by alum workings. Good fossils may sometimes be found in the rocks on either side of the bay. The Cleveland Way leads east from Whitby along the clifftop to a small stretch of sand between the rocky promontories of Saltwick Nab and Black Nab.

㉘ Whitby

The stark brooding ruins of 13th-century Whitby Abbey (EH) have a spectacular setting on the clifftop above Whitby. The abbey was built on the site of an earlier monastery dedicated to St Hilda, which housed both monks and nuns and produced nine saints, five local bishops and the Saxon poet Caedmon.

The large Church of St Mary, beside the abbey, has a Norman tower but was substantially altered in Georgian times. The clifftop graveyard is set with straggling rows of headstones, pock-marked with salt erosion, and can be reached from the harbour below by a steep flight of 199 steps. Steps, graveyard and abbey ruins all feature in Bram Stoker's novel *Dracula*, and melodramatic tastes are catered for at the Dracula Experience on Marine Parade.

The harbour town's superb setting can be viewed in a sweeping panorama from the bridge that spans the estuary of the Esk. The river divides the eastern side of the town from the Victorian West Cliff development. Surveying the lively harbour from the western side of the estuary is the statue of Captain Cook, whose great ships of exploration were all built at

Whitby. The Captain Cook Memorial Museum, set in a house where Cook once lodged, has rooms containing furniture of the period, model ships, and drawings from artists who travelled on the explorer's voyages.

Near the statue of Captain Cook is an arch made from the jawbone of a whale, erected to commemorate what was one of Whitby's major businesses in the 18th and 19th centuries. Local captain William Scoresby, inventor of the 'crow's nest' ship's lookout, accounted for an extraordinary 533 whales in his career. Whitby remains a working fishing port, and herrings are still smoked over oak to produce kippers.

Whitby Museum in Pannett Park has one of Britain's finest fossil collections as well as jewellery carved from jet found on the local shore, which has been used since the Bronze Age; you can also visit the Museum of Victorian Whitby and the Lifeboat Museum in Pier Road.

Holiday activities include sailing, sea and river fishing, and seaside amusements on the fine Whitby Sands. Two miles inland, at Ruswarp,

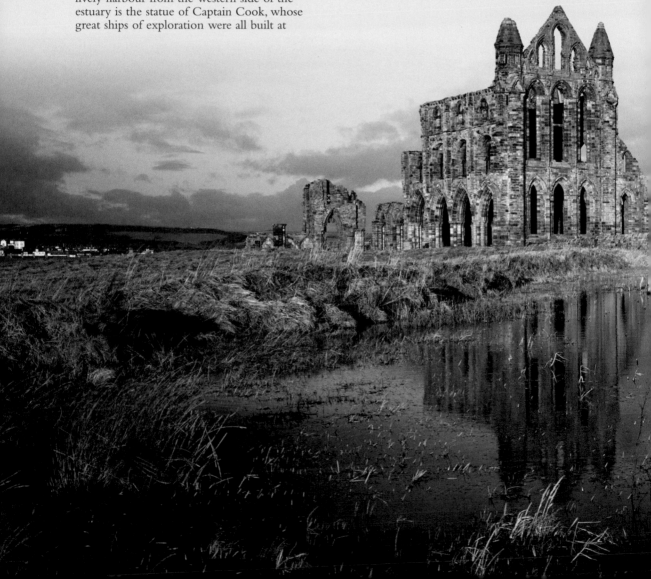

you can hire rowing boats to explore the Esk, or take a miniature steam railway that travels round a half-mile circular track.

29 Sandsend

The cliffs at Overdale Wyke and Sandsend Ness, north of the village, reveal some of the area's oldest alum workings, dating from 1607. Jet was also mined at Sandsend, to be worked by carvers in Whitby. The small but popular resort of Sandsend has a sandy beach that stretches for more than 2 miles to Whitby. Part of the Loftus–Whitby railway line has been absorbed into the Cleveland Way footpath. The former Sandsend railway station is now a private house, but the foundation pillars of the viaducts that crossed two streams, Mickleby Beck and East Row Beck, can still be seen. A footpath beside each stream leads into the beautiful Mulgrave Woods, and the owner allows walkers to roam the paths on Saturdays, Sundays and Wednesdays, except in May. In the woods are the ruins of 13th-century Mulgrave Castle.

30 Kettleness

The entire village of Kettleness disappeared into the sea in 1829. Close to the former railway station, now a private residence, stands a half-ruined chapel, and on high ground between these buildings and the nearby hamlet of Goldsborough is the site of a Roman military post. It was excavated in 1919 to reveal the skeletons of three men and a dog; the latter is thought to have died trying to protect its master from an attacker. Coins found date the incident to some time after AD 423.

31 Runswick Bay

During the 1680s an earlier village of Runswick slipped into the sea overnight. Modern Runswick consists of houses wedged into the unstable hillside at the northern end of a fine crescent of sand, and it is popular as a small sailing resort and holiday village.

32 Port Mulgrave

A row of cottages, built in the 1850s for miners from the local ironstone mines, is perched on the clifftop overlooking the harbour and reached by a very steep flight of steps. The cottages were once connected to the coast by a series of tunnels. Most of the railway and pier were dismantled in the 1930s, and the breakwater was destroyed by Royal Engineers during the Second World War to prevent the harbour being used by an invasion fleet.

INSPIRATION FOR BRAM STOKER'S DRACULA
WHITBY ABBEY

�33 Staithes

James Cook was a haberdasher's apprentice in Staithes in the mid 1740s, when 50 fishing cobles sailed out daily from the village. In the 19th century Staithes could fill three trains a week with cod, haddock and mackerel. Only a few cobles still fish regularly now.

Interest in Captain Cook is tapped by a heritage centre, sited in a refurbished former chapel built for Primitive Methodists in 1880. Near the centre is the start of a circular walk to Port Mulgrave, taking 2 to 3 hours.

Staithes is reached via a narrow valley that runs down to a small harbour, surrounded by high cliffs and protected from the open sea by a large breakwater and a protective wall of boulders. From the top of the hill near the entrance to the village, streets of closely packed houses, separated by narrow alleys with names such as Slippery Hill and Gun Gutter, wind steeply down to the harbour.

�34 Boulby

At 203m (666ft) above sea level, Boulby Cliffs are the highest point on England's eastern coast. They descend to the sea by stages rather than in a vertical drop, but the summit footpath still affords an exhilarating view. In the spring the cliffs provide nesting sites for kittiwakes, fulmars and house martins. Like Skinningrove, Boulby had both alum and ironstone mines; and jet, a form of fossilised wood much valued by the Victorians for making jewellery, was also found here.

Inland is a large mining complex where potash is extracted and refined for use as a fertiliser. Workings extend 1150m (3774ft) underground and stretch for up to 2 miles under the seabed.

�35 Skinningrove

The discovery of ironstone in 1848 introduced more than a century of mining, iron-making and steel-making to the small fishing village. A few traditional flat-bottomed

STAITHES

cobles still fish part time from the rocky beach and the Corus works near the museum now makes specialised products from Teesside steel, such as the sculptures along the Cleveland Way footpath. The works reflect the social history of the area with images including fish, horses and hammers.

Although the area's last ironstone pit closed in the mid 1960s, the small stream running through the village is still rust-coloured from iron-ore waste. The Cleveland Ironstone Mining Museum, at the former Loftus ironstone mine, offers visitors an opportunity to experience the underground working conditions of the past.

36 Saltburn-by-the-Sea
Britain's oldest hydraulic cliff lift, built in 1884, is a reminder of the town's Victorian heyday. The advent of the railway in 1861 began Saltburn's transformation from a small fishing hamlet into a holiday resort. The town retains its (shortened) pier and many fine

examples of Victorian architecture. To the south, beside the wooded banks of Skelton Beck, lie the remains of Marske Mill, an 18th-century watermill that went out of use in the 1920s.

37 Marske-by-the-Sea
A former fishing port, Marske-by-the-Sea has a fine stretch of sand that draws many holidaymakers. Errington Wood, on a prominent hillside in New Marske to the west, has a woodland trail, while a few miles southwest is Tocketts Mill, Cleveland's last working watermill, which is open every Sunday in summer.

38 Redcar
A traditional 'bucket-and-spade' seaside resort, Redcar is also a busy working fishing port. The town's attractions include a racecourse and the RNLI Zetland Museum.

To the west is Coatham Marsh Nature Reserve, where sedge warblers are common in summer and herons can be seen throughout the year. The conservation area of Kirkleatham, to the south, features the Old Hall Museum of local history, opened in 1709 as a Free School, and the Owl Centre with flight displays by birds of prey.

39 Hartlepool
Once a thriving shipbuilding centre, Hartlepool's old docks are now a marina, and include a collection of historic ships. A museum tells the story of Hartlepool from Saxon times, and next to it is a reconstruction of a seaport of the early 1900s, known as Historic Quay. The Headland museum explains the town's maritime past, and nearby is the fine early 12th-century Church of St Hilda.

To the south of the town is the popular resort of Seaton Carew. A long stretch of sandy beach leads onto North Gare Breakwater and the Teesmouth National Nature Reserve. The reserve's mudflats and sand dunes are a staging post for migrating waders such as knots and redshanks, and support a small population of grey seals.

Dividing the reserve into two separate areas is Hartlepool nuclear power station.

Visitor information

Bridlington ☎ (01262) 673474
Hartlepool ☎ (01429) 869706
Hornsea ☎ (01964) 536404
Hull ☎ (01482) 223559
Humber Bridge ☎ (01482) 640852
Middlesbrough ☎ (01642) 729700
Saltburn ☎ (01287) 622422
Scarborough, Filey, Whitby ☎ (01723) 383636

CASTLE EDEN DENE TO BERWICK-UPON-TWEED

Isolated Holy Island, cut off from the mainland at high tide, looks out onto a shoreline dotted with tiny fishing villages

Seaham developed around the cliffside harbour, built in the early 19th century as an outlet for local mines.

③ Sunderland

The industrial city's ancient origins are evident at St Peter's Church, built in AD 674 as a monastery and which featured the first glass to be made in Britain. Sunderland subsequently became a glass-making centre. The National Glass Centre on the north bank of the river houses galleries and exhibitions, while Sunderland's history is chronicled at the town's museum and art gallery. Sunderland's industrial identity is symbolised by the parallel road and railway bridges spanning the River Wear.

Monkwearmouth Station Museum, to the north of the town, has a large collection of rail memorabilia, and northwest is the 15th-century Hylton Castle (EH), displaying medieval heraldry.

Also north of the town, on the seafront of suburban Roker, stands a memorial to the Venerable Bede, born in the area in AD 673. And nearby is St Andrew's Church, built in 1907, with fittings produced by Arts and Crafts artists.

④ Whitburn

A sandy bay stretches south of the neatly tended village of stone houses, whose Church of St Mary has been a coastal landmark since it was built in the 13th century. The clifftop path to the north, towards Lizard Point and South Shields, is edged with wild flowers.

⑤ South Shields

Excavations have revealed the remains of the Roman fort of Arbeia on a hill commanding the south bank of the Tyne, where South Shields now stands. Digs at the site have exposed the foundations of the granaries that supplied the troops stationed along Hadrian's Wall, and one gate has been reconstructed.

At the foot of the headland, South Pier projects a mile into the sea, protecting the sands of Littlehaven Beach, while south of the pier is long, sandy Sandhaven beach; strong currents at the northern end make swimming dangerous.

A path leads south across the grassy slopes of The Leas (NT), where the shore is rocky, and onto the sandy arc of Marsden Bay. Souter Lighthouse (NT) is open to visitors.

① Castle Eden Dene

The local nature reserve of Castle Eden Dene is an unusual feature in the former mining landscape south of Seaham. A waymarked footpath runs 3 miles through a wooded ravine from the coast to the south-western edge of Peterlee, skirting a fast-flowing stream. The 18th-century castle in the centre of the forest is privately owned.

② Seaham

The Saxon Church of St Mary in the old village has a 13th-century font and 16th-century pulpit. The old village lies to the north of modern Seaham. Also to the north is a clifftop promenade and a wide sandy beach. Modern

⑥ Jarrow

The ruins of a Saxon monastery where the Venerable Bede lived and worked can be traced in the ruins of a later Norman foundation in this small riverside town. Above the chancel arch of St Paul's Church is the original Saxon dedication stone of AD 685, and one of the windows in the chancel contains stained glass from the same period, made in the monastic workshops. Nearby Bede's World tells the story of Northumbria in the early Middle Ages; the museum includes a reconstruction of an Anglo-Saxon farm.

The town has earned a place in history on two other accounts: the hunger marchers set out from Jarrow in 1936 and the novelist Catherine Cookson was born there in 1906.

⑦ North Shields

Tyneside's connection with the pioneering days of the railway are recalled at the Stephenson Railway Museum, which includes one of the early locomotives of engineer George Stephenson. The museum is linked to the Metro railway network by the North Tyneside Steam Railway. Both the museum and the railway are open on summer weekends.

Early in the morning, trawlers sell their catches from stalls on the Fish Quay of North Shields, a mile upriver from Tynemouth.

⑧ Tynemouth

The atmospheric ruins of Tynemouth Priory and Castle (EH) stand high on a grassy headland north of the Tyne. The fortified priory, built in 1090 on the site of a 7th-century monastery, had battlemented walls and a powerful gatehouse. It was in military use until after the Second World War, and you can still see the gun battery and magazine. Below the priory, a huge statue of Newcastle-born Admiral Collingwood, Nelson's second-in-command at Trafalgar, gazes out over the Tyne. A fine wide street of mainly 18th-century houses leads up to the priory gates, and there is the Blue Reef aquarium on the promenade, which extends northwards along the wide beach of Long Sands.

⑨ Whitley Bay

Sheltered from the open sea by rocks, the beach of Whitley Sands is linked to St Mary's Island by a causeway which can be crossed on foot at low tide. There are fine views along the coast from the top of the lighthouse, which houses a visitor centre.

Connected with Newcastle by the Metro railway, Whitley Bay is the city's main seaside lung. Hotels and guesthouses line the seafront, and gardens decorate the slopes between the road and the beach.

The former small fishing village of Cullercoats, just to the south, has been absorbed by Whitley Bay. A cluster of old houses survives round the stone walls of the tiny harbour.

⑩ Seaton Sluice

The tiny harbour at the mouth of Seaton Burn is lined with massive stones that were put in place in 1660, when a port was created for the export of coal and salt. The harbour's name comes from a long-vanished sluice gate between the harbour and Seaton Burn.

One mile inland is the imposing mansion of Seaton Delaval, designed by Sir John Vanbrugh in the early 1700s; there is limited public access at present.

⑪ Newbiggin-by-the-Sea

Once a working port, Newbiggin is now a haven for pleasure boats and a few fishing cobles, with the large Church of St Bartholomew standing alone on a windswept promontory at the north end of the main street. The sandy beach here is backed by a wide promenade and a massive sea wall; the tide-line is black with coal dust and small nuggets of sea-coal.

Neighbouring Woodhorn is the site of a Colliery Museum, while the former Woodhorn Colliery itself forms part of the Queen Elizabeth II Country Park, where one of Britain's largest spoil heaps has been turned into a leisure lake surrounded by extensive woodland.

Woodhorn's Saxon church, said to be the oldest on the Northumberland coast, is now the Church Museum and features carved stones and changing exhibitions.

⑫ Druridge Bay

A 6 mile crescent of magnificent sandy beach, backed by grass-covered dunes, is the setting for an environmental effort aimed at protecting and enhancing wildlife habitats.

Until 1989 Ladyburn Lake, in Druridge Bay Country Park, was an opencast mine; it is now a venue for watersports. The park, which has a large visitor centre, embraces 3½ miles of beach and dunes, with rocks and rock pools at its northern end.

⑬ Amble

On the north side of the harbour a spit of land juts out seawards from Warkworth, whose castle stands on the skyline. The beach on the seaward side of the spit is a mix of sand, shingle and rock.

A busy coal-shipping port until the 1960s, Amble is now a small residential and resort town, with a marina, and a boat-builder's yard beside the River Coquet. To the south of the town is the local nature reserve of Amble Dunes.

A mile offshore, a lighthouse marks Coquet Island, the home of eider ducks, roseate terns and many other sea birds. The island is an RSPB nature reserve and cannot be visited, but you may take a boat trip round it from Amble.

⑭ Warkworth
Enclosed by a horseshoe loop of the meandering Coquet, Warkworth's main street leads steeply up from the river to its splendid 15th-century castle (EH), set high on a grassy mound; Harry Hotspur was born there in 1364. A short walk upstream leads to a landing stage on the south bank of the Coquet, from where English Heritage's only ferryman rows visitors to the Hermitage, a 14th-century chapel cut out of a cliff.

⑮ Alnmouth
The village of colour-washed houses at the mouth of the Aln was an important port before the harbour silted up in 1806. With two golf links and a wide inland haven for small boats, Alnmouth is still popular with golfers and sailing enthusiasts. South of the river is a 3 mile stretch of sand, bordered by dunes but bathing is dangerous near the river mouth.

⑯ Boulmer
A gap in the offshore rocks between Longhoughton Steel and Seaton Point makes Boulmer a natural harbour. The hamlet is a fishing community, with fishing cobles moored off the beach overlooked by a row of fishermen's cottages; the large sandy beach is sheltered by a reef of rock offshore. A fighter aircraft stands menacingly at the gates of RAF Boulmer, whose yellow air-sea rescue helicopters are often seen hovering over the coast.

⑰ Howick
Just outside the Victorian hamlet stands the classical 18th-century mansion Howick Hall, with its superb terraced gardens which are open to visitors. The gardens give way to an idyllic woodland, full of rhododendrons, through which a path follows the course of the stream as it meanders for 1½ miles to the sea.

⑱ Craster

Overlooking Craster's little harbour are the smoking sheds where the village's famous kippers are produced. The harbour, which empties of water at low tide, is now used by leisure boats and a few cobles that fish for lobsters and crabs. Behind the car park is the Arnold Memorial Nature Reserve, where you can sometimes see bluethroats and other rare birds in the lush woodlands.

⑲ Dunstanburgh Castle

The commanding ruins of the castle are perched on a ledge of basalt rock. The only way to reach Dunstanburgh Castle (NT and EH) is by foot. Cars should be parked at Craster to the south.

Northumberland's most ethereal and enigmatic castle, it was begun in 1313 by Thomas, Earl of Lancaster, and the original great gatehouse, with twin towers and walls several feet thick, was converted into the castle keep in 1380 by John of Gaunt, once the most powerful man in England. From the top of one of the towers there are panoramic views over the castle and down the steep incline of the castle rock to the rolling fields beyond.

⑳ Low Newton-by-the-Sea

The Newton Pool Nature Reserve (NT) is a summer breeding ground for more than 30 species of birds, including black-headed gulls, little grebes and mute swans. From the car park above Low Newton, the road leads steeply down to fishermen's cottages and a pub looking over a sandy beach.

You can reach the sandy crescent edging Embleton Bay on foot from Low Newton, or across the golf course from Dunstan Steads. A coast path leads round the bay to Dunstanburgh Castle.

BROODING RUINS AND PANORAMIC VIEWS

DUNSTANBURGH CASTLE

㉑ Beadnell

The strange fortress-like structure beside the sea with round, honey-coloured stone towers is actually 18th-century limekilns (NT). The harbour, with an entrance hardly wide enough for a dinghy, provides moorings for a small fleet of cobles; fishermen stow their crab pots below the arches of the kilns. From the harbour, the sands of Beadnell Bay sweep south for 2 miles to the rocks of Snook Point, and there is a 3½ mile walk beside the dunes to Low Newton.

㉒ Seahouses

Terraces of grey stone houses overlook the little port of Seahouses, where fishing cobles and a few larger vessels land their catches, and fish boxes and crab pots line the quayside. Trips to the Farne Islands leave from Seahouses in summer.

The life of a Northumbrian fishing community at sea and ashore is vividly portrayed in the Marine Life Centre and Fishing Museum.

㉓ Farne Islands

A scattering of rocky outcrops, within 4½ miles of the mainland, the Farne Islands (NT) form a nature reserve that attracts many nesting sea birds, including puffins, kittiwakes and most breeds of tern. The Farnes are also one of the grey seal's principal breeding grounds. Boats tour the islands from Seahouses harbour, but visitors can land only on Inner Farne and Staple Island.

The largest of 28 islands is Inner Farne, where in AD 676 St Cuthbert built himself a cell of stone and turf and

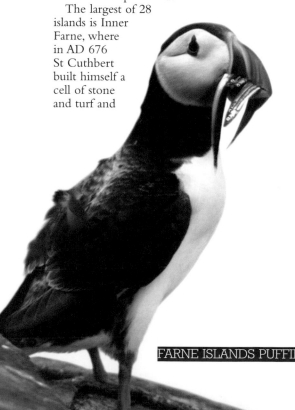

FARNE ISLANDS PUFFIN

lived alone there for eight years. A 14th-century chapel dedicated to him stands near Prior Castell's Tower, built in 1500, and which may mark the site of the saint's cell. The lighthouse and small cottage on Longstone Island are associated with Grace Darling, heroine of a famous sea rescue in 1838.

㉔ Bamburgh

An outcrop of rock rises 46m (150ft) above the sandy bay of Bamburgh and continues into the pink stone walls and battlements of majestic Bamburgh Castle, which towers above the village and the rolling dunes on either side. First fortified by the early kings of Northumbria, Bamburgh became the Northumbrian capital under King Oswald, who ruled in the 7th century, though the castle was later pillaged by the Danes. A deep well, possibly dating from the 8th century, is Bamburgh Castle's oldest feature, and the 12th-century keep retains its original walls, as thick as 3m (11ft) in places.

The village has a row of 18th-century cottages overlooking a tree-shaded green. In the churchyard of the fine Early English Church of St Aidan is a memorial to Bamburgh's own heroine, Grace Darling, who is also commemorated by a small museum run by the Royal National Lifeboat Institution. The museum's centrepiece is the fishing coble in which she and her father rescued the crew of the paddle-steamer *Forfarshire* in 1838.

㉕ Budle Bay

Almost cut off from the sea by a ridge of sand, Budle Bay consists at low tide of weed-covered mudflats that form a sanctuary for flocks of sea birds, which you can watch from roadside parking. It is dangerous to walk far out on the flats because of fast incoming tides. Swans and ducks visit the stream flowing into the bay at derelict Waren Mill, whose history goes back to Saxon times.

㉖ Ross Back Sands

The 3 mile stretch of deserted sands give wonderful views of the fairytale outline of Lindisfarne Castle and Bamburgh Castle in the foreground. To protect the environment, visitors are not widely encouraged onto this splendid sandy beach, which makes up part of the Lindisfarne National Nature Reserve, but it can be reached after a mile-long walk across the rolling dunes of Ross Links.

㉗ Holy Island

The fretted and worn red sandstone ruins of Lindesfarne Priory (EH) stand on a wide peninsula of sand, which is cut off from the mainland for 11 out of 24 hours at low tide and is a bountiful feeding ground for birds.

Christianity came to the island in AD 634, when the monk Aidan crossed the sands to found a monastery, subsequently destroyed by the Danes in the 9th century. One magnificent relic survived from the monastery, the Lindisfarne Gospels, a masterpiece of English Celtic art, and now one of the treasures of the British Library. Lindisfarne Priory was begun in 1093 and the priory museum gives a vivid picture of the life of the isolated Holy Island monks.

Outside the priory walls, the tight-knit houses of Lindisfarne village look onto small squares and narrow streets, and the jetty is still used by a few fishermen who go out after crabs and lobsters.

Beyond the harbour, Lindisfarne Castle (NT) is dramatically sited on a cone of rock. Built in 1550, it was restored from a ruined site in 1902 by the architect Edwin Lutyens. East of the castle are the remains of limekilns, and on the north side of the island are wide strips of dunes backing fine sandy beaches.

28 Lindisfarne National Nature Reserve
A vast area of dunes, salt marsh and mudflats, the reserve stretches from Goswick Sands in the north to Budle Bay in the south. It is internationally known for the large flocks of wildfowl and waders, and in winter the sheltered waters round Holy Island teem with ducks, geese – including pale-bellied Brent geese – and whooper swans. Bar-tailed godwits, redshanks and dunlin are among the more common waders that winter on the flats. You can also see grey and common seals here sometimes.

29 Beal
From a cluster of farm buildings, the road to Holy Island descends gently to the shore, where it becomes a causeway, impassable for about 3 hours either side of high tide; tide tables stand beside the road. From the car park, visitors have a choice of footpaths round Lindisfarne National Nature Reserve.

30 Cheswick
A few cottages and farmhouses make up the village, and a lane across the railway leads to dunes on the edge of vast sands that stretch at low tide for 4 miles across to Holy Island. Treacherous tides and currents make it dangerous to walk to the island, but walkers on the shore can enjoy exhilarating views.

31 Cocklawburn Beach
Paths lead over the dunes down onto the sandy beach, with craggy outcrops and rock pools at both ends. Cocklawburn Dunes Nature Reserve is visited by turnstones, oystercatchers and purple sandpipers; near the

shore are the huge remains of 18th-century limekilns, with lime-loving plants such as vetch growing on nearby spoil heaps.

32 Spittal
Flocks of swans haunt the mudflats at the mouth of the Tweed, which separates Berwick from the tiny resort of Spittal. The village has a grey-stone, Victorian main street, a promenade and a sandy beach, from where fishermen net salmon in season. A coastal path leads 1½ miles south to Seahouse.

33 Berwick-upon-Tweed
Standing on a peninsula between sea and river, Berwick has the best-preserved Elizabethan town walls in Britain. During medieval times it passed back and forth between the English and the Scots; today it is an English town situated north of the natural border of the Tweed, a superb salmon river.

A small fishing fleet and a few commercial vessels are based at Tweedmouth; the stone pier north of the river, and the southern end of Spittal beach are good places from which to watch the fishermen at work. Three bridges cross over the Tweed at Berwick: the pink stone Jacobean Bridge (1611–35); the four-arched Royal Tweed Bridge (1925–8); and the grey Royal Border Bridge, built by Robert Stephenson in 1847, to take the railway.

Berwick Barracks (EH), constructed in 1721, houses the regimental museum of the King's Own Scottish Borderers as well as the borough's museum and art gallery. The Main Guard holds local history exhibitions, while in the 18th-century Town Hall is a cell block with grim reminders of past punishments.

Between the town ramparts and the sea is an open expanse of grassland called Magdalene Fields. The shore here is mainly rocky, but just north of the pier there is a small sandy beach.

Visitor information

Alnwick ☎ (01665) 511333
Amble ☎ (01665) 712313 (summer)
Berwick-upon-Tweed ☎ (01289) 330733
Craster ☎ (01665) 576007
Newcastle ☎ (0191) 277 8000
North Shields ☎ (0191) 200 5895
Seahouses ☎ (01665) 720884
South Shields ☎ (0191) 454 6612
Sunderland ☎ (0191) 553 2000
Whitley Bay ☎ (0191) 200 8535

Scotland

Off the mountainous west coast lie the rugged and beautiful Hebridean Islands while sandstone cliffs on the east coast shelter dozens of fishing villages, with craggy castles perched on the headlands.

Key
— Motorway
— Principal A road
(See 'Finding your way', page 7)

Cairngorms
National Park

Grampian Mountains

Loch Lomond
& The Trossachs
National Park

Places

Durness
Thurso
Wick
Lairg
Ullapool
Tain
Fraserburgh
Peterhead
Elgin
Nairn
Inverness
Aberdeen
Portree
Kyle of Lochalsh
Newtonmore
Braemar
Mallaig
Fort William
Pitlochry
Forfar
Dundee
Oban
Crianlarich
Perth
St Andrews
Stirling
Kirkcaldy
Lochgilphead
Dumbarton
Edinburgh
Glasgow
East Kilbride
Coldstream
Irvine
Kilmarnock
Hawick
Jedburgh
Ayr
Moffat
Dumfries
Stranraer
Kirkwall
Lerwick
Stornoway

EYEMOUTH TO GRANGEMOUTH

As well as being a golfer's paradise, East Lothian's coastline, with its storm-sculpted cliffs alive with sea birds, boasts some fine sandy beaches

❶ Eyemouth

Trawlers and seine-netters tie up at quaysides well back from the outer harbour in this major fishing port. Although white fish account for most of the town's multimillion-pound landings, it also exports prawns, crabs and lobsters.

The local museum tells Eyemouth's story since 1298, with a tapestry commemorating the 189 fishermen lost in a ferocious storm on October 14, 1881 – Eyemouth's 'Disaster Day'. Although local boats no longer catch herring, a week-long Herring Queen Festival is still held in July, when the fishing fleet, decorated with brightly coloured bunting, escorts the newly elected queen from St Abbs to Eyemouth.

An informative town trail identifies notable buildings such as the Georgian mansion of Gunsgreen House, which was once a smugglers' headquarters. The golf course here spreads out over a breezy plateau, and you can take coast walks in both directions.

❷ St Abbs

Rows of neat cottages overlook a harbour, and the towering reefs and rock stacks offshore are alive with sea birds. Fishing trips start from the harbour, which is used by sub-aqua divers as a base for the exploration of the marine reserve off St Abb's Head.

The fishing village takes its name from a Northumbrian princess who became the abbess of a nearby nunnery in the 7th century.

❸ Coldingham

White-capped breakers roll in at Coldingham Sands, and beach huts line the dunes. The Coldingham to Eyemouth coast path winds through steep grassy hills, while smaller tracks circle and zigzag around them.

The priory at Coldingham is one of the glories of this part of Scotland. Now used as a parish church, it evolved from the restored choir of a ruined medieval priory, most of which was demolished by Cromwell's cannons in 1648. The most notable interior feature of the building is the delicate arching and arcading of the north and east walls. In happier times, a thousand retainers of Mary, Queen of Scots, were accommodated in the priory during her 1566 progress through the Borders.

❹ St Abb's Head

Kittiwakes and guillemots, herring gulls, fulmars and puffins throng the cliffs and rock stacks of the superb national nature reserve of St Abb's Head (NTS). Swans, grebes and tufted ducks are also attracted to the reedy Mire Loch, in a low-lying geological fault. Footpaths and a road from the visitor centre lead to the large natural amphitheatre of Pettico Wick, and climb the sheep-cropped grassland towards Harelaw Hill, which offers wide views to the Cheviots and the Lomond hills of Fife.

Scotland's only voluntary marine reserve lies offshore. Run by local people, its aim is to conserve the marine environment and increase

A SUPERB NATIONAL NATURE RESERVE

ST ABB'S HEAD

public awareness; wardens conduct 'rock-pool rambles' in summer, describing the wildlife found there. On the cliffs to the northwest are the ruins of medieval Fast Castle.

❺ Pease Bay
Beyond the cove of red cliffs and tawny sands lie the glorious wooded glens of Pease Dean and Tower Dean. Pease Dean is a wildlife reserve of predominantly oak and ash woodlands, where sun-dappled pathways follow the course of burns. Here you may hear woodpeckers, warblers and wood pigeons above the chattering streams. In spring and summer the reserve is covered in a carpet of wild flowers including campions, primroses and tormentils, and the air is full of the garlic scent of ramsons.

❻ Cove
The harbour's most unusual feature is a 55m (60yd) tunnel that cuts through the cliffs, wide enough for a horse and cart. It was built to give fishermen access to a now-disused curing house on the south side. Perched on top of the cliffs, the tiny village was once linked to the harbour below by a steep road

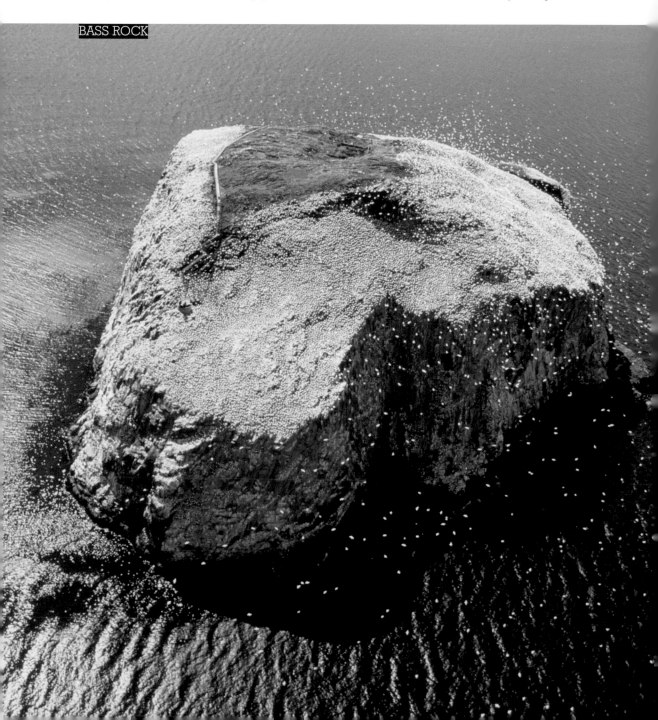

BASS ROCK

carved out of the rock. The road was closed to traffic in 1991 after a landslip, hastening the decline of Cove Harbour, where only small catches of lobsters are still landed.

The Southern Upland Way, which runs for 212 miles from Portpatrick in Dumfries and Galloway, reaches the east coast at Cove.

⑦ Dunbar

The ancient burgh of Dunbar was inhabited in Iron Age times, as shown by exhibits at the 17th-century Town House. Many of its buildings date from the 18th and 19th centuries, the most substantial being Lauderdale House; it was once a rich magnate's mansion and is now flats. John Muir's birthplace in the High Street is a museum, and a clifftop walk bears his name.

The 19th-century Victoria Harbour was created by hacking through Dunbar Castle, now little more than a nesting cliff for gulls and kittiwakes. Harbour-side dwellings and old warehouses built for a long-gone shipping trade have been restored, and there is a lifeboat museum. The Battery, raised in 1781 on natural basalt columns, is an excellent viewpoint. Sub-aqua divers and sea anglers frequent Dunbar, but the most popular recreation here is golf.

⑧ John Muir Country Park

The park has 8 miles of beaches, dunes, salt marsh, pinewoods and open grassland. Named after the Dunbar-born pioneer of the US National Parks movement, it serves as a recreational area as well as a wildlife sanctuary. Footpaths follow the coastline, where you may see shelduck, mallard, teal, plover and wigeon.

⑨ Bass Rock

The core of an ancient volcano, offshore Bass Rock is a mile in circumference with almost perpendicular cliffs. Noted for its gannetry, the rock gave the gannet its scientific name, *Sula bassana*. Among the other sea birds you may see here are fulmars, cormorants, razorbills and puffins. Additional attractions are a lighthouse dating from 1902, the ruins of a 16th-century chapel and the remains of a fort that was used as a state prison from 1673 to 1701. Boat trips around the rock start from North Berwick.

⑩ North Berwick

Famous for its golf, the town boasts sandy beaches on both sides of a restored harbour, crammed with yachts and lobster boats. It blossomed as a bracing holiday resort when the railway opened in 1850.

The Scottish Seabird Centre's remote cameras allow visitors to view off-shore bird colonies, while in summer, weather permitting, you can take a cruise round Fidra and Bass Rock. Steps and footbridges lead to a wave-lapped point on the narrow peninsula stretching north from the town; there are views of the rock of Craigleith offshore.

North Berwick Law is a towering volcanic remnant, its magnificent summit viewpoint marked by an archway made from a whale's jawbones. To the east, Tantallon Castle (HS) was a stronghold of the Douglases until, like so many of the region's castles, it was bombarded by Cromwell during the Civil War.

⑪ Dirleton

With its neat parish church and cottage gardens bordering a triangular green, Dirleton has been described as the most 'English-looking' village in Scotland. The tranquil scene is overlooked by the dramatic ruins of a castle, dating in part from the 13th century; its grounds have a 16th-century dovecot.

Yellowcraig nature trail explores woodlands and shoreline dunes, and offers views of Fidra, a puffin colony island. To the south of Dirleton, Fenton Barns farm offers local produce, and has an archery centre and an archery museum.

⑫ Gullane

Muirfield, one of the village's five golf courses, was founded in 1891 by the Honourable Company of Edinburgh Golfers and has hosted several Open championships.

Ruined St Andrew's Church, abandoned in the 17th century after it was engulfed by windblown sand, is a reminder of the natural hazards here. The dunes at Gullane Bents have been stabilised thanks to the planting of coastal grasses and bushes, and the village has one of the finest beaches around.

⑬ Aberlady

Among the maritime relics of Haddington's former seaport is the 17th-century custom house, while the high street has distinctive 18th and 19th-century houses, many with Gothic detailing. A 'loupin'-on' stone outside the parish church allowed riders to mount their horses in a seemly manner.

Aberlady Bay, with its long wooden footbridge, is a nature reserve, whose visitors include ospreys and Montagu's harriers. South-west of the village, 18th-century Gosford House is bordered on its seaward side by dramatic banks of trees; it is open at weekends from mid June to early August. Myreton Motor Museum stands inland among fields.

⑭ Longniddry

Some attractive older cottages recall the appearance of this trim commuter village before the arrival of the railway in 1846. To the north is a golf course, and the dunes and scrubland of Longniddry Bents, a D-Day training area. The village's western boundary is marked by a woodland path in Longniddry Dean, and a 4½ mile walk along a disused railway track strikes east from Longniddry to Haddington.

⑮ Prestonpans

A modest cairn to the east of the town commemorates the Battle of Prestonpans, which was fought here in 1745. The town is named after salt pans that once ran along the shoreline. The parish church looks seawards over gardens and, set back from the waterside, the 17th-century market cross is surmounted by a royal unicorn. There is a huge, well-preserved dovecot close by from the same era, and the ruins of 15th-century Preston Tower survive in a walled garden.

To the southwest of the town is the industrial museum of Prestongrange, which includes a beam engine and several colliery locomotives, 'in steam' on summer Sundays.

⑯ Musselburgh

Known as the 'honest town' since 1332, when its people cared for the dying Regent of Scotland, the Earl of Moray, without any thought of reward, Musselburgh retains a fine legacy of 18th and 19th-century buildings and monuments and a town trail recalls the many battles in which Musselburgh played a part, and explores the roles of such figures as Oliver Cromwell and Sir Walter Scott in its history.

There is a 3 mile riverside walk along the Esk southeast to Whitecraig, while the harbour at Fisherrow is popular with yachting enthusiasts. Formed round artificial lagoons, Levenhall Links has watersports areas, a bird reserve and a golfing practice ground. Inland, quiet Inveresk is home to the gardens of Inveresk Lodge (NTS).

⑰ Portobello

Victorian and Edwardian day-trippers flocked to Edinburgh's beach resort, given its exotic name by its founder, a veteran of the 1739 battle of Puerto Bello in Panama. The town has been spruced up in recent years and its once-polluted sands are now cleaned every day; several impressive buildings on the promenade have been refurbished.

⑱ Leith

Moored in the harbour of Edinburgh's port is the Royal Yacht *Britannia*, which was decommissioned in 1997 and is open to visitors. It cost more than £2 million to build and was crewed by 244 officers and men on royal tours and holidays around the world.

Leith's docks are still flourishing and the quaysides near the Water of Leith have been neatly restored. The Clan Tartan Centre at Leith Mill has an exhibition of Highland dress.

⑲ Cramond

In AD 142 the Romans built a fort near the mouth of the River Almond, whose excavated site you can see behind Cramond Kirk. Yachts share the narrow river here with swans and mallards, and a wooded path follows the Almond upstream. A walk along the breezy esplanade leads past picnic lawns to Granton, 2½ miles to the east. Uninhabited Cramond Island can be reached on foot across the mudflats at low water, but walkers should beware of fast incoming tides.

About half a mile inland is Lauriston Castle, a turreted 16th-century tower house.

⑳ Dalmeny House
Home of the Earl of Rosebery, the splendid Gothic Revival mansion, built in 1815, includes 18th-century porcelain, paintings by

artists such as Gainsborough, and a room devoted to Napoleon. To the west, 12th-century Dalmeny Church is probably Scotland's finest example of a Norman parish church.

㉑ Queensferry
Towering over the town is the magnificent mile-long Forth Rail Bridge, a triumph of Victorian engineering. Built in 1890, trains still speed past its cantilevered girders. The town was named after a long-running ferry service across the Forth, which was in turn named after

FORTH RAIL BRIDGE, QUEENSFERRY

Queen Margaret. The ferry was eventually superseded in 1964 by the Forth Road Bridge, an awesome structure just over 1½ miles long with a central span of 1006m (3300ft).

There is an attractive tolbooth in the high street, and a nearby yacht harbour gives the best views of the bridges. Queensferry Museum tells the story of the ferries, the bridges and the town. One display features the strange costume of the Burry Man, the central figure in the annual Ferry Fair, who is covered from head to foot in burrs and collects money for charity.

Robert Louis Stevenson wrote part of *Kidnapped* at Hawes Inn, and incorporated both it and Queensferry into the plot. To the west, at Port Edgar, is a large marina and watersports centre, while at Hawes Pier, in summer, cruises leave for Inchcolm Island.

㉒ Hopetoun House

The seat of the Marquess of Linlithgow, this elegant stately home still contains many of its 18th-century furnishings, tapestries, portraits and porcelain. The original house, built by Sir William Bruce, was later enlarged and extensively modified by William Adam and his sons and finally completed in 1702. Several separate exhibitions are housed there.

The grounds include walks through woodland, nature trails and a beautiful, spacious park where you can see red deer and Hebridean sheep. On the edge of the grounds, Abercorn Church dates partly from the 12th century; however, masonry has been found here from the 7th-century monastery of Abercurnig, which once occupied the same site when this area was part of the kingdom of Northumbria.

㉓ The Binns

In 1944 the spacious 17th-century house was the first country mansion taken over by the National Trust for Scotland. Its name is from the Gaelic *beinn*, meaning 'mountain', although the house stands on only a modest slope.

This is the ancestral home of the Dalyell family, the most noted of whom was Thomas or Tam. A royalist during the Civil War, he became a commander in the Russian Tsarist army and, finally, was a scourge of the Presbyterian Covenanters back in Scotland. He founded the Scots Greys regiment at the Binns in 1681, and many mementos of him are preserved in the house. The house is also noted for its moulded plaster ceilings in four of the rooms.

A short woodland walk leads you northeast to the panoramic Tower Viewpoint, which looks out over the Forth and the surrounding hills.

㉔ Blackness

One of Scotland's most important artillery fortifications between the 16th century and the First World War, Blackness Castle (HS) looks out across the River Forth to the naval dockyards of Rosyth. It fell out of use after this time but has been restored to its pre-1870 appearance.

The village's natural harbour became the seaport for Linlithgow in the late 14th century. Now it is used only by a sailing club. A ridge of parkland stretches from the village to the castle; together with the beach beyond these make ideal picnic places. There are also shoreline walks west to Bo'ness and east to Hopetoun House.

㉕ Bridgeness and Carriden

A replica of a distance slab from the Antonine Wall can be seen in Harbour Street in this large suburb of Bo'ness, which was once two separate villages. Bridgeness Tower, built in 1750 as a windmill and later adapted as an observatory, has been restored, although it is not open to visitors.

In Kinningars Park, an unusual 18th-century colliery winding-house remodelled as a dovecote is overlooked by modern homing-pigeon lofts. Carriden Church, the latest of four churches that have occupied the present site, was built in the early 1900s but includes several Norman-style features.

㉖ Bo'ness and Kinneil Railway

A fine collection of steam locomotives and rolling stock are on show at Bo'ness station, now the headquarters of the Scottish Railway Preservation Society.

A journey by steam train to Birkhill, taking 17 minutes, can be combined with guided tours of Birkhill Fireclay Mine, where clay used to make fire-resistant bricks was processed until 1980. The fossils of giant tree ferns living 300 million years ago can also be seen in the mine.

㉗ Bo'ness

The town flourished during the Industrial Revolution, and became Scotland's third most important port. Its prosperity came from coal, iron-founding, salt, whaling and pottery-making, and this is recalled in Kinneil Museum in the Kinneil estate.

Walks starting at the museum take in the sites of a Roman fortlet, a village that was abandoned as Bo'ness grew, and the ruined cottage, built in 1769, where James Watt experimented with steam engines.

A town trail in Bo'ness identifies many 18th and 19th-century houses and commercial buildings. Walks by the pebbly shore and scrubland lead a mile east and 3 miles west along the Firth of Forth, and cross the territory of birds such as skylarks and goldfinches. Terns fly offshore, while wildfowl and waders favour the tidal mudflats.

28 Grangemouth

Clouds of steam and flames belch out from the cooling towers of BP's refinery and petrochemical works here, set against a backdrop of romantic hills.

The town was originally established as the eastern terminal port of the Forth and Clyde Canal, which opened in 1790. Although shipbuilding has ended here and dockside buildings have been cleared, Grangemouth still has considerable commercial traffic. The town's history, including that of its short-lived airport, which was used as a training ground during the Second World War, is described in the local museum.

Half a mile away is the Museum Workshop, which has displays of restored vehicles, along with domestic, agricultural and industrial machinery; visits are by appointment only.

Visitor information

Bo'ness, Edinburgh, Old Craighall, Musselburgh
all covered by **Visit Scotland** ☎ 0845 225 5121
Dunbar ☎ (01368) 863353
Eyemouth ☎ (018907) 50678
Falkirk ☎ (01324) 620244
Linlithgow ☎ (01506) 844600
North Berwick ☎ (01620) 892197

Beside the golf course at Polmonthill, southeast of the town, a dry ski slope plunges down parallel to the course of the Antonine Wall, built by the Romans around AD 142. The wall was a rampart of soil and turf on a stone foundation, which originally ran from Old Kilpatrick on the Clyde to Carriden on the Forth. Parts of the wall and the ditch that ran alongside it can still be seen.

BO'NESS AND KINNEIL RAILWAY

80105

KINCARDINE TO MONTROSE

The Kingdom of Fife's gentle shoreline is home to St Andrews, the cradle of golf, as well as a number of villages and burghs that were once bustling ports

❶ Kincardine

Ornamental wall plaques and 'marriage lintels' marking the date when couples moved into their homes adorn attractive 18th-century houses in the oddly angled lanes of this intriguing town. The former fishing, trading, ferry and salt-panning port also has a well-preserved 17th-century Mercat Cross, or market cross, indicating that the town was given a charter to hold a market. The green where cattle drovers grazed their herds before ferrying them to the great 'tryst', or livestock sale, at Falkirk, survives as a public park.

The graveyard of the partly restored 17th-century Old Kirk of Tulliallan contains headstones carved with symbols of trades and professions. Tulliallan Castle, built as a mansion in the 19th century, is now a police training school.

❷ Culross

Red-tiled roofs, crow-stepped gables and cobbled streets, all beautifully restored, recall the heyday of the village in the 16th and 17th centuries, when it was Scotland's wealthiest town. Salt and coal exports made a fortune for Sir George Bruce, the 17th-century laird of Culross, pronounced 'Cooross'. Bruce's

mansion, completed in 1611, was so grand that it became known as The Palace. Here you can see rare wall and ceiling paintings and a massive strong-room. In 1932, this was the first building bought by the National Trust for Scotland, at a cost of £700.

Much conservation work has been carried out in Culross. The NTS visitor centre, with an exhibition and video presentation outlining the burgh's history, is located in the Town House, and another restored house conceals an electricity substation. The House with the Evil Eyes takes its name from the window design high on its Dutch gable.

Sir George Bruce and his family are buried in partly restored Culross Abbey, now the parish church, and many of the gravestones here bear the royal warrant symbol of the Culross Hammermen, who for generations until the mid 18th century held the monopoly on making all of Scotland's iron-baking 'girdles', or griddles.

❸ Valleyfield

A 'deep, romantic and richly wooded glen', the former estate of the Prestons of Valleyfield was laid out by the English landscape gardener Humphry Repton in the

CULROSS

early 19th century but is now overgrown. The mansion was knocked down in the 1940s, and the walled garden, one of the features of the estate, has returned to the wild. The woodland is home to jays, coal tits, goldcrests and kingfishers, and walkers here may catch glimpses of roe deer.

Footpaths follow the narrow valley of the Bluther Burn north of the former mining village of Valleyfield.

④ Charlestown

For what is now a quiet residential village, Charlestown has unexpectedly complex harbours. They and the village itself were founded in the mid 18th century by the 5th Earl of Elgin to exploit the lime deposits on his Broomhall estate.

In the harbour is a sailing club, just to the north is a vast array of derelict limekilns, and beyond that is the original 'model village'. Broomhall, to the east of the village, is still the family seat, and is not open to visitors.

⑤ Limekilns

There are some fine cottages in the lanes of this old trading and ferry port, the location for an episode in Robert Louis Stevenson's novel *Kidnapped*. The village's oldest building, the 14th-century King's Cellar, once a store for the court at Dunfermline, is now a meeting hall.

An embankment walk leads past Bruce Haven, an old harbour area, to the breezy site of ruined Rosyth Church.

⑥ Rosyth

Britain's largest Royal Naval dockyards was developed on a green field site in 1909 by what was then the village of Rosyth. Work still goes on, but Rosyth's scale of operations was drastically reduced in 1994. Although now privatised, the dockyard still refits naval vessels, and a ferry service to Zeebrugge operates from here.

⑦ Inverkeithing

One of Scotland's oldest royal burghs, the town has been home to many famous people. Samuel Greig, the admiral who created the Russian Navy for Catherine the Great, was a native of the town, and temporary residents have included the 18th-century lawyer and author James Boswell, the 19th-century missionary and explorer David Livingstone, and Lord Raglan, commander of the British forces in the Crimean War.

The elegant 15th-century market cross is crowned by a royal unicorn carved in 1688 as a test for entry to the local company of masons, while Inverkeithing's St Peter's Church was consecrated in 1244, and some Gothic elements survive in the present building. Part of the

INCHCOLM ABBEY, OFF NORTH QUEENSFERRY

medieval friary houses the local history museum, and the friary gardens are an attractive public park, looking out across waterside sports fields and the old shipbreakers' yard where the German Grand Fleet, scuttled at Scapa Flow, was broken up for scrap after the First World War.

8 North Queensferry

The atmospheric ruins of 12th-century St Colm's Abbey stand on Inchcolm Island in the Firth of Forth, reached by a summer ferry service from North Queensferry. Seals, seagulls and puffins are the island's only inhabitants today but old tunnels and gun emplacements are a reminder of its sterner wartime role.

A heritage trail in North Queensferry takes in places of interest from busier days, including inns, a hexagonal Signal House and a remarkable number of wells. An old quarry lagoon is now home to the Deep Sea World aquarium.

9 Dalgety Bay

The Fife Coastal Path runs through this residential town, to the west of which are First World War gun emplacements at Downing Point. A side path leads to the ruined 18th-century Donibristle Chapel. The coastal path skirts Ross Plantation, a half-flooded alder woodland where bulrushes and other moisture-loving plants thrive.

Farther along the rocky bay is 13th-century St Bridget's Church, the burial place of the Seton Earls of Dunfermline. An oil and gas terminal lies over a wooded point to the east.

10 Aberdour

From the main beach there are fine views over the firth to Edinburgh Castle, with the ruins of Inchcolm Abbey in the foreground. Golf, yachting, windsurfing and walking are the favourite activities in the trim resort.

Above Silver sands beach, footpaths on the Hawk Craig headland end at the top of a vertical cliff. A driveway leads from the village to 14th-century Aberdour Castle, once a stronghold of the Douglases, and its impressive garden terraces. The castle was built on the site of a 12th century towerhouse, the remains of which can still be seen among the castle ruins.

⑪ Burntisland

At the little town's parish church in 1601 James VI of Scotland, later James I of England, announced his plan to publish a new version of the Bible, which became known as the Authorised Version. Some 30 years later, his son Charles I was highly indignant when many of his courtiers, and part of the royal treasury, were lost from a boat that foundered off Burntisland.

Above the sandy beach of Pettycur Bay is a large public park known as Burntisland Links, and overlooking the docks is Rossend Castle, a royal residence over several centuries, now restored as offices. An exhibition in the town hall, open in summer, explains Burntisland's history.

⑫ Kinghorn

South of Kinghorn's harbour conservation area are a sailing club and a small sandy beach, from which footpaths zigzag up a grassy hill towards the village. The old ferry port of Pettycur is used by fishermen as a base for sea angling, while the sands of Pettycur Bay stretch away to the west. The lighthouse island of Inchkeith lies 2½ miles from the shore.

On the road to Burntisland is a monument to Alexander III, Scotland's last Celtic king, who fell from the cliffs to his death in 1286.

⑬ Kirkcaldy

One of the biggest street fairs in Britain, the Links Market is held in Kirkcaldy each April. The town has a generous supply of parks and green spaces. Ravenscraig Park, on a clifftop site with extensive sea views, includes ruined Ravenscraig Castle, while Dunnikier Park is given over to sports fields and a golf course. Beveridge Park to the south has a road network that once formed a car and motorcycle racing circuit. Nearby Raith Lake is stocked with rainbow trout and American brook trout.

Kirkcaldy was the birthplace in 1728 of the architect and interior designer Robert Adam, and, five years earlier, of Adam Smith, political economist and author of *The Wealth of Nations*.

By the harbour is the restored 15th-century Sailors Walk, Kirkaldy's oldest building, and nearby are a modern maltings and a flour mill. Paintings from Scottish artists and local pottery feature in Kirkcaldy Museum and Art Gallery, while the 16th-century Merchant's House is a tourist information centre with gardens.

⑭ Dysart

Dysart's trim little harbour has a collection of pleasure craft and lobster boats and is reached from the northern end of the village by a lane called Hot Pot Wynd. The 17th-century fishermen's houses in Pan Ha', another quaintly named street, have been restored by the National Trust for Scotland, and colour-washed houses surround the large 17th-century tolbooth and the battlemented tower of the Church of St Serf. The restored Harbour Master's House is now open to the public, and at the John McDouall Stuart Museum you can find out about the 19th-century explorer of the Australian interior, who was born in Dysart.

A walk along the harbour cliff here gives panoramic views of the village and the firth.

⑮ Coaltown of Wemyss

Houses with typical crow-stepped gables are a feature of this model village, which was created in the mid 19th century to house local miners. Coaltown of Wemyss, pronounced 'weems', is one of a trio of similarly named villages on this strip of the coast.

Colour-washed houses overlook a small disused harbour at West Wemyss, where fulmars nest on ledges in a cliff, and the delicate tolbooth has a gilded swan as its weather vane.

At East Wemyss, the disused Michael Colliery lies derelict above the sea, and nearby stands a memorial to the men who died in a fire at the colliery in 1967. At the northeastern end of the village are the ruins of the 11th-century Macduff's Castle.

There are several caves in the cliffs along the rocky shore below the castle, but rockfalls make them and the path that leads to them rather hazardous.

⑯ Buckhaven and Methil

A substantial North Sea oil construction base and its docks and power station complete the industrial seafront at Methil. To the southwest is the former sea-angling and lobster-fishing centre of Buckhaven.

The town's theatre is housed in a redundant church that was originally located in St Andrews; local fishermen bought the church in 1869, then had it dismantled and brought in pieces by boat to Buckhaven to be re-erected.

⑰ Leven

The little resort town has two excellent golf courses, one of which is a qualifying course for the Open championship. The broad sandy beach and promenade offer estuary views, and park and woodland walks can be found just north of Leven at Letham Glen and to the northeast at the Silverburn estate.

⑱ Lower Largo

A statue in the old rivermouth port commemorates Alexander Selkirk, born here in 1676. Selkirk's adventures as a castaway on the deserted island of Juan Fernandez, off the coast of Chile, were the inspiration for Daniel Defoe's novel *Robinson Crusoe*.

The area is good for sailing and windsurfing, and dinghies can be launched from the shingle beach. Lower Largo merges with the resort of Lundin Links, where the Victorians built seaside villas and laid out gardens and a golf course.

From Kirkton of Largo, or Upper Largo, a footpath leads you to the 290m (952ft) mound of Largo Law, which was once a volcano. The summit is a splendid point for views across the Firth of Forth.

⑲ Elie and Earlsferry
The harbour of the former fishing port of Elie and the old market town and ferry port of Earlsferry have long been united as one burgh. Today the harbour is devoted to watersports of all kinds, and Elie Golf House Club presides over a classic golf course, whose history goes back to 1589.

A stroll along Wood Haven beach leads to Elie Ness, where you can take in a white lighthouse, built in 1908, on one low headland. The Lady's Tower was the summerhouse of Lady Jane Anstruther, an 18th-century beauty who sent a bellman through the streets to warn the lower orders not to steal a look while she was bathing.

High basalt cliffs at Kincraig Head support ledge and grassland wild flowers, which attract many species of butterfly. Fulmars and house martins nest on the rock, and kestrels soar above.

⑳ Isle of May
An outstanding national nature reserve, the largest island in the Firth of Forth is reached in summer by ferry from Anstruther harbour. Paths explore the narrow central plateau. Guillemots, razorbills and kittiwakes nest in great numbers, and the island has a large puffin population. You can also see eider ducks and grey seals around the shore.

From the 8th to 16th centuries the island was an important religious site, and the ruins of a 12th-century monastery survive, as do old military fortifications and domestic ruins. Scotland's first manned lighthouse was built there in 1636.

㉑ St Monans
Once a busy boat-building centre, St Monans' harbour is now a haven for yachts and shellfish boats. Overlooking the rocky shore, the sturdy, square-built Church of St Monan, with its many historic and heraldic features, stands on one of the oldest religious sites in Fife, dating from at least the 11th century. St Monans Windmill, near the coast path, was built in the 18th century to pump seawater into coal-fired salt pans. Partly restored, the mill has displays relating to the salt-panning industry, which died out in the 1820s.

㉒ Pittenweem
The 'weem', or cave, reputedly lived in by the 7th-century missionary St Fillan, is carefully preserved in the stepped Cove Wynd, which descends from the high street to the harbour. The town is the home port of the East Neuk fishing fleet.

Kellie Lodging, built in 1592, was the town mansion of the Earls of Kellie, whose inland home, Kellie Castle (NTS), 2 miles northwest, was built in the 16th and 17th centuries and has a fine walled garden.

㉓ Anstruther
The harbour is home to the evocative Scottish Fisheries Museum although Anstruther's fishing fleet is now based at Pittenweem. Housed in 18th and 19th-century buildings that were once used as a chandlery and net loft, the museum depicts the lifestyle and history of a fishing community.

㉔ Scotland's Secret Bunker
A simple and unobtrusive house hides a top-secret command centre, where Britain's government and military commanders would have been based in the event of a nuclear war. Marked on detailed maps simply as a communications mast, this astonishing place was revealed after its declassification in 1992. The house, now part of a museum, hides the entrance to a 229m (250yd) approach tunnel. You can venture deep underground to explore the labyrinthine complex, built on shockproof foundations and protected by a 5m (15ft) thick concrete ceiling.

㉕ Crail
From the tolbooth and the market cross to the pretty harbour area, the townscape of this little burgh remains unspoiled, conserved by individual property owners and the National Trust for Scotland. The museum and heritage centre tells the story of Crail's involvement with royalty, fishing, golf and the air station on the road to Fife Ness.

The parapet Castle Walk, which follows the remains of a castle wall along a cliff path, gives views of the harbour and, in clear weather, St Abb's Head, 30 miles to the south.

㉖ Fife Ness
A Second World War Royal Naval air station lies derelict beside the road to the rocky headland of Fife Ness. A kart-racing circuit has been laid out there, and a side road leads to a picnic area. The coast path leads through grassland and wild flowers, and you may see terns, eiders, puffins and gannets, as well as migratory birds, in spring and autumn. Balcomie golf course is at the end of the Fife Ness road.

27 Kingsbarns

The older houses in Kingsbarns display the neat proportions and delicate detail work for which Fife's district of East Neuk is famous. The village was used to store grain for royal residences in the county. There is a grassy picnic area down by the sea, with rock pools at low tide, while Cambo Gardens, which were laid out in Victorian times, sit beside a tumbling burn.

28 St Andrews

Named after Scotland's patron saint, St Andrews is internationally recognised as the home of golf, and today has the British Golf Museum and no fewer than six golf courses. The Old Course is on the northern edge of the town, in full view of several streets; a right of way called Grannie Clark's Wynd crosses the 1st and 18th fairways.

Running parallel to the Old Course is West Sands, one of the town's two extensive beaches, while East Sands stretches beyond the rivermouth harbour, which shelters lobster boats. South Street, entered through a 16th-century gateway, has narrow alleys known as 'rigs' branching off it. The street leads to the ruin of 12th-century St Andrews Cathedral (HS), and you can climb the tower for a fine view across the city. Other attractions at St Andrews include the university, founded in 1410 and the third oldest in Britain, an aquarium, the Victorian Botanic Garden, and St Andrews Castle (HS), built around 1200, with a forbidding dungeon.

Two miles inland, Craigtoun Country Park features a Dutch-style model village, built in 1918 on a lake island.

29 Leuchars

Every September, the massive RAF base here is the scene of Scotland's biggest air show. The base was first used in 1911 for military balloon experiments. In the attractive old part of Leuchars village, the Church of St Athernase, dating from about 1180, is one of the loveliest Norman churches in Scotland; much of the arches, arcades and apse remain.

30 Tentsmuir Forest

Extensive and almost entirely level plantations of Scots and Corsican pine are the home of roe deer, squirrels and crossbills. Special roosting sites have also attracted several species of bat including pipistrelles, common long-eared bats and Natterer's. Walks leading from the car park by the beach at Kinshaldy Bay take in dunes, forests and open heaths, and an abandoned 19th-century ice house survives beside an old salmon pond, with a wildlife observation hide.

31 Tayport

A shoreline walk gives full views across the Tay to Dundee, with the Sidlaw Hills on the skyline. Originally known as Ferryport-on-Craig, the burgh of Tayport was the southern terminal for the widest Tay ferry crossing until the opening of the Tay Road Bridge, which can be reached by a shoreline walk. At Scotscraig, southwest of the village, there is a golf course.

32 Newport-on-Tay

From the splendid Victorian fountain on top of a steep bank there are views across the Tay to Dundee. Newport-on-Tay is bounded by the road bridge and railway bridge, beside which stand the remains of an ill-designed earlier bridge, which collapsed during a storm in 1879. All 75 people on board a train at the time died as it plunged into the sea.

33 Balmerino

The ruins of Balmerino Abbey (NTS) stand in grounds noted for a 450-year-old Spanish chestnut tree. Founded in 1229, the abbey was on the pilgrim route from St Andrews to Arbroath. The village of Balmerino contains many neatly restored houses in peaceful lanes, set on a sweeping hillside of farms and woodlands overlooking the Tay.

Coast paths lead west to Newburgh and east to Wormit, and outside the shooting season walks are possible on the Birkhill estate.

34 Newburgh

Originally a market town, the royal burgh of Newburgh was 'new' in the 13th century. Weaving and spinning, quarrying and fruit farming were some of many industries that brought prosperity to the town, and the Laing Museum has displays on the town's ancient and modern history. Ruined Lindores Abbey, founded in 1178, stands on the town's eastern outskirts.

In hilly Pitmedden Forest, to the southwest, you can take walks through larch, spruce and pine plantations with views of the Lomond Hills to the south.

35 Carse of Gowrie

The finest views of this low-lying landscape of fruit farms and agricultural land are from the hill roads. The roads serve villages such as Kinnaird, with its dramatically placed parish church, and Rait with its antique shops. There is also a Railway Heritage Centre at Errol Station, though trains no longer stop here.

Inchture is an old stagecoach halt, while Baledgarno is an attractive 18th-century estate village at the gates of the privately owned Rossie Priory.

㊱ Dundee

Once a city of 'jute, jam and journalism', Dundee retains only its magazine publishing industry. The royal burgh has not always been well served by modern planners, but some impressive older buildings survive. Claypotts Castle (HS) is an amazingly complete 16th-century tower house, while the Victorian Gothic McManus Galleries feature local history and Scottish paintings.

St Mary's Church dates partly from the 14th century; or you can tour the Verdant Works, a 19th-century jute and flax mill restored to celebrate the great days of the textile industry, as well as the traditional Shaw's Dundee Sweet Factory. The Mills Observatory, opened in 1953, is Britain's only full-time public observatory.

Dundee is also home to two notable historic ships, both of which you can visit. The frigate *Unicorn*, launched in 1824, is one of Britain's oldest ships still afloat, while the Royal Research Ship *Discovery* was built in 1901 for Captain Scott's voyages to the Antarctic. Discovery Point Visitor Centre entertains visitors with audiovisual displays of the ship.

In the heart of the city, Dundee Law, a 174m (571ft) hill, offers a panorama extending across the city and its many open spaces, which include the university's Botanic Garden and Camperdown Country Park with its excellent wildlife centre. North of Camperdown lie Templeton Woods and Clatto Country Park.

㊲ Broughty Ferry

Many of Dundee's wealthiest Victorian businessmen built grand houses in this suburb, and helped to found both the Royal Tay Yacht Club and Forfarshire Cricket Club. Broughty Castle (HS), originally a 15th-century fortress, is now an excellent museum of local history. Extensive sandy beaches border the esplanade, and Reres Park offers an unexpectedly wild wooded hill amid a residential area.

㊳ Carnoustie

The golfing centre providing three famous courses is also a holiday resort with long, sandy beaches and a sailing club. The War Memorial Gardens here are an impressive blaze of colour in spring and summer, while north-west of Carnoustie are Barry Mill (NTS) and Monikie Country Park, based on a reservoir.

㊴ Arbroath

Raucous calls of sea birds announce the early morning fish landings at a port famous for the Arbroath 'smokie', haddock cured slowly over a beechwood fire. Until the end of the 19th century, the town was principally a trading harbour. Today Arbroath is a holiday resort, with attractions such as Kerr's

Miniature Railway, which has been operating since 1935. Beyond the Kings Drive promenade, Arbroath Cliffs nature trail, leading towards Auchmithie, takes in sea-bird nesting grounds, wild-flower havens and spectacular rock formations.

Arbroath Abbey (HS), now a well-preserved ruin, was built in 1178 and dedicated by the Scottish king William the Lion to his martyred friend Thomas Becket. The Declaration of Arbroath, signed here in 1320, was a re-affirmation of Scotland's independence The Signal Tower now houses an Arbroath history museum.

⓸⓪ Lunan Bay
Standing on a hilltop overlooking the bay is the rust-coloured ruin of aptly named Red Castle, thought to have been built in the 15th century. A long, sandy beach cut in half by the mouth of Lunan Water, Lunar Bay stretches south from Boddin Point, with its substantial limekiln and Elephant Rock, a rock eroded into the shape of an elephant's head.

⓸① Montrose
The Georgian heritage of this bustling town is evident in the handsome golden-domed Montrose Academy, which is closed to the public, and the Montrose Museum, while the soaring spire of the 1834 parish church is a landmark for miles around.

Located on the estuary of the South Esk, Montrose is centred on a port and a North Sea oil supply base, although grassy expanses between the town and its sandy beach provide space for two golf courses, playing fields and strolling areas. The Air Station Heritage Centre has displays on Britain's first military air station, established at Montrose in 1912.

The brackish tidal waters of Montrose Basin are a winter reserve for many species of bird, including greylag and pink-footed geese.

Four miles west of Montrose, the House of Dun (NTS) is a stately mansion, designed by William Adam and built in 1730. The Caledonian Railway, nearby, operates steam-hauled trains on summer Sundays from Brechin, west of Montrose, to Bridge of Dun station.

Visitor information

Anstruther ☎ (01333) 311073
Arbroath ☎ (01241) 872609
Carnoustie (library) ☎ (01241) 859620
Crail ☎ (01333) 450869
Dundee ☎ (01382) 527527
Kirkcaldy ☎ (01592) 267775
Perth ☎ (01738) 450600
St Andrews ☎ (01334) 472021

Kincardine to Montrose

SCOTLAND

ST CYRUS TO CULLEN

At Fowlsheugh reserve, looking out over the North Sea, 100,000 birds congregate, making this wild and fascinating coast home to one of Britain's greatest sea-bird colonies

One mile north of the town, the Mill of Benholm, a restored, working water-powered meal mill, is open to visitors in summer. Two miles inland, Damside Garden Herbs and Arboretum has seven gardens with displays of herbs, whose origins date back to Celtic times.

❸ Gourdon

This is one of the last fishing villages in Scotland where 19th-century trawling methods are used, and you can buy fish straight from the filleting sheds. At the harbour a barometer built into a granite pillar is a Victorian memorial to the seafaring men of Gourdon.

❹ Inverbervie

The most famous son of 'Bervie', as the town is known locally, was Hercules Linton, designer of the great tea-clipper _Cutty Sark_. A rose-garden memorial to him was opened by Sir Francis Chichester on the 100th anniversary of the ship's launch in 1869. Bervie Bay's curving, wave-sculpted pebble beach is fringed by a picnic area, and behind it the old railway line between Inverbervie and Montrose is now a cycleway and footpath south to Gourdon and Johnshaven.

Two miles inland, The Grassic Gibbon Centre commemorates James Leslie Mitchell who wrote, using the pseudonym Lewis Grassic Gibbon, _Sunset Song_, _Grey Granite_ and _Cloud Howe_, an evocative trilogy of novels about The Mearns, the agricultural area around nearby Laurencekirk.

❶ St Cyrus

Riverbanks, salt marshes, sand dunes, cliffs and a sandy beach make up one of Britain's most fascinating national nature reserves. The visitor centre here, originally a 19th-century lifeboat station, illustrates the wonderful variety of birdlife, wild flowers and butterflies within the reserve, which can be reached by a footbridge built in 1985 by a troop of Gurkhas.

A short but steep path from the beach climbs to the village of St Cyrus, where a clifftop viewpoint looks out over the sea and to Montrose to the south. From the village an exhilarating path leads north to Woodston, where a tractor track swoops down to the sea again.

❷ Johnshaven

In the early 18th century, Johnshaven was a highly productive fishing port, but many of its young men moved away, partly because of the dangers of the coast, and partly because of the navy press gangs. There is a working harbour here, where you can buy lobsters and salmon.

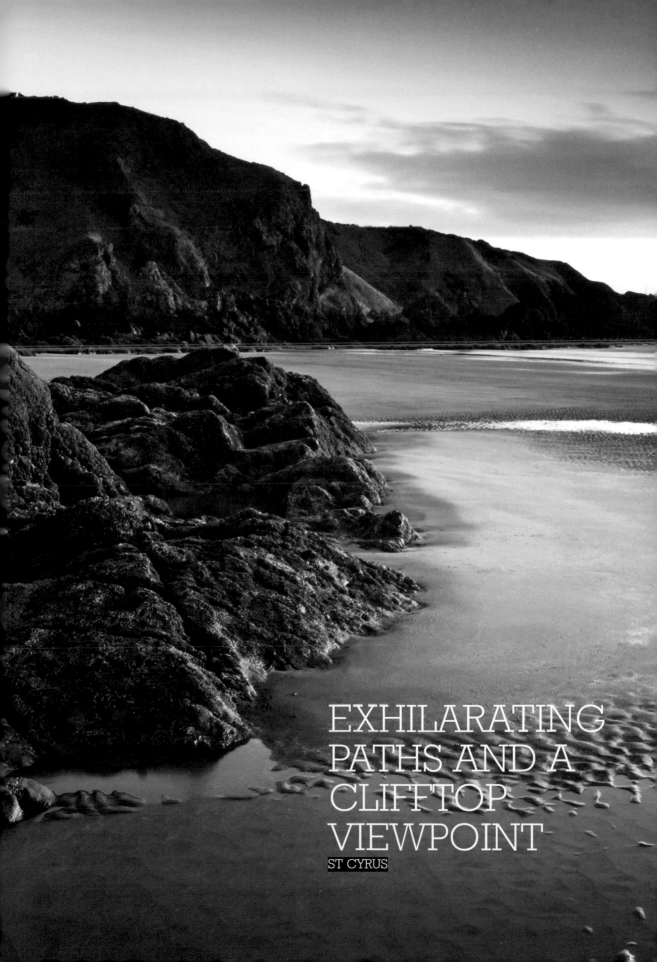

EXHILARATING PATHS AND A CLIFFTOP VIEWPOINT

ST CYRUS

⑤ Old Kirk of Kinneff

Overlooking the sea, the Old Kirk outside Kinneff village once held Scotland's best-kept state secret. In 1651 Cromwell's troops forced the surrender of Dunnottar Castle, 7 miles up the coast, where the Honours of Scotland – the royal crown, sword and sceptre – were thought to be in safe keeping. But they had been smuggled out by the parish minister's wife and hidden in the Old Kirk. Only in 1660, with peace restored, were the Honours returned to the state's ownership. The church dates from 1738, but there has been a church on the site since around AD 700.

⑥ Catterline

A grassy amphitheatre, bright with wild flowers in summer, plunges down to a tiny harbour in Catterline. Houses originally built for fishermen and coastguards stand on the clifftop and, although Catterline's fishing may have declined, the village's charming setting is still popular with artists, while ornithologists come to photograph the sea birds on the cliffs and offshore islets. A clifftop path leads to Crawton, 1½ miles to the north.

⑦ Fowlsheugh RSPB Reserve

More than 100,000 kittiwakes, fulmars, razorbills, guillemots and other species make this reserve one of Britain's greatest sea-bird colonies. A footpath from Crawton village leads to a grassy clifftop that looks down on inlets, towers and rock stacks, where the cries of sea birds constantly echo; seals, porpoises and dolphins swim offshore.

⑧ Dunnottar Castle

The ruined 14th-century fortress stands on an impregnable rock, separated from the mainland by a deep ravine. The castle was involved in many historical episodes, and was virtually demolished after the 1715 Jacobite Rising, before being partly restored in 1925. A tunnel entrance leads up towards the top level where the surviving buildings stand.

⑨ Dunnottar Woods

Shady paths run through this mainly broadleaved woodland, and Gallow Hill, an old execution place, provides views of the woodlands to the south. On the Burn of Glasslaw, Lady Kennedy's Bath is a stonework bathing pool, created for one of the ladies of long-gone Dunnottar House.

Sir Walter Scott once came upon a man restoring a memorial stone to a group of Covenanters near Dunnottar Kirk. The man, Robert Paterson, became the model for the hero of Scott's novel *Old Mortality*. The Covenanters' Stone is still in place.

⑩ Stonehaven

Yachts and fishing boats shelter in the harbour of the old town of Stonehaven, reached by a breezy promenade across Carron Water. The town is centred around the elegant Market Buildings of 1826. The Tolbooth Museum recalls that in 1748 a group of imprisoned Episcopalian ministers secretly baptised children brought to their cell window by fishermen's wives. A path climbs towards a war memorial, where there are fine views.

The old royal burgh of Cowie, north of Stonehaven, has a separate fishing quarter, and Boatie Row, a seafront street of cottages, leads to a stake-net drying green. From there a stepped footpath continues along the clifftop to the ruins of 13th-century St Mary of the Storms Church and a dramatic sea view.

⑪ Skatie Shore

The sandy bay on an otherwise rocky coast is reached by a path from the car park that leads along the foot of the cliffs. Garron Point marks the eastern end of the great Highland Boundary Fault, a fracture in the rock that runs almost arrow-straight across Scotland towards the Firth of Clyde on the west coast.

⑫ Newtonhill

Down a curving flight of steps, fishermen's huts stand out of sight of the village houses in this clifftop fishing village, which is well preserved despite much development in recent years. A plank bridge over the Burn of Elsick forms part of a circular walk.

⑬ Portlethen

Lobster boats still work from a pebbly cove in the old fishing settlement, which is reached from the modern town of Portlethen. Most of the cottages at Portlethen Village have been restored as commuter homes. The neighbouring fishing village of Findon is known for 'Finnan haddie' – haddock split and smoked over a peat fire. This was produced here until the 1870s, although the method of smoking continues in other eastern coast towns in Scotland.

⑭ Aberdeen

The capital of the North Sea oil industry, Aberdeen's harbour is crammed with oil-platform supply vessels. As well as being a popular seaside resort, Scotland's third largest city is also a fishing, fish-processing and general trading port, and ferry services operate to Shetland and the Orkneys. Extensive public parks include Hazlehead, with its giant maze, and Duthie Park, which has one of the largest Winter Gardens in Europe.

The local granite is evident in much of Aberdeen's imposing architecture, including Marischal College, part of the city's university, with its exuberant neo-Gothic frontage. Founded in 1593, the college has a museum devoted to its history. The Maritime Museum is in Provost Ross's House (NTS), while 16th-century Provost Skene's House contains the city museum. King's College Chapel, in the once-separate burgh of Old Aberdeen, has a majestic 17th-century crown tower. Nearby St Machar's Cathedral (HS) originates from the 15th century.

Within the city boundaries, Cove is a fishing village, while Footdee, pronounced 'Fittie', boasts a sandy beach.

15 Bridge Of Don
The River Don, which flows through the Aberdeen suburb of Bridge of Don, is crossed by two bridges. The early 14th-century Brig o' Balgownie, which is reached from a row of restored cottages dating back to 1600, is closed to road traffic. Instead, vehicles use the Bridge of Don, built in 1829.

The Scotstown Muir Nature Reserve is an area of heathland, gorse thickets, woodland and marshes, and here you can spot a variety of birds and wild flowers from a network of footpaths. The Donmouth Nature Reserve at the river mouth is visited by wildfowl all year round.

A mile southwest, the Crombie Woollen Mills visitor centre tells the story of the renowned Crombie cloth, once made there.

16 Balmedie Country Park
Vast sandy beaches and huge dunes stretch between the Don and the Ythan estuaries. The park is home to waders, which include redshanks, ringed plovers and sanderlings.

17 Forvie National Nature Reserve
A visitor centre in the reserve describes this fascinating area of cliffs, beaches, salt marsh, mudflats and sandhills. The reserve has some of the largest dune systems in Britain, and stretches from Collieston to the mouth of the River Ythan, with fulmars, kittiwakes and herring gulls on the cliffs. Thousands of greylag and pink-footed geese winter here, and terns come to nest, together with the greatest concentration of eider ducks in Britain.

Footpaths from the car park on the reserve's western side lead for 3 miles east to the site of a lost village engulfed in 1413 by wind-blown sand. All that survives is ruined Forvie Kirk.

18 Collieston
An amphitheatre of cottages encloses the harbour at Collieston, which used to be noted for 'speldings' – salted and sun-dried whiting. The rocky inlet called St Catharine's Dub took its name from the *Santa Catarina*, a Spanish ship wrecked in 1590 while bringing arms for the Earl of Erroll's failed rebellion. Later on, Collieston was also a famous haunt of smugglers.

19 Cruden Bay
The eerie ruins of Slains Castle, built in 1597, are said to have been the inspiration for Bram Stoker's *Dracula* in 1895; the novelist was a regular visitor to Cruden Bay. The ruins of the castle can be reached along a path from the car park at Cruden Bay.

The original fishing village at Cruden Bay was transformed when the railway arrived in 1897. A palatial hotel was built, and excellent golf courses were laid out behind the magnificent sandy beach. Although the railway and hotel have gone, Cruden Bay remains an appealing holiday and golfing resort.

The great stone font inside 18th-century St James's Church probably came from an earlier church, founded by Malcolm II in 1012, while the monument in the main street remembers the Norwegian aviator Tryggve Gran, whose solo flight in 1914 from Cruden Bay to Stavanger in Norway was the first flight across the North Sea.

North Sea oil is unobtrusively piped ashore to a terminal near the fishing hamlet of Whinnyfold, south of Cruden Bay.

20 Bullers of Buchan
Visible from the cliff path is a huge granite cauldron called the Pot, into which the tide pours through a natural archway. Walkers should take great care walking along the path. Fishermen used to live in the tiny clifftop hamlet, and their boats were kept at the foot of frightening cliffs, where fulmars and kittiwakes nest.

21 Peterhead
For a century until 1893, Peterhead was Britain's major whaling port and the story of its fishing and whaling heritage is brought to life in the Arbuthnot Museum, together with its political and historical associations. Although fishing has declined, it is still one of the largest white-fish ports in Europe.

Peterhead Bay is contained within the great Harbour of Refuge, and the story of the town is told at the Maritime Heritage Centre. The Fish House, near the mouth of the Ugie, dates from 1585 and still smokes trout and salmon.

A statue of Field Marshal Keith, one of Frederick the Great's commanders, stands in front of the 18th-century Town House, built from the pink granite that characterises Peterhead. Nearby, the Reform Monument's heraldic arms and Latin inscriptions celebrate the passing of the Reform Bill in 1832. The Reform Tower is another reminder of the same event.

㉒ Crimond

The village has a church clock that, due to an error by the clockmaker, shows 61 minutes in the hour. Northeast of Crimond, the Loch of Strathbeg RSPB reserve was a saltwater bay until its sea exit was blocked by the build-up of dunes in the 1720s; the reserve attracts tufted ducks and water rails.

㉓ Rattray Head

High, grassy dunes line miles of beach round Rattray Head, a fine place for watching wading birds and Arctic skuas. The lighthouse was built on a tidal platform, with an elegant shore station behind the dunes. Shoreline walks lead to Inverugie, 6 miles south, and to St Combs, 5 miles northwest.

All that remains of Old Rattray is the ruined chapel of St Mary, dating from the 13th century.

㉔ Fraserburgh

Named after its 16th-century founder, Alexander Fraser, Fraserburgh is the biggest fishing port after Peterhead on Scotland's northeast coast. Its market cross, carved soon after the Union of Crowns in 1603, shows the royal arms of both Scotland and Great Britain.

Kinnaird Head lighthouse, built into the structure of 16th-century Fraserburgh Castle, is now the Museum of Scottish Lighthouses. Adjacent to the museum is the Heritage Centre.

A sandy beach, fringed by dunes and reached from the Water of Philorth picnic site, stretches to the east, while the line of the old light railway to the villages of Cairnbulg, Inverallochy and St Combs is now part of the Formartine and Buchan Way. Cairnbulg Boathaven is an excellent viewpoint over Fraserburgh Bay, and you can visit Cairnbulg Castle by appointment.

㉕ Rosehearty

Surrounding a peaceful harbour, the village was a flourishing fishing port from around the 14th century until its narrow harbour entrance could no longer cope with larger vessels; its fleet is now based at Fraserburgh.

The fine 15th-century ruin of Pitsligo Castle is preserved by a local trust, while Rosehearty war memorial, which looks across spectacular cliffs, provides the district's finest viewpoint. Pitsligo parish church, on the edge of Peathill, includes beautiful woodcarvings from its 17th-century predecessor, whose ruins stand alongside.

㉖ Aberdour Bay

The pebble beach of this popular tourist spot is backed by red sandstone cliffs, pierced by caves, that stretch beyond a grassy pass to Boat Shore. St Drostan's Well marks the spot where a 6th-century missionary from

Caithness is said to have landed, and the Jane Whyte memorial commemorates the heroine of a shipwreck of 1884. The ruins of Old Aberdour Church, part of which is Norman, sit on a site that was consecrated in St Drostan's time.

Northfield Farm Museum, about 3 miles southwest, has a collection of farm machinery and household implements.

27 Pennan
Cliffs noisy with sea birds surround the handsome village of Pennan, whose hotel and a red telephone box featured in the film *Local Hero*. The box now has a preservation order on it and is one of the most famous in Scotland.

Cullykhan Bay's sandy beach is reached by a flight of steps, while a path leads to the Bronze Age promontory settlement of Fort Fiddes, from where you may walk with caution to the intimidating sea cliff tunnel called Hell's Lum.

28 Gardenstown
Built on a series of terraces set into the dramatic cliffs of Gamrie Bay, the village rises behind a well-maintained harbour. Gardenstown gained prosperity in the 19th century through its fishing industry, although most locally owned fishing boats operate from larger ports today.

A clifftop path heads north to Crovie, pronounced 'Crivie', a 10 minute walk away. This village is crammed so tightly against the cliffs that there is no room for a public street.

On the west side of Gamrie Bay, ruined St John's Kirk was founded in the 11th century to mark the defeat of an invading Danish army.

29 Macduff
Boat trips, sea-angling and diving expeditions can all be arranged in this fishing port, set beyond the sandy mouth of the Deveron. The town cross on the Hill of Donne stands in front of Doune Church, whose clocktower has a blank west face. It was designed in this way as a gesture to the people of Banff, who had moved their own clocks forward on the day of James MacPherson's execution, to minimise the chance of a last-minute reprieve.

30 Banff
A royal burgh and county town, Banff preserves many town houses of 17th and 18th-century landed families. The grand mansion of Duff House (HS), built around 1740, houses a magnificent collection of art from the National Galleries of Scotland, and there are many impressive tombstones and memorial sculptures in the churchyard of ruined St Mary's. Banff Museum has exhibits of local silverware.

James MacPherson, a notorious troublemaker, was hanged in 1700 at the Plainstones area of the town. The song he wrote in jail, starting 'I have spent my life in rioting', was rewritten by Robert Burns as *MacPherson's Farewell*.

31 Whitehills
The ancient Red Well here is fed by a spring containing iron salts. Immense cliffs rise to the east of the independent fishing village, which retains its own fish market.

32 Portsoy
Restored 17th-century warehouses stand tall by the waterside of the Moray Firth's oldest harbour, now used by pleasure craft and lobster boats. One of the warehouses is a workshop for Tortsoy marble, a red-and-green serpentine used in the construction of parts of the Palace of Versailles.

33 Sandend
One of Scotland's smallest harbours is the focus of this traditional fishing village, whose short streets run at right angles to the sea. A fine, sandy beach occupies the head of Sandend Bay, drawing sea birds.

In Fordyce village, 3 miles inland, 13th-century St Tarquin's Church is an intriguing, partly restored ruin with elegant canopied tombs, while Fordyce Joiners Workshop celebrates the expertise of Victorian rural craftsmen.

34 Findlater Castle
Perched on a headland are the hazardous ruins of this 15th-century fortress, which was abandoned soon after 1600. A clifftop path from a car park at Barnyards of Findlater leads past a restored dovecote and overlooks the ruins. Westwards, the coast path dips down to the sandy beach at Sunnyside.

35 Cullen
Cullen Skink – fish soup with a smoked haddock base – was devised in Seaton, the lower village in the cheerful resort of Cullen, which is built on two levels. Within the square of the upper village stands an ornate market cross, dating from 1696. Paths along disused railway viaducts provide views over restored Seatown. The Auld Kirk, dating from at least the 14th century, has fine 16th and 17th-century interior details.

> **Visitor information**
>
> **Aberdeen** ☎ (01224) 288828
> **Banff** ☎ (01261) 812419
> **Fraserburgh** ☎ (01346) 518315
> **Stonehaven** ☎ (01569) 762806

PORTKNOCKIE TO BALINTORE

There are plenty of opportunities to view bottle-nosed dolphins along this stretch of coast, while salmon are synonymous with the Spey, returning here instinctively, the place of their birth, to spawn

❶ Portknockie

A quiet former fishing village, Portknockie sits on a cliff high above the harbour and is an excellent haven for small boats. From the cliff path to the east, strangely shaped rocks such as the Bow and Fiddle can be seen spearing out of the sea just offshore, while Preacher's Cave, one of several caves along the rocky foreshore, was used as a church during the religious revival of the early 19th century.

A 1½ mile clifftop walk west to Findochty offers superb views across the Moray Firth to the Black Isle.

❷ Findochty

Brightly painted houses give a cheerful appearance to this former fishing village, which now attracts pleasure craft. The older part of Findochty, pronounced 'Finnechty', borders a little bay, overlooked by a First World War memorial to the west and the 19th-century Hythe's Church to the east.

Dolphin-watching boat trips leave from the harbour in summer, and a coast path follows a smugglers' route westwards for a mile, past hidden coves and caves. To the east of the harbour is a sheltered sandy cove, with a clifftop path leading eastwards to Portknockie.

❸ Buckie

Buckie is a thriving fishing port and one of the few places in Scotland where traditional fishing boats are still made. Stretching for 2½ miles along the coast, from Buckpool in the west to Portessie in the east, it has a morning fish market, at its busiest on Thursdays and Fridays.

From the turn of the century to the 1930s Buckie was the base of a large herring fleet, but today the catch is mainly of shellfish, supplying markets in France and Spain, as well as in Britain. In summer boat trips are available round the harbour, or along the coast to observe bottle-nosed dolphins, which you can often see in groups of 20 or more.

❹ Portgordon

The late 18th-century village of Portgordon clusters round its tiny harbour, once used by salmon fishermen but now visited only by pleasure craft. A 2½ mile walk along the sand and shingle foreshore leads west to Spey Bay.

Just over a mile inland, at Leitcheston, stands a dovecot built to provide pigeon meat and eggs for a nearby castle, no trace of which remains. The dovecot is clearly visible from the A98.

To fishermen, the River Spey means salmon. The fish spend most of their adult lives, usually about two to three years, in the North Atlantic, but swim for thousands of miles back to the river of their birth to spawn, from November to early January. It is thought that some form of in-built 'compass' may enable salmon to steer by the Earth's magnetic field, or even by the stars. In coastal waters each fish can 'smell' its own river.

❺ Spey Bay

Set at the mouth of the Spey, the village was once an important centre for salmon fishing. Although commercial fishing has ceased, salmon are still caught by individual fishermen. Tugnet Ice House, a warehouse built in 1830 to store salmon before it was sold, has exhibits from the Whale and Dolphin Conservation Society.

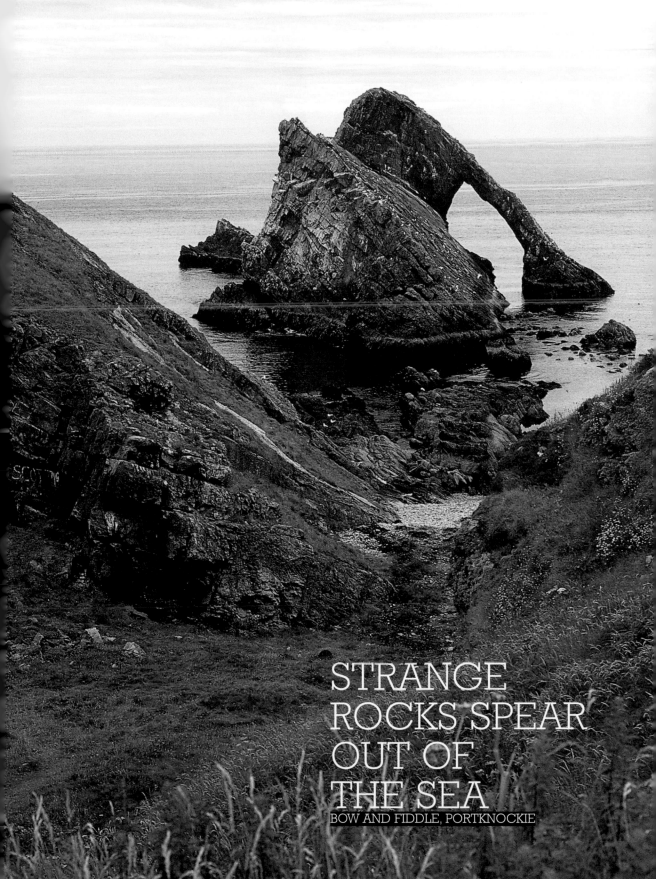

STRANGE
ROCKS SPEAR
OUT OF
THE SEA
BOW AND FIDDLE, PORTKNOCKIE

The river estuary and long shingle beach are rich in slack and freshwater marsh vegetation, including coral-root orchid and burnet rose, and this is a good place to view summer-feeding birds such as ospreys. The village is at the northern end of the Speyside Way to Aviemore.

⑥ Lossiemouth

Shellfish and some white fish are landed at this busy fishing town, and a fish market operates most weekday mornings. There are excellent sandy beaches to the east and west, and the east beach often has good conditions for surfing. Britain's first Labour prime minister, Ramsay MacDonald, was born in Lossiemouth in 1866; a memorial, erected on the centenary of his birth, offers spectacular views over Spey Bay.

Three miles inland are the ruins of 15th-century Spynie Palace (HS), once the home of the Bishops of Moray.

⑦ Duffus

Towering above a Norman mound on the edge of flat land that was formerly a loch are the ruins of Duffus Castle (HS). There has been a castle on this spot since 1150, although the most recent building was abandoned in the 18th century.

Like many of the villages along this coast, the quiet, pretty hamlet of Duffus was planned and built in the 19th century. The original village was centred on 13th-century St Peter's Church, now a ruin. In the churchyard, is a small gravewatcher's hut, built in 1830.

⑧ Hopeman

The quiet, unspoilt fishing village, founded in the early 19th century, is built on a gentle slope overlooking the sea, and the small sheltered harbour is used by pleasure craft. There are sandy beaches east and west of the harbour; a 5½ mile walk eastwards, mostly along cliffs, leads to Lossiemouth.

⑨ Burghead

Every January 11, a blazing tar barrel known as the Clavie is carried round the village in a celebration of the New Year under the Julian calendar, which was replaced by the Gregorian calendar in 1752. The barrel's charred remains are placed on the Clavie Stone, not far from the well. The visitor centre explains the Clavie tradition, and displays some Pictish stones engraved with the figure of a bull that were found in the area.

The village is built on a promontory jutting into the Moray Firth, and near the tip is Burghead Well (HS), which may have provided water for a nearby Iron Age fort. The well is enclosed, but the key to the gateway is available from a neighbouring house.

RANDOLPH'S LEAP, FINDHORN

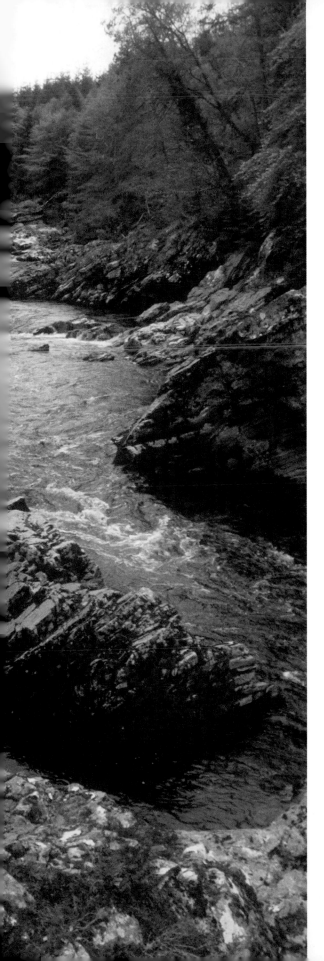

Stone-built granaries lining the harbour here date from the time when Burghead was Moray's foremost grain-shipping port. Now the harbour is used by fishing boats and pleasure craft.

There are walks and a picnic area in Roseisle Forest, bordering the 5 mile sandy beach southwest of the town.

🔟 Findhorn

Grey and common seals live in the bay, and migrating wildfowl visit the extensive tidal mudflats in this former port which is now a centre for watersports and sailing. A heritage centre that occupies a converted ice house explains the natural and human history of the area, while east of the village, paths lead from the long sandy crescent of Burghead Bay into Roseisle Forest.

⑪ Culbin Forest

For centuries, the area where Culbin Forest now stands was a desert of sand created by storms during the 17th century. The sands buried the village of Culbin, which had stood at the heart of rich farmland. In the 1920s the Forestry Commission started planting Scots and Corsican pines on the sands, and the forest now extends along some 9 miles of coastline. Its varied wildlife includes rare species such as ospreys, wild cats and capercaillies, Britain's largest game bird.

There are walks through the forest to shoreline dunes, and bordering the forest on its northwestern shore is the Culbin Sands RSPB Reserve, where you can see birds such as bar-tailed godwits, knots, shelduck and greylag geese.

⑫ Nairn

Nairn was once a prosperous herring port and behind the harbour are the narrow streets and tightly packed cottages of the old fishing district of Fishertown. The industry declined in the 1930s and the harbour is now used mainly by pleasure craft.

The history of this popular holiday town which dates back to the 12th century when Alexander I granted it a royal charter, is explained in the Nairn Museum, housed in a Georgian mansion. In the grounds is a statue of Dr John Grigor, who did much to promote Nairn as a health resort in the 19th century. The early 19th-century Old Courthouse, in the town centre, has an impressive bell tower that was added in 1860.

There is a sandy beach to the east of the harbour, and another to the west, with entertainments including croquet; there are also walks along both sides of the River Nairn. Highland games are held here in mid August.

⑬ Fort George

Standing at the tip of a promontory jutting into the Moray Firth, Fort George is one of the finest 18th-century artillery fortresses in Europe. It was built after the Battle of Culloden as a garrison fortress for the Hanoverian army of George II and is protected by almost a mile of mighty ramparts. Every approach is covered by at least two cannon-lined walls.

The fort is still an army barracks, but you may explore several buildings, such as the main guardrooms, a powder magazine, an armoury and the garrison chapel, and walk the ramparts for views of the Moray Firth. At the entrance to the fort is a visitor centre, while in the grounds, but independently run, is the Regimental Museum of the Queen's Own Highlanders.

⑭ Cawdor

Made famous by Shakespeare's MacBeth, Cawdor Castle is set amid woods of beech and oak and has been the home of the Thanes, later the Earls, of Cawdor for many centuries. The 14th-century keep was extended in the 17th century, and the mellow stone house now contains a superb collection of family portraits, as well as tapestries and some excellent furniture. There are nature trails in the impressive grounds, which include a Walled Garden dating from around 1600.

A small river flows by the hamlet of Cawdor, separating it from the Cawdor estate to the east. West of Cawdor, on the north bank of the Nairn, is the 15th-century Kilravock Castle. The grounds are open to visitors in summer; on Wednesdays and Thursdays you can take a tour of the castle, which includes a small museum of clan-related objects.

⑮ Culloden Moor

Open farmland and dark forest cover Culloden Moor (NTS), the site of the bloody battle of 1746 in which the Duke of Cumberland's army defeated that of Charles Edward Stuart, Bonnie Prince Charlie, and ended the Stuart dynasty's last chance of regaining the English throne. A visitor centre explains the history of Culloden, the last major battle fought on mainland Britain, and guided tours of the moor can be arranged in summer.

A pleasant forest walk of about 2 miles passes near the Prisoners' Stone, where 17 officers of the losing army were executed after the battle. Earlier historical remains can be seen southeast of the visitor centre at Clava Cairns (HS). The cairns, surrounded by rings of standing stones, are thought to be more than 4000 years old. On the western edge of the moor is ancient St Mary's Well, whose waters were once believed to have curative powers.

⑯ Inverness

The Highlands' unofficial capital, straddling the Caledonian Canal and the River Ness, sits on a level plain fringed by tidal mudflats. On a hilltop overlooking the east bank of the Ness is the town's 19th-century castle, now the court house. The nearby Gothic-style Town House was the scene in 1921 of an emergency Cabinet meeting to discuss the Irish Treaty, called by the prime minister, David Lloyd George, who was on holiday in the area.

Castle Wynd houses an art gallery and a museum telling the history of the Highlands. On the river's west bank is the mid 19th-century St Andrew's Cathedral, which has fine stained glass. A pedestrian bridge crosses the Ness to the Old High Church, dating from the 14th century but substantially rebuilt 400 years later.

Inverness has many opportunities for gentle walks, such as around the Ness Islands south of the town. The islands are joined to each other and to the riverbanks by a series of bridges. Pleasure craft abound in this part of the Caledonian Canal, which links the Beauly Firth to Loch Ness; it is possible to hire a boat here.

⑰ Craig Phadrig

The 169m (556ft) hill, just west of Inverness, can be explored by a network of paths through attractive woodland. On the summit are the remains of an Iron Age fort, from where there are superb views, eastwards across the Moray Firth and westwards over the Beauly Firth and to the mountains beyond. The easiest way to reach Craig Phadrig is from the car park at its southern end.

⑱ Beauly

The town grew up around 13th-century Beauly Priory (HS), whose ruins dominate the main street. Set at the head of the Beauly estuary, its name comes from the French beau lieu, meaning 'beautiful place'. To the west is a large crafts centre where knitwear, jewellery, pottery and glassware are displayed.

Southeast of Beauly is a winery based in a mansion known as Moniack Castle, which produces wines made from elderflower and silver birch. The house is a private residence, but you can visit the fermenting rooms, vats and bottling room, which have been converted from the former stables and laundry. A nearby walk follows a stream along Reelig Glen.

⑲ Muir of Ord

Until the opening of the Kessock Bridge the Muir of Ord was the main gateway to the Black Isle peninsula. The number of roads converging on it bears witness to the fact that it was once an important market town.

One of Scotland's major agricultural events, the Black Isle Show, is held at Muir of Ord on the first Thursday in August. To the northwest of the town is the Glen Ord Distillery, where whisky has been produced since 1838. Tours are available, and a visitor centre traces the history of the area.

⑳ North Kessock
You can listen to dolphins and seals in the firth using underwater microphones at a centre in this small village at the entrance to the Beauly Firth just north of Kessock Bridge. Near the centre is a picnic area offering fine views. Paths nearby climb the 191m (626ft) summit of Ord Hill.

A watersports centre at Craigrory, 2½ miles west of North Kessock, offers waterskiing, sailing and windsurfing.

㉑ Munlochy
The quiet village is set on high ground at the head of Munlochy Bay, whose mudflats attract large numbers of birds, including herons and geese. Ornamental waterfowl are the principal attraction of the Black Isle Country Park, 2 miles south of Munlochy; you can also see meerkats, llamas and wallabies and other exotic animals.

From the park, a lane leads east to the hill of Craigiehowe, which overlooks the bay's southern entrance. The hill is home to a herd of wild goats.

㉒ Avoch
Old cottages cluster round the harbour of the bustling fishing village of Avoch, pronounced 'Ock'. The churchyard of Old Avoch Church contains the grave of Sir Alexander MacKenzie, the 18th-century Scottish-born explorer of Canada, who spent some time in the village after his retirement.

Avoch and the village of Fortrose are linked by a 4½ mile circular walk, part of which follows a disused railway line near the banks of the Moray Firth.

㉓ Fortrose
Lying at the foot of steep hills, the harbour of this former fishing village is often busy with pleasure craft. Fortrose was made a Royal Burgh in 1455 by James II, and in the village are the ruins of the red sandstone Fortrose Cathedral (HS), which includes parts of the 14th-century south chapel and aisle, and of the 13th-century chapter house.

East of the harbour is a small beach, beyond which a long, narrow peninsula protrudes into the Moray Firth. Its tip, Chanonry Point – Fortrose was once called Chanonry – is approached by a road across a golf course.

Secrets of the sandstone

Hugh Miller, born at Cromarty in 1802, was a stonemason whose lasting interest in geology began in the early 19th century when he was working in quarries on the Black Isle. During his relatively short life, his interests and influences were wide-ranging, but as a self-taught expert in palaeontology, he discovered many fossils that were then unknown to science, and the 6000 or so specimens he accumulated now form the basis for an important collection at Edinburgh's Royal Scottish Museum.

At the Old Red Sandstone rock formation at Eathie, Miller found a winged fish, later named in his honour as *Pterichthyodes milleri*. This and other fossils he discussed in his book *The Old Red Sandstone*, one of many acclaimed books and papers written on geology, the history of the earth and other subjects by Miller, who also worked as an Edinburgh newspaper editor.

His years spent as a stonemason caused Miller to be plagued by silicosis all his life, and that coupled with debilitating headaches eventually led him to commit suicide in 1856. The funeral of this much-loved man was one of the biggest that Edinburgh had ever seen.

▶ Cromarty ㉕, page 184

At the point, and next to a whitewashed lighthouse, stands the Brahan Seer Stone, which commemorates Kenneth MacKenzie, a 17th-century seer who was condemned to death as a witch. Superb views extend from the point, across the firth to Fort George, and west towards Inverness.

㉔ Rosemarkie
Housed in the Groam House Museum and Pictish Centre is the Rosemarkie cross-slab, with its enigmatic Pictish symbols. The museum, located in the tiny main street, recalls the history of the area and includes a collection of local photographs.

The popular resort comprises a collection of small cottages and two-storey houses by a sandy beach. At the northern end of the village, the car park marks the start of a walk leading through Fairy Glen Nature Reserve, so called because some claim to have spotted fairies there.

Portknockie to Balintore

SCOTLAND

CROMARTY

Managed by the RSPB and local landowners, this wooded area extends some 2 miles inland along the Rosemarkie Burn, and features two waterfalls, many varieties of woodland plant, and birds such as dippers, grey wagtails, buzzards and willow warblers.

㉕ Cromarty
The town is notable for its variety of 18th and 19th-century architecture, and many of its old buildings have been restored. Before Dingwall, Cromarty was the administrative centre of the peninsula known as the Black Isle, so called, some say, because it is seldom whitened by snow.

Hugh Miller's Cottage (NTS) was the birthplace of a remarkable 19th-century stonemason who was also a geologist, folk historian, accountant, newspaper editor and churchman. You can also see Miller's memorial nearby. The nearby Cromarty Courthouse, originally built in 1773, has been converted into a museum, complete with prison cells, a trial room and exhibits on local history. The East Church here dates back to at least the 17th century and features a plaque commemorating the eccentric Sir Thomas Urquhart, the mid 17th-century Laird of Cromarty, who claimed to have traced his ancestry back to Adam and Eve. At the town's southern end is a chapel, built for the Gaelic-speaking worshippers who moved to Cromarty in search of work in the 1770s.

A walk along the foreshore leads to the South Sutor headland, which offers wide views of the North Sea and the Cromarty Firth, as well as over the narrow channel to the North Sutor on the Nigg peninsula. Another walk, starting at Eathie Mains to the south, leads to fossil beds on the shore of the Moray Firth, where Hugh Miller made several discoveries. Boat trips from the harbour explore the Cromarty Firth, where you may see numbers of bottle-nosed dolphins, and a ferry runs to Nigg Ferry opposite.

㉖ Udale Bay
The national nature reserve of Udale Bay is an important resting point for migrating birds. From the RSPB hide in a lay-by to the west of Jemimaville, you can view large numbers of waders, ducks and geese.

Inland, the remains of medieval St Michael's Chapel are situated in Kirkmichael burial ground, at the east end of a loop road. This road passes the cluster of pretty cottages that make up the village of Balblair, and provides a pleasant 2 mile circular walk, with good views.

㉗ Conon Bridge
There is excellent fishing for salmon and sea trout on the fast-flowing Conon, and you can take tranquil walks upstream along its southern banks. Once a separate community, Conon Bridge now merges with its neighbour Maryburgh, to form a large residential area.

The ruins of 17th-century Brahan Castle, 3 miles inland, lie within peaceful gardens that offer magnificent views along the Conon valley.

㉘ Strathpeffer
The beautiful little town was distinctive in the 19th century for its spa, and it is still possible to sample the sulphurous waters in a pavilion in the town square. The former railway station building now houses a craft centre and the Highland Museum of Childhood, which has dressing-up costumes for children, as well as displays of toys and photographs.

A short walk through the eastern part of the town leads to the Eagle Stone, a fine example of Pictish art dating from the 7th century.

㉙ Dingwall
The town is the birthplace of General Sir Hector MacDonald, the hero of the Battle of Omdurman in 1898. His considerable military career began in the Gordon Highlanders and is retold in the town's museum, housed in the partly 18th-century Town House. A tower erected in MacDonald's name in 1907, four years after his death, stands within the cemetery on top of Mitchell Hill.

There has been a settlement here since Viking times. The name Dingwall comes from the Norse Thing vollr, meaning 'place of the parliament', and the market town continues to play a major administrative role in the district.

㉚ Evanton
The quiet village is overlooked by Cnoc Fyrish, a hill crowned by the Fyrish Monument. This structure, a replica of an Indian gate, was commissioned by General Sir Hector Munro in 1782, partly in celebration of his military success at Negapatam, in India, in 1781, and partly because its construction provided employment in the area. The monument can be reached from a forest walk that starts from the car park on the Boath road.

Half a mile inland from Evanton lies the spectacular Black Rock Gorge, a 61m (200ft) deep chasm carved by the River Glass as it storms down from Loch Glass towards the Cromarty Firth.

㉛ Alness
The town sits astride the River Averon, which flows through woodlands to reach a mud and shingle shore. It has expanded greatly as a result of the industrial growth brought by the oil business. Alness has two distilleries, one of which, Dalmore Distillery, is open to the public.

㉜ Invergordon
Oil rigs are as much a part of Invergordon as the undulating hills behind it. The town prospered in the 1970s and 80s from both rig-fitting and aluminium smelting, and it still refits and maintains rigs. Now a popular stopping place for cruise liners, the harbour also has a yacht club.

The stony foreshore, part of which forms the Nigg Bay RSPB Reserve, is a good place to spot wading birds. You can take walks from Invergordon along the shore for about 2 miles northeast to Saltburn and 4 miles west to Alness.

㉝ Nigg Ferry
An RSPB reserve on the Sands of Nigg provides a haven for a wide range of ducks, geese and waders; a walk along the southern shore eventually climbs the cliffs of North Sutor, on which stands ruined 12th-century Dunskeath Castle. A two-car ferry crosses the Cromarty Firth from Nigg Ferry to Cromarty.

㉞ Nigg
Nigg Old Church, restored from near-dereliction, houses the Nigg Stone, a Pictish cross-slab that once stood in the churchyard. Engravings feature complex interlacing motifs, and the figures of St Paul and St Anthony.

㉟ Balintore
The magnificent Clach a' Charridh, a tall Pictish cross-slab with carvings of angels, huntsmen, warriors and animals, and abstract patterns, stands to the south of Shandwick, a seaside village that merges into Balintore. In Balintore's harbour, local boat owners provide fishing and sea-bird viewing trips, while to the north, at Hilton of Cadboll, are the remains of the ancient Our Lady's Chapel (HS); the Pictish stone that originally stood next to the chapel is now in Edinburgh's Royal Museum of Scotland.

Visitor information

Elgin ☎ (01343) 542666
Forres ☎ (01309) 672938
Inverness ☎ (01463) 234353
Nairn – Visit Scotland ☎ 0845 225 5121
Strathpeffer and North Kessock –
  Visit Scotland ☎ 0845 225 5121

Lifelines across the water

The islanders of Scotland would struggle to survive without ferry links to the mainland. Bridges, too, are vital routes for the Scots.

The October 1995 opening of the road bridge across the Sound of Sleat from Kyle of Lochalsh to the Isle of Skye should have been the catalyst for universal celebration. No more sickening sea crossings, no more waiting for a ferry, no more nightly closure of the means of access – and escape. But not everyone was happy.

Many folk welcomed the bridge, but plenty of others did not. Under the grumbling about inflated tolls and the new-fangled look of the structure was a subtler cause for lamentation. Somehow the bridging of that 1,000m gap had robbed Skye of some of its romantic appeal – epitomised in the Skye Boat Song. You might technically still be able to travel 'over' the sea to Skye, but where was that famous 'bonny boat' to speed you, 'like a bird on the wing', to the isle of Bonnie Prince Charlie and Flora Macdonald? Gone, in a stroke of absolute pragmatism, to the disappointment of the dreamy, the poetic and the sentimental traveller.

Preserving the island life

To islanders, an island is just the place they live and work. An islander takes a purely practical view of the link between island and mainland – whether it is free or cheap, does it work round the clock and operate in all weathers. But to outsiders islands are places of romance, and the means of reaching them are touched with magic, too. There is something special, a nobility as well as a dogged determination, about the sight of one of Caledonian MacBrayne's salt-rusted ferries butting out in a storm to the isles of Raasay, Islay or Lewis and throwing up a bow wave of agitated white water – 'with a bone in its teeth', as the islanders say. Crossing the sea by boat shuts a door on the humdrum mainland and opens another on the captivating isles in a manner that bridges just cannot rival.

Not that the majority of the inhabitants of the Western Isles, the remote northwestern island chain also known as the Outer Hebrides, have any such reservations about the chain of bridges and causeways that have been built piecemeal since the 1940s to connect up the main islands of their archipelago. Improved access and communications have played a large part in reversing a seemingly unstoppable decline in the population of the Western Isles, and few islanders have anything negative to say about that.

Engineering conquers the sea

The island ferries may be romantic, but they do not have a monopoly on the enchantment of travel around the coasts of Scotland. Bridges,

it seems, can exude glamour too, even if they do not join islands to each other or to the mainland. The railway bridges that stride across the wide firths or estuaries of Forth and Tay to the north of Edinburgh are the epitome of Victorian building genius and confidence. The Forth Bridge of 1890, more than a mile and a half long, is upheld on three mighty cantilevers like the backbone of a monstrous dinosaur. It ought to look ugly and intrusive, yet all who see the bridge admire it, for its daring shape and legendary strength as much as for its brilliance as an engineering success story. In a London & North-Eastern Railway's 1928 poster the Forth

Bridge is a brooding dark presence against a night-time sky, the red glare of the locomotive's fire and the yellow glow of the carriage windows reflected among the girders high overhead. It captures perfectly the sense of heightened expectation generated by crossing this wide stretch of water in the days if steam over such an awesome structure.

Great tragedy and small triumph

Of course, it is tales of bridge disasters rather than accounts of engineering triumphs that live on longest in the collective imagination. The present Tay railway bridge is the second to be built across the Firth of Tay – the first will always be associated with tragedy. Thomas Bouch's great Tay bridge took 600 men six years to build, consumed 2 million rivets and 10 million bricks, and cost nearly half a million pounds and the

lives of 20 workmen. It was opened on September 26, 1877, to universal acclaim. Bouch was knighted for his feat. Yet a little over two years later, on December 28, 1879, the central girders of the bridge collapsed in a ferocious winter storm, sending a train plummeting into the water and killing 75 passengers and crew. Bouch died soon afterwards, a broken man.

Directly across Scotland as the crow flies is a crossing of much more modest engineering. The 18th-century Clachan Bridge arches gracefully to reach the isle of Seil on the west coast. The slender stone bow is otherwise known as the 'Bridge Over the Atlantic' – a serious case of rose-tinted spectacles, since the gap it spans is less than 21m (70ft). And yet the 500 inhabitants of Seil still have the proud right to call themselves islanders just as much as their more numerous counterparts do to the north on Skye.

CROSSING THE SEA BY BOAT OPENS A DOOR TO THE ISLANDS

OBAN HARBOUR, SCOTLAND

TARBAT NESS TO BALNAKEIL

The most northerly part of mainland Britain became the home of many who were cast out during the Highland Clearances; with its towering cliffs, it still provides a vital and dramatic landscape

❶ Tarbat Ness
A tall slender lighthouse stands at the tip of Tarbat Ness, guiding ships past the sandbar of Gizzen Briggs in the Dornoch Firth. A finger of rolling farmland which culminates in an area of heath and grassland and a rocky shore, Tarbat Ness is an important landfall for migrating birds from Scandinavia.

❷ Portmahomack
An arc of houses looks out over tall marram grass and a sandy shore to a bay popular with windsurfers. The oddly domed tower of Tarbat Old Church dominates the village where, in the 18th century, Lord Tarbat built a pier beside what had been 'a handful of cottages on an empty heath'.

At its northern end, a breakwater shelters craft engaged in lobster and crab fishing. Boats can be chartered here for fishing trips, and you may spot dolphins and porpoises in the firth. A short walk leads you to the diminutive village of Rockfield, tucked away beneath imposing cliffs, and the ruined grandeur of 16th-century Ballone Castle.

❸ Inver
The wide plain surrounding this quiet village is cluttered with the shells of disused military buildings. During the Second World War there were plans to use the area for D-Day practice. Tidal shifts of sand and water channels made this impossible, and the idea was abandoned in favour of a shooting and tank training range. The area is still used for military exercises, and there is no access to the flatlands northwest of the village.

❹ Tain
The town's importance as a place of pilgrimage dates from about AD 1000, when St Duthus, or Duthac, was born there. He established a chapel, whose ruins stand near the shore of Dornoch Firth. The 13th-century St Duthus Church, in the centre of the town, was frequented by James IV, who paid his last visit there only a few weeks before his death at the Battle of Flodden in 1513.

Next to the 18th-century Tolbooth is the Court House, built in the 19th century with turrets and crenellations to match the Tolbooth's candle-snuffer pinnacles. The royal burgh's history is explained at the District Museum, which also houses the Clan Ross Centre.

❺ Edderton

Ancient cairns and field systems in the gentle hills behind the small village suggest that this area was extensively settled in prehistoric times. In a field on the western edge of the village is a 3m (10ft) standing stone, probably of Bronze Age origin, featuring Pictish symbols in disc and Z-shapes. You must ask for permission to enter the field from the neighbouring farmhouse.

In the old village churchyard is a cross-slab, a stone on which is carved the outline of a cross, with Pictish engravings of figures on horseback carrying shields and spears.

Two miles to the east, a picnic area marks the start of an extensive network of woodland walks.

❻ Bonar Bridge

The village lies on the north side of the Kyle of Sutherland as it enters the Dornoch Firth, and the river is spanned by a bridge of the same name. To the northwest are forest trails in Balblair Wood, while immediately south of the bridge is a picnic site with a riverside walk and an open-air display of types of rock found in northern Scotland.

Nearby Ardgay is the site of the Clach Eiteag, a massive white boulder that used to be moved from parish to parish to mark the location of local markets and fairs; it was finally set here on the site of an annual cattle market held throughout the 19th century.

❼ Spinningdale

Standing by the shore of an inlet, like an ancient castle, are the ruins of an 18th-century cotton mill. En route to the tiny village of Spinningdale from Dornoch is the hamlet of Ospisdale and the tall Ospis Stone, which take their names from a Norse chieftain. To the northwest, down a small lane, are Ledmore and Migdale Woods, where paths through pine and oak woods afford views of small Loch Migdale. On a promontory 2 miles southwest of the village stands the Iron Age fort of Dun Creich.

❽ Dornoch

The compact royal burgh has its roots in the 6th century, when a chapel was founded by St Barr, or Finbarr. The site of the chapel is marked at the east end of what is now the cathedral churchyard. The cathedral itself, originally built in the 13th century, was badly damaged by fire in 1580, but was much restored in the 17th and 19th centuries. The

16th-century Bishop's Palace across the road has been converted into a hotel, and next door is the Town Jail centre and craft centre.

The Royal Dornoch Links attract many golfers, but the long, sandy beach backed by dunes remains relatively quiet. The sandbanks of Dornoch Firth draw many wintering wading birds and wildfowl, and common and grey seals can often be seen at low tide.

❾ Loch Fleet

Salmon moving in from the sea to spawn gather in a pool at the narrow western end of this saltwater basin, crossed by a causeway called The Mound. When rising water shuts the sluice gates the salmon wait here until the path upriver is open. Their main run is in July.

Loch Fleet is a nature reserve, and here you can view common seals, terns, kittiwakes and cormorants from a number of lay-bys. Above one of these stand the ruins of 14th-century Skelbo Castle, which is not open to the public. A car park in Skelbo Wood is the starting point for several forest trails.

❿ Golspie

A huge statue of the first Duke of Sutherland stands on the 394m (1293ft) summit of Beinn a' Bhragaidh, reached by a steep 2 mile track from the village.

The administrative centre of the district of Sutherland lies between a long sandy beach and a range of hills. At the northern end of the village is the 19th-century Golspie Mill, once the meal mill for the Dunrobin estate and still used for milling flour. Next to the mill is the start of a mile-long walk along the tree-lined Golspie Burn to a waterfall, beyond which the path continues along the burn for another 3 miles. Highland rocks and crystals are displayed at the Orcadian Stone Company workshop.

⓫ Dunrobin Castle

The castle and its luxuriant formal gardens command far-ranging views. Since the 13th century Dunrobin castle has been in the hands of the Earls and Dukes of Sutherland, whose family played a leading role in the Highland Clearances. Its original massive keep has been embellished with turrets and pinnacles, first in the 19th century by Sir Charles Barry, architect of the Houses of Parliament, then by Sir Robert Lorimer after a fire in 1915. The castle museum contains Pictish stones and a number of mementos of the Victorian era.

⓬ Carn Liath Broch

The well-preserved Iron Age Carn Liath Broch (HS) stands on a knoll looking out to sea. Some dwellings were built into its outer wall at the time of original construction, while others came later, one of them from the remains of a fallen wall.

⑬ Brora
Crofters evicted from the Sutherland estate in the 1800s settled here and established a whisky distillery. The village had been a coal-mining centre from the 16th century but coal-mining ceased here in the early 1970s. However, the Clynelish Distillery still produces a fine single malt, and you can pay a visit.

South of the harbour mouth, a large car park overlooks a rocky outcrop popular with gulls, gannets and basking seals. To the north a sandy shore stretches for more than a mile to Kintradwell Broch.

There is good fishing for salmon and trout in the area, as well as an 18-hole golf course, and impressive scenery along the shores of Loch Brora, 3 miles to the northwest.

⑭ Helmsdale
Situated at the mouth of the Helmsdale salmon river, the former fishing village is surrounded by crofts and steep-sided hills. Located in the village is the Timespan Visitor Centre, where Highland history and lore is brought alive through a number of tableaux and audiovisual presentations.

Helmsdale is the starting point for a spectacular 38 mile drive northwest to Melvich, following the Strath of Kildonan and Strath Halladale through the great expanse of peat bogs, known as the 'Flow Country', which covers much of north Sutherland and Caithness.

⑮ Ord of Caithness
The coast road twists and climbs up the Ord of Caithness, where a narrow pass crosses a natural bastion of rock. From the 229m (750ft) summit of the Ord, which marks the boundary between the districts of Caithness and Sutherland, the views of the coast in all directions are superb.

Below the northern slope lie the workshops of Ousdale Weaving, open to visitors throughout the year.

⑯ Badbea
A path by a lay-by leads to a ruined clifftop settlement, built in the early 19th century by families evicted from their homes during the Highland Clearances. A plaque on one building records that children and animals had to be tethered to stakes to keep them from being blown off into the sea. Most occupants eventually left for New Zealand, from where one descendant later returned to erect a tablet bearing the names of the emigrants.

⑰ Dunbeath
The former fishing village has a heritage centre covering the history and wildlife of the area. From the centre there are views of the distant platforms of the Beatrice Oil Field, the only oilfield visible from the Scottish mainland. Dunbeath Castle, built on a sheer cliff south of the village in the 15th century, was one of the strongholds of the Earls of Caithness. It is still inhabited, and is not open to the public.

Dunbeath is the starting point for several walks, one of which follows Dunbeath Water for 4½ miles to a standing stone and a cairn. The coast road south of the village passes the hamlet of Berriedale, where a trail follows Berriedale Water into a broad moorland.

⑱ Laidhay Croft Museum
A traditional Caithness thatched long-house, standing on land worked as a croft until 1968, has been converted into a museum of local life. The building combines living quarters with stables and a byre, while agricultural implements are displayed in a barn whose roof, incorporating driftwood and old oars, is supported by tree-trunk crucks known locally as 'Highland couples'.

LAIDHAY CROFT MUSEUM

⑲ Latheron

The 18th-century kirk houses the Clan Gunn Museum, which documents the claim that a Gunn reached the Americas a century before Christopher Columbus. Just north of Latheron are two fine Bronze Age standing stones, and to the south is the snug harbour of Latheronwheel and a small picnic area, from which a path across a partly overgrown bridge leads to clifftop walks.

⑳ Whaligoe

A flight of some 360 often slippery flagstone steps leads down to a minuscule quay bordering wave-lashed rocks in the tiny village. The boats of the 19th-century herring fishers had to be pulled into Whaligoe Cove stern first, and heavy gear and baskets of fish were carried up and down the steps by the women of the village. About 3 miles southwest, on the Hill o' Many Stanes (HS), are hundreds of small Bronze Age standing stones.

㉑ Wick

Wick consists largely of stone houses arranged according to a medieval street plan, most connected with the fishing trade that has been the community's mainstay. The origin of the town's name is Viking, vik denoting a sheltered bay or creek in Old Norse.

The heritage centre near the harbour includes a kippering shed and a fully functioning reconstructed lighthouse, while Old Wick Castle (HS), on a peninsula to the south, dates from the 12th century and is one of Scotland's oldest castles.

㉒ Castle Girnigoe and Castle Sinclair

Two magnificent ruined fortresses balance precariously on a cliff overlooking Sinclair's Bay. Built by the Sinclairs, Castle Girnigoe dates from the 15th century; Castle Sinclair was added in the early 17th century. Neighbouring Ackergill Tower, another of the Sinclair strongholds, is one of the oldest inhabited houses in the north of Scotland.

㉓ Keiss

A quayside warehouse built in 1831 was once a store for salt, barrels, nets and fish, and newly delivered catches were preserved in the nearby ice house. Crab fishing is now Keiss's main occupation.

Perched on the edge of a sheer cliff, 16th-century Keiss Castle, belonging like so many other properties in the area to the Sinclairs, was abandoned in 1755 in favour of a three-storey mansion, which you can see just behind the original; the mansion is not open to the public. A 3 mile beach edging Sinclair's Bay forms the most extensive stretch of sands on the Caithness coast.

The Northlands Viking Centre at Auckengill covers local history from prehistoric times through the Pictish era to the late Norse period and has a model of a Viking settlement.

㉔ Duncansby Head

The lighthouse on the headland guards the entrance to the Pentland Firth. A path from the car park, giving views of the chasms, arches and stacks carved out of the sandstone cliffs, descends to a shingle beach. At low tide it is possible to walk through a natural doorway in the rock towards Duncansby Stacks, remnants of an ancient cliff line eroded by the sea and rowdy with gannets, fulmars, skuas, guillemots and puffins.

㉕ John o' Groats

A jumble of houses, hotels and shops, John o' Groats is named after Jan de Groot, an immigrant Dutchman who was commissioned by James IV in 1496 to set up a ferry service between the mainland and Orkney. De Groot's original octagonal house is now no more than a grassy mound supporting a flagstaff, but there is still a passenger ferry service to South Ronaldsay in summer. Birdwatching trips round the coast are also available from the harbour.

The Last House in Scotland Museum exhibits local memorabilia and photographs of shipwrecks in the Pentland Firth, and has displays relating to life on the nearby island of Stroma.

㉖ Mey

A fearsome sight can be seen at the Men of Mey off St John's Point when the ebb tide throws gouts of roaring water 9 to 12m (30 to 40ft) high and blows spume far inland.

The Castle of Mey was built on the site of a stronghold of the Sinclairs in the 16th century. In 1952 it became a summer residence of the late Queen Elizabeth, the Queen Mother, and the castle and gardens are open in summer; in the village of Mey, the Castle Arms Hotel displays colour photographs of the Royal Family taken during visits to Caithness.

East of Mey, at Kirkstyle, is the Old Canisbay Kirk of St Drostan, whose oldest parts date from the 15th century. In the porch is a grave slab dedicated to the memory of members of the Groot, or Groat, family who gave their name to the settlement 2½ miles to the east.

㉗ Brough

Thrusting up from the centre of the cove is Little Clett, a rugged sea stack that is noisy with sea birds.

The pier in the rocky little bay, reached by a steep path from Brough village, was built in the early 19th century to serve boats taking supplies out to Dunnet Head and other isolated lighthouses. This task was superseded by helicopters until the lighthouses were automated.

㉘ Dunnet Bay

Standing more than 91m (300ft) above the sea, the head offers superb views, and gives you the feeling of being at the edge of the world. Marked by a lighthouse, the most northerly point on the British mainland is reached by a road from Dunnet which winds over the high moors.

You will find a natural history visitor centre at the northern end of Dunnet Bay; ranger-guided walks start at the centre and lead through the nearby forest, home to several species of butterfly. The walk continues through Dunnet Links Nature Reserve, where terns, gannets and auks can be seen. In Dunnet village, Mary-Ann's Cottage, named after a former occupant, shows life on an early croft, and is open to the public.

㉙ Castletown

In and round the small settlements of Scotland's northeastern tip, field walls and even the smallest garden are typically made of Caithness flagstones. During the 19th century the easily split sedimentary rock of the area provided paving material for towns and cities throughout Britain, and as far afield as Calcutta and Melbourne, until the development of cheaper concrete virtually destroyed the trade. Workings in Castletown have closed, but an industrial trail follows the course of a stone from quarry to shipment from the harbour. A heritage centre is being developed in phases.

㉚ Thurso

Oats and barley were shipped from the town as far back as the 13th century; later on, beef, hides, fish and timber were transported. In the 1950s the population more than trebled with the opening of Dounreay nuclear power station, 10 miles west. The decommissioning of the plant has made Thurso's future uncertain.

A statue in the main square commemorates Sir John Sinclair, a local landlord who played a major part in agricultural improvements in the 18th and 19th centuries, while the skeletal 13th-century Church of St Peter stands near the restored fishing quarter of Fisherbiggins, and a promenade has views north towards Orkney. Thurso Bay is often lively with windsurfers; east is the ruin of Thurso Castle, closed to the public.

DUNNET HEAD

The Highland brochs

The remains of stone towers, or brochs, can be seen in many parts of the Highlands. Built by Iron Age people between 500 BC and AD 100 to defend against rival tribes, each had just one small, easily defended entrance, so could be used as a refuge in times of trouble. The towers were circular and built at heights of 9m (30ft) or more, with walls as thick as 5m (18ft). Inside was a living area about 9m (30ft) across, in which timber partitions surrounded a central hearth.

③① Scrabster

Boats can be hired for sea anglers in search of shark, pollack, coalfish, skate and halibut at Scrabster's port, which was originally developed for the export of Caithness flagstones but today operates vehicle ferry services to Stromness on Orkney. There is also a modern fish market in the port. It was from Scrabster that Lord Kitchener set out during the First World War aboard the ill-fated HMS *Hampshire*, which sank off Orkney.

③② Crosskirk

This hamlet by a small pebbly bay is home to the 12th-century Chapel of St Mary, whose sturdy walls stand roofless. Its sloping jambs and doorway lintel, unfamiliar in the Highlands, probably owe much to the influence of the Orkney Norsemen, who also ruled this part of Scotland. Just south of the little church is an ancient well, and the nearby fields are dotted with the remains of cairns and brochs.

③③ Reay

In the 17th century, MacKay of Farr, clan chief and owner of vast tracts of mountains and deer forest in the area, took the village name and became Lord Reay. The village church, rebuilt in the 18th century after being buried by sand dunes for more than a century, still has the 'laird's loft'. Set into the wall of the chapel in the old burial ground is the Reay Stone, carved in relief with a cross and ornamental knot-work; it is probably 10th century. The church opens in summer to visitors.

The shoreline to the east is dominated by the metallic sphere of Dounreay nuclear power station, in the process of being decommissioned.

North of Reay is Sandside Bay, where an information panel by the car park tells of Pictish and Viking settlements lying buried deep beneath the shifting dunes. On the western side is the hamlet of Fresgoe, whose boats fish mainly for cod, coley and lobster. Each year some 2500 salmon are taken from the bay by dragnets.

③④ Melvich Bay

A profusion of tiny wild orchids in the grass can be seen on the clifftop walks here in early summer. The villages of Melvich and Portskerra run together above the dunes of a sandy bay and the Halladale River.

A footpath down to the neck of the strath faces the grey stone mansion of Bighouse, which was once home to a branch of the Clan MacKay.

③⑤ Strathy

Impressive cliffs offer views over miles of coastline from the lighthouse at Strathy Point. On a fine day you can see Cape Wrath to the west, Dunnet Head to the east, and the Orkney islands to the northeast. The headland is on the migration route of many bird species, including gannets, skuas and storm petrels.

③⑥ Bettyhill

Set on hummocks of rocky moorland, Bettyhill overlooks impressive sand dunes in Torrisdale Bay on one side, and Farr Bay on the other. Farr Bay is an expanse of unbroken golden sand that can be dizzying in bright sunshine, flanked by splintered rocks striped and inlaid with vivid colours and pastel shades.

The town developed largely as a result of the Highland Clearances. One theory attributes its name to Elizabeth, Countess of Sutherland and the wife of the Duke of Sutherland, some of whose tenants were resettled there after being evicted from the Strathnaver valley in the early 19th century; but older tradition tells of one Betty 'Cnocan' who ran an inn at the top of the cnoc, the Gaelic word for 'hill'.

The village's 18th-century church has become the Strathnaver Museum, with displays on the Clearances and the archaeological treasures of cairn, broch and abandoned clachans, or hamlets, a few miles to the south in Strathnaver. The museum retains the church's handsome pulpit and reader's desk, and has a room with mementos of the Clan MacKay. In the churchyard stands the Farr Stone, a 9th-century Celtic cross-slab with carved patterns on one side only – possibly because it was once set against a wall.

On the western side of the Naver estuary is the Invernaver National Nature Reserve, where rare mountain plants grow almost down to sea level. The entrance to the reserve is on its western side, from the road leading north to Skerray off the A836.

About 3 miles south of Bettyhill, along a minor road leading to Skelpick, are chambered cairns, a ruined broch and remains of a pre-Clearance village. A panel explains their history.

The nearby B871 runs along Strathnaver, nearly deserted save for salmon fishers.

③⑦ Tongue

This surprisingly wooded oasis in an otherwise bleak landscape is a good centre for hillwalking, and for fishing in Loch Loyal, 4 miles to the south. In the village is a white-harled, or roughcast, church built in the late 17th century and dedicated to St Andrew. The church has a 'laird's loft', or raised gallery where the laird and his family worshipped, and was once used by chiefs of the Clan MacKay, who dominated the area.

From the village a footpath leads to Castle Varrich, a roofless tower reputed to have been a Viking lookout but more likely to be of 14th-century origin.

About 8 miles east of Tongue is the Forestry Commission's Borgie Forest, a conifer plantation with woodland and riverside walks passing some of the tallest trees in Sutherland.

③⑧ Kyle of Tongue

Dun na Maigh, a broch whose remaining wall rises clear of tumbled stones, stands on a ridge at the southern end of the long inlet known as the Kyle of Tongue. The entrance of the broch leads to a crumbling stairway and an inner cell. From parking spaces on the causeway crossing the inlet, visitors can watch flocks of waders such as redshanks and herons.

The bleak moorland west and south of the Kyle of Tongue is dominated by the mass of Ben Hope and the shapely peaks of Ben Loyal.

③⑨ Talmine

Some crofting families evicted during the Highland Clearances were resettled here and managed to scrape a living by fishing and quarrying flagstones. The community survived for more than a century, but finally gave up the struggle against the inhospitable land. Holiday cottages have replaced the old crofts, looking out towards the uninhabited Rabbit Islands.

④⓪ Loch Eriboll

During the Second World War the deep loch, sheltered by steep hills, was an assembly point for North Atlantic convoys, whose crews dubbed it Loch 'Orrible. The small island in the middle was used as target practice by bombers assigned to destroy the German battleship *Tirpitz* in a Norwegian fjord of similar shape. At the end of the war, crews of German U-boats surrendered to the British Navy on Loch Eriboll.

On Ard Neackie, a rugged outcrop protruding into the east side of the loch, stand four massive limekilns built in 1870 and a crumbling pier, which once served a nearby quarry.

Choraidh Croft Farm Park at Laid, on the loch's western shore, is home to more than 30 breeds of rare and unusual farm animals, including Soay sheep from the Outer Hebrides.

④① Durness

The village stands on a limestone outcrop that supports richer grazing than the neighbouring moorlands. Outside the visitor centre, which houses the tourist information office, a geological display explains the region's rock formations. Inside, a mural painted by children depicts episodes from local history.

By the coast road east of the village, a curving flight of steps, followed by stepping stones, leads down to the vast Smoo Cave, whose name derives from the Norse word *smjuga*, meaning 'narrow cleft'. A wooden walkway extends into a second chamber, where the Allt Smoo burn falls 24m (80ft) from an opening in the roof. A third chamber is practically inaccessible by foot, but can be visited by boat trips in summer.

④② Balnakeil

At the southern end of the sandy bay, the ruin of a 17th-century church has a tombstone decorated with skull and crossbones built into a niche in a wall. It commemorates a highwayman said to have paid £1000 to be buried there, as protection against enemies who might desecrate a more exposed grave. In the churchyard is a monument to the Gaelic poet Rob Dorm Calder, whose works were published after his death with a foreword by Sir Walter Scott.

Military installations that once formed part of an early warning system have been transformed into Balnakeil Craft Village, where you can watch workers creating leather goods, ceramics and other products.

A 3 mile walk north through the 'Faraid Desert', a long stretch of dunes edging the eastern side of Balnakeil Bay, leads to the narrow headland of Faraid Head, home of nesting puffins and other sea birds.

> **Visitor information**
>
> **Dornoch, John o' Groats, Thurso, Wick,** all covered by **Visit Scotland** ☎ 0845 225 5121

ORKNEY AND SHETLAND

This is the place to get away from it all, with only a quarter or so of Orkney's 70 islands populated and Shetland lying over 100 miles from the north coast of Scotland

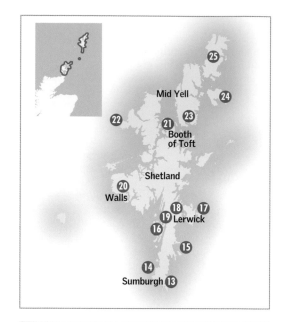

❶ South Ronaldsay
In a clifftop setting east of Burwick is the excavated Tomb of the Eagles, so called because of the sea eagles' talons found there among the human burials. The fishing township of St Margaret's Hope takes its name from seven-year-old Margaret, 'Maid of Norway', who died there on her way to marry the son of Edward I of England. The island's Smiddy Museum displays blacksmiths' metalwork.

❷ Hoy
Towering sandstone cliffs and a 137m (450ft) sea stack known as the Old Man of Hoy, greet travellers passing the island by ferry from Scrabster. Reached by a 2 mile footpath from Rackwick, the stack is within the North Hoy RSPB Reserve, notable for its spectacular high cliffs and heather moorlands, and rare red-throated divers can be seen there in summer. Hoy is also distinctive for its myriad wild flowers that grow at low altitudes. The Dwarfie Stane (HS), a tomb carved from a sandstone block around 3000 BC, stands beside the road to Rackwick, while Lyness Naval Cemetery and Interpretation Centre recall events on Hoy during two world wars.

❸ Scapa Flow
The great natural harbour was a British naval base during both world wars. Sunken German warships, scuttled there in 1919, are explored by diving enthusiasts. Early in the Second World War a German U-boat torpedoed HMS *Royal Oak* at anchor in Scapa Flow, and a large buoy marks as an official war grave the point where the vessel sank. The attack prompted Winston Churchill to order the building of concrete barriers to block the eastern approaches; a causeway constructed across the barriers now links three islands to Mainland.

During the Second World War, prisoners of war converted Nissen huts on Lamb Holm into a place of worship, with medieval-style wall paintings. Today most ships here are oil tankers serving the terminal on the island of Flotta.

❹ Kirkwall
The 'capital' of Orkney's most impressive building is the Cathedral of St Magnus, dedicated to an 11th-century earl canonised after his murder. During rebuilding work, an ancient skeleton was found with an axe cleft in its skull; the injury matched that from which the earl is believed to have died. The Bishop's Palace (HS) was founded around the same time as the cathedral, while neighbouring Earl's Palace (HS) is a fine example of a French Renaissance-style building. Tankerness House museum has displays of Orkney life, and a wireless museum covers military communications from 1930.

❺ Stromness
Most of the harbourside houses here have jetties and moorings for small boats. A plaque beside Login's Well recalls that for over 200 years this port was the last watering place

for vessels of the Hudson's Bay Company, who traded in fur with Native North Americans. Captain Cook's ships *Resolution* and *Discovery* made their first British landfall here after his death, and the ill-fated Franklin expedition in search of the Northwest Passage set out from the port in 1845.

Stromness Museum has displays of these and other historical records, while the Pier Arts Centre has a collection of 20th-century British art. Sea-angling trips operate to Scapa Flow or the Pentland Firth.

❻ Skara Brae

For centuries the 4500-year-old village of Skara Brae (HS) was buried beneath dunes until it re-emerged during a storm in 1850. Sand had preserved the walls of stone houses and their domestic furniture, including food boxes lined with clay to act as refrigerators. There are even what appear to have been lavatories. The village was home to people whose way of life was more sophisticated than that of many 19th century crofters.

❼ Loch of Harray

Standing on the southern edge of the loch are the Stones of Stenness (HS), a 3rd-century BC stone circle of which only four monoliths survive. The nearby Ring of Brodgar (HS) is a wider circle of 27 stones. Orkney's largest freshwater loch, Loch of Harray offers plentiful fishing for brown trout.

To the southeast is Maes Howe (HS), a huge cairn with the world's largest collection of runic inscriptions in one place. Corrigall Farm Museum, off the A986, re-creates an 18th-century farmstead.

❽ Brough of Birsay

During spring the Brough of Birsay (HS) is aglow with sea pinks. Reached by a causeway at low tide, it offers many historical remains, including Pictish and Viking farmsteads, and a 12th-century Romanesque church, while the 16th-century Earl's Palace (HS) in Birsay village was built in Renaissance style. Birsay Moors and Marwick Head are two of several RSPB reserves on Mainland.

❾ Rousay, Egilsay and Wyre

These three neighbouring islands offer a wealth of ancient sites which are managed by Historic Scotland, like many others in Orkney. Dominating Egilsay is the 12th-century round-towered church dedicated to St Magnus, who was martyred nearby, while on Wyre is the castle of Cubbie Roo, a 12th-century Norse chieftain.

Along the southern shore of Rousay, the Westness Walk leads from the huge Mid Howe

Broch to a chambered cairn known as 'The Great Ship of Death'. The shell of a church, together with Norse antiquities, including a cemetery and longhouses, have been uncovered. Sea birds and seals inhabit the Bay of Swandro.

A vehicle ferry from Dingwall on the mainland links the three islands.

❿ Sanday

Seals can be seen basking on the skerries, or rocky isles, around the southern tip of this island of shining beaches. At Northwall, waders and ducks are joined in winter by whooper swans and goldeneyes.

Many human societies have also flourished on Sanday. Tofts Ness has a prehistoric complex of 500 burial mounds, while Quoyness (HS) is a chambered tomb dating from 2000 BC. There are Viking graves by the Ness of Brough, and the ruined Cross Kirk stands on the site of another Viking settlement.

⓫ Westray

The heavily fortified Noltland Castle (HS) was built by Gilbert Balfour, who was implicated in the murder of Lord Darnley, husband of Mary, Queen of Scots. He was forced to flee the country, only to be executed in Stockholm in 1576 for plotting against the Swedish king. The name of Noltland Castle is derived from the Old Norse word for 'cattle land', evidence that farmsteads have occupied this fertile island for many centuries.

Neighbouring Papa Westray is called after the 'Papae', Celtic priests who once lived there. Its North Hill RSPB Reserve, together with the surrounding maritime heath and dunes, supports an abundance of wild flowers and is visited by ducks, cormorants, Arctic skuas and Arctic terns. Knap of Howar (HS), a prehistoric two-roomed farmhouse, is considered to be the oldest preserved dwelling in north-western Europe.

⓬ North Ronaldsay

The sheep which populate Orkney's northernmost island feed on seaweed instead of grass; the flat cultivated land is protected from the depredations of these animals by an enclosing stone dyke. Near a broch, to the south, are the remains of an ancient dyke, a forerunner of the present one.

⓭ Sumburgh

South of the village lies Jarlshof, one of Britain's most remarkable archaeological sites. Trim, grassy mounds, walls, doors, hearths and passageways are the remains of 3000 years of settlement, from the Stone Age through the Bronze and Iron Ages to Viking times. The interpretation centre shows finds excavated at Jarlshof. At Boddam, to the north, is a 19th-century croft house restored as a museum. At Sumburgh Head sea birds roost by the thousand, and seals clamber on and off the rocks below. To the west lies the sandy Bay of Quendale, and beyond towers a 274m (900ft) hill, Fitful Head. An arduous walk leads to a radar dome at the summit, from where there are magnificent views over Mainland's cliffs, inlets and rolling inland hills. Nearby is the Loch of Spiggie RSPB Reserve, an important winter wildfowl refuge.

⑭ St Ninian's Isle
Despite its name, St Ninian's is not an island, but is linked to Mainland by a narrow isthmus formed by two beaches of pure sand back to back. On the hillside facing Mainland are the remains of a 12th-century chapel. There, in 1958, archaeologists found 27 Celtic silver pieces dating from around AD 800. Replicas of the coins can be seen at the Shetland Museum in Lerwick.

⑮ Mousa
The most complete example of an Iron Age broch can be found on this small uninhabited island, which is reached by boat from Sandwick. The tower rises 13m (43ft) on walls that are 4m (12ft) thick at the base. Inside, a clan of Picts constructed a 'wheelhouse' of thatched wooden rooms set in a circle.

⑯ East and West Burra
The road to these islands leads south from Scalloway over a narrow causeway and provides dramatic views of Clift Hills on Mainland. Hamnavoe, a small fishing village, is the islands' principal community. In good weather there are views of the spectacular cliffs of Foula, 24 miles to the west, and its 418m (1370ft) summit, The Sneug. An air service to Foula operates from Tingwall, and passenger ferries leave from Walls.

⑰ Isle of Noss
The uninhabited island, a national nature reserve, is one of Europe's greatest sea-bird colonies. In the course of a walk around the small island, taking 2 to 3 hours, visitors can see eider ducks, Arctic terns and great skuas, and ledges provide nesting sites for gannets, kittiwakes and guillemots. The walk also includes the 181m (594ft) Noup of Noss cliff.

⑱ Lerwick
Every January, a replica of a Viking longship is paraded and ceremonially burned as a prelude to a night of revelry as part of the festival of 'Up Helly Aa', adapted from a Norse feast called Uphalliday. These traditions in Shetland reveal the traces of Norse settlement between the 9th and 15th centuries.

Shetland's capital, and the islands' only town, was a Dutch settlement in the 17th century. It became a thriving fishing port after Fort Charlotte was founded in 1653 to exploit the military potential of Bressay Sound. The oil boom of the 1970s brought dramatic growth, but the old town along the waterfront is intact.

On an islet in the Loch of Clickimin, are the remains of a broch dating from the 4th century BC, which can be reached by a causeway. The new Shetland Museum on the waterfront in Lerwick contains replicas of Celtic silver treasures and Norse artefacts. The tourist centre issues permits for inland fishing, and you can also hire boats for sea angling.

⑲ Scalloway
The former capital of Shetland is dominated by the towering, gaunt ruin of a castle built in 1600 by Earl Patrick Stewart, who forcibly replaced Norse law by Scottish feudal law. The key to the castle is available from a local shop on weekdays and the Royal Hotel on Sundays.

Close to the castle is the harbour, busy with fishing vessels. During the Second World War, Scalloway was the main base for Norwegian patriots who smuggled saboteurs in and refugees out of their homeland, in an operation known as 'the Shetland Bus'.

⑳ Walls
Set by a fine natural harbour visited by pleasure craft in summer, the village of Walls is western Mainland's principal settlement. The A971 from Lerwick cuts through moorland inhabited by sheep and dotted with inland lochs, and the coast is reached by minor roads, such as the B9071, which heads south, passing a beach of red sand at Reawick before ending by granite cliffs around Westerwick. Towards Sandness is fertile crofting land.

The area offers good walking, trout fishing and birdwatching.

㉑ Sullom Voe
In this deep, ice-scoured fjord, or 'voe' in the Shetland dialect, is one of the largest oil and liquefied gas terminals in Europe. Pipelines from the East Shetlands Basin, emerging from the ocean 2 miles away across a peninsula, deliver oil to huge tanks, ready for transfer to tankers in the voe. Seals and otters can often be seen.

㉒ Esha Ness
Fulmars soar over the ragged cliffs, and puffins burrow in the soil below on this headland, one of Shetland's many startling

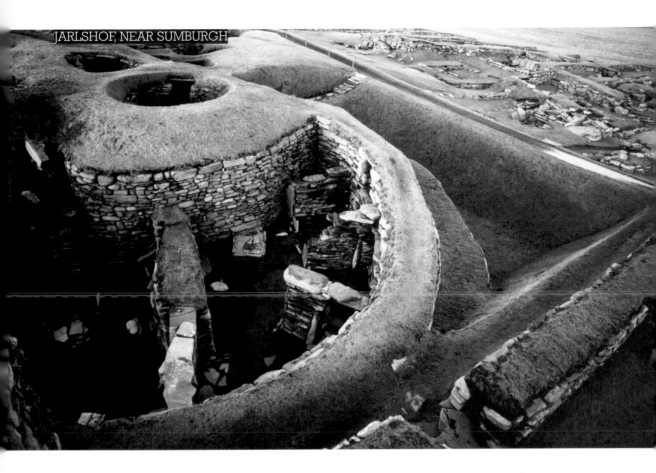

clifftop viewpoints, and one of the few accessible by car. The road leads to a lighthouse and car park over a high, barren, peat plain strewn with lava boulders.

North of the lighthouse are the Holes of Scraada, a series of blowholes that have been carved out of the cliffs by the sea. You can take fine walks over the springy turf here. Ronas Hill, 7 miles to the northeast, is Mainland's highest point at 450m (1475ft).

㉓ Yell
On the second largest island in Shetland, rolling peat hills are speckled with lochs and surrounded by cliffs. West Sandwick, however, has a fine sandy beach, and 3 miles north is Whale Firth, which has shingle beaches.

The Lumbister RSPB Reserve, set amid moorland, has a thriving otter population. Frequent car ferries link Mainland to Yell, and Yell to Fetlar and Unst.

㉔ Fetlar
The island is well known to ornithologists, particularly for its Arctic and great skuas and storm petrels. In 1967 a pair of snowy owls began to breed there, an event that caused a large part of Fetlar to be declared an RSPB reserve. In 1975 the only male vanished, and there are now no resident owls. Otters, common seals and grey seals abound, however.

Fetlar's Interpretive Centre, in Houbie, the island's main settlement, contains items relating to local social and natural heritage.

㉕ Unst
A place of screes and stony outcrops, Britain's northernmost island also has the densest population of Shetland ponies. In the southeast stand the ruins of 16th-century Muness Castle, while at the island's northern tip is the Hermaness National Nature Reserve. The cliff ledges are crowded with guillemots and razorbills, and wheeling above are kittiwakes and fulmars.

> **Visitor information**
>
> **Kirkwall** ☎ (01856) 872856
> **Lerwick** ☎ (01595) 693434
> **Stromness** ☎ (01856) 850716

SCOTLAND
Orkney and Shetland

CAPE WRATH TO MINGULAY

From wild and raging Cape Wrath to the poetic island of Mingulay, the northwest corner of Britain boasts a diverse geography and a rich historical past

Isle of Lewis

0   5 Miles

Scourie

Ullapool

Gairloch

Skye

Kyle of Lochalsh

North Uist

South Uist

Barra

① Cape Wrath
The lighthouse, built here on mainland Scotland's northwestern tip in 1828, crowns a windswept headland battered by raging seas; to the east, the highest cliffs on the British mainland rise to 280m (920ft) at Clò Mor.

Cape Wrath can be reached by a passenger ferry across the Kyle of Durness and then a track crossing The Parbh, a huge wilderness. In summer a minibus takes visitors along the 10 mile route. The cliffs and track lie within a Ministry of Defence bombing range, and walkers should check on restrictions.

② Sandwood Bay
A mile-long stretch of sands backed by rolling dunes makes Sandwood Bay one of the finest beaches in Britain. Its unspoiled nature owes much to its remoteness: the track from Blairmore is impassable to cars, and it is a 4 mile walk across the deserted peat and heather. On the southern edge, a finger of rock known as Am Buachaille rises sheer out of the sea.

③ Kinlochbervie
The small village of Kinlochbervie has an impressive modern harbour and is one of Scotland's most important fishing ports. To the north, at Oldshoremore and Oldshore Beg, wide sandy bays are backed by rolling grassland, with stunning views along the coast.

④ Handa Island
Some 30 species of birds, including puffins and guillemots, nest on this uninhabited cliff-girt sanctuary. A summer ferry from Tarbet crosses to Handa, and a bothy, or hut, is available for overnight accommodation. From Fanagmore, north of Tarbet, short boat trips explore the islands and seal colonies of Loch Laxford, which is also noted for its salmon.

⑤ Scourie
A sandy beach, hotels and a campsite make this village an attractive centre for visitors in an otherwise sparsely populated area. You can explore the wild and rocky shoreline on foot or by boat trip from the harbour, and there is trout fishing nearby. In Loch a'Mhuilinn National Nature Reserve, to the south, woods of rowan, birch and oak slope down to the shore.

⑥ Kylesku
The bridge across the narrows of Loch a' Chairn Bhain is a good place from which to appreciate an immense landscape of lochs and mountains. During the Second World War this was a training area for midget submarines.

In summer, there are boat trips to the spectacular waterfall of Eas a Chùal Aluinn, the highest in Britain with a 198m (650ft) drop.

⑦ North Assynt

A narrow road follows the spectacular coastline of Assynt, an area of low hillocks dotted with numerous lochs and lochans. West of the pink sands of Clashnessie Bay, a lane leads to the Stoer lighthouse; climbers swim out 46m (50yd) laden with their kit to scale the Old Man of Stoer, a 60m (200ft) sandstone pinnacle.

Along the peninsula's southern shore are fine sands at Clachtoll and Achmelvich. Unusually for a Highland estate, North Assynt is owned by local crofters and run as a cooperative enterprise.

⑧ Lochinver

The heart of Assynt's largest village is its modern fishing harbour, and boats from as far afield as France regularly land their catches at Lochinver for sale at the evening fish market. There are craft shops and a visitor centre in the village, while at Baddidarach, on the loch's northern shore, you will find a pottery.

A path runs beside the River Inver, noted for its angling; the track up Glen Canisp is a starting point for climbers planning an assault on Suilven, one of Sutherland's most dramatic mountains.

⑨ Inverpolly

Mountain wilderness and lochs stretching to the sea make up Inverpolly National Nature Reserve. The sandstone peaks of Cùl Mor, Cùl Beag and Stac Pollaidh offer a challenge to walkers and rock climbers.

From Knockan Visitor Centre, trails explore the diverse habitats of the reserve and the complexities of its geology, and nearby is Knockan Cliff, a site that revolutionised Victorian ideas of how mountain ranges were formed. To the north, at Elphin, Highland cattle are some of the traditional farming animals at the Highland and Rare Breeds Farm.

⑩ Enard Bay

The 'Mad Road of Sutherland', following the coast south of Lochinver, offers views that are as breathtaking as many of its bends. From Inverkirkaig, a crofting village on a sand-and-shingle bay, a walk follows the river to the Falls of Kirkaig and the wild slopes of Suilven. The little road meanders on through woods and mountain glens until, beyond the River Polly, it enters barren moorland.

By Achnahaird, along the south shore of Enard Bay, lies a huge sandy beach in a sheltered inlet.

⑪ Achiltibuie

Fishing nets hang out to dry along the shore at Achiltibuie, the largest of a string of crofting 'townships' that overlook the uninhabited Summer Isles. In the village is an experimental indoor garden, the Hydroponicum, where vegetables and flowers are grown without soil. You can take cruises round the islands and deep-sea angling trips from the pier, situated about a mile north of the village. Farther north is the secluded harbour of Old Dornie.

The road leading south from Achiltibuie peters out at Culnacraig, where the shore is dominated by the towering peak of Ben Mór Coigach.

ENARD BAY

⑫ Ullapool

Shops and whitewashed cottages overlook Loch Broom in this lively little harbour town, established in 1788 as a herring port and curing station. Despite a major slump in the herring industry, fishing still continues here, and in winter factory ships from eastern Europe anchor in Loch Broom to buy the local catch.

A car ferry to Lewis keeps the harbour busy, and there are local cruises and sea-angling trips. Ullapool Museum, housed in the old parish church, has displays relating to local history.

⑬ Little Loch Broom

The massive crags of An Teallach tower above the loch's southern shore. One of many walks in the area starts from the hamlet of Ardessie and passes a series of waterfalls as it follows the course of a mountain stream.

About 2 miles southeast of Dundonnell, a narrow lane climbs north through a wooded glen before continuing through barren hills. From the road's end, 6 miles away at the small village of Badrallach, a path leads to Scoraig, an 'alternative' community that relies on wind turbines for its power supply.

The frequency of the passenger service from Scoraig to Badluarach varies from once a day to once a week, depending on the time of year.

⑭ Gruinard Bay

A sweep of coves and sandy beaches, and a horizon of entrancing beauty, can be enjoyed from a viewpoint on Gruinard Hill. The largest beach, on the southern side of the bay, has pink sands formed of red sandstone. The sheltered waters are home to colonies of black-throated divers, and are sometimes frequented by porpoises. In the middle of the bay is Gruinard Island, used for experiments in germ warfare during the Second World War, when it was contaminated with anthrax. The island is now considered safe, but it is privately owned.

At Laide, on the bay's western shore, is a tiny ruined chapel said to have been founded by St Columba in the 7th century; the present building dates from the early 18th century. Nearby is a cave that was long used as a place of worship.

A minor road from Laide leads north to a wide beach of pure white sands at Mellon Udrigle, and halfway between Laide and Mellon Udrigle, by Loch na Beiste, a track heads west for 3 miles to the ruined village of Slaggan.

⑮ Inverewe Garden

In 1861 Osgood Mackenzie inherited the Inverewe estate, then a barren wilderness, and turned it into a subtropical Eden. Taking advantage of the North Atlantic Drift which

A WILDERNESS OF SAVAGE SPLENDOUR
TORRIDON

gives the northwest coast of Scotland its mild, humid weather, Mackenzie planted trees as shelter-belts against the prevailing winds, improved the soil, and over the next 60 years created an internationally renowned environment in which subtropical plants could flourish. The gardens, now owned by the National Trust for Scotland, are crisscrossed by a maze of paths that meander through woodland, shrubberies and water gardens. They are most colourful in spring and early summer when the rhododendrons and azaleas are in flower but autumn brings an equally dazzling display.

⑯ Gairloch
The romantic scenery here was much admired by the Victorians, who travelled to the fashionable resort by steamer. Overlooked by a golf course is a long, sheltered sandy beach, and pleasure cruises and sea-angling trips leave from the pier. The Gairloch Heritage Museum has an excellent local history collection.

⑰ Redpoint
From the hamlet of Redpoint there are spectacular views across to Skye and Lewis. A footpath to the south of the car park in Redpoint passes magnificent sands before continuing for about 9 miles along the coast to Diabaig. Redpoint is about 2 miles south of Gairloch along a minor road which passes through woodland glens and a tranquil anchorage at Badachro where small boats can be hired.

⑱ Diabaig
This village has a pretty harbour on a bay enclosed within a natural amphitheatre of enormous hills. The narrow road to Torridon twists through hairpin bends said to be the steepest in Britain as it climbs the exposed Pass of the Winds, a glacial desolation of moorland and scoured rock.

⑲ Torridon
A wilderness of savage splendour, dominated by the massive quartz-capped peaks of Liathach, Beinn Alligin and Beinn Dearg, rises behind a scattered lochside village. The Countryside Centre at Torridon estate (NTS) has information on the region's walks and natural history, and you can view tame red deer in enclosures at the nearby Deer Museum.

About 2 miles west of the village, on the north shore of Upper Loch Torridon, a waterfall is the starting point for several waymarked hill walks. A short distance to the west is the former fishing harbour of Inveralligin.

⑳ Applecross

The coast road from Shieldaig to Applecross begins with splendid views across the loch to Torridon's spectacular mountains, composed of sandstone that, at more than 600 million years old, is among the oldest in the world. Crofts strung along the peninsula's western shore were extraordinarily remote until the road was built in the 1970s.

The little village is set on a sheltered bay, and wooded hills make it a haven in a bleak environment. The road east out of Applecross climbs into the lunar landscape of the 610m (2000ft) high Bealach na Bà, or Pass of the Cattle, where there can be blizzards even in midsummer. Following the hairpin bends that twist down to Loch Kishorn can be a memorable and challenging experience.

㉑ Loch Carron

The landscape of sheltered Loch Carron is welcoming and gentle, with rose bushes by the cottages along its shore, in contrast to the wilds of Applecross. The yard on nearby Loch Kishorn where oil rig platforms were once constructed closed in 1987, and Lochcarron village now relies for its income on visitors attracted by the tranquil loch. The Smithy Heritage Centre has a local history section.

South of the village are the ruins of Strome Castle (NTS), a MacDonald stronghold destroyed by the MacKenzies in 1602.

㉒ Plockton

Palm trees line the waterfront of this delightful village, a favoured haunt of artists, naturalists and sailors. You can hire small boats or take a trip to see the seal colonies on islands round the rocky headland. Pine martens and golden eagles can be spotted in the woods and hills to the south of Plockton, and to the east Craig Highland Farm has rare breeds of domestic animals.

㉓ Kyle of Lochalsh

A ferry point before the Skye bridge spanned Kyle Akin, the bustling little town has the air of a place of transit. The Lochalsh Woodland Garden (NTS) at Balmacara has exotic shrubs planted beneath magnificent old trees, and inland are several woodland walks.

㉔ Butt of Lewis

The northern tip of Lewis is a windswept spot, exposed to the unleashed power of the waves. Some 45 miles north is the island nature reserve of North Rona and beyond are the Faeroes; to the east, the seas rage around Cape Wrath on Scotland's north-western tip; and 3000 miles due west lies northern Newfoundland and the entrance to Hudson Bay.

In Eoropaidh, the island's northernmost village, is the 12th-century St Moluag's Chapel, built on the site of an earlier chapel. From nearby Port of Ness, where there is a sandy beach, each September the men of the parish sail to the island of Sulisgeir, 30 miles to the north, to harvest the young 'gugas', or gannets, which are a local delicacy.

In the village of Siadar, 10 miles to the south-west, are the ruins of Teampull Pheadair, a 12th-century chapel, the Steinacleit stone circle and the vast monolith of Clach an Trushal.

㉕ Arnol

The Blackhouse Museum at Arnol is the best example in the Hebrides of this traditional form of building, giving a picture of life in these thatched homes with stone walls up to 2m (6ft) thick. The house had no chimney, and the smoke from the peat fire in the centre of the floor stained everything a rich black. Straw mattresses in the box beds, the kettle hanging on a hook above the flames, and the neat crockery on the wooden dresser are all as they were when the house was last lived in, in the 1960s.

At Bragar to the west, a whale's jawbone, from an animal killed around 1920, arches over an otherwise humble gateway, and in nearby Siabost, a crofting museum displays traditional agricultural, fishing and domestic equipment.

To the southwest of Arnol, lanes lead off the coast road to Dalbeg and Dalmore bays, where Atlantic rollers crash between jagged rocky headlands onto wide sweeps of sand.

㉖ Carloway Broch

The Iron Age broch, or fortified tower, standing on a crag by the hamlet of Dun Charlabhaigh is a testament to the skills of its masons. Some 2000 years after they were erected, the dry-stone walls are still 9m (30ft) high in some places. The central courtyard is 8m (25ft) across and surrounded by double walls containing galleries, chambers and flights of stairs. In nearby Garenin, a traditional thatched 'blackhouse' is now a renovated hostel.

㉗ Stornoway

The fishing port, ferry terminal and market town retains a gentle air, despite the fact that car ownership per head on this island of scattered settlements is among Europe's highest, and a large percentage of the Lewis and Harris population of 20,000 comes here to work.

Stornoway's architecture recalls the boom days of the late 19th century; a grandiose Edwardian town hall and wide avenues of imposing villas speak of more affluent times, when a herring fleet crammed into the harbour. Close to the town centre, Museum Nan Eilean mounts varied exhibitions on the history of the Western Isles.

A small river feeds into the harbour mouth, and standing on its western bank is the mock-Tudor Lews Castle, built in the 1840s by the business magnate Sir James Matheson. Matheson spent a fortune on schools and new industries, but the islanders were resistant to his plans and the enterprise failed. In 1918, the industrialist Lord Leverhulme bought the estate and tried to transform Stornoway into a great fishing port, but he met with indifference, and departed for Harris.

East of Stornoway, the road leads over the isthmus to the Eye Peninsula, passing the derelict 14th-century St Columba's Church and the graveyard of Ui, where 19 MacLeod chieftains are buried. From the Tiumpan Head lighthouse at the tip of the peninsula, you can sometimes see basking sharks and whales.

㉘ Callanish Stones

The standing stones outside the hamlet of Callanish rival those of Stonehenge and Carnac in the majesty of their setting – and in their inscrutability. Standing some 6m (20ft) high on a hill above East Loch Roag, the

Callanish Stones (HS) were quarried locally and erected about 4000 years ago in roughly the form of a Celtic cross, with a chambered cairn in the centre. Their meaning will probably never be known, but they appear to have astronomical significance and they align with other standing stones and circles in the area.

South of Callanish, the B8011 runs through rugged, near-deserted terrain. Where the road bends sharply round the tip of narrow Little Loch Roag, a rough and often muddy 2½ mile path leads to the remains of a group of curious 'beehive' dwellings, a rare example of a primitive Hebridean form of housing in which stones were positioned to form a hollow hillock about 2m (6ft) high. Continuing on are the sandy beach of Uig Sands, where in 1832 a set of Norse chess pieces were discovered in the dunes.

㉙ Hushinish

In early summer the machair, the sandy lowlands unique to the western coasts of the Hebrides, is covered in flowers. The Hushinish beaches and machair are reached by a rollercoaster road which runs west through North Harris by the southern foothills of Clisham, at 804m (2637ft) the highest peak in the Outer Hebrides, past the remains of an old whaling station at Bun Abhainn Eadar and the privately owned castle at Abhainn Suidhe, pronounced 'Avinsooi'. Across a narrow but treacherous stretch of water from Hushinish lies uninhabited Scarp Island.

㉚ Tarbert

Harris's capital is only a village but its ferry terminal, bank, shops and hotels give it the feel of a small town. The island has just one road, and the lighthouse at Eilan Glas can be reached only on foot. To the east lies the island of Scalpay, now linked to Harris by a bridge.

South of Tarbert, the narrow road runs round the inlets and sea lochs of South Harris's bare and rocky eastern coast, winding in and out of fishing villages where vegetables are still grown in 'lazy beds' – plots of earth created by hand, out of peat, manure, rotting seaweed and sand.

By contrast, the west coast of Harris is a fertile expanse of machair, stretching between the breathtaking sandy beaches of Tràigh Losgaintir and Tràigh Sgarasta.

㉛ Rodel

The handsome little port at the very tip of South Harris is home to the finest example of ecclesiastical architecture in the Hebrides. Its small Church of St Clement, built by the MacLeods of Dunvegan in the 16th century, contains three monuments to the family. The finest, carved in sparkling black local gneiss, shows the eighth chieftain, Alastair Crotach.

㉜ North Uist

Ferries from Skye or Harris weave through a jumble of islands and headlands on their approach to Lochmaddy, the 'capital' of North Uist. A few yards from the ferry pier is the island's main hotel, and the nearby outdoor centre is often busy with walkers, climbers, sailors and divers. In the east of the island, where there is more water than land, hundreds of freshwater and saltwater lochs teem with trout.

Prehistoric remains abound on North Uist, as they do throughout this chain of islands. Three miles northwest of Lochmaddy, and half a mile from the road, is a group of stones called Na Fir Bhreige, or 'The False Men' – according to one legend, they are wife-deserters turned to stone.

Evidence of continuous occupation of the island from the Bronze Age has been discovered on the sandy peninsula of Machair Leathann in the northwest; Dun an Sticar, a small Iron Age fortress near Newton Ferry, is known to have been lived in until 1602. Bernerary can be reached by a causeway where a ferry crosses to Leverburgh on Harris.

The elusive corncrake and the rare red-necked phalarope are among the numerous birds you can see at the Balranald RSPB Reserve; a nature trail starts from the visitor centre at Hougharry.

Near Carinish are the impressive remains of the 13th-century Teampull na Trionaid, or Trinity Temple, where the sons of medieval chieftains were educated. North of Clachan-a-Luib, just off the A867, is the 5000-year-old chambered cairn of Barpa Langass, which contains a large burial vault. Otter-watching tours are run from Langass Lodge Hotel.

㉝ Benbecula

On the southern slopes of Rueval is reputed to be Prince Charlie's Cave, where Charles Edward Stuart managed to hide himself before fleeing to Skye, on June 28, 1746, with Flora MacDonald, disguised as her Irish maid.

Causeways link the Uists to Benbecula, which is dominated by the army rocket range headquarters, RAF base and airport at Balivanich, both socially and economically. However, crofting and fishing activities continue to occupy many of the island's inhabitants, and there is a flourishing crafts industry.

The vast community school at Liniclate houses a library, a museum, a restaurant and a theatre, as well as a swimming pool and sports centre, all of which are open to visitors.

㉞ South Uist

On a hill beside the main road near West Gerinish is the 9m (30ft) granite statue of Our Lady of the Isles, by Hew Lorimer, erected in 1957. She and the infant Jesus gaze over a rocket range, where test missiles are fired towards the Atlantic and tracked by a base on St Kilda, 45 miles to the west. Small shrines, statues and votive offerings are scattered throughout the island which is Catholic, unlike most of the Western Isles.

The west coast of South Uist is a 20 mile beach broken only by a few rocky headlands, while the east is riven by deep fiords and lochs. One of the largest, freshwater Loch Bee, almost bisects the island and is famed for its mute swans. Loch Druidibeg National Nature Reserve is a breeding ground for greylag geese, and a sanctuary for other birds, including corncrakes.

Down a footpath behind a house on the main road north of Mingary a cairn marks the birthplace of Flora MacDonald, and nearby is the Kildonan School Museum, containing local artefacts and archaeological finds.

Lochboisdale is the main settlement and ferry port of South Uist.

㉟ Eriskay

The fishermen, crofters and seafarers of Eriskay are renowned for their poetry and songs. Now linked to South Uist by a causeway, this romantic island is famed for its beauty, for the haunting 'Eriskay Love Lilt', and for the farcical 'Whisky Galore' episode. In 1941 the SS *Politician*, bound for New York with 243,000 bottles of whisky, foundered in the shallow sea north of Eriskay. Most of the cargo was salvaged by locals, to be drunk, fed to livestock and used to light fires. Sir Compton Mackenzie's book on the incident was filmed on Barra.

㊱ Barra

The strange charm of Barra immediately strikes visitors who fly here and land, tides permitting, not on a runway but on an immense beach of firm white sand.

The 14 mile road encircling much of this strikingly beautiful island makes it easy to explore. Several side roads wander off to the bays and beaches or into green glens beneath the central hills.

At Cille-bharra, is the 12th-century Church of St Barr, where a restored chapel contains a replica of a unique grave slab featuring both Norse runic markings and a Celtic cross. Sir Compton Mackenzie is buried there.

The main town and ferry port of Castlebay in the south is dominated by Kisimul Castle, which rises straight out of the waters of the bay. This is the home of the MacNeil of Barra, whose forebears were the terror of the western seas for hundreds of years until the 16th century. When they had dined, a bard would announce from the battlements: 'The MacNeil has supped; now the princes of the world may sit down to eat.' There are guided tours of the castle in summer.

On the steep slopes of Heaval is a statue of the Madonna and Child, on a site offering spectacular views over the bay and beyond to Vatersay, Sandray, Pabbay, Mingulay and Berneray.

With a healthy income derived from tourism, fishing and seafood-processing, Barra is one of the most prosperous communities in the Western Isles. Perfume is also made on the island, and shell grit is supplied for masonry paint. A children's festival is held here every July.

㊲ Vatersay

On the dunes in the 'waist' of the island stands a monument recording the tragedy of the *Annie Jane*. The ship was taking victims of the Highland Clearances to America when it was swept onto the surrounding rocks and all its passengers killed.

The island is now linked to Barra by a causeway, making it easier for the inhabitants to get to and from the 'mainland', but leading to some loss of its independent character.

In 1908 a group of landless men from Barra 'raided' the island, trusting in the old custom that anyone building a home and lighting a fire in it all in a day was entitled to tenure. The owner, Lady Cathcart, had ten of them put in prison, but the national outcry led to their release, and a year later the Congested Districts Board bought the island and divided it among the raiders.

㊳ Mingulay

Sailors used to sing the shanty 'Homeward Bound for Mingulay', but the only inhabitants of the island today are sea birds, seals and rabbits. Natural historians, artists and birdwatchers delight in the rugged surroundings, bordered on the western side by sheer 229m (750ft) cliffs, but the locals on Barra talk of ghosts rising from the moor of Macphee's Hill, and the abandoned village in the east bay is an eerie spot.

Boat trips to Mingulay and to Berneray can be arranged from Castlebay harbour on Barra.

Visitor information

Castlebay ☎ (01871) 810336
Gairloch – Visit Scotland ☎ 0845 225 5121
Kyle of Lochalsh – Visit Scotland
  ☎ 0845 225 5121
Lochboisdale ☎ (01878) 700286
Lochinver ☎ (01571) 844330
Lochmaddy ☎ (01876) 500321
Stornoway ☎ (01851) 703088
Tarbert ☎ (01859) 502011

SKYE TO MULL

Scotland's western coast is a treasure trove of islands, from the dark peaks of Skye to cheerful, colourful Mull, and the many fascinating little isles in between, not least Staffa, site of the amazing Fingal's Cave

❶ Kylerhea

In summer Kylerhea is linked to Glenelg on the mainland by a romantic and exciting journey on a six-car ferry with one ramp, whose deck revolves to allow cars to disembark. The 5 minute trip is often made across a fierce tidal flow that sweeps the ferry down the narrows like a twig in a stream. Incredibly, cattle were once swum across these straits.

Just north of the ferry is the Kylerhea Otter Haven, where a hide allows you to watch eagles, falcons, buzzards, herons, seals and a huge variety of sea birds, as well as otters.

❷ Kyleakin

For almost a century the landing point for the Kyle of Lochalsh ferry, the fishing village of Kyleakin is now bypassed by a bridge half a mile to the north. The bridge leapfrogs Eilean Ban, the lighthouse island where the author Gavin Maxwell lived for a year before his death in 1969.

Watching over the bay is the ruin of 15th-century Castle Moil, said to have been built by a Norwegian princess called Saucy Mary who ran a chain across the straits to sink any ship failing to pay her toll. Seal-spotting cruises leave from Kyleakin in summer.

❸ Broadford

Drambuie was first brewed at Broadford, following a secret recipe of Charles Edward Stuart, Bonnie Prince Charlie, around 1745; the liqueur is no longer made on the island. The largest settlement in the south of Skye includes an environmental centre, incorporating the International Otter Survival Fund, which is open to visitors, while a serpentarium has snakes, lizards and insects.

❹ Loch Sligachan

Loch Sligachan serves as a base camp for mountaineers and hill-walkers venturing into the Cuillin Hills, with its large campsite and hotel. Climbers planning assaults on the fearsome crags and pinnacles of the Skye Ridge start from Glen Brittle, in the west of the island, where there is another campsite and a hostel. Anyone tempted to go into the hills without a professional guide should inform the Mountain Rescue Service in advance.

Visitors in search of gentler pursuits might prefer a round of golf at Sconser, near the mouth of Loch Sligachan. The Sconser Inn is believed to have been the place where MacDonald of Clanranald pleaded, unsuccessfully, with MacDonald and MacLeod chieftains to support the Jacobite uprising.

❺ Raasay

The beautiful, remote island of Raasay includes moorland, beaches, ravines, cliffs, woods, luxuriant gardens and fascinating buildings and ruins. The islanders supported the Jacobite cause in 1745, and the government razed their houses.

Only 13 miles long and with a population of about 200, the island is reached by ferry from Skye. Raasay House, former seat of the MacLeods of Raasay, is an outdoor pursuits centre and home to a local history society. Behind the house is a 13th-century chapel dedicated to Raasay's patron saint, Moluag.

You can see remains of the island's iron industry at East Suisinish, near the ferry pier, and on the road east from Inverarish, at the foot of the track up to the flat summit of Dun Caan.

To the north are the ruins of Brochel Castle, and from here the track is known as Calum's Road. Calum MacLeod, who lived at Arnish, built a 2743m (3000yd) stretch of road to his village single-handedly but died in 1988, aged 77, soon after completing the task. A memorial cairn marks the route.

❻ Portree

The Royal Hotel in Skye's capital stands on the site of McNab's Inn, where Bonnie Prince Charlie said farewell to Flora MacDonald in 1746 after the failed rebellion. The story and the island's cultural history are explored at the Aros Heritage Centre.

The eastern coast of the Trotternish peninsula north of Portree is remarkable for its spectacular cliffs, such as Kilt Rock and the 91m (300ft) Mealt Falls, as well as for the monstrous rock formations known as the Old Man of Storr and The Quiraing, both of which stab jagged spires into the bellies of the clouds.

❼ Kilmuir

It was at Prince Charles's Point, on the shore below Monkstadt house, now a gaunt ruin, that the fugitive prince hid after his journey in an open boat from Uist, while Flora MacDonald went to get help; Flora is buried nearby.

The Museum of Island Life, a group of refurbished 'blackhouses', illustrates the hardships once faced by the islanders, while on the cliffs to the north are the ruins of Duntulm Castle, home until 1730 of the MacDonalds of the Isles; it is said to be haunted by the ghost of a child accidentally dropped to the rocks by a nurse.

❽ Uig

From this pretty, bowl-shaped bay, partly lined with trees, ferries leave for the Outer Hebrides. The only buildings of note are a bold white hotel and a 19th-century folly tower.

The surrounding countryside is dotted with ruined brochs, duns and forts, standing stones and the remains of ancient settlements. Among these is Caisteal Uisdean, near the mouth of the Hinnesdal, a fortress built in the 17th century by the treacherous Hugh, a cousin of the MacDonald chieftain. It had no doors or windows, so that the only entrance was through the roof. Uig is also a centre for canoeing, wind-surfing and horseriding.

❾ Trumpan

The ruins of Trumpan Church stand high up on the west coast of the Waternish peninsula. On a Sunday morning in 1578 a raiding party of MacDonalds from Uist set fire to the church, killing all but one of the congregation of MacLeods. But the ebbing tide beached the raiders' boats; they were caught and almost annihilated by a MacLeod force that, some say, was strengthened by spirits summoned by the waving of the Fairy Flag. The dead of both sides were buried beneath a toppled wall.

❿ Dunvegan

For nearly 800 years the MacLeod chieftains have lived in Dunvegan Castle, making it the oldest house in Britain to have been continuously occupied by the same family. The imposing building has a clan exhibition, and is home to many MacLeod treasures, including the famous Fairy Flag. You can take boat trips to see Loch Dunvegan's seal colony, and north of the castle are the coral beaches at Claigan.

A museum in Dunvegan is dedicated to Angus MacAskill, at 2.4m (7ft 9in) the tallest recorded true giant, and on the peninsula to the west is Borreraig, home of the MacCrimmons, hereditary pipers to the MacLeods. A monument marks their achievements.

The Borreraig Park Musem displays traditional farming implements and machinery, while to the south, the ancient dwelling at Colbost Croft Museum, with a traditional peat fire in the middle of the floor and no chimney, makes it clear how 'blackhouses' got their name. Another museum, at Glendale, is devoted to toys.

To the south are the flat-topped basalt mountains known as MacLeod's Tables. On one, Healabhal Bheag, a chieftain is said to have entertained to dinner some mainland lairds who had wagered that he could not provide a larger table than that in the king's court in Edinburgh.

⓫ Talisker Distillery

Skye's only distillery stands on the shore of Loch Harport and is fed by the peaty waters of Carbost Burn. Both the sea and the burn leave their mark on the smoky single malt whisky, which you can sample before taking a fascinating tour of the aromatic building.

⑫ Elgol

The boulder-strewn bay at the end of the Strathaird peninsula is a fine point from which to view the Cuillin Hills to the north and the islands of Soay, Canna, Rùm and Eigg to the west and south. Boat trips round the peninsula and to the islands start from Kirkibost.

⑬ Armadale

A wooded road lined in summer with bluebells leads down the Sleat peninsula, the lush 'Garden of Skye', to Armadale, where the Mallaig ferry docks. Armadale Castle houses one of Skye's major attractions, the Clan Donald Visitor Centre and its Museum of the Isles.

Up the coast at Ostaig you can take a short course at the flourishing Gaelic College in Gaelic, music and culture; or from the Aird of Sleat, a 2 mile walk up a dirt track leads to remote Point of Sleat's lighthouse and harbour.

On the northern coast of the peninsula are beaches of coral sand at Tarskavaig and Ord; between the two beaches stand the dangerous ruins of Dunsgaith Castle, the former residence of the MacDonalds of Sleat.

⑭ Eilean Donan Castle

The battlements and turrets of a romantic castle rise from a rocky islet at the meeting place of three lochs. Eilean Donan was built in the 13th century as a Highland stronghold of the Scottish kings, and was later held by the MacKenzies and their loyal followers, the Macraes. After centuries of turbulent clan warfare, the castle was finally destroyed by British forces during the abortive Jacobite uprising in 1719. The ruins were fully restored in the early 1900s, and you can see Macrae portraits and furniture.

⑮ Kintail Forest

The wild and mountainous estate of Kintail (NTS), which includes the dramatic but isolated waterfalls of Glomach, is open to walkers even during the deer-stalking season; an unmanned visitor centre at Morvich displays details of local walks. From Shiel Bridge, the A87 heads inland along Glen Shiel, overlooked by the peaks of the Five Sisters of Kintail.

⑯ Mam Ratagain Pass

The narrow road from Shiel Bridge to Glenelg, built as a military road in the 18th century, climbs 335m (1100ft) in a series of breathtaking zigzags to cross a wild pass. Through clearings in the forestry plantations there are views you might normally get only from the cockpit of an aircraft. The descent to Glenelg passes a string of working crofts.

⑰ Glenelg

Just outside Glenelg are the crumbling ruins of Bernera Barracks, built by the English after the 1719 Jacobite uprising, and garrisoned until 1790. North of the remote hamlet is a summer car ferry service to Skye.

EILEAN DONAN CASTLE

To the southeast, along Gleann Beag, are two of Scotland's finest Iron Age brochs, or fortified towers, Dun Troddan and Dun Telve. Their hollow dry-stone walls, which house stairs and galleries, still stand 9m (30ft) in height some 2000 years after they were built.

⑱ Sandaig
The tiny hamlet of Upper Sandaig was home to the naturalist and author Gavin Maxwell, who lived in a waterside house dubbed Camusfeàrna in his books. The house has gone but visitors from around the world leave shells and pebbles on memorials to Maxwell and his pet otter Edal, the inspiration for Maxwell's novel *Ring of Bright Water*. Wild otters are often seen along this beautiful shore. A 2 mile track from the hamlet through a forestry plantation leads to a rocky bay.

⑲ Loch Hourn
The dark and claustrophobic 'Loch of Hell', flanked by high barren mountains, bites deep into the coast. A narrow road from Glenelg runs for some miles along the northern shore, and determined drivers can reach Kinloch Hourn at the loch head by a 30 mile twisting lane of wilderness from Glen Garry. At journey's end there is nothing but an eerie silence.

⑳ Knoydart
The Knoydart peninsula, between Loch Hourn and Loch Nevis, remains an utterly remote area of unspoilt wilderness. Inverie has a shop, a school, a restaurant and a pub, even a small library – but no road to connect it to the rest of the world. Day trips or longer visits must be made by boat from Mallaig.

Quite unlike the landscape of Loch Hourn, the shoreline of Loch Nevis is an open and a bright place, a paradise for walkers and escapists.

㉑ Mallaig
The busy harbour village has a backdrop of dramatic hills and magnificent views over the Sound of Sleat to the jagged Cuillin Hills of Skye. The catch, mainly of shellfish, is landed on the quay for the evening market. Mallaig's history is recalled at the Heritage Centre, which has exhibits and photographs.

Summer car ferries run to Skye and to South Uist, and there are boat trips to Hebridean islands including Rùm, Eigg, Muck and Canna.

㉒ Morar
The hilly village looks out over the Morar estuary, which has pure white sands. Only half a mile in length, its river is an anchorage for pleasure craft. It flows to the sea from Loch

Morar, which is 11 miles long, more than 305m (1000ft) deep and said to be the lair of a monster called the Mhorag; venturesome fishermen can hire boats on the loch.

㉓ Traigh Beach

Extensive sands, crystal-clear water and rock pools make this one of the most attractive beaches on this stretch of coast. Both Traigh and the beach at Camusdarach, situated a mile to the north, are backed by dunes.

㉔ Arisaig

In contrast to the nearby wilderness of high bare hills, the wooded glens round the village of Arisaig form a gentle landscape that encourages leisurely, undemanding exploration. In summer there are boat trips to Rùm, Eigg and Muck, which was a major harbour on a remote coast until the railway opened in 1894. An ancient ruined chapel by St Mary's Church has gravestones with medieval carvings, including scenes showing hunters.

The ruined pier at Rhu, 3 miles west of Arisaig, is a good place for watching seals or admiring sunsets over Rùm and Eigg.

㉕ Loch nan Uamh

A memorial cairn stands on the shore of Loch nan Uamh, where Charles Edward Stuart, or Bonnie Prince Charlie, landed at the start of the 1745 rebellion, and departed 14 months later, following the Jacobite defeat at Culloden. Before the prince and his fellow fugitives left for France, they sheltered from the English redcoats in a cave below Arisaig House, now a hotel.

On a headland to the south are traces of an Iron Age fort, whose stones were vitrified, or fused together by terrific heat – probably caused by the accidental burning of timbers used to strengthen the walls.

㉖ Moidart

The road to this wild and sparsely populated area between Loch Ailort and Loch Shiel offers an exhilarating coastal drive. A narrow lane branches off the main road by Glenuig Inn, and runs behind sandy beaches.

At Kinlochmoidart, seven beech trees known as 'the Seven Men of Moidart' commemorate the band of Jacobites who landed with Bonnie Prince Charlie in 1745.

㉗ Castle Tioram

A sand spit, occasionally covered by high water, connects the romantically sited island fortress of Castle Tioram with the wooded shores of Loch Moidart. The castle is said to have been built in 1353, though the curtain wall is probably far older, and for centuries it was the home of the chieftains of Clanranald. In 1715, it was deliberately burnt down when the 14th chieftain departed to fight beside James Edward Stuart, the Old Pretender, convinced – rightly, as it turned out – that he would not return alive.

The Silver Walk, along which buried treasure was once found, leads along the cliffs of Loch Moidart and then inland to the abandoned settlement of Port á Bhàta, whose inhabitants were transported to Australia in 1853 during the final stages of the Highland Clearances.

㉘ Kentra Bay

On the northern side of the bay, beyond a bleak expanse of peat bog, are the sandy beaches of the Ardtoe peninsula and, at the end of the road, a fish-farming research centre. A 3 mile track along the southern shore of Kentra Bay leads to the Singing Sands of Camus an Lighe, so called because they are said to emit an eerie sound when trodden on.

㉙ Ardnamurchan

The tip of this long peninsula, the Point of Ardnamurchan, is mainland Britain's most westerly point, and local time, according to the sun, is 30 minutes behind Greenwich Mean Time. A lighthouse stands on the clifftop.

From Salen, the road along the peninsula passes through lush woods and rhododendron thickets beside Loch Sunart before crossing desolate moors round Ben Hiant, the core of an extinct volcano; the Natural History Centre at Glenmore has displays relating to local wildlife. From the scattered village of Kilchoan a car ferry operates to Tobermory on Mull.

Sanna Bay, northeast of the Point of Ardnamurchan, has a sandy beach sheltered from the winds by dunes covered by machair grass, while Kilmory, on the peninsula's wild, isolated northern coast, has an ancient burial ground, and sandy beaches flanked by caves.

㉚ Strontian

The lochside village gave its name to the metallic element strontium, which in 1808 was isolated from a mineral mined in the nearby hills. Silver, lead and zinc were also extracted there in the 18th and 19th centuries.

Nearly 2 miles inland is Ariundle Oakwood, a national nature reserve noted for its wild flowers and mosses, and with attractive walks leading to abandoned lead mines. The minor road through Scotstown leads up to a high mountain pass that gives extensive views across Loch Doilet.

㉛ Lochaline

The only road that crosses the lonely Morvern peninsula, bounded by great sea lochs, meets the coast at Lochaline.

Intricate Celtic stone carvings are displayed inside the Church of Keil.

At the head of Loch Aline, 3 miles from the village, Kinlochaline Castle is a 14th-century tower, once the seat of the chiefs of Clan MacInnes, restored in 1890. Its exterior can be seen from the grounds of Ardtornish House, a Victorian Gothic mansion; it is not open to the public, but you can visit its woodland gardens.

32 Canna

The basalt rocks of the cliffs here are so magnetic that they distort compass readings on craft as far away as 3 miles. Despite these curious navigational hazards, the deep-water harbour on the 5 mile long island of Canna (NTS) is popular in summer with small-boat sailors.

The island has a population of about 15, consisting of estate workers, crofters and lobster fishermen. In the 1840s, during the Highland Clearances, about two-thirds of the inhabitants were shipped to Canada. Previously there had been a township here called A'Chill; you can see its scant remains, including a Celtic cross, a curious pink standing stone and a burial ground, near the pier.

33 Rùm

Wild and mountainous, the island rises steeply from the sea to peaks of 700m (2300ft) and more. Few people have lived there since 1826, when almost the entire population was shipped across the Atlantic to Newfoundland in Canada.

In 1957, Rùm became a national nature reserve. Two signposted nature trails start from the dock, near the head of Loch Scresort. One follows the loch's southern shore, part of which is frequented by otters, and ends 1½ miles away at Port nan Caranean, an abandoned village where eider ducks and gulls nest among the ruins. The other trail heads inland for about 2 miles.

Red deer are everywhere; there are also wild goats here, and little Rùm ponies bred on the island to carry deer carcasses down from the hills. You may also spot golden eagles and, more rarely, sea eagles. The latter, which has a wingspan of 2.7m (9ft), became extinct in Britain early in the 20th century but was reintroduced to Rùm in the 1970s.

Grey and common seals hunt for fish in the bay, and in the long summer evenings Manx shearwaters gather on the waves by the thousand, before returning to their mountaintop nests, where they rear their young in burrows.

34 Eigg

The island's most interesting feature are the Singing Sands at Camas Sgiotaig, which squeak when walked upon, or even emit a long, continuous moan when the wind is in the right direction. With a population of about 70, Eigg is the most crowded island in the Small Islands Parish. There are sandy beaches to the south of the Singing Sands and to the north of Galmisdale. For visitors interested in geology there are fine walks round the cliffs of An Sgurr, and bicycles, mopeds, ponies and dinghies may be hired.

SCOTLAND
Skye to Mull

213

TOBERMORY

35 Muck

The meadows on this fertile, low-lying island are bright with wild flowers in summer. Muck has a relatively mild climate, thanks to the North Atlantic Drift and its sheltered position in relation to its higher and bigger neighbours. The small island's name comes from the Gaelic word Muc, which means variously a heap, a pig or a sea-pig, or porpoise.

The island is home to a few dozen people. In 1828 Muck's landlord evicted most of the crofters and sent them to Nova Scotia, Canada, where some descendants still speak Gaelic.

36 Coll

Much of the west coast of the 12 mile long island is made up of bright shell-sand, blown into dunes of 30m (100ft) and higher, their slopes knitted by grass to form machair, on which cattle graze.

From the deck of the Oban ferry, the eastern seaboard of the island looks inhospitably craggy. But once the boat penetrates Loch Eatharna to dock at Arinagour pier, an expanse of gentle, heathery moorland, dotted with slaty-dark lochans, comes into view. There are plenty of sandy, secluded coves here, and Arinagour, ablaze in summer with flowers, includes a craft and pottery shop. At the southwestern end of the island is an RSPB reserve where you may hear corncrakes in summer. Otters live along the coast, and you can see common seals in the many sheltered bays.

37 Tiree

The sunniest place in Britain in May, Tiree has the air of a tropical isle with empty beaches of pale sand and good surfing conditions. The island's name means 'Land of Corn', and the fertility of the machair helps to houses, shops, a tea room and an inn neatly sandwiched between a wooded cliff, a pier and a coast path.

Just over a mile south of Craignure are Torosay Castle and Gardens. The castle, reached by road, woodland path or miniature railway, is a handsome Victorian mansion in the Scots baronial style. It contains family portraits from 1840 and other photographic displays. Its terraced gardens and the Italian statue walk are glorious, with views of the Appin coast extending from Ben Cruachan to Ben Nevis.

At Fishnish Point, 6 miles northwest of Craignure, a car ferry crosses to Lochaline, on the remote Morvern peninsula on the mainland. You may see otters from the picnic area near the ferry terminal.

39 Salen
A collection of snug stone cottages, a ruined pier, a general store and a post office make up Salen. The village was created at the beginning of the 19th century by Major General Lachlan MacQuarie, a native of the island of Ulva who later became Governor of New South Wales; his mausoleum can be seen 3 miles southwest of Salen.

On a headland above a sandy bay north of Salen are the battered remains of Aros Castle, last occupied in 1608. The castle was one of a chain of great fortifications built throughout the Inner Hebrides and western mainland, and was used by the Lords of the Isles, rulers of the Western Isles and part of the western mainland from the mid 14th century to the late 15th century.

40 Tobermory
The main town of Mull is a place of colour-washed houses and hotels, with shops selling items such as ship chandlery, fishing tackle, diving gear and guns. Tobermory was built in the 1780s, when the British Society for Encouraging Fisheries founded a port on the natural harbour. Fishing boats are now joined by pleasure craft and boats offering fishing trips for skate and mackerel, and, except in midwinter, a ferry to Kilchoan on Ardnamurchan peninsula.

In Aros Park, woodland walks lead past rhododendrons and waterfalls; on its edge, at Druimfin, the Mull Little Theatre is establishing a new production centre.

41 Dervaig
The road from Tobermory to Dervaig is steep and single-tracked, and seems to wind through a hundred hairpin bends as it skirts small lochs or leaps over tiny stone bridges.

Dervaig village, at the head of a narrow, rocky inlet, was built by Maclean of Coll in 1799, and consists mostly of low stone houses, some whitewashed, with brightly painted windows

support a population of about 770. Apart from three bumps at its western end, Tiree is so low-lying that it looks from a distance like a pencil stroke on the horizon. Although there are carpets of wild flowers in early summer, there are no trees; the 120 knot gales that come off the Atlantic in winter make their growth impossible.

Tiree's villages include Scarinish, south of sandy Gott Bay, and Balemartine on Hynish Bay. In the 1840s, labourers constructing the Skerryvore lighthouse were housed at Hynish, to the south of Balemartine; the granite buildings are now holiday accommodation. Balephuil, to the west, is set in a bay, attractively flanked by Ben Hynish and the steep headland of Ceann a' Mhara.

38 Craignure
The 40 minute ferry trip from Oban to Craignure on Mull presents an ever-changing vista of mountains, islands and sea. Craignure itself is an attractive collection of

and doors. Cruises departing from the village give opportunities to observe local wildlife, including sea birds, dolphins, porpoises and whales. The Old Byre Heritage Centre, a mile south, relates Mull's history from the Bronze Age.

㊷ Calgary
The tiny settlement stands on one of Mull's loveliest bays with peaceful white sands and a grassy plain behind. The tranquillity is broken in summer, as the holiday crowds flock, but the beauty of the bay remains unchanged.

In 1822, during the Highland Clearances, the people of several townships round Calgary Bay emigrated to Canada after being evicted from their homes.

The views from the roads to and from Calgary are as grand as any in the Hebrides, embracing Coll and the Treshnish Isles to the west, and Skye and Ardnamurchan to the north.

㊸ Ulva
Scattered throughout Ulva are many ruins of settlements whose inhabitants were evicted in the late 1840s. An information centre explains the history of the island, which you can reach by passenger ferry from Mull. There are several waymarked trails around Ulva, including a 2 hour woodland walk and a 5 hour walk that leads across a bridge to Gometra.

㊹ Staffa
Resembling a cathedral, with its huge walls formed from hexagonal basalt columns, Fingal's Cave on the isle of Staffa provided the inspiration for Mendelssohn's overture *The Hebrides*. In the first half of the 19th century, the lonely grandeur of the tiny uninhabited island attracted visitors such as Tennyson, Turner, Wordsworth and Queen Victoria. Legend has it that the giant Torquil MacLeod was building the Giant's Causeway in Ireland and took home a sackful of his work, but the sack burst and the rocks were scattered, the largest being Staffa. You can reach the island by boat from Fionnphort, Ulva Ferry and Oban.

㊺ Treshnish Isles
Puffins, skuas, gannets, guillemots and razorbills are among the many birds on the string of uninhabited islands. Day cruises from Oban and Ulva Ferry include landings on Lunga, the largest island at just over a mile in length; here you may see seals, black rabbits and rare varieties of orchids.

⑯ Iona

St Columba called the 3½ mile long island 'Iona of my heart', and chose it as the site of his monastery. Of the original building of AD 563, which is thought to have been built of wattle and daub, nothing remains. In the Dark Ages the monastery was raided on several occasions by Vikings, and its community massacred. Because Iona was such a holy place, 60 kings were buried there, including Macbeth and Duncan, the 11th-century Scottish kings on whom Shakespeare based his characters.

Iona's oldest building is St Oran's Chapel, built by Queen Margaret in 1080; the restored 13th-century abbey is the home of the Iona Community. Outside the abbey church is the beautifully carved St Martin's Cross, 5m (17ft) high and more than 1000 years old.

The 100m (328ft) hill of Dun I gives superb views to the Hebrides beyond. There is a ferry from Fionnphort, and day trips from Oban.

⑰ Lochbuie

Standing stones and stone circles left by early settlers populate the fertile plain at the head of Loch Buie. A 5½ mile walk along the north side of the loch leads to massive cliffs at Carsaig Bay.

Visitor information

Broadford ☎ (01471) 822361
Craignure ☎ (01680) 812377
Kilchoan – Visit Scotland ☎ 0845 225 5121
Mallaig – Visit Scotland ☎ 0845 225 5121
Portree ☎ (01478) 612137
Strontian – Visit Scotland ☎ 0845 225 5121
Tobermory ☎ 08707 200625

⑱ Duart Castle

Of all the fortresses in the Western Isles, none is more expressive of the power and majesty of the medieval chieftains than Duart Castle. The forbidding clifftop building dates from the 13th century, with additions made towards the end of the 14th century by the Macleans. In 1912 the castle was restored from a ruinous state to its former grandeur, and to its position as rallying place of the Clan Maclean.

Inside are a collection of family relics, an exhibition on chiefs of the clan, and a Scouting exhibition; the 27th clan chief was for many years leader of the Scout movement in the Commonwealth. The views from the Sea Room are especially breathtaking.

FINGAL'S CAVE, STAFFA

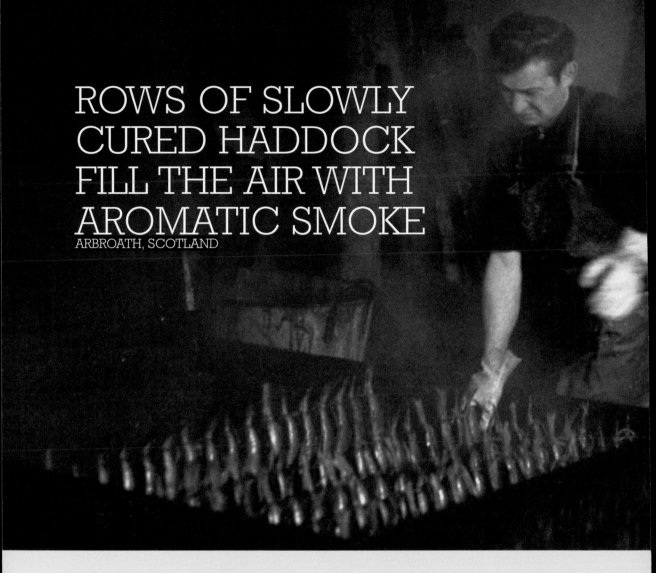

ROWS OF SLOWLY CURED HADDOCK FILL THE AIR WITH AROMATIC SMOKE
ARBROATH, SCOTLAND

Fishy tales

Through the ages, fishing has been the lifeblood of the Scottish coast, famed for Arbroath 'smokies' and Anstruther herring girls

The rugged east coast of Scotland with its sandstone cliffs and deep little bays facing the North Sea is peppered with fishing villages. And you couldn't find a more archetypal small fishing town than Arbroath on the Angus coast. Arbroath is built of weathered pink sandstone. The town lies low, sloping towards the harbour. Everywhere you go you notice a thick, sweetish reek on the air – the tang of the celebrated Arbroath smokies.

Haddock caught by the local fishermen are still smoked the traditional way over smoking pits, imparting a beautiful taste. Whole families are still involved in the smokie business here as they have traditionally been – catching, gutting,

smoking, packing, selling. You can buy a pair from any one of a dozen smokeries, ready-wrapped in plastic to take away with you. 'Slap them with butter and put them in the microwave for two minutes,' say the experts. 'It keeps them nice and moist.'

A casual stroll through Arbroath, and you might come away with the impression that life in the Scottish fisheries is rosy. In fact the industry is in a state of crisis, due mainly to over-fishing in the past. The great spring runs of herring that used to pour southwards down the coast have dried up. So has the work they brought for generations of herring girls, itinerant fish-gutters who would follow the fishing boats as they, too, flocked south after the 'silver darlings'. The big Scots fleets, and those who worked them, have been diminished by quotas and other conservation measures. In the old days there was a fishing-related job, at sea or on shore, for every fisherman's son or daughter. Nowadays those who can get a place on one of the huge deep-sea trawlers working out of Fraserburgh or Peterhead count themselves lucky.

Music on the waves

Up in the Shetland Isles the fishermen used to work six-oared rowing boats known as 'sixareens'. Shetlanders are famous fiddle-players, but the sixareen fishers found that taking a conventional wooden fiddle to sea was asking to have it smashed. They refused to be parted from their musical instruments, however, claiming that they were also instruments of navigation because so many tunes composed on them were named after headlands, bays and inlets. So the ingenious islanders took to making their own special sea-

going fiddles out of indestructible tin, reckoning that being able to go on playing music at sea was compensation enough for the somewhat harsh tone of a tin fiddle.

The devastation of Eyemouth

But the fishing industry had a human cost. One of the worst of a host of catastrophes to befall Scottish fishing fleets in the days of sail was the Eyemouth Disaster of 14 October 1881, when a hurricane arose out of a calm blue sky and fell on the fishing village of Eyemouth in the Berwickshire cliffs, a few miles north of the English border. 'The sky suddenly thickened with dark, heavy clouds,' wrote the Rev Daniel McIver. 'A fierce wind arose which was as wild in its fury as the calm was quiet; the sea began to heave its threatening bosom, like a man in whose heart passion was rising, and what between sudden darkness – it was then between eleven and twelve of the day – the shrieking of the hurricane as it drove at the creaking masts and ripping sails, and the thunderous roar of a boiling ocean, the poor fishermen thought that the Judgment Day had come.'

Altogether 189 fishermen died that day, 129 of them from Eyemouth, drowning or smashed to death in the surf in full view of their horrified families on the shore. The village lost one in three of its men. 'Eyemouth is a scene of unutterable woe,' reported the Berwickshire News. 'The fleet is wrecked, and the flower of the fishermen have perished.'

In Eyemouth's museum hangs a tapestry made in the village in 1981 to commemorate the centenary of the disaster. It is embroidered with images of the fishermen overwhelmed by the tempest, the fish that they and so many like them lost their lives in harvesting, and a radiant sunrise to symbolise the hope and optimism that still infuses these tough, resilient fishing communities of the Scottish coast.

A fishing heritage remembered

The Scottish Fisheries Museum on the harbour-front in Anstruther takes you on a comprehensive journey through the dramatic story of Scotland's fishing communities, from whale harpooners to herring lassies. Here you will find beautifully laid out displays of boat models, shark jaws and sawfish blades, paintings and photographs, real boats in a boatyard, and the deep-sea lines and crab pots and whale harpoons that were and still are the tools of the fishing trade. One harpoon head has been bent into a corkscrew by its victim's struggles. Tableaux run the gamut from the wheelhouse of a trawler to the front room of a fisher family's cottage. Such exhibitions paint a poignant picture of a way of life that is fast disappearing.

FORT WILLIAM TO CRARAE GARDEN

Climbers delight in the many high peaks, including Ben Nevis, in and around this winding coastline, while peaceful retreats, such as gentle Islay, lie offshore

① Fort William

Oliver Cromwell established fortifications at Inverlochy, which were later expanded and renamed Fort William after King William III. The town is a busy holiday centre, attracting walkers and climbers; Ben Nevis, Britain's highest summit, is 4 miles east of the town and is bounded on its south side by the gorge of Glen Nevis, which is enclosed by dramatically plunging slopes. Other visitors come to cruise on the Caledonian Canal, which opened in 1847 to link the lochs of the Great Glen.

The West Highland Museum displays Jacobite relics, including a 'secret' portrait of Prince Charles Edward Stuart, or Bonnie Prince Charlie, revealed only when reflected onto a curved and polished surface. Treasures of the Earth, 4 miles northwest at Corpach, is a collection of gemstones, crystals and fossils.

② Glen Coe

The dark summits towering over 'the Narrow Glen' provide some of Britain's most testing challenges for mountaineers. Near the eastern end of the glen are ski slopes served by tows and by a chairlift, operating in summer as well as during the skiing season. Its 732m (2400ft) high terminus gives wide views of the glen and over Rannoch Moor, a vast expanse studded with lochans.

In the village of Glencoe to the west, a folk museum is housed in a group of thatched cottages. Some of its displays recall the infamous massacre of February 1, 1692, when members of the MacDonald clan, who had been slow to renounce the Jacobite cause and to sign an oath of allegiance to William III, were butchered by Campbells of the Argyll militia. The killers had spent the previous 12 days accepting the unsuspecting MacDonalds' hospitality.

A National Trust for Scotland visitor centre, 2 miles southeast of the village, is the starting point for guided walks through the glen in the summer months.

③ Loch Linnhe

Mountains rise steeply from the waters of Loch Linnhe, a long inlet of the sea, crossed at its narrowest point by the Corran ferry.

At South Ballachulish, close by the bridge that spans Loch Leven's narrow outlet into Loch Linnhe, is a monument to James Stewart, hanged on this spot in November 1752 for complicity in the murder of Colin Campbell, a land agent employed by the English to evict suspected pro-Jacobites. Robert Louis Stevenson's novel *Kidnapped* presents the case that Stewart could not have been guilty, and was put to death only because his accusers and the jury were under Campbell domination.

❹ Portnacroish
Standing on an islet in the bay to the south is the tall rectangular Castle Stalker; the Gaelic name is *Caisteal an Stalcair*, 'Castle of the Hunter', for it was often used by James IV as a hunting lodge. You can arrange a visit in summer.

Portnacroish is a yacht marina and wind-surfing centre. In the churchyard a memorial stone recalls a battle in 1468 between the feuding Stewarts and MacDougalls 'in which many hundreds fell'.

❺ Lismore
Lismore can claim to have been one of the earliest Christian sites in the Highlands. The parish church of Kilmoluag was once the choir of a cathedral founded in the 13th century and dedicated to St Moluag, who was a contemporary of St Columba and arrived there in about 560; the rest of the building was destroyed during the Reformation.

The island consists of a narrow 10 mile strip of fertile grazing land. By virtue of its central position in Loch Linnhe, Lismore has far-ranging views, including Ben Nevis, Mull and Morvern. The road that runs from end to end is joined roughly halfway along by a side road from Achnacroish, where the Oban car ferry lands.

❻ Scottish Sea Life Sanctuary
Sharks, octopuses, jellyfish and crabs are just some of the inhabitants of the earliest of Britain's sealife centres, which opened in 1979 on the southern shore of Loch Creran. Other attractions include seal pools, a nursery for rescued seal pups, and shoals of herring.

Near Barcaldine, 1½ miles east of the sanctuary, there are waymarked forest walks.

❼ Loch Etive
A ruined chapel is all that remains of a 13th-century foundation at Ardchattan Priory (HS) on the northern shore of Loch Etive. The priory was the scene in 1308 of a meeting of one of Robert Bruce's National Councils, the last to be conducted in Gaelic. Nearby, Ardchattan Garden has formal gardens overlooking the loch, and a wild garden with some 180 varieties of shrub.

Summer cruises to the remote head of the loch, which is dominated by the gaunt summits flanking Glen Coe, start from Loch Etive's

southern shore, near Taynuilt village. Buoys mark the headlines, or ends, of ropes from which some 200 tons of mussels are harvested annually, and seals bask on a long tongue of rock.

Bonawe Iron Furnace (HS), near Taynuilt, is a charcoal blast furnace, established in 1753 and now restored.

❽ Connel
The village stands beside the narrow mouth of Loch Etive, which is crossed by a cantilever bridge built as a railway viaduct but now carrying road traffic. Below are the Falls of Lora, impressive rapids created by a submerged ridge over which, at ebb tide, waters from Loch Etive thresh and swirl towards the Firth of Lorn.

❾ Dunstaffnage Castle
Set upon a rocky outcrop in a commanding position near the mouth of Loch Etive, and defended by 3m (10ft) thick outer walls, Dunstaffnage Castle (HS) was founded in the mid 13th century by the MacDougalls.

In 1309 the castle was captured by Robert Bruce and for some years remained a royal property. Later it was granted to the Earls and then Dukes of Argyll, as hereditary Captains of Dunstaffnage. Flora MacDonald spent ten days there before being sent for trial in London for helping Bonnie Prince Charlie in his flight after Culloden. The nearby chapel dates from the 13th century and has intricate carving in its windows.

❿ Kerrera
Perched on a pillar of rock in a bay of low cliffs at the southern end of the island is the ruined Gylen Castle, a 16th-century MacDougall stronghold sacked by Covenanters during the Civil War. It is a 2½ mile walk from the jetty where the passenger ferry from Oban docks. The island offers excellent walks, with fine views of Mull, Oban and Lismore.

⓫ Oban
The town rises steeply from its bustling waterfront to McCaig's Tower, built at the end of the 19th century by a local banker and resembling the Colosseum in Rome. The tower was to have been a museum and art gallery, but remains an unfinished shell around a pleasant garden, with a viewing platform looking out over the harbour; nearby Oban malt whisky distillery provides tours. The Argyllshire Gathering, held each year in late August, features traditional Highland games. Ferries sail from the town to Mull and other Hebridean islands; some give dramatic views of Dunollie Castle, a creeper-choked tower house.

At Oban Rare Breeds Farm Park, 1½ miles east, you can see pigs, sheep and cattle that are no longer found on modern farms.

BOWMORE CHURCH, ISLAY

⑫ Seil

The island is reached by Clachan Bridge, which, although only some 46m (50yd) long, is known grandiosely as 'The Bridge over the Atlantic'. On the west coast, Easdale has craft shops and art exhibitions, and gives views of the southern part of the Firth of Lorn and the islands. A ferry makes the short journey to Easdale Island, whose folk museum evokes life in the heyday of the local slate industry, which existed until 1965, while on the east side of Seil Sound, Ardmaddy Castle Gardens encompass woodlands and a walled garden.

⑬ Arduaine Garden

Rhododendrons, azaleas, shrubberies, lawns and a wilder woodland garden on the higher slopes make up Arduaine Garden (NTS). It is reached from the Loch Melfort Hotel by a path offering views of neighbouring islands and the marina at Craobh Haven.

⑭ Luing

Grazed by a breed known as Luing cattle, and surrounded by backdrops of other islands – as well as by treacherous currents – Luing is reached by ferry from the south end of Seil. Once a slate-quarrying area, the island has

rugged scenery in the north and gentler terrain farther south. Semi-precious stones may be found on the rocky shores.

⑮ Colonsay

White, empty beaches, standing stones and seal colonies on the islets and skerries are just some of the attractions this island has to offer. Colonsay and Oronsay become one 10 mile island for 3 hours at low tide, when they are linked by a sandy beach known as The Strand. Together, the islands enjoy almost as much sunshine as Tiree, Scotland's record-holder, and a much lower rainfall than the mainland. Wild goats live at the north of Colonsay, and on Oronsay; the long-horned, black-fleeced creatures are said to be descended from goats that swam here from the Spanish Armada, which were wrecked offshore in 1588. Rabbits abound, and golden eagles soar high above.

Kiloran Bay, backed by dunes, is one of the island's finest beaches; a long headland protects it from the full force of the Atlantic, though strong westerly winds can provide rollers for surfing. At nearby Kiloran Gardens palm trees and rhododendrons flourish in the mild climate.

Almost alone among the Hebrides, Colonsay suffered no forced evictions during the Highland

Clearances and so is free of the sad, almost haunted quality that possesses so many other Scottish islands. Some 110 people live there.

Only a handful of people live on Oronsay, where St Columba is said to have landed on his way from Ireland to Iona in the middle of the 6th century. Substantial ruins of a priory on the island date from the 13th century, and include a Celtic cross, a high altar and tombstones bearing the carved portraits of warriors and priests.

⑯ Islay

The island's healthy economy is almost entirely the result of a thriving whisky industry and the reason for the high level of employment among its 3500 people. Islay, pronounced 'I-la', has eight distilleries, most of them open to visitors.

Some 7 miles northeast of Port Ellen is the 9th-century Kildalton Cross, a magnificent example of Celtic carving. A mile's walk to the west of Port Ellen leads to the Carraig Fhada lighthouse and the Singing Sands, so-called because of the swishing noise created when you walk through the dry sand. To the southwest is a headland, whose name, The Oa, shares with Bu on Orkney and Ae in southern Scotland the distinction of being one of Britain's shortest place names. A monument at the tip of the headland is in memory of American sailors who drowned nearby during the First World War.

The long, straight road from Port Ellen to Bowmore runs inland from Laggan Bay, whose 5 miles of dune-backed sand is the largest of Islay's many beautiful beaches. Bowmore's unusual round church was built in 1767.

To the northeast, Loch Finlaggan's main island was where the MacDonald chiefs held parliament from the 12th to the 16th centuries; excavations have revealed traces of buildings, a paved road and timber defences. Islay's history is explained in the Museum of Islay Life at Port Charlotte.

In autumn, thousands of barnacle and Greenland white-fronted geese arrive to spend winter at the Loch Gruinart RSPB Reserve. The marsh fritillary is among the butterflies you can see there. Choughs and corncrakes breed on the reserve and elsewhere on Islay.

⑰ Jura

Most of the island is mountainous and inhabited only by deer – the name Jura comes from the Norse _Dyr Oe_, meaning 'Deer Island'.

Although the ferry crossing from Islay to Jura lasts only slightly longer than the time it takes to buy the ticket, there could hardly be a greater difference between the two islands. While Islay is well populated and largely flat, 27 mile long Jura has only 160 inhabitants and is a wilderness of rock, moor and peat bog.

Craighouse, the island's only village, has a whisky distillery that you can visit, while Jura House Walled Garden, 3½ miles southwest, has plants from Australia and New Zealand that flourish in the mild climate of this part of the island. Three peaks in the south, rising to around 762m (2500ft), are known as the Paps of Jura.

One of the most difficult and winding A-class roads imaginable leads most of the way along Jura's east coast, and ends near the hamlet of Ardlussa. In the cemetery are the graves of a woman who died aged 128, and a man 'who kept 180 Christmases'. A small track continuing beyond Ardlussa passes tiny Barnhill, where the author George Orwell wrote his novel *1984*.

To the north lies the roaring, seething whirlpool of the Gulf of Corryvreckan, which separates Jura from small, uninhabited Scarba.

⑱ Inverliever Forest

The huge conifer plantation cloaking the northern slopes of Loch Awe is a haunt of red, roe and sika deer, as well as of buzzards, ospreys and golden eagles. Along the road that runs parallel to the shore, several car parks provide starting points for walks that take in waterfalls and viewpoints.

⑲ Kilmartin

The Church of St Martin of Tours contains the 10th-century Kilmartin Cross, an early Celtic image of Christ. Housed in a shelter in the churchyard are a number of tombstones carved in the 14th and 15th centuries.

Kilmartin lies close to one of the largest concentrations of ancient ritual and burial monuments in Scotland, dating from before 3000 BC to about 1200 BC. A track leads south-westwards past Nether Largie Linear Cemetery (HS), a series of burial chambers dating from 2300 BC and in use for about a thousand years. Also nearby are the two Temple Wood Stone Circles (HS), erected before 3000 BC.

A mile north of Kilmartin are the imposing ruins of 16th-century Carnassarie Castle (HS).

⑳ Dunadd Fort

Believed to have been the inauguration site of the kings of the ancient kingdom of Dalriada, Dunadd Fort (HS) was founded about AD 500 and is strategically sited on a hillock, and defended by four tiers of walls. Enigmatic rock carvings on a slab at the summit depict a boar and a footprint. The fort is surrounded by a waterlogged peat bog, which once lay under the sea and is known as Moine Mhor. Part of it forms a national nature reserve.

To the east, Kilmichael Glassary (HS) is another ancient site, where mysterious 'cup and ring' markings – hollows surrounded by rings – were cut into rock in the Bronze Age.

㉑ Crinan

The village lies beside a marina busy with sleek yachts and net-festooned fishing boats. Sweeping views extend over the Crinan Basin to the islands of Jura and Scarba, and boats leave in summer on seal and birdwatching trips.

Opened in 1801, the Crinan Canal forms a 9 mile short cut between Crinan and Ardrishaig, linking the Sound of Jura with Loch Fyne and saving a journey of 120 miles round the Kintyre peninsula. 'Clyde Puffers' were vessels specially built for the Forth and Clyde and Crinan canals. A few craft still carry passengers on cruises.

㉒ Tayvallich

Tucked into a sheltered inlet among the heavily wooded promontories and bays that bound the upper end of Loch Sween, Tayvallich attracts small-boat sailors. South of Tayvallich, Taynish National Nature Reserve has Scotland's largest surviving remnant of oak forest.

㉓ Kilmory

Farm buildings and holiday homes cluster around a ruined 13th-century chapel that contains more than 30 medieval grave slabs carved with warriors, chiefs and hunters. Outside stands the 15th-century MacMillan's Cross.

To the south, the Point of Knap is a gentle jut of land that separates Loch Sween from Loch Caolisport. Two miles northeast of Kilmory, from the road to Achnamara, a path leads to the bleak ruins of Castle Sween.

㉔ Gigha Island

The island's gentle landscape is dotted with small farms, ancient duns, or forts, and prehistoric standing stones. South of the port of Ardminish, Gigha's only village, are the gardens of Achamore House, where azaleas, rhododendrons and palms flourish in the mild climate. The tiny ruined church dedicated to St Cattan dates from the 13th century.

㉕ Glenbarr Abbey

Despite its name, Glenbarr Abbey is an 18th-century Gothic house, home to members of the Clan MacAlister, whose 500 year history is chronicled in a visitor centre in the building. Walks and nature trails start from the house.

㉖ Mull of Kintyre

A steep and twisting 7 mile drive through spectacular hill scenery leads from a point just west of Southend towards the peninsula's south-western tip, though the last few hundred yards to the lighthouse must be walked. The Antrim coast lies just 12 miles away, making this the closest point to Ireland on mainland Britain.

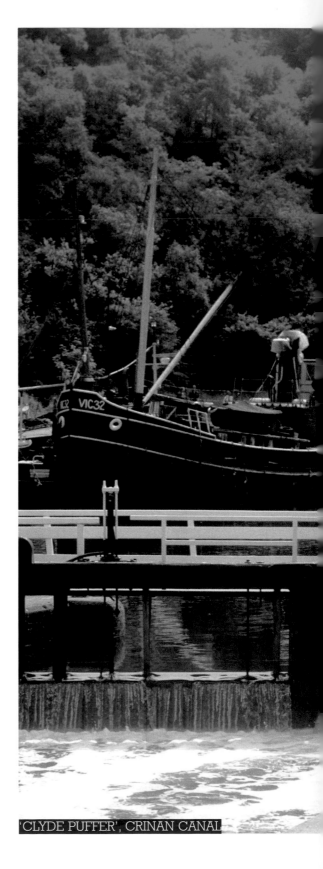

'CLYDE PUFFER', CRINAN CANAL

㉗ Southend

Carved in a rock in the churchyard are St Columba's Footsteps, where the saint is believed to have stood. St Columba visited the area in AD 561, two years before establishing a monastery on Iona. His name is also given to a holy well near Keil Point. Three small bays bite into the nearby coast, their sands coloured red.

㉘ Campbeltown

Hills rise behind the harbour and a cluster of stone buildings. Herring fishing has declined since its 19th-century heyday, but the town is now a sailing and holiday resort. Whisky, too, has played a role in Campbeltown's history, though today just two distilleries remain. In summer there are tours of the Springbank distillery; these must be booked at the Whisky Shop. You can reach The Island Davaar, at the mouth of Campbeltown Loch, from the mainland by walking along a causeway exposed for 3 hours either side of low tide.

㉙ Saddell

In a quiet glen just off the main road at Saddell stand fragments of a Cistercian abbey founded about 1160. Among gravestones protected under a shelter are examples of 14th to 16th-century stone carvings. The nearby beach can be reached through the grounds of 16th-century Saddell Castle, though the castle itself is not open to the public.

㉚ Carradale

The tranquil holiday village and its small fishing harbour have sweeping views up the coast and across to Arran. You can follow woodland walks from the Network Carradale Heritage Centre, just west of the village, and in Carradale Forest to the north. Walkers may also venture southwards to Carradale Point, where there are remains of a fort dating from 1500 BC.

㉛ Lochranza

A jumble of painted cottages fringed by a pebbly beach and spread round the loch from which it takes its name, the village is set by the remains of twin-towered Lochranza Castle (HS), begun in the 13th century as a two-storey hallhouse. On the other side of the loch, footpaths pass Ossian's Cave, named after a legendary Irish warrior and poet.

㉜ Blackwaterfoot

A 2 mile walk northwards along the coast from the small village leads to King's Cave, believed by some to have been the place where Robert Bruce was inspired by the perseverance of a spider weaving its web. On Machrie Moor are a large number of Neolithic and Bronze Age monuments, including Auchagallon stone circle.

㉝ Whiting Bay

Whiting Bay is the starting point for two forest walks, one to the Glenashdale Falls, the other to the chambered cairns of Giants' Graves. Another chambered cairn, possibly dating from as long ago as 4000 BC, can be seen outside Lagg.

㉞ Lamlash

The hamlet stands in a sheltered bay popular with small-boat sailors and anglers. Presiding over it all is the towering mass of Holy Island, home to a community of Tibetan monks, and to feral ponies, sheep and goats. In summer, ferries cross to it from Lamlash and Whiting Bay.

㉟ Brodick

Arran's largest village is the port for the ferry crossing to Ardrossan, on the mainland. Dinghies, canoes and waterskis can be hired near the broad sandy beach. The Isle of Arran Heritage Museum examines the island's past and its unusually complicated geology.

About a mile north is 13th century Brodick Castle (NTS), now the focus of a country park. At 874m (2866ft), Goat Fell is Arran's highest peak and a popular 2½ hour climb from Brodick.

㊱ Tarbert

A popular sailing centre, scene of Scotland's largest regatta each May, Tarbert was once the hub of the Loch Fyne herring industry. Although this activity has declined, Fish Quay is still busy in the morning as boats unload their catches. Much of the village is Victorian, but the castle's earliest visible remains are 13th-century.

Two miles north, the gardens of Stonefield Castle Hotel contain Himalayan rhododendrons and exotic shrubs.

㊲ Crarae Garden

Within sheltered woodland gardens, by the northern shore of Loch Fyne, rhododendrons and azaleas dazzle in spring and summer; deciduous trees continue the colours into autumn. Paths climb the hillside, and footbridges span a plunging gorge, while to the south, waymarked walks thread through the tranquil plantations of Kilmichael Forest.

Visitor information

Ballachulish ☎ (01855) 811866
Bowmore ☎ (01496) 810254
Brodick ☎ (01770) 303776
Campbeltown ☎ (08707) 200609
Fort William – Visit Scotland ☎ 0845 225 5121
Lochgilphead – Visit Scotland ☎ 0845 225 5121
Oban ☎ (01631) 563122
Tarbert ☎ (01880) 820429

INVERARAY TO BALLANTRAE

Much here has been immortalised by Robert Burns, Scotland's national poet, who lived and worked along this stretch of coast, which is also home to many popular holiday resorts

❶ Inveraray

A splendid example of 18th-century urban planning, the town stands by the waters of a sheltered bay on Loch Fyne. Inveraray Castle was built at the same time as the town, to be the home of the third Duke of Argyll, chief of the Campbells. Its magnificent interior is open to visitors, and in the grounds are woodland walks to a hilltop folly.

The old Inveraray Jail is now a museum of 19th-century crime and punishment, while at the nearby pier, a small maritime museum is based in the schooner *Arctic Penguin*, a former Irish lightship. All Saints' bell tower, built in 1925 as the Clan Campbell war memorial, has a fine ten-bell peal and an exhibition on bell ringing.

An adventure centre provides attractions such as pony trekking and climbing walls.

❷ Auchindrain

Auchindrain's open-air museum is a monument to a communal farming system, which was all but wiped out during the Highland Clearances of the 1830s. Twelve tenants paid their rent jointly to the Duke of Argyll, sharing the arable and grazing land at Auchindrain, and the practice continued in the same way until the 1930s. Cottages here have been refurnished in period style, and barns, byres, a stable, a smithy and other buildings have been preserved.

❸ Loch Fyne

Measuring some 40 miles from its north-eastern tip to its mouth, Loch Fyne is one of Scotland's longest lochs. Its eastern shore provides dramatic views of forested ridges sweeping up from the water's edge.

In Cairndow, by the loch's head, the woodland gardens at Ardkinglass House are open throughout the year. South of the 'Heart of Argyll', a traditional gypsy wedding site, are the quiet villages of St Catherines and Strachur, once served by steamer services.

An exhilarating lochside road continues south past the ruined hulk of 15th-century Castle Lachlan, skirting the rocky shoreline to Otter Ferry, named from the Gaelic *oitir*, the great shingle bar that is exposed at low tide. At Kilfinan, a pre-Reformation church stands near the village's restored stagecoach inn.

From Millhouse, a small road heads west to Portavadie, an industrial 'ghost village' of the 1970s with a car ferry service to Tarbert. A picnic area just north of the village is the starting point for a hilly woodland trail.

❹ Tighnabruaich

A spectacular mountainous landscape surrounds Tighnabruaich and Bute's rumpled northern moorlands. The village dates from the 1850s, when a resort grew up as steamer traffic was developed. This is a superb yachting area, with a busy sailing and wind-surfing school, and pleasure cruises in the surrounding lochs. Other popular activities include golf, birdwatching, fishing, walking and shinty, a game similar to hockey.

To the north of the village, on the A8003, a magnificent viewpoint looks out over Loch Riddon and both the eastern and western Kyles of Bute.

❺ Colintraive

The airy village, whose name rhymes with 'strive', was once a place to which cattle destined for mainland markets swam over from Bute. Now the narrows are crossed by a vehicle ferry.

To the east, Loch Striven lies among hill farms and forests. Once a wartime midget submarine training area, the loch is now a 'park' for redundant merchant ships, and home to a naval fuel depot.

❻ Isle of Bute

Central Bute is a charming combination of Victorian coastal resort, farms, nature trails, angling lochs and western sea bays with superb views towards the granite peaks of Arran.

Rothesay, the island capital and car-ferry port, is flanked on either side by the Skeoch and Bogany Woods, and close to the shore are the substantial ruins of 13th-century Rothesay Castle. Bute Museum illustrates the history, archaeology and wildlife of a fascinating island. From the centre of the town, Serpentine Road climbs through 13 closely packed hairpin bends to Canada Hill viewpoint and colourful Ardencraig Gardens.

South of Rothesay is the 18th-century mansion of Mount Stuart, the hereditary seat of the Marquess of Bute, which is open to visitors. In the hills to the south are the atmospheric ruins of the Church of St Blane (HS).

❼ Dunoon

Each year in late August, Dunoon is the site of the Cowal Highland Gathering, which features the traditional tossing of the caber as well as athletics and Highland dancing competitions.

As the town's Castle House Museum illustrates, in the Clyde steamer era Dunoon and its neighbours Kirn and Hunter's Quay were the Cowal peninsula's busiest resorts. Car ferries still operate to Gourock from here, and there are many summer cruises on offer.

Sea anglers tackle cod and coal-fish, plaice and conger eel, and you can also try your hand at inland loch and river fishing, as well as hill and forest walking, and golfing. South of the town you can take woodland walks through Morag's Fairy Glen.

The fragmentary remains of an ancient royal fortress lie in Dunoon's breezy park on Castle

MOUNT STUART, BUTE

Hill. Nearby is a statue of Robert Burns's sweetheart, 'Highland Mary', or Mary Campbell, who was born in Dunoon in 1764.

8 Holy Loch

The sailing village of Sandbank, located on the southern shore of a sea loch that used to be a US Polaris submarine base, is where the boats *Sceptre* and *Sovereign*, Britain's unsuccessful challengers for the America's Cup sailing race in 1958 and 1964 respectively, were built.

On the northern shore, footpaths through the broad-leaved trees and conifers of the Kilmun Arboretum, part of the Forestry Commission's Argyll Forest Park, climb a soaring ridge. Earls, dukes and the only Marquess of Argyll all lie in the family mausoleum at the Church of St Munn, which features a curious water-powered organ.

Off Strone Point, you can see feeding gannets crash-diving into the sea.

9 Ardentinny

Beautifully situated at the foot of Glen Finart, the hamlet faces the massive Trident missile base at Coulport on Loch Long's eastern shore, which is hidden from view from other angles.

Gairletter Point, 2 miles to the south of Ardentinny, is a good location for birdwatching.

10 Loch Eck

One of the grandest inland waterways in Scotland lies at the foot of the rugged hillsides of Cowal. Summertime cruises start from Coylet Inn.

To the north, Lauder Forest Walks explore oakwoods and conifer plantations, and lead past waterfalls, while to the south, an avenue of giant redwoods is a feature of the Younger Botanic Garden. Close by, a series of footpaths and footbridges climb the spectacular 250m (820ft) Puck's Glen.

11 Lochgoilhead

Loch Goil curves through a fiord-like landscape, and the village at its head looks across small-boat moorings to a towering skyline. The holiday village at Drimsynie includes a leisure centre open to visitors.

A forest path leads north along a mossy glen to Rob Roy's Cave, named after the 18th-century highland rebel who is said to have hidden there.

About 5 miles south, the village of Carrick Castle stands beside the ruins of the 14th-century Campbell tower, which gave it its name. You can often see herons along the shoreline here.

12 Arrochar

Set cosily among the mountains and forests at the head of Loch Long, the rural village of Arrochar was the heartland of the MacFarlanes, notorious cattle-raiders, from around the 11th century. The clan territory was sold in 1784, and the family died out in 1866.

Rock climbers can enjoy scaling the 'Arrochar Alps', especially Ben Arthur, known as the Cobbler because of the silhouette of its summit, while an easy walk over the range leads to the Cruach Tairbeirt path.

13 Loch Long

The 17 mile fiord-like sea loch slices deep into the Arrochar mountains. Its steeply banked upper reaches attract sea anglers.

Between Garelochhead and Arrochar, the West Highland Railway runs high above the lochside road. South of a Ministry of Defence jetty, the oil terminal at Finnart is one of the deepest water-tanker berths in Europe. Oil is pumped to Grangemouth's refinery, 57 miles away.

14 Rosneath Peninsula

Buzzards, hen harriers and sparrowhawks patrol the high plantations and grazing pastures, and early morning travellers may sometimes catch sight of roe deer. Much of the land on the peninsula, together with the modern road to Coulport, is Ministry of Defence property, although you may drive along the road. Cove Park's artists on residency development offers a range of events and talks.

Ferries and cruise boats, bound for Gourock and Helensburgh, leave from Kilcreggan Pier.

15 Gare Loch

On the eastern bank of the Gare Loch are the attractive villages of Rhu and Garelochhead. The Royal Northern and Clyde Yacht club has its headquarters at Rhu, and uphill from the separate Rhu Marina is Glenarn, a woodland garden with scenic walks. A hillside viewpoint above Garelochhead reveals the huge Clyde submarine base at Faslane Bay.

16 Helensburgh

The town of tree-lined streets is set out on a grid pattern and tucked in behind a promenade. Gulls, oystercatchers, redshanks, knots and turnstones feed along the water's edge among the yachts, sailboards and dinghies of Helensburgh's sailing club. A regular ferry service, which calls at the pier, sails to Kilcreggan and Gourock, and you can also arrange boat trips to Gare Loch and Holy Loch. A seafront obelisk commemorates Henry Bell, designer of the *Comet*, the world's first seagoing steamboat, launched in 1812.

John Logie Baird, the television pioneer, was born at Helensburgh in 1888. There is a small display explaining his life and works in the library, and a memorial window in West Kirk.

The Helensburgh Upland footpath, which starts at the top of Sinclair Street, passes through the car park of Hill House (NTS), Charles Rennie Mackintosh's Edwardian masterpiece. East of Helensburgh, the tidal bays at Ardmore provide fine opportunities for birdwatching.

⑰ Dumbarton

Presiding over the town from the shore, Dumbarton Rock has steps and pathways leading to mainly 18th-century fortifications, while the higher summit of Castle Rock, next to it, offers commanding views of the Firth of Clyde.

East of Castle Rock, a foreshore walk passes a launching ramp, all that remains of a wartime flying-boat factory. The pebbles, mudflats and reed beds attract redshanks, shelduck and reed buntings.

Denny's Ship Model Experiment Tank, a reminder of the town's successful ship design company, survives in the town centre as part of the Scottish Maritime Museum.

⑱ Bowling

The village marks the western end of the Forth and Clyde Canal, opened in 1790. The canal runs across Scotland for 35 miles and its banks are popular with coarse anglers, walkers and cyclists. Berths for pleasure craft are available at Bowling harbour, where locks, bridges and the old Custom House survive.

⑲ Port Glasgow

The building and launching site of Henry Bell's *Comet,* Port Glasgow was originally the seaport for the city of Glasgow, until the Clyde was deepened in the 1700s, although shipbuilding here has now dwindled to one fully operational yard. Newark Castle (HS), nearby, is a 16th-century mansion. Finlaystone, off the road between Port Glasgow and Langbank, has gardens, woodland walks and picnic areas.

⑳ Greenock

As the birthplace in 1736 of James Watt, who perfected the steam engine, Greenock was, in a sense, the cradle of the Industrial Revolution. The town prospered between the 17th and 19th centuries, but it has now declined as a port and shipbuilding centre. The Watt Library and the McLean Art Gallery and Museum tell the story of Watt and the town. The museum in Greenock's stately Georgian Custom House recalls literary figures from Chaucer to Burns who were once employed by the Customs and Excise service.

㉑ Gourock

The town is associated with James Watt and the old yarn that Watt's interest in the power of steam was roused when, as a boy, he watched a kettle boil. Ferries sail from Gourock to various points along the Clyde, and Prince's Pier has a direct rail link with Glasgow.

Yacht races are held in summer off West Bay, the base of the Royal Gourock Yacht Club.

㉒ Inverkip

Larch and pinewood ridges swoop down to the village of Inverkip, once a smugglers' haunt and now marked by the pontoon moorings of the Clyde's oldest marina, built in 1971. Nearby Lunderston Bay has a sandy beach with rocky outcrops, and a picnic site.

East of the village, on a road signposted to Loch Thom, is the Cornalees Bridge Visitor Centre, where you can take glen and moorland walks around a historic reservoir system.

㉓ Wemyss Bay

A red sandstone cliff, with the deep ravine of Kelly Burn, is the bay's great landscape feature. Once Glasgow's gateway to resorts along the Clyde, Wemyss (pronounced 'Weems') Bay is still a ferry port, and a path from the elegant Grade A listed railway station descends to the departure point for the Rothesay ferries. Beyond Kelly Burn, Skelmorlie village has hotels and villas. A golf course and trout fishery, open to visitors, occupy the hills above.

㉔ Largs

The Viking heritage of this popular holiday resort is celebrated every September at a Viking Festival. The Vikingar! exhibition tells the story of the Viking influence in Europe, especially Scotland, while the 'Pencil' monument, overlooking Largs Yacht Haven, commemorates the Scots' victory over the Vikings there in 1263. The local museum stands near the 17th-century Skelmorlie burial aisle, all that remains of the old parish church. The town also offers seafront walks, picnic spots, watersports and golf courses. There is a magnificent viewpoint at the top of Douglas Park, to the southeast of the town, from where, in clear weather, the peaks of Jura can be seen.

㉕ Great Cumbrae Island

One of the loveliest resorts on the Clyde, is home to the Victorian Cathedral of the Isles, Scotland's smallest cathedral. Millport, the island's only town, is a traditional resort curving round an islet-studded bay. The Museum of the Cumbraes tells the stories of the islands, while a house known as The Wedge, in Stuart Street, has a street frontage of only 119cm (47in), the narrowest in Britain.

㉖ Seamill

Long, sandy beaches start near Seamill Hydro, the last of the district's Victorian 'hydropathic' hotels, which were popular with middle-class Glaswegians as places to indulge in luxuries such as seawater baths. The coast road overlooks the boulder-strewn sands of Ardneil Bay. From a fine golf links, footpaths lead north to Portencross, whose ruined castle lies southwest of a vitrified Iron Age fort.

㉗ Saltcoats

A seaside resort with a sandy beach, the harbour in Saltcoats has a lookout tower and a walk along the sea wall. The town's main activity in the 16th century was evaporating seawater in coal-fired salt pans, hence its name.

㉘ Irvine

This old quayside town has close connections with Robert Burns, with a Burns museum and the Burns Club and Museum; the latter was founded in 1826 and is one of the oldest clubs in the world dedicated to the poet.

㉙ Troon

Ringed by six golf courses, Troon is also a major sailing resort and has a ferry link to Larne in Northern Ireland. Its marina occupies part of the old harbour where, in the early 19th century, the first railway in Scotland brought coal from inland. There is a pleasant stroll along a path backing the curving sands of South Beach.

㉚ Prestwick

The oldest burgh in Scotland, Prestwick was granted its status in AD 987, and Old Prestwick was the first home, from 1860 to 1872, of golf's Open Championship. In one of the many public gardens is Bruce's Well, a 13th-century healing well from which Robert Bruce is said to have drunk.

㉛ Ayr

The town described by Robert Burns in *Tam o'Shanter* as 'Auld Ayr wham ne'er a town surpasses for honest men and bonie lasses' is now Scotland's main west-coast resort, with 2 miles of sandy beaches. Sea-fishing trips from the harbour, at the mouth of the River Ayr, yield dogfish, tope, haddock and whiting; good shore fishing can be had along Newton Shore.

㉜ Heads of Ayr

On cliffs south of Ayr Bay, where an Iron Age fort once stood, are the ruins of Greenan Castle, a 16th-century stronghold

A HUGE PLUG FROM A LONG-EXTINCT VOLCANO
AILSA CRAIG

of the Kennedy family. The nearby Heads of Ayr Farm Park has a collection of exotic wildlife.

33 Dunure
In this bright little village stand a well-preserved dovecot and the ruins of a castle that belonged to the Kennedy family. Here in 1570 the lay abbot of Crossraguel Abbey, 5 miles southeast, was slowly roasted alive over a fire in a successful attempt to persuade him to transfer his lands to the 4th Earl of Cassilis.

Robert Bruce is said to have landed at Dunure from Irish exile in 1307 to begin the campaign that freed Scotland from English rule for a period of 400 years.

34 Electric Brae
This disconcerting stretch of road gives drivers the impression of going downhill when actually going uphill, and vice versa. Properly known as Croy Brae, the road was dubbed Electric Brae because of a theory that the effect was due to magnetism. In fact it is an optical illusion caused by unusual configurations of the land on either side.

35 Culzean Castle
Until the mid 18th century Culzean, pronounced 'Cullain', was a simple medieval tower house perched on a cliff edge. In 1777 the 10th Earl of Cassilis engaged Robert Adam to transform the building and its interior. The finest features of Culzean Castle (NTS) include an oval staircase and the round drawing room with views over the Firth of Clyde. A flat at the top of the castle was given to General Eisenhower in recognition of his achievements during the Second World War; he stayed there four times, and an exhibition covers his time in Britain.

A visitor centre in Adam's Home Farm is the focal point of a country park with a swan pond, deer centre, walled garden and playground.

36 Turnberry
Fine silver sands stretch for 1½ miles at Turnberry, and behind them are the golf courses for which the village is best known. The Ailsa course has a tee close to the beach known as Woe-be-Tide, and the Arran course has fine views of the Isle of Arran, 14 miles away.

The fragment of castle north of the golf courses was the home of Robert Bruce's mother and, like several other sites, lays claim to having been his birthplace. In conflict with Dunure, it also claims to have been the place where he landed before launching his campaign against the English.

37 Girvan
More than a mile of sands lie to the south of the colourful harbour in this small resort, which has several floral gardens. Boat trips to

Ailsa Craig, and for sea angling between Girvan and Bennane Head, leave from the harbour. Plaice and flounder can be caught from the pier.

38 Ailsa Craig
Ten miles offshore, the huge plug of a long-extinct volcano dominates the view from most of this coastline. Ailsa Craig is more than 335m (1100ft) high but measures only just over 2 miles in circumference. Its granite was long used to make what were regarded as the finest stones for use in the sport of curling.

The island is home to guillemots and kittiwakes, but they are outnumbered by thousands of gannets, which breed here every summer. Former tenants of the island used to pay their rents in gannet feathers.

39 Lendalfoot
Above the tiny settlement with its shingle beach, rises the ruined tower of Carleton Castle. There is an old tale that one of its owners, Sir John Cathcart, made a habit of marrying heiresses and then pushing them off a cliff at Games Loup, southwest of the castle. The eighth heiress, a Kennedy of Culzean, turned the tables by pushing Sir John off the same cliff.

From Lendalfoot, the coast road heads southwest towards Bennane Head. Below is Sawney Bean's Cave, once reached by a footpath now too dangerous to use. The cave was home in the 16th century to the Bean family, said to prey on travellers, killing and eating them. Around 1600 James VI had them hunted down and publicly dismembered.

40 Ballantrae
Dominating the southern end of Ballantrae are the jagged ruins of Ardstinchar Castle, where Mary, Queen of Scots, spent a night in August 1566; below, a graceful old bridge, closed to traffic, crosses the River Stinchar. When the water is low, you may see salmon in pools, waiting for enough water to get them upstream to spawn.

The shingle spit and lagoons at the mouth of the river form the Ballantrae Nature Reserve.

Visitor information

Ayr ☎ (01292) 290300
Balloch ☎ 08707 200607
Dunoon ☎ (01369) 703785
Helensburgh – Visit Scotland ☎ 0845 225 5121
Inveraray – Visit Scotland ☎ 0845 225 5121
Largs ☎ (01475) 689962
Milton, Dumbarton – Visit Scotland
  ☎ 0845 225 5121
Rothesay ☎ 08707 200619

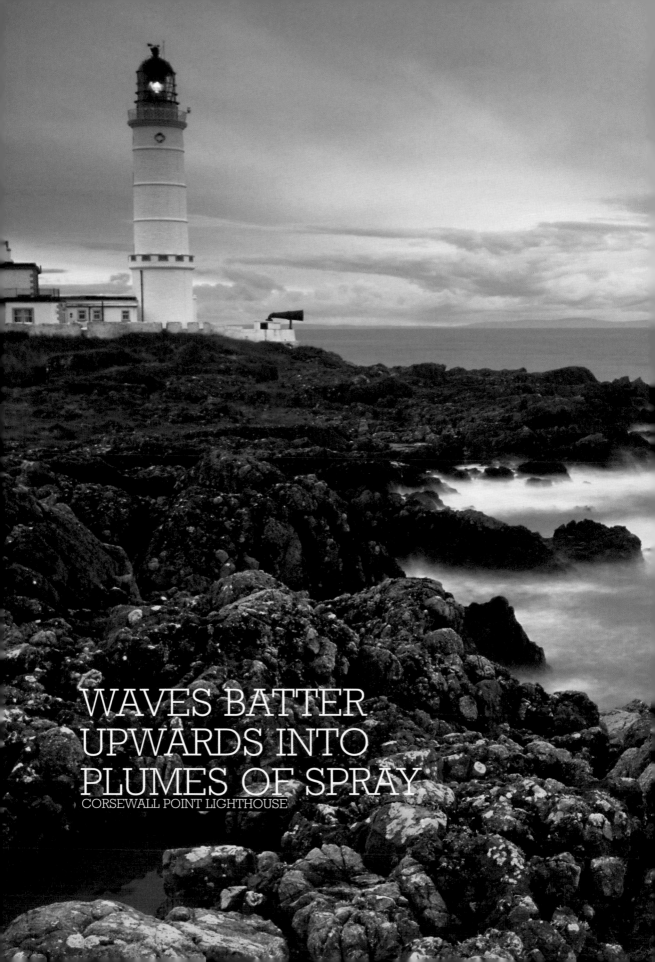

WAVES BATTER
UPWARDS INTO
PLUMES OF SPRAY
CORSEWALL POINT LIGHTHOUSE

CAIRNRYAN TO GRETNA

Southwest Scotland is home to a number of luxuriant and exotic gardens, some with thriving subtropical plants, thanks to its fertile land and the influence of warm ocean currents

❶ Cairnryan
During the Second World War Cairnryan became a military port handling supplies of food and ammunition from the USA. The wartime harbour has now given way to a small ferry terminal for vehicle, passenger and freight services to Larne in Northern Ireland.

Finnarts Bay, to the north, offers some of the best local sea fishing, especially for tope and other types of shark.

❷ Castle Kennedy Gardens
Landscaped terraces, wooded gardens and tree-lined walkways lie between the ivy-clad ruin of Castle Kennedy, mostly destroyed by fire in 1716, and the privately owned 19th-century Lochinch Castle, which is not open to the public. The gardens include grassy mounds and embankments created in the early 18th century by troops of the 2nd Earl of Stair to resemble contemporary military fortifications.

❸ Stranraer
In its sheltered position within Loch Ryan, Stranraer became, in 1872, the main terminal for steam packets to Northern Ireland. Today it has regular ferries to Larne, and a high-speed catamaran service to Belfast.

The Castle of St John in the centre of the town was built in 1500 beside a medieval chapel,

demolished in the early 18th century. For a time, after 1682, it was the headquarters of 'Bluidy' Claverhouse during his persecution of the Covenanters. The castle has also served as a courtroom and prison cells, and as a police station, and it has exhibits on law and order.

On the waterfront, the hotel known as North West Castle was built by Sir John Ross, the 19th-century explorer of the Canadian Arctic.

❹ Kirkcolm
The former fishing village sits inland from the bay of The Wig, where there is a slipway once part of a flying boat and seaplane base in both world wars. The slipway now serves Lochryan Sailing Club, and The Wig and curving spit of The Scar attract nesting terns, eider ducks and oystercatchers.

To the north, Clachan Heughs woodland has trees planted in the exact formation of Sir John Moore's troops as they lined up to fight at Corunna in 1809; the Moore family lived nearby at Corsewall House, which is privately owned. Lady Bay has a sandy shore and picnic area.

❺ Corsewall Point
At the north-western tip of a windswept almost treeless peninsula, deep-cut rock fissures bring the waves battering upwards into plumes of spray. On the headland above

stands the white tower of Corsewall lighthouse; opened in 1816, it was designed by Robert Stevenson, the grandfather of the writer Robert Louis Stevenson and is now a hotel.

6 Portpatrick
A holiday resort sparkling with colour-washed villas and hotels, Portpatrick has a small sandy beach, backed by cliffs, on the top of which are two golf courses. The northern cliff marks the western end of a coast-to-coast footpath, the 212 mile Southern Upland Way, which reaches the North Sea at Cockburnspath. For centuries boats sailed from Portpatrick to Donaghadee in Northern Ireland.

In 1774 John Smeaton was commissioned to build a pier, lighthouse and breakwaters along the shore at Portpatrick, but storm tides wrecked his work. The later efforts of Thomas Telford and John Rennie were also defeated by the weather, and in the mid 19th century shipping to and from Ireland was re-routed via Stranraer.

To the south, a dizzying but well-fenced walk along the clifftop, with fine views out to sea, leads to ruined 16th-century Dunskey Castle.

7 Port Logan
Stormy seas put an end to plans to develop a small harbour here in the early 19th century. Colonel Andrew McDouall, a local resident behind the idea, had hoped to profit from the Irish cattle trade. Though the harbour was soon abandoned, a few fishermen still go out in search of herring in June and July.

North of the village and its whitewashed cottages, wooden stairways descend to a sandy shore; from here a short walk leads to Logan Fish Pond, excavated in 1800 from the rocks behind the shore to provide a stock of fresh fish for the kitchen at nearby Logan House. The fish became so tame that they would answer a bell to be fed. The pond holds around 30 fish, mainly cod, and they are still so tame that they can be enticed to feed from visitors' hands.

8 Mull of Galloway
The southernmost tip of Scotland narrows between wave-beaten cliffs before rising to a high promontory from which one of Robert Stevenson's lighthouses looms 82m (270ft) above.

The Mull of Galloway's cliffs form an RSPB reserve and in summer the ledges teem with crowds of rowdy sea birds such as guillemots, razorbills, kittiwakes and shags, which you can see from certain lookout points along the clifftop.

9 Drummore
A snug little holiday resort of whitewashed cottages overlooking a sandy beach, Scotland's southernmost village originated in the early 19th century as a harbour for importing

coal and lime from the north of England, and shipping out agricultural produce. The village is one of several local centres for tope fishing.

10 Logan Botanic Garden
An exotic walled garden has been arranged round the ruined keep of Balzieland Castle. The warming effect of the Gulf Stream enables many plants native to the Southern Hemisphere, such as eucalyptus, cabbage palms and tree ferns, to be grown here.

11 Ardwell Gardens
The woodland gardens of Ardwell House offer seasonal displays of daffodils, azaleas, rhododendrons and a variety of other flowering shrubs, and are reached from the A716 south of Sandhead. The gardens include three ponds, one giving views across Luce Bay.

12 Luce Sands
Sandhead's parking and picnic area overlooks an 8 mile stretch of golden sands, but a bombing range 2 miles east puts the sands beyond out of bounds to the public.

Starting from the B7084 towards Glenluce, a 1½ mile walk wanders through the spruces and pines of Bareagle Forest. The walk ends at a picnic area with a view over Luce Bay from Ringdoo Point.

13 Glenluce
Set on the Water of Luce, the village has an imposing but derelict viaduct that once carried the railway line from Carlisle to Stranraer. A road under one of the viaduct's arches leads to Glenluce Abbey (NTS), a ruined 12th-century Cistercian abbey and chapter house rebuilt in the 15th century.

In the village, a shaded stroll beside a burn leads through the glen that lies between the main street and the bypass.

14 Stair Haven
Apart from its beach of rocks and sand, Stair Haven consists of little more than a lonely cottage, a small harbour and a ruined pier, now used only by local fishermen and visitors. Species in the bay include crab, flounder, mullet, mackerel and skate.

A narrow coastal road to Stair Haven from Glenluce gives uninterrupted vistas of Luce Sands and the bay.

15 Auchenmalg Bay
At the northern end of a sandy bay stretching south to Craignarget is the hamlet of Auchenmalg. Boats can be hired for the fishing of crab, flounder, mullet and skate. Sinniness Barracks, a private house, was built in the 1820s to house a group of revenue men, sent

to stamp out the Solway smuggling trade, while in a walled enclosure beside the road south to Port William are the low foundation walls of a 10th or 11th-century pilgrims' chapel dedicated to an Irish bishop, St Finian of Movilla.

16 Port William
The village was established in the late 18th century as a shipbuilding and fishing centre, and became a haunt of smugglers. Near the shore of pebbles and splintered rock are parking and grassy picnic sites, and boats can be hired for tope and porbeagle fishing.

17 Monreith
Trim cottages cluster round a sandy bay. On a headland, above the village and near a golf course, an otter sculpture commemorates Gavin Maxwell, author of *Ring of Bright Water.* Many of Maxwell's family are buried beside the ruins of Kirkmaiden Church, which cling to the cliff below.

A mile to the south is Monreith Animal World, whose attractions include an otter family.

18 St Ninian's Cave
From Kidsdale Farm, a path leads to the cave to which St Ninian retreated. The saint lived during the 4th and 5th centuries, and was the first Christian missionary to come to Scotland. Christian crosses have been carved into the cave walls.

19 Isle of Whithorn
A causeway from the village leads to a rocky peninsula, once a genuine isle, where there is a 13th-century ruined chapel named after St Ninian. The village, a sailing and sea-angling centre with boats for hire, is the base of the Wigtown Bay Sailing Club.

Four miles inland at the town of Whithorn, archaeological finds associated with the saint, such as crosses and stones, are displayed at the Whithorn Museum (HS) and at the Whithorn Story Visitor Centre. Both buildings are in the same complex.

20 Garlieston
Laid out around 1760 in two crescents of colour-washed cottages facing the sand and shingle bay, the village prospered from shipbuilding, sailmaking and cattle trade with Ireland. Today the harbour is used by small craft, and there are fishing trips for salmon.

Walks to the shore join a short coastal path that leads past Galloway House Gardens to Cruggleton Castle ruins. The gardens have many fine old trees, and seasonal displays of azaleas and rhododendrons.

America's 'Man of War'

John Paul Jones was a Scotsman who became a hero to the Americans after he joined their naval forces during the War of Independence. He made daring raids on the British Coast and, in 1779, won a singular victory over a superior British force in the North Sea.

Generally regarded as the founder of the American naval tradition, he was described by Thomas Jefferson as 'the principal hope of America's future efforts on the ocean'. He later served Catherine the Great in the Russian Navy.

▶ Arbigland Gardens 35, page 238

21 Wigtown
In summer the flats and salt marshes of Wigtown's sandy bay are breeding grounds for lapwings, curlews and common terns.

A royal burgh since 1292, Wigtown has a spacious town square, with a bowling green in the middle of it. The town's harbour silted up early in the 20th century, but it has been renovated with quays, parking and picnic areas along the River Bladnoch.

A path across a disused railway embankment leads to a grim memorial honouring two female Covenanters who, in 1685, refusing to change their religious allegiance, were tied to stakes offshore and drowned by the rising tide.

22 Kirroughtree Forest Garden
The arboretum includes beeches, whitebeams and red oaks. There are also forest trails, a wildlife pond and views of the heights of Cairnsmore of Fleet, which features briefly in John Buchan's novel *The Thirty-Nine Steps.*

23 Creetown
A dazzling collection of gemstones, crystals and minerals is housed in the Gem Rock Museum in this little port. In the 19th century the port exported granite from nearby quarries.

The Scottish historian and essayist Thomas Carlyle once assured Queen Victoria that the only road finer than that between Gatehouse of Fleet and Creetown was that between Creetown and Gatehouse of Fleet. The road, watched over by the relic of 16th-century Carsluith Castle (HS), 3½ miles south of Creetown, is still a visual delight, with magnificent seascapes on one side and lush greenery on the other.

㉔ Cairn Holy

The two chambered cairns of Cairn Holy (HS) date from 4000–5000 years ago and are located up a lane from the A75. The larger of the two has an exposed burial chamber as well as a small courtyard in which ritual ceremonies took place. The smaller cairn was robbed for building stones in the 18th century.

㉕ Gatehouse of Fleet

Planned on a grid pattern by James Murray of Broughton and Cally in the late 18th century, the town developed as a cotton manufacturing centre, and its history is explained at the Mill on the Fleet Heritage Centre. On a rocky mound above the Water of Fleet, which divides the town in two, is the 15th-century tower of Cardoness Castle (HS).

South of the town, in the grounds of James Murray's old home, now the Cally Palace Hotel, the Fleet Oakwoods interpretive trail is a 2 mile woodland walk, with trees identified by markers.

㉖ Sandgreen

The bay is the most popular of a series of sandy coves, separated by grassy headlands, that stretch southwards along the coast opposite the Islands of Fleet.

At low tide walkers can cross from the hamlet of Carrick's bay to the biggest of the islands, Ardwall, inhabited in the late 18th century by a family who kept open house for smugglers.

㉗ Kirkcudbright

From the harbour, where boats land the small scallops known as 'Kirkcudbright queenies', visitors can book sea-angling trips. Pronounced 'Kirkoobree', the town's name probably derives from St Cuthbert, who converted much of Scotland to Christianity.

MacLellan's Castle (HS), a ruined 16th-century mansion, was built largely from the ruins of neighbouring Greyfriars monastery, while the medieval Tolbooth, in the largely Georgian high

CAIRN HOLY

her last night on Scottish soil, on May 15, 1568, before crossing the Solway to seek help from Queen Elizabeth I of England. Among the abbey's fine sculptures is a large-size group depicting a murdered abbot and his assassin.

29 Auchencairn
The steep little village of whitewashed cottages and pebble beaches was once a haunt of smugglers and during the 18th century it was an iron-mining centre.

Hestan Island and its lighthouse lie a mile offshore. During the Middle Ages the island was owned by the monks of Dundrennan Abbey, and you can still see still traces of their fishpond near the causeway.

30 Balcary Point
Built by 18th-century smugglers as a headquarters and a storage place for contraband, Balcary House is now a hotel. A footpath crosses the fields to Balcary Point, where you can see sea birds such as oystercatchers, curlews, redshanks, dunlin and shelduck. In summer, common sandpipers abound.

31 Palnackie
The estuary offers good fishing for flat-fish, and each summer hosts the World Flounder Tramping Championships on the mudflats of the Glen Isle peninsula. Contestants may use only their feet and a three-pronged spear to catch the fish.

The village was once a busy port on the Urr estuary, until its tiny harbour silted up; several of the houses in Palnackie were built with two storeys to accommodate sailors from the trading ships that used to ply the coast.

Southwest of the village, 15th-century Orchardton Tower (HS) is the only surviving Scottish tower house built in the cylindrical style common in Ireland. A spiral staircase within its walls leads up to an airy parapet walk.

32 Kippford
Hillside houses surround the small resort of Kippford and its pebble beach. The former shipbuilding centre is now the base of the Solway Yacht Club.

A clifftop walk following the mile-long Jubilee Path (NTS) to neighbouring Rockcliffe offers views of the Galloway Hills and, on clear days, St Bees Head in Cumbria and the peaks of the Lake District. On nearby Scaur Hill is the Motte of Mark, a 6th-century Celtic fort so savagely burnt by raiders that its stones vitrified.

A shingle spit leads at low tide from the southern end of the village to Rough Island (NTS), a bird sanctuary where terns and

street, retains on its outer walls the manacles to which wrongdoers were fastened to receive public beatings. Now the Tolbooth Arts Centre, it houses craft studios and an exhibition devoted to the town's long-established artists' colony.

Broughton House (NTS), bequeathed to the town by the painter E.A. Hornel (1864-1933), has a collection of his paintings and sculptures.

North of the harbour is the start of the 6 mile Dee Walk, while Galloway Wildlife Conservation Park, 2 miles northeast of Kirkcudbright, works for the conservation of rare breeds, such as Scottish wildcats, lynx and Arctic foxes; you can take guided tours.

28 Dundrennan Abbey
A 13th-century chapter house and some Norman stonework are the remains of Dundrennan Abbey (HS), founded by Cistercians in 1142. It was here that Mary, Queen of Scots, having abdicated in favour of her infant son James VI, is believed to have spent

oystercatchers nest in May and June. In summer, the National Trust for Scotland organises ranger-conducted tours from Kippford and Rockcliffe.

㉝ Rockcliffe

With its shore of sand and rock pools, broken by jagged shoulders of rock in a sheltered bay, the village developed as a smart resort in Victorian times. A short footpath follows the edge of Rough Firth to the summit of Castlehill Point, with wide views across the Solway Firth to Cumbria. Shore and clifftop paths continue to Port o' Warren and Portling; at low tide you can explore a number of smugglers' caves around the latter. Farther east, at Sandyhills, is a complex of stake-nets used to trap salmon.

㉞ Southerness

On the foreshore stands a lighthouse dating from the 18th century. The wide sands that surround it have given rise to a large holiday village. Walkers here should take care when venturing seawards, as the tide can sweep in faster than walking pace.

㉟ Arbigland Gardens

The gardens reach down through a succession of glades, featuring a range of semitropical shrubs and trees, to a sheltered, sandy beach. In 1768 the head gardener's son, John Paul Jones, became the captain of a Dumfries trading vessel. Soon afterwards, he departed for America and

CAERLAVEROCK CASTLE

became a founder of the American navy. His birthplace, Paul Jones' Cottage, is now a tiny museum.

36 New Abbey

Set among woods by the New Abbey Pow River, the village and surrounding landscape are dominated by Criffel, a hill that rises to 569m (1868ft). The summit can be reached by a 1½ mile track at Ardwall, and from the top you can see the Nith estuary and the Isle of Man. Sweetheart Abbey (HS) was founded in 1273 by Devorgilla, the wife of John Balliol, a Scottish king. The abbey is so named because after Balliol's death Devorgilla carried his embalmed heart with her, and was buried with it.

Shambellie House (HS) is a museum of mainly Victorian and Edwardian costume in period surroundings; in the 18th century its owner built the nearby water-powered Corn Mill, now restored. Bordering the road to Dumfries is Mabie Forest, with picnic areas and walks, including one through the nature reserve of Lochaber Loch, noted for its butterflies and oaks.

37 Caerlaverock Nature Reserve

Barnacle geese from Spitsbergen come to spend autumn and winter on the nature reserve at the Caerlaverock Wetland Centre, along with pink-footed geese from Iceland and other wildfowl. There is also a large colony of rare natterjack toads. At East Park Farm, viewing towers and hides are open to the public all year round, and between May and August you can take guided walks.

The deep red sandstone ruins of Caerlaverock Castle (HS), overlooking the Merse saltings, are reflected in its moat. Built in the late 13th century, the castle changed hands several times between English and Scots. One of its most remarkable features is a 17th-century row of interconnecting buildings that looks more like a Renaissance mansion than part of a fortress.

38 Ruthwell

In the secluded village is a 7th-century stone cross carved with Biblical scenes and verses from *The Dream of the Rood,* the oldest-known English poem. Broken up as an idolatrous monument in 1640, it was later restored in 1820 by Dr Henry Duncan, the parish minister, and it now stands in the church apse. He also founded the first Trustee Savings Bank, remembered in the village's Savings Banks Museum.

West of the village is Brow Well, to which in early June 1796 Robert Burns came in the hope of curing his ailments by drinking the well waters, which contain salts of iron.

39 Annan

The village of red sandstone buildings stands on the eastern bank of the River Annan and is the main market town in the region. The tidal river provides anglers with good catches of salmon and trout. Commercial fishing is done from February to September with haaf-nets and stake-nets.

40 Gretna

From the mid 18th century, neighbouring Gretna Green flourished as a place for couples eloping from England to marry without parental approval and under the age of consent. Overlooking the estuary of Kirtle Water is the 2m (7ft) high Lochmaben Stone, which may once have formed part of a prehistoric stone circle.

Visitor information

Castle Douglas ☎ (01556) 502611
Dumfries ☎ (01387) 245555
Gatehouse of Fleet ☎ (01557) 814212
Gretna Green ☎ (01461) 337834
Kirkcudbright ☎ (01557) 330494
Newton Stewart ☎ (01671) 402431
Stranraer ☎ (01776) 702595

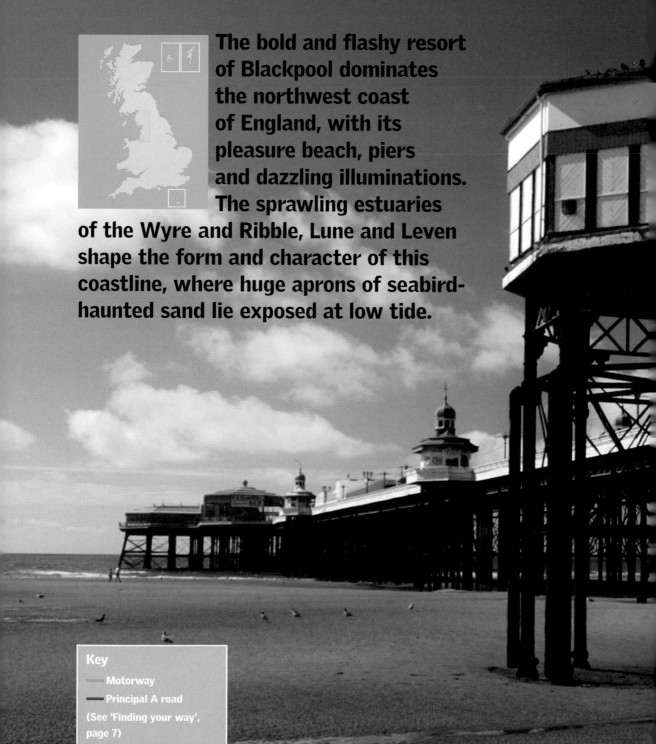

Northwest

The bold and flashy resort of Blackpool dominates the northwest coast of England, with its pleasure beach, piers and dazzling illuminations. The sprawling estuaries of the Wyre and Ribble, Lune and Leven shape the form and character of this coastline, where huge aprons of seabird-haunted sand lie exposed at low tide.

Key

Motorway

Principal A road

(See 'Finding your way', page 7)

BURGH BY SANDS TO DUDDON SANDS

Once a thriving mining area, the coast surrounding the timeless and secluded Solway Firth is overlooked by wild, lonely beaches, while farther inland there are nature reserves aplenty

0   5 Miles

❶ Burgh by Sands
The stone-and-brick cottages of Burgh, pronounced 'Bruff', stand on the site of a Roman fort. St Michael's Church was built with stones from the Roman defences, but its Norman doorway is its earliest architectural feature. A refuge from marauders as well as a place of worship, its 14th-century tower has no outer doorway.

A mile north of the village, the Edward I Monument is prominent amid the lonely saltings of Burgh Marsh. It marks the spot where Edward I died in 1307, aged 68, while setting out on a campaign against the Scots.

❷ Drumburgh
The small village originally marked the site of the next Roman fort to Bowness along Hadrian's Wall. Although the fort has gone, the road through Drumburgh still twists along the line of its outer walls, and to the east, the sea wall follows the line of the original turf rampart.

❸ Bowness-on-Solway
A compact village of narrow streets lined with sandstone cottages, Bowness was founded by the Romans as their fortress of Maia. It lies at the western end of Hadrian's Wall, built across the neck of England to the Tyne at the northernmost limit of the Roman Empire, and the present-day road through the village still follows the line of Maia's central thoroughfare. From there a chain of 'milefortlets' and towers extended 40 miles farther down the coast.

Two miles south is Glasson Moss, part of the South Solway Mosses National Nature Reserve, an expanse of peat bog and sphagnum moss, where insect-eating sundews and bog rosemary grow on treacherous terrain.

❹ Herdhill Scar
Until 1935, a mile-long railway viaduct connected the headland of Herdhill Scar to the Scottish shore. The line was opened in 1869 to link the iron-ore mines of Cumbria with the smelting furnaces of Lanarkshire. Trains ran across the viaduct until the 1920s.

Campfield Marsh RSPB Reserve, to the west of the promontory, is a huge area of tidal mudflats and a major site for a variety of water birds, including oystercatchers and curlews, as well as a feeding ground for migrating pink-footed geese.

❺ Newton Arlosh
Founded as a new settlement by the monks of Holm Cultram, the straggling village, was for centuries under threat from Scottish marauders. During raids, cattle were driven inside the nave of 14th-century St John's Church for safety.

❻ Abbeytown
The farming village gets its name from the Cistercian abbey of Holm Cultram, which was founded in 1150. As well as growing grain, the monks raised large flocks of sheep and

established a thriving trade in salt from the Solway Firth. In 1322 the abbey was sacked by Robert Bruce, but was later rebuilt. Although it was dissolved by Henry VIII in 1538, part of the nave survives and is still used as a parish church, dedicated to St Mary.

To the south, a series of grassy ridges and depressions marking the foundations give an indication of the size of the former abbey.

⑦ Skinburness

Most of the original village was swept away by a flood in 1303, and the villagers moved inland to a safer site at Newton Arlosh. The sea has since retreated, leaving a tract of salt marsh on which sheep and cattle graze.

During his Scottish campaigns in the early 14th century, Edward I made the village his supply base. Linked to Silloth by a mile-long promenade, today it consists of a large hotel and a handful of houses.

Grune Point, to the northeast, gives a wide view of the estuary. Antennae belonging to the NATO radio station at Anthorn dominate the skyline to the east.

⑧ Silloth

Wide, tree-lined streets give the small resort, with its sand and shingle beach, a spacious air. At the centre is The Green, an expanse of flowerbeds and rose bushes, fringed by pines and facing across the Solway Firth.

Silloth became popular with holidaymakers after the railway arrived in the 1850s, though the branch line is now defunct. The harbour, opened in 1859, was once a departure point for steamers to Liverpool and Dublin. Today it is used by pleasure craft and small coasters.

The town's name dates from when the monks of Holm Cultram Abbey cultivated grain on the fertile Cumbrian fields. Granaries, or 'laths', were used for storage, and the granary by the sea became known as 'Sea-lath', altered down the years to 'Silloth'.

⑨ Allonby

Vast areas of sand and rock pools, thronged with sea birds, are exposed at low water in this village, where the tide goes out more than a mile. It can be unsafe to venture far from the shore when the tide turns, but the bay is popular with windsurfers. Fishermen's cottages are scattered along the coast, with wide stretches of grass between the houses.

⑩ Crosscanonby Saltpans

At the foot of Swarthy Hill, 2 miles south of Allonby, you can see the square stone foundations of 17th-century salt pans. Solway salt was made there by a process called 'sleeching', whereby salt was extracted from sand

raked from the beach, rather than directly from seawater. On a mound across the road are the overgrown remains of the 'kinch', the circular stone enclosure where the sleech was processed.

Steps lead up the hill to the remains of a small Roman fort, one of a chain of 'milefortlets' built to guard the Solway south of Hadrian's Wall.

⑪ Maryport

The town owes its name to Mary Senhouse, the wife of an 18th-century entrepreneur who built the docks and harbour to serve the Cumbrian coal trade. In the 19th century, ships from Maryport were loaded with iron rails, made in Cumbria for railways all over the world. Near the harbour-side is the Maritime Museum, where reminders of Maryport's seagoing past include several exhibits on Fletcher Christian, leader of the mutiny on the *Bounty* in 1789.

High up on the north side of the town are the remains of the Roman fort of Alauna, built to prevent seaborne raiders from outflanking the defences of Hadrian's Wall. It is now just a faint outline in a field on private land. Next to it, however, the Senhouse Roman Museum has a magnificent collection of Roman inscriptions.

⑫ Workington

A grid of streets surrounds Portland Square, where 18th-century cottages overlook an expanse of tree-shaded cobbles, although much of the rest of Workington bears a distinctively industrial look. Mine tunnels once ran deep under the sea from the collieries around Workington, and Cumbrian coal used to be shipped from its deep-water harbour. The steel rails made in the town were exported around the world.

In a public park above the Derwent stand the imposing ruins of Workington Hall, where Mary, Queen of Scots, spent her last few days of freedom in May 1568, after fleeing from Scotland across the Solway Firth. Workington's past is conjured up inside the Helena Thompson Museum, a Georgian house opposite the hall.

A mile north, the Siddick Pond Nature Reserve is a bird sanctuary with a lakeside hide.

⑬ Whitehaven

Laid out in the 17th century on a grid pattern and retaining a Georgian elegance, Whitehaven was Britain's first post-medieval planned town, and the docks and harbour, built in the 18th and 19th centuries, are used today by fishing boats, pleasure craft and coasters. The Whitehaven Beacon, a museum by the harbour, tells the stories of the town's sailors, miners, slave traders and tobacco merchants. Exhibits include a superb enamel goblet made in 1763. Whitehaven is also the western end of the 140 mile C2C cycle route.

⑭ St Bees

An Irish princess called St Bega established a nunnery here around AD 650. Destroyed by the Vikings, it was refounded as a Benedictine priory in 1120. Nearby is St Bees School, founded in 1583 by Edmund Grindal, Archbishop of Canterbury, and looming over the long sandy beach is St Bees Head cliff. The RSPB reserve on the headland has one of the largest sea-bird colonies on England's west coast, and is the only breeding ground in England for black guillemots.

⑮ Egremont

Every September, the town holds a Crab Fair, so called because, when it was founded in 1267, crab apples were given away to visitors. The fair's 'World Gurning Championship' is won by the contestant who pulls the ugliest face. In the park are the ruins of Egremont Castle, which dates from the 12th century; part of the gatehouse, great hall and outer wall survive.

⑯ Sellafield

In 1956, Calder Hall became Britain's first nuclear power station to generate electricity on a commercial scale. The remains of Calder Hall are being decommissioned and are just one part of the nuclear processing plant of Sellafield. Two miles away are the riverside ruins of 12th-century Calder Abbey.

⑰ Ravenglass

Narrow-gauge steam-hauled trains head northeast for 7 miles through unspoiled scenery from this village, the terminus of the Ravenglass and Eskdale Railway. A museum in the station tells the story of the line, built in 1875 to carry iron ore to the coast.

Ravenglass was the site of the Roman naval base of Glannoventa. The ruins of its bathhouse lie a few minutes' walk from the village.

⑱ Muncaster Castle
Built on a hillside above the Esk, Muncaster Castle has 14th-century origins but was substantially rebuilt in the mid 19th century. Its gardens include azaleas, rhododendrons and a terrace almost a mile long, and the Owl Centre in the grounds conserves endangered owls.

⑲ Hodbarrow RSPB Reserve
The dramatic stretch of brackish water was formed when the Hodbarrow iron mines were flooded after the last mine closed in 1968. Great crested grebes, tufted ducks, oystercatchers and little terns gather at the water's edge, and kestrels and barn owls hunt here.

⑳ Millom
The quiet Victorian town on the Duddon estuary grew prosperous from iron mining. During the late 19th century its mines had 11 working shafts, making them the largest and busiest in Britain; the last closed in 1968.

Displays at Millom's Folk Museum include a reconstruction of a miner's cottage kitchen, and a replica of part of the Hodbarrow iron mine at Haverigg.

㉑ Duddon Sands
Low tide in the Duddon estuary reveals a stretch of sand 2 miles across at its widest point but treacherous sands and fast incoming tides mean the sands should only be crossed with local guidance. The mudflats on both sides of the estuary attract huge numbers of oystercatchers, lapwings and other wading birds.

> **Visitor information**
>
> **Carlisle** ☎ (01228) 625600
> **Cockermouth** ☎ (01900) 822634
> **Egremont** ☎ (01946) 820693
> **Maryport** ☎ (01900) 702840
> **Silloth** ☎ (016973) 31944 (Solway Coast Discovery Centre)

A BREEDING GROUND FOR BLACK GUILLEMOTS
ST BEES HEAD

ISLE OF WALNEY TO CLEVELEYS

Curving round the magnificent arc of Morecambe Bay, this stretch of coastline contains a number of sandy beaches and popular resorts; it was also once home to the biggest steelworks in the world

❶ Isle of Walney
The 12 mile strip of land provides the shelter that makes Barrow such a fine harbour. A wide expanse of water, dotted with rocks and islets, offers moorings for pleasure craft on the island's landward side, while on the seaward side is a sandy beach over 10 miles long.

The North Walney National Nature Reserve is an area of dunes and grassland where birds such as redshanks and stonechats congregate, and where the natterjack toad is also found. At the island's southern end, a sand and shingle bank, with ponds formed by old gravel workings, forms another nature reserve, home to one of Europe's busiest lesser black-backed and herring gull colonies.

❷ Piel Island
Built in the 16th century by the monks of Furness Abbey, Piel Castle (EH) played an important role in Barrow's defences from the 12th century and parts of the massive keep and walls survive. Set midway between Roa Island on the mainland and the southern tip of the Isle of Walney, you can reach the island on foot, with care, from South Walney at low tide, or by ferry service from Roa Island.

The narrow finger of land southeast of Roa Island is occupied by Foulney Island Nature Reserve, reached along a 1½ mile shingle causeway, flooded at high tide. It attracts birds such as terns, eider ducks and dunlin.

❸ Barrow-In-Furness
Local deposits of iron ore transformed Barrow in the early 19th century from a country village into a thriving industrial and shipbuilding centre. High-grade ore was shipped to steelworks all over England, and by 1870 Barrow's own steelworks, now closed, were the biggest in the world. The town centre, with its wide streets and huge, red sandstone town hall, is a monument to Victorian civic pride.

Though Barrow's great days of shipbuilding are over, Trident nuclear submarines have also been built there, in a hall whose vast white bulk looms over the port area. Across the road is the Dock Museum, which tells the story of Barrow's industrial past. Today there are plans for a marina and a new shipbuilding facility.

In a peaceful green valley on the north side of the town are the sandstone ruins of Furness Abbey (EH), built by Cistercian monks in the 12th century. You can also see the remains of a warehouse used to shelter goods traded from the abbey, such as food, wine and wool.

❹ Dalton-in-Furness
The small town lies in an area honeycombed with old iron-ore quarries and mine workings. Here, Dalton Castle (NT) is a squat 14th-century tower with a small museum, open only on Saturday afternoons in summer. Across the road from the castle is the huge Victorian Church of St Mary, while the South Lakes Wild Animal Park is the place to see giraffes, rhinos and baboons.

Three miles northwest of Dalton is the Sandscale Haws Nature Reserve (NT), where natterjack toads breed in spring and Arctic birds visit in summer. Walks along the shore give superb views of Black Combe and other fells of the southern Lake District.

5 Gleaston Water Mill

The 18ft water wheel and machinery at this mill, built in 1774, have been restored to working order. Archaeologists have unearthed flint tools there, dating from 5000 BC, now displayed along with milling artefacts inside the mill.

The 14th-century ruin of Gleaston Castle is not open to the public but you can see it from the road between Gleaston and Scales.

6 Aldingham

Recorded in Domesday Book, the village has been gradually lost to the sea over the centuries. Little remains of the original Aldingham, except for the Church of St Cuthbert, protected from the sea by a wall, and 19th-century Aldingham Hall, which is not open to the public. Notable features of the 12th-century church include two carvings in the chancel portraying a demure bride and a bashful bridegroom.

7 Baycliff

The village is set on top of the low banks that border the west side of Morecambe Bay. North of Baycliff the elevated, bracken-covered expanse of Birkrigg Common gives panoramas of the bay and has a well-preserved Bronze Age stone circle.

8 Bardsea Country Park

The strip of coast beside the road from Baycliff to Ulverston has fine views looking out across Morecambe Bay towards Heysham, has picnic spaces and waymarked footpaths. Sea Wood, the site of a nature trail, includes ancient woodland as well as oaks planted to provide timber for ships built at nearby Barrow-in-Furness.

Conishead Priory stands in extensive grounds to the north of the country park; an Augustinian priory once stood on the site in the 12th century, but the present mansion is a 19th-century Gothic fantasy run as a centre for Buddhist studies. The temple is open to the public most weekends in summer and the gardens are open all year.

9 Ulverston

The comedian Arthur Stanley Jefferson, better known as Stan Laurel, was born in Ulverston in 1890 and is celebrated in the Laurel and Hardy Museum.

Ulverston flourished as a port in the early 19th century after the opening of a canal to the coast at Canal Foot. On top of Hoad Hill stands a 30m (100ft) monument in the form of a lighthouse. It was erected in 1850 to commemorate Sir John Barrow, an explorer and Secretary to the Admiralty, who was born here.

Just outside Ulverston, Swarthmoor Hall was in the 17th century a safe house for Quakers, who were a persecuted sect. The hall belonged to Judge Fell, a sympathiser; George Fox, the founder of the Quaker movement, stayed there. The staircase has one step deliberately made higher than the others, so that intruders would stumble over it and unwittingly alert the occupants. The hall, now owned by the Quakers, is usually open to the public.

10 Greenodd

Once linked with Lake Windermere by a branch line of the Furness Railway, all that remains of the track in this sleepy backwater is a 3½ mile section from Haverthwaite, 2 miles to the northeast, along the Lakeside and Haverthwaite Railway. Steam locomotives proceed farther northeastwards to Lakeside, where there is a steamboat connection on Lake Windermere.

To the east of Greenodd, Bigland Hall is set amid parkland, beside a lake. The hall and grounds are a centre for country pursuits such as riding and fishing.

11 Holker Hall

The grounds of the hall are home to one of Britain's oldest herds of fallow deer, which can be viewed from woodland walks. The grounds also include formal and rose gardens, fountains and a splendid tree-lined, limestone cascade.

The hall itself dates from 1604, although the part of the building open to the public was rebuilt in extravagant mock-Elizabethan style in 1874 after a fire. Its interior possesses a magnificent cantilevered oak staircase with intricately carved balusters.

You can see vintage Buicks and Bentleys, as well as an array of antique motorcycles and car memorabilia, in the Lakeland Motor Museum, which is also in the grounds of the hall.

12 Flookburgh

Now separated from the sea by reclaimed marshland, Flookburgh was once so close to the shore that high tides would bring waves washing along the main street. It remains a fishing village, however, with shrimps and flukes – the local name for flounders – sold at local cottages. The fishermen cross the sands on tractors from nearby Sand Gate and Humphrey Head to net their catches.

13 Humphrey Head

The limestone cliff extends for about a mile into the flat expanses of Morecambe Bay, and rises to 52m (172ft). The head includes the Joy Ketchen Nature Reserve, which has a range of grassland plants and trees, including the rare Lancastrian white-beam. At the foot of the cliffs is the holy well of St Agnes, celebrated by pilgrims for centuries for its curative powers.

⑭ Grange-over-Sands
Substantial Edwardian houses, arcades of shops, ornamental gardens, a lake and a bandstand recall a sedate age. There are children's amusements and bowling and putting greens near the mile-long waterfront promenade here, while paths climb to Hampsfield Fell, whose 222m (727ft) summit is capped by a 19th-century hospice, built as a refuge for travellers.

⑮ Cartmel
Dwarfing the village is the cathedral-like Priory Church of St Mary and St Michael, part of an Augustinian establishment founded in the 12th century. It has a huge east window, a fine set of misericords and an ornately carved tomb built to commemorate the first Lord Harrington, who died in 1347, and his wife; he is thought to have built the south choir aisle of the church. The 14th-century priory gatehouse flanks Cartmel's central square.

⑯ Arnside
A holiday resort and sailing centre, the village hugs the lower slopes of Arnside Knott, whose summit is reached on foot and has wonderful views across the Kent estuary. A siren sounds at Arnside when the tide starts to come in; under certain conditions it rushes in at such a pace that you can hear it from the village as a distant roar. When the tides are safe, guided walks head across the bay to Grange-over-Sands and Kents Bank.

The train journey from Arnside to Ulverston crosses low viaducts, built over Warton Sands and Cartmel Sands, with superb coastal panoramas.

⑰ Silverdale
The village has a long tradition as a resort, with the novelists Charlotte Brontë and Mrs Gaskell among its 19th-century visitors. A house above the shore was built as a bathhouse where Victorians could enjoy in comfort the fashionable benefits of immersion in the sea, while the swathe of turf along the foreshore used to be harvested for bowling greens and tennis courts.

At one time the village stood beside the River Kent, and steamers cruised there from Morecambe, but in the 1920s the river changed its course northwards, leaving Silverdale high and dry. The winding lanes round Silverdale give occasional glimpses of the sea, and the village is an excellent centre for walking. Eaves Wood (NT), just north of Silverdale, includes ancient woodland with species such as oak, ash and

small-leaved lime. The wood is a haven for rare butterflies including the high-brown fritillary and pearl-bordered fritillary.

A mile to the east of Silverdale is Leighton Moss RSPB Reserve, an area of reed beds, meres and woodland, where you can see otters and red deer. Among the reserve's many birds is the elusive bittern, whose booming cry may be heard from late January to mid June.

⑱ Jenny Brown's Point
The point is strikingly solitary in character, and the origins of its name remain a mystery, though it is known that a man called Brown farmed there in the 16th century.

This was once a centre for copper smelting, but all that remains of the industry today is an old stone chimney stack. You can reach it from Silverdale along a lane signposted to a farm called Gibraltar.

⑲ Carnforth
Until 1931 the town had a steelworks that processed Cumbrian iron ore, and after this closed Carnforth remained a busy railway junction. The Lancaster Canal, on the other side of the town, is now used for recreation but was once crowded with barges carrying sand and gravel. Completed in 1819, it connected Preston and Kendal; its towpath gives a 27 mile walk from Lancaster to Kendal. A waterbus runs between Carnforth and Lancaster in summer.

The visitor centre at Carnforth station recalls David Lean's 1945 film *Brief Encounter*.

⑳ Bolton-le-Sands
The Packet Boat Hotel was a stopping point on the canal for fast passenger boats capable of speeds of more than 10mph. The old village of Bolton-le-Sands lies to the east of the busy A6, which runs through the modern village, while the newer village overlooks salt marshes that attract waders and waterfowl on their early autumn migrations southwards.

㉑ Hest Bank
A wide expanse of open foreshore gives fine views across Morecambe Bay to the hills of the Lake District in this residential suburb of Lancaster. However, because of hazardous quicksands and a shift in the course of the river it is no longer possible to walk across the sands to Kents Bank, near Grange.

㉒ Morecambe
The town's success was built on sea, sand and entertainment, and it remains a lively place today, with a 4 mile promenade. The resort was born with the coming of the railway, in the mid 19th century, providing cheap travel for thousands of workers

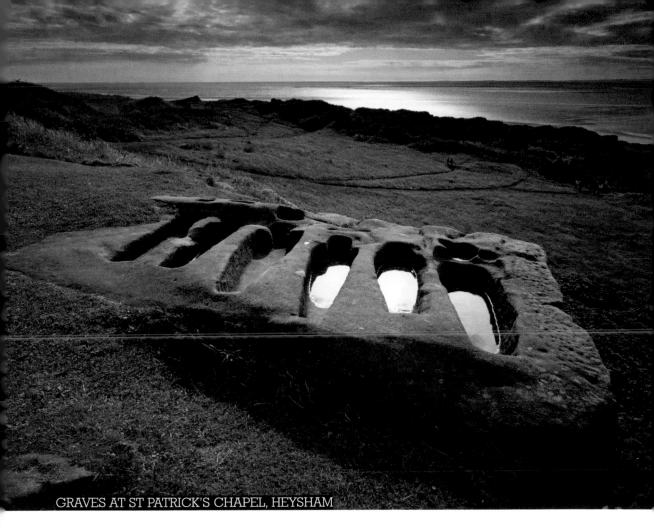

GRAVES AT ST PATRICK'S CHAPEL, HEYSHAM

from the industrial towns. Sunsets are a memorable feature of Morecambe Bay but the town is also vulnerable to storms; sea defences have been strengthened, and an old stone jetty, built in 1850, has been extended. Boats land catches of shrimps.

23 Heysham

High on a headland, looking out across Morecambe Bay's sands, stand some solitary graves, including one of a child, cut out of the rock. The graves stand beside the ruins of tiny St Patrick's Chapel, whose thick walls were built in the 8th and 9th centuries. Just below the chapel is the Church of St Peter, dating from the 10th century.

Modern Heysham is focused on the harbour, the starting point for a vehicle ferry to the Isle of Man, and the base of support vessels for the Morecambe Bay gas field, discovered in 1974.

To the south of the harbour, and visible for miles, is the square block of Heysham's nuclear power station. Beside the power station is a nature reserve where you can see many butterflies and moths.

24 Sunderland

In the early 18th century this was a busy shipping port where cargoes from the West Indies were unloaded and transferred to smaller vessels for the onward journey to Lancaster. Traffic declined with the growth of Glasson Dock, across the Lune estuary, and in the 19th century the village became known for sea bathing.

The only road into Sunderland leads across a narrow causeway that is flooded at high tide; at low tide the road traverses a maze of muddy channels.

25 Glasson

A lively mix of working docks, a barge-lined canal and a yacht basin, Glasson, unlike many of the other small ports in the area, has not declined to become a historical curiosity. A port since the late 18th century, its fortunes improved when it was linked to the main Lancaster Canal in 1826 and shipped raw materials for Lancaster's mills.

A 6 mile path leading along the Lune estuary as far as Lancaster offers some excellent opportunities for birdwatching.

26 Cockersand Abbey

Cows graze among the scattered ruins of Cockersand Abbey, once one of the great religious houses in northwest England. The squat tower of the 13th-century chapter house, and a few stunted walls, are all that remain of the abbey, built in the early 12th century on the tip of a remote tongue of land at the mouth of the River Lune. You can also see the remnants of a fish trap built by the monks at low tide.

A few hundred yards from the shore is a small lighthouse topped by a black cone; the bulk of Heysham nuclear power station looms on the far shore, and beyond are the Lakeland hills. A narrow lane leads to the shore, from where a pleasant 10 minute stroll leads you to the abbey.

27 Knott End-on-Sea

Knott End is a small, quiet place with trim bungalows, a wide beach of sand and stretches of mud. Sailing boats are moored in the Wyre estuary, opposite Fleetwood docks, and beside the landing stage for the passenger ferry that in summer links Knott End and Fleetwood. From the quay, a path leads south along the riverbank past a golf course to the two nature reserves of Barnaby's Sands and Burrows Marsh, set in the last large areas of ungrazed salt marsh on the Lancashire coast.

A car park and picnic site at Lane Ends, 4½ miles east of Knott End, is an ideal spot for birdwatching, and gives broad views over Morecambe Bay.

② Skippool Creek

High tides on the River Wyre regularly reach up to 9m (30ft) in depth, filling a maze of creeks such as Skippool. The creek, a haven for birds, including herons, ducks and lapwings, is also a popular sailing centre, with moorings and jetties. There is a picnic area near the narrow path beside the creek, while another path that floods at high tide leads north to Stanah, almost 2 miles away.

In the 16th century, Skippool was the port for the ancient market town of Poulton le-Fylde, a mile inland. In the 1750s, the port's trade is said to have been greater than that of Liverpool. Imports included wine, tobacco, timber and guano from Africa for use as fertiliser on Fylde farms.

ONCE A GREAT RELIGIOUS HOUSE
COCKERSAND ABBEY

② Stanah

In winter large flocks of lapwings, golden plovers and redshanks can be seen with oystercatchers near the estuary mouth. Many other birds can be seen on the mudflats and sandbanks on the estuary throughout the year. Located at the entrance to Wyre Estuary Country Park, the Wyreside Ecology Centre provides visitors with information on the wildlife of the estuary.

③ Fleetwood

Once a major fishing port, Fleetwood could have been as elegant as Bath if plans for a new town, prepared in 1840 by the architect Decimus Burton, had been completed. Traces of his grand design survive, as does a great railway hotel, the North Euston; the hotel was built for travellers to Scotland, who took a boat from Fleetwood to Ardrossan and travelled on from there to Glasgow by train. The centrepiece of Burton's plan was The Mount, a grassy hill surmounted by a clock tower, which overlooks a long promenade with a boating lake, a pier, bowling greens and the Marine Hall entertainment centre, set in gardens.

Modern Fleetwood is a lively mix of resort and fishing port, and it is the only town in the UK that boasts three lighthouses, with the Pharos Lighthouse located well inland. The Wyre Dock has been redeveloped as Harbour Village, a retail and shopping area.

Trams run between Fleetwood and Blackpool; in summer, there are passenger ferries to Knott End across the Wyre, and vehicle ferries to Larne in Northern Ireland.

③ Cleveleys

Cleveleys is quieter than its neighbour Blackpool and offers a range of more modest attractions, including amusement arcades and the Jubilee Gardens behind the promenade. The beach is sand and shingle.

The red sails of Marsh Mill, turning slowly above the village of Thornton, 1½ miles inland, are a landmark in the area. Built in 1794, the 21m (70ft) mill produced flour for bread, and crushed barley for animal feed, until 1922. It has now been restored to working order, and also houses a clog museum. Beside the mill, shops are grouped round a courtyard where events such as brass-band concerts are staged.

Riddle of the sands

The northwest is home to miles and miles of sand that has the ability both to nurture life or take it away in an instant

Morecambe Bay is not the innocuous sweep of sand that it can seem when the tide is out and the weather fair. The bay contains 117 square miles of tidal flats, and – in such an enormous area of sand and mud – is not as flat as it looks, consequently appearances are deceptive. Horizons that appear to be only a few hundred metres off can in reality easily be as much as four or five miles away. With its sinking sands and hidden gullies, its rivers that can switch course overnight from one side of the bay to the other, its secret channels where the tide comes creeping round to cut off unwary travellers, Morecambe Bay is one of the most treacherous (as well as one of the most beautiful and compelling) sections of coast in Britain. The riddle of these Great Sands of Lakeland, like the other vast sands that fringe the northwest coast of England, is that they support bird and invertebrate life in gigantic numbers, yet can take human life away in the blink of an eye.

Perilous crossing

Three rivers – Kent, Leven and Duddon – flow into the Irish Sea from the southernmost tip of the Lake District. Travellers have always been tempted to avoid the long journey round the shore by taking a short cut across the sands that form the floors of the three tidal bays, and there has been a steady toll of death and disaster down the centuries from quicksands, storms and high tides. The monks of nearby Cartmel Priory provided a guide service of sorts in the early Middle Ages, as did the state from the reign of King John onwards.

Crossing the sands remained a perilous venture: records show that 140 bodies of drowned travellers were retrieved between 1559 and 1880, and many more victims were never found. A particularly poignant double accident in the 19th century befell a jaunting cart. A young couple, due to be married the next day, were drowned along with seven friends when the cart tipped over in the notorious Black Scar hole. Then, some years later, a dozen young men on their way to Lancaster Fair in the same conveyance were sucked down to their deaths in quicksand when the cart capsized in exactly the same location.

These days there is a guide to shepherd leisure walkers across the open sands on official guided walks. This guide has also saved the lives of many a lone venturer after spotting that they had got themselves into difficulty. In spite of the dangers they pose to humans, the sands of Morecambe Bay mean life and wellbeing to millions of seabirds and countless numbers of shellfish, marine worms and other organisms on which birds feed. Every year huge flocks of knot and dunlin and large groups of bar-tailed godwit, pintail and pink-footed geese join the resident oystercatchers and curlews to spend the winter in the sheltered bay. Birdwatchers straggle out onto the sands to observe them, and sometimes need a sharp reminder from local people about just where it is and is not safe to go.

For sheer loneliness and a taste of the unique atmosphere of immense sands and mud under open skies, it is hard to beat the estuaries of the

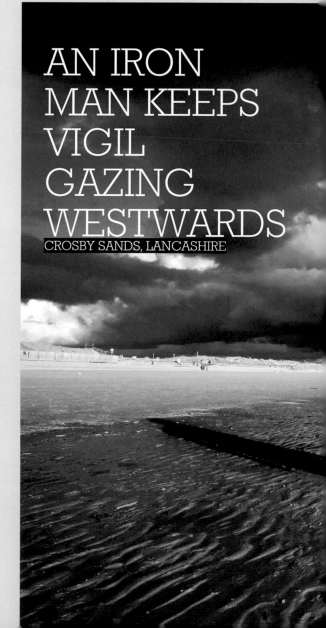

AN IRON MAN KEEPS VIGIL GAZING WESTWARDS
CROSBY SANDS, LANCASHIRE

rivers Lune and Ribble, south down the coast from the Great Sands of Lakeland. The Lune has Lancaster on its banks, and the Ribble has Preston; but these cities cast no urban or industrial shadow on the estuaries where the broad muddy waters curve out to sea between piled mudbanks that gleam at low tide like sliced chocolate, then flow through long, low hills of sand that appear as flat as those in Morecambe Bay, but are equally deceptive.

One of the most poignant resting places imaginable is that of Sambo, a young West African servant who landed at Sunderland Point, near Heysham, with his employer in 1736, and soon died of 'a broken heart' – probably from pneumonia. He lies in the corner of a field beside the sea wall in a grave always neatly tended and furnished with fresh flowers.

Another place

Great sands and big skies opening on a sea horizon always raise images of travelling over that skyline to another place. And 'Another Place' is the title that sculptor and installation artist Antony Gormley chose for the work that he sited on Crosby Sands at the entrance to the River Mersey just downstream of Liverpool's dockland. A hundred iron men, each one a naked casting of the artist himself, stand on the sands, some up near the dunes, others out in the tideway so that they emerge from under the sea at each fall of the tide. Rusting, salt-streaked and festooned with seaweed, they keep their enigmatic vigil, gazing out westwards as if expecting something as yet unfathomable to arrive out of the infinite wastes of the wild Atlantic.

ISLE OF MAN

Much of the self-governing Isle of Man's east coast is mild and low-lying, while the west of the island, exposed to the Atlantic, can be a wilder place, with good fishing

❶ Blue Point

A narrow turning swings down the face of an ancient earthwork in a double hairpin to reach a small car park behind the dunes. Here a flat beach of sand and some shingle stretches southwestwards for 12 miles, and northeastwards past Rue Point to the island's northernmost tip, the Point of Ayre.

The 4 mile stretch of coast between Rue Point and Point of Ayre is called The Ayres, from the old Norse meaning a bank of sand or gravel. A visitor centre is the starting point for a nature trail that illustrates the geology and natural history of this wild and lonely part of the island.

❷ Point of Ayre

The lighthouse on the point gives a wide-ranging view of sea and low-lying land round three-quarters of the horizon. It is reached by a 3 mile road from the village of Bride. Behind is the frowning bulk of the mountains in the island's interior.

❸ Ramsey

The mild climate of Ramsey, and its sheltered position in the centre of the long sweep of Ramsey Bay, allows palm trees to grow on the seafront. Pleasure craft pack the harbour, in the estuary of the Sulby, and there are sandy beaches on either side of the river mouth. Ramsey is the northern terminus of the Manx Electric Railway, whose trams run to Douglas.

The Albert Tower, on a hill behind the town, was built to commemorate the visit of Queen Victoria and Prince Albert in 1847.

❹ Maughold Head

The pretty little village of Maughold is set back from the clifftops of Maughold Head. From the churchyard a path leads to the top of the headland and lighthouse, with good views.

❺ Dhoon Glen

One of the most spectacular glens on the Isle of Man, Dhoon Glen is formed by a fast-running stream that cuts its way down through the cliffs to the sea at Dhoon Bay. The path to the shore crosses the glen by a series of rustic bridges, passing two steep waterfalls, each of which drops 18m (60ft) or more.

❻ Laxey

One of the Isle of Man's best-known sights is the huge Laxey Wheel, a mighty water wheel, also known as the 'Lady Isabella'. It was constructed in 1854 to pump water out of the lead-mine workings under Snaefell, the island's highest mountain, and was named after the wife of the then lieutenant governor of the island. It has a diameter of 22m (72ft 6in) and a circumference of 66m (217ft), and it still pumps water – when running at top speed a complete revolution takes 30 seconds. Visitors can follow trails past former mine workings.

On the opposite side of the valley from the wheel, the Snaefell Mountain Railway runs in a long spiral up to the 621m (2036ft) summit of Snaefell. The journey, which takes about half an hour, ends at a spectacular viewpoint.

❼ Groudle Glen

Paths descend narrow Groudle Glen through groves of beech, larch and pine and past rocky cliffs and rushing rapids; at the bottom you will find a small stony beach. The

GROVES OF BEECH, LARCH AND PINE
GROUDLE GLEN

Groudle Glen narrow-gauge steam railway runs through the glen on summer Sundays and some weekday evenings.

⑧ Onchan

Electric trams of the Manx Electric Railway pass through the village of Onchan on their route between Douglas and Ramsey, and there are also regular services to Douglas by horse-drawn Victorian trams. The village is virtually an extension of Douglas and spreads around the rocky mass of Onchan Head at the northern end of Douglas Bay.

⑨ Douglas

The island's capital and largest town spreads along the 2 mile curve of Douglas Bay, which forms a fine natural harbour. Ferries tie up at the docks at the southern end of the town, under the shelter of Douglas Head. The busy promenade looks out over a beach where sand is exposed at low water, and in summer horse-drawn trams run the length of the promenade; the service began in 1876, and uses about 35 horses.

Near the harbour is the terminus of the Isle of Man Steam Railway, a 3ft gauge steam-hauled line that in summer runs to Port Erin on the southwest coast of the island. The railway was inaugurated in 1874.

The Manx Museum in Douglas recounts the story of 10,000 years of turbulent Manx history, and has an extensive collection of artefacts covering all aspects of island life, including the oldest surviving double-decker horse tram. In Nobles Park on the northern side of the town are the grandstands that mark the start and finish of the famous annual Tourist Trophy (TT) motorcycle race.

⑩ Port Soderick

A small stream flows between grassy slopes at Port Soderick Glen, along which a path runs for 1½ miles. The path starts at the car park next to an east-facing shingle beach.

⑪ Derby Haven

A curving sandy bay, Derby Haven is separated from the larger Castletown Bay by the rocky headland of Langness. There are fine views of the island's coastal scenery from Dreswick Point lighthouse, at the southern end of Langness, and from the old fort on St Michael's Island, at the northeastern tip of the headland. Good sea fishing can be had from boats off Langness.

⑫ Castletown

The town's narrow twisting streets seem to huddle for protection round the medieval fortress of Castle Rushen. Castletown was the island's capital until 1874, and a building now occupied by the local authority councillors was used for meetings of the House of Keys, the elected lower house of Tynwald, the Isle of Man parliament.

On the edge of Castletown's inner harbour is the Nautical Museum, which includes a sailmaker's workshop and model ships ranging from mid 18th-century sailing craft to modern diesel vessels. Among the exhibits is *Peggy*, last in a line of clippers made in the Isle of Man in the 17th and 18th centuries.

To the south of Castletown is the Scarlett Visitor Centre, which has displays of the island's plants and animals, and a nature trail that follows part of the coastline.

⑬ Port St Mary

Once a fishing village, Port St Mary is now popular with yacht owners because of the deep-water moorings close inshore. The village shelters between the twin headlands of Kallow Point and Gansey Point and offers sandy beaches at Chapel Bay, and the wider sweep of Bay ny Carrickey, on the other side of Gansey Point.

Paths lead westwards to the spectacular cliff scenery of The Chasms and Spanish Head, and eastwards to Black Rocks. You will find good sea fishing off The Carrick, a rock in the bay.

⑭ Cregneash

The open air Cregneash Village Folk Museum recalls the old Manx way of life. From the car park, you can walk to a group of old thatched cottages, which include a smithy, a weaving shed and a turner's workshop with an old treadle lathe. Harry Kelly's Cottage is an old crofter's home, built more than 150 years ago and named after a Manx-speaking crofter. Demonstrations of wool spinning and smithying are given regularly in summer.

⑮ Calf of Man

Isle of Man's southwestern tip overlooks the treacherous, rock-strewn passage of Calf Sound. To the south is the massive cliff of Spanish Head and straight ahead are the islets of Kitterland. Behind the islets is the uninhabited island known as Calf of Man. The island is a nature reserve supporting large colonies of guillemots, razorbills, kittiwakes and puffins; you can also see smaller groups of hooded crows and choughs. In settled weather, boat trips run to the island from Port Erin or Port St Mary.

⑯ Port Erin

Sheltered by the high cliffs of two headlands, the small resort of Port Erin is the western terminus of the Isle of Man Steam Railway, which runs

Thrills on two wheels

Early in June, 38 miles of roads on the Isle of Man are closed to ordinary traffic for the annual Tourist Trophy (TT) motorcycle races. The gruelling course, which starts and finishes at Douglas, includes such testing hazards as the hump-backed Ballaugh Bridge, a sharp hairpin bend at Ramsey, and the road over Snaefell, which twists up to a height of 425m (1400ft).

round the southern end of the island to Douglas. Port Erin's Railway Museum, situated in part of the old train storage shed, includes the first and last engines to enter service on the line. The town also has a variety of seaside amusements.

A footpath round Bradda Head gives a panoramic view of Port Erin, and you can get magnificent views out to sea from Milner's Tower, a monument built by a local locksmith in 1884 in the shape of a key. The path skirts the edge of Bradda Hill to the north, and eventually rejoins the road to Fleshwick Bay.

⑰ Fleshwick Bay
The road to Fleshwick Bay ends at a grassy slope overlooking a beach of shingle amid clusters of rocks. The bay faces northwards towards the cliffs that line the coast all the way to Peel.

⑱ Niarbyl Bay
A minor road from the village of Dalby reaches the sea by a group of cottages. A path climbs round the cliff face to the south, above Niarbyl Bay and eventually reaches a lane at the top of the slope. This lane rejoins the main road 3 miles farther south, near the summit of Cronk ny Arrey Laa.

⑲ Glen Maye
A path winds down the glen in this steep-sided narrow valley, past a magnificent waterfall; it follows the course of a stream that reaches a pebbly beach through steep cliffs. The path starts in front of the Waterfall Hotel.

A footpath from the glen's lower end heads south along the coast over Contrary Head and on to Peel, 3 miles away, with superb views all the way.

⑳ Peel
An old fishing harbour, with narrow, winding streets, is dominated by the massive fortress of Peel Castle on St Patrick's Isle; the 'isle' is in fact linked to the mainland, forming a protective arm at the western end of the harbour. The castle's main walls are 14th century, and within are a huge round tower and a ruined 13th-century cathedral.

On the eastern side of the harbour a promenade overlooks a sandy beach. There is good fishing for mackerel at the entrance to the harbour, and for mullet, skate, pollack, conger eel and flatfish from the breakwater beyond the castle. Manx kippers, cured over fires of oak woodchips, are produced in the town.

Tynwald Hill, 3 miles southeast of Peel at St John's, was the traditional meeting place of Tynwald, the island's parliament, which has its origins in Viking times. Tynwald still meets there on July 5 each year, to hear details of the year's new Acts, which are read in both Manx and English by the island's two 'deemsters', or high court judges.

㉑ Glen Mooar
The beach at the seaward end of the Glen Mooar is the southern limit of a long stretch of sandy cliffs that gives way to sand dunes beyond Jurby Head, several miles to the north. A narrow lane off the coast road, nearly a mile southwest of Kirk Michael, leads to a small car park at the glen, and a lane on the opposite side of the coast road leads to the waterfall of Spooyt Vane, or 'White Spout', above Glen Mooar.

Cooildarry, a deep wooded valley just south of Kirk Michael, is a nature reserve with a variety of woodland habitats. Wood warblers are among the birds you can see there.

㉒ Ballaugh
Ballaugh Bridge is a favourite viewpoint for spectators on the northern part of the Tourist Trophy (TT) motorcycle course. About 1½ miles to the north is a hamlet called The Cronk, whose Church of St Mary de Ballaugh dates back to before the 13th century.

At the Curraghs Wildlife Park, about a mile east of Ballaugh, you can see tailless Manx cats and the multi-horned Manx sheep known as loaghtan, as well as flying foxes and lemurs.

> **Visitor information**
> **Douglas** ☎ (01624) 686801

BLACKPOOL TO NESTON

Holiday resorts, including the most famous of them all – Blackpool, an English institution with its autumn illuminations – sit alongside a wealth of nature reserves, including one of Europe's most important sites for wintering wildfowl and waders, at Hilbre Island

❶ Blackpool

More than 10 million visits are made to Blackpool each year, by people drawn by the 158m (518ft 9in) Tower, and the huge Pleasure Beach, with some 150 rides. Every inch of the seafront between the North and South piers is packed with hotels, bars, pubs and entertainments. There are 3500 hotels, guest houses and self-catering units in the resort, which has 120,000 holiday beds – more than the whole of Portugal.

From early September to early November the illuminations dispel the autumn darkness with more than 500,000 lamps. The best way to see them is from one of the trams that trundle along the seafront to Cleveleys and on to Fleetwood.

❷ St Annes

St Annes was built in Victorian times as a holiday resort for the better-off, offering traditional resort attractions. It has a pier, bandstand and sandy beach, and its flat sands are ideal for sand-yachting.

Fairhaven Lake, used for rowing, wind-surfing and other watersports, is also a good vantage point for watching migrant birds on the Ribble estuary, while sand dunes at the Blackpool, or northern, end of town form a nature reserve with a small interpretative centre. A memorial in St Annes records a lifeboat disaster that took place in 1886, with the loss of 27 crew.

❸ Lytham

A windmill, built in 1805, stands on Lytham Green, a stretch of close-cropped turf behind the promenade. The mill produced flour until 1919, and now houses an illuminating exhibition of milling and of local life. Next to the mill, the dramatic story of Lytham's lifeboat service is displayed in the former lifeboat house;

the new lifeboat building overlooks the wide Ribble estuary and the muddy beach.

Placid and peaceful, the town has fine golf links, including the championship course of Royal Lytham and St Annes.

❹ Freckleton

The sprawling village, set back from the narrow thread of the River Ribble, has a small brick church, built in 1837, with box pews and a fine Jacobean pulpit. A footpath leads from the village along the edge of an inlet to marshland that was the site of a battle in the Civil War, and nearby Naze Mount is thought to have been a Roman port. Freckleton hosts a classical and folk music festival each December.

❺ Longton Brickcroft

A wetland nature reserve occupies the site of a former brickworks, where ponds have been created from flooded claypits. The south pond is part of a recreation area popular for walking and picnics, while the north pond is a wildlife conservation area. Occasional guided walks start from a visitor centre.

6 Ribble Marshes National Nature Reserve

Stretching along the south bank of the Ribble estuary are the salt marsh, mudflats and sandbanks of the reserve. Thousands of ducks, geese, gulls and terns depend on the varied habitat for feeding and breeding, and each spring and autumn up to 80,000 waders, including knots, dunlins and oystercatchers, arrive at Ribble Marshes on their way to and from Arctic breeding grounds.

To the north, a footpath leads along Banks Marsh embankment. Fortnightly spring tides can cause flooding, making the salt marsh dangerous.

7 Southport

In the 18th century a local man, William Sutton, made the first bathing house from local driftwood in this popular resort, lined by a 7 mile stretch of sand. There has been a pier here since 1860, and today a train takes holidaymakers from amusement arcades at the landward end to the sun decks and bars nearly a mile away.

Victoria Park, to the east of the esplanade, is the site of the Southport Flower Show, held every August. Paths through the park provide access to a nature trail that explores part of the vast area of dunes running south to Crosby; you can walk along the Sefton Coastal Footpath to Hightown, 11 miles away, and return by train.

8 Ainsdale Sand Dunes

High rolling dune ridges, valleys and hollows characterise the national nature reserve that lies at the centre of one of Britain's largest dune systems, stretching from Southport to Crosby.

A marked trail traces a circular route through the sands, where display boards describe the local wildlife and landscape. Natterjack toads live in the low hollows, known as slacks, in the dunes; on spring and summer nights the mating calls of the male toads create such a chorus that they have been nicknamed the 'Southport nightingales'. Waders flock to the beach and dune area, and the reserve supports many sand-loving plants, such as dune helleborine, as well as butterflies.

The 21 mile Sefton Coastal Footpath runs the length of the dunes, from Crossens in the north to Crosby Marine Park in the south. Industrial and urban development has destroyed part of the dunes, which once stretched all the way from the mouth of the Ribble to Liverpool, but repair work started in the late 1970s, and marram grass has been planted to stabilise them. Flood banks also protect the land behind the dunes from tidal surges. Just inland, large pine plantations from the early 1900s provide habitats for a variety of wildlife, including red squirrels.

BLACKPOOL PLEASURE BEACH

⑨ Formby

High grassy dunes separate the town of Formby from its beach, and there are splendid walks with views of the ships entering and leaving the Mersey, backed by the distant mountains of North Wales.

Lifeboat Road takes its name from Britain's first lifeboat station, built here in 1776, and you can see the ruins of a later station built in 1809 on the beach.

In the porch of the 19th-century Church of St Luke is the gravestone of Richard Formby, the 7ft armour-bearer to Henry IV and Henry V known as 'Richard the Giant'. A cross in the churchyard, which once stood on the village green, is believed to have been used during the Great Plague of 1665; its hollows were filled with vinegar so that coins could be disinfected.

⑩ Crosby

The town's impressive Regency crescents and terraces were built by wealthy local merchants in the 18th and 19th centuries. About a mile inland is the original hamlet of Little Crosby with its 17th-century cottages and the Georgian Crosby Hall.

An expanse of open grassland by the southern end of the sandy beach contains Crosby Marine Park, where beginners can learn to sail. Strong currents and the proximity of shipping lanes make it dangerous to swim in the Crosby Channel.

'Another Place', an installation of 100 cast-iron figures by sculptor Antony Gormley, spreads for 2 miles along Crosby beach. Although originally intended as a temporary display, it looks set to stay.

⑪ Seaforth

Roosting colonies of cormorants and Arctic terns can be seen in the two lagoons which form the centrepiece of Crosby Marine Park, located to the north of the busy Seaforth Container Terminal. You may also see kittiwakes and Mediterranean gulls in the nature reserve.

⑫ Bootle

The towpath of the Leeds and Liverpool Canal runs northwards from Bootle for 7 miles as far as Aintree racecourse, and south for 2 miles to the locks of Liverpool's Stanley Dock. The four locks were built in the early 19th century by Jesse Hartley, who also built Liverpool's Albert Dock.

⑬ Liverpool

The city was one of the most important ports in the world by the end of the 19th century, when some 40 per cent of the world's trade was carried in Liverpool ships. It had begun to prosper and develop as far back as the early 18th century when the silting up of the Dee cut off the thriving port of Chester. With

HIGH GRASSY DUNES AND SPLENDID WALKS

FORMBY DUNES

the shift to containerisation and bulk-carriers, however, port activity moved north to the more modern docks at Bootle and Seaforth, and Liverpool's Albert Dock was closed in 1972. Albert Dock is now a heritage area, and its huge Victorian warehouses include attractions such as Tate Liverpool, a museum of 20th-century art, and the Beatles Story.

As European Capital of Culture in 2008, Liverpool invested heavily in new and refurbished museums including the International Slavery Museum and HM Revenue and Customs Museum, housed in the same building as the Maritime Museum. The new Museum of Liverpool is due to open in 2010/11.

The huge Royal Liver Building at Pier Head, built in 1908 by the Royal Liver Assurance Company, measures 98m (322ft) from the ground to the top of the two statues of the fictitious Liver Birds. Its ground floor was once a shipping hall, and parts are open to visitors.

In the city centre are the Walker Art Gallery, with its collection of European art from the 14th century to the present day, and the World Museum Liverpool, which includes a natural history centre and planetarium. Nearby is the 19th-century neo-classical building of St George's Hall, a former concert hall and Crown Court now restored and with a heritage centre.

South of the city centre are two cathedrals. Liverpool's Anglican cathedral, the largest in Britain, took more than 70 years to build and was completed in 1978. The Metropolitan Cathedral of Christ the King, a Roman Catholic cathedral completed in 1967, is remarkable for its circular design.

⑭ Otterspool

To the south of Liverpool, a 3 mile riverside promenade gives wide views across the Mersey to the Wirral shore. Inland are Sefton Park with its boating lake and Victorian palm house, and Sudley House, a Victorian shipowner's home with 18th and 19th-century paintings and furniture. At Liverpool's Botanic Gardens, a mile northeast, is a museum of Victorian artefacts.

⑮ Speke Hall

Construction of the intricately decorated, half-timbered Speke Hall (NT) began in 1490, but much of what you see today dates from refurbishment in Victorian times. The Tudor Great Hall remains, and many panelled rooms contain furnishings and wallpaper designed by the 19th-century craftsman William Morris.

⑯ Hale

At the centre of a great paw of land jutting out into the Mersey is a quiet village of whitewashed cottages and country gardens. In the 17th century, Hale was the home of John Middleton, better known as 'the Childe of Hale'. It is claimed that he grew to 2.8m (9ft 3in), and that he won a contest with James I's champion wrestler. He is buried in St Mary's churchyard.

A lane leads south from the village to a stretch of mudflats and rocky sand; a lighthouse at the tip of the promontory is now part of a private riverside residence. About a mile northeast of Hale, a former waste tip has been reclaimed and the area has been transformed into the Pickerings Pasture Nature Reserve. Riverside and meadow walks explore the reserve, and there is a hide from which to watch the birds of nearby Hale Marshes, closed to the public.

To the northwest of Hale is the Halewood Country Park, where miles of walking and cycling routes have been developed along a disused railway track.

⑰ Widnes

The town played an important role in the region sometimes referred to as the cradle of the British chemical industry. In 1845 a complex incorporating a railway, canals and docks was established in the strip of land known as Spike Island, to develop soap and soda-ash works; it fell into disuse in the early 20th century.

Now the works have been replaced by meadows and woodland, and paths follow the old railway lines. Birds of prey, including hen harriers and short-eared owls, hunt over the marshes to the east, and migrating birds such as teals visit in winter. A visitor centre explains the history and wildlife of the area, while the nearby Catalyst Science Discovery Centre explores the region's industrial heritage.

⑱ Runcorn

The town is best known today for its chemical works, which at night light up the sky like a space-age city. It was once a resort that attracted day-trippers from Liverpool. Then the soap and chemical industries were established and, in the late 19th century, thousands of people arrived to work on the Manchester Ship Canal.

In the sandstone outcrops of the former quarry on Runcorn Hill, to the south of the town, fossilised dinosaur footprints were found in 1848. The area is now a nature reserve with a 'quarry trail' and visitor centre.

To the east of Runcorn, Town Park is the start of a 2 mile circular walk that takes in the remains of a 12th-century castle at Halton. Nearby are the ruins and gardens of Norton Priory, where a museum traces the development of the medieval priory first into a Tudor manor house, then a Georgian mansion.

⑲ Ellesmere Port

A boat museum containing the world's largest collection of traditional canal boats is housed in old warehouses by a disused dock basin at Ellesmere Port. The now little-used port stands at the junction of the Shropshire Union Canal and the Manchester Ship Canal, in an industrial area.

⑳ Port Sunlight

The town is a splendid example of enlightened 19th-century town planning. It was created by the soap magnate and philanthropist William Hesketh Lever, later Lord Leverhulme, whose aim was to provide for his workforce 'a new Arcadia, ventilated and drained on the most scientific principles'. The village is now a conservation area.

㉑ Birkenhead

The first settlement on the site was attached to an ancient priory, and it was the monks who in the 12th century established a ferry to Liverpool. Birkenhead grew with the advent of a steam ferry service in the early 1800s, after which Liverpool merchants developed shipyards and docks, and built houses inland. The Wirral Museum is housed in the 1887 Old Town Hall.

Most shipping activity has moved to Seaforth, north of Liverpool, but Birkenhead's industrial heritage can still be seen at Shore Road Pumping Station, which houses a large Victorian steam engine used to prevent flooding of the Mersey rail tunnel. The nearby Church of St Mary offers dramatic views of Liverpool and the Wirral from the top of its tower.

㉒ New Brighton

The ferry from Liverpool brought thousands of Victorian day-trippers here, and with the construction in 1898 of the 189m (621ft) New Brighton Tower, then Britain's tallest structure, the town's future looked set.

However, the tower fell into neglect during the First World War and was demolished in 1921, and the pier used by the ferries was closed some time later. The sands were scoured away by changes in currents, though new breakwaters to the north have encouraged the build-up of sand and the town still offers a range of attractions.

At the mouth of the Mersey, a causeway leads to privately owned Perch Rock Fort, built in the 19th century. The fort's small aviation archaeology museum, containing Second World War aircraft wreckage, is open every weekend.

㉓ Hoylake

The Royal Liverpool Golf Links is Hoylake's main attraction, but a close second is its beach. From the 18th century, shifting sands filled the lake from which the small town takes its name, creating a broad sandbank that at low tide extends some 2 miles north from the promenade.

㉔ Hilbre Island

Hilbre is the largest of three small sandstone islands at the mouth of the Dee estuary, one of Europe's most important sites for wintering wildfowl and waders. The island was used as an outpost by the Romans, and Benedictine monks built a monastic cell there in the 12th century. A signalling station was also established in the 19th century.

Hilbre Island Bird Observatory was formed in 1957, and the islands are now a nature reserve, where basking seals can often also be seen. It is an hour's walk from West Kirby to the islands, which are cut off by the tide for 3 hours either side of high water.

㉕ Parkgate

Parkgate was once one of the main departure points for Ireland and a fashionable resort. The sea has left it stranded, though, and the promenade and harbour wall now look out over a large stretch of salt marsh.

In the marshes and mudflats west of Parkgate is the Gayton Sands RSPB Reserve, where large flocks of wintering waders include pintails and bar-tailed godwits. Peregrines, merlins and hen harriers hunt along the foreshore.

㉖ Neston

From the small town, a path skirting the edge of the flats and marshland to the south offers wide views over the Dee estuary to the hills of North Wales. East of Neston, the Wirral Country Park follows a disused railway line, offering footpaths and bridleways through tranquil farmland.

The former Hadlow Road station has been preserved much as it was when the last train operated in 1956, and to the south are Ness Gardens, with a large collection of heathers, willows and exotic plants.

Visitor information

Birkenhead (telephone enquiries only)
☎ (0151) 666 3188
Blackpool ☎ (01253) 478222
Chester ☎ (01244) 402111
Cleveleys ☎ (01253) 853378
Fleetwood ☎ (01253) 773953
Liverpool ☎ (0151) 233 2459
Lytham St Annes ☎ (01253) 725610
Preston ☎ (01772) 253731
Southport ☎ (01704) 533333

Wales

South Wales boasts the Glamorgan Heritage Coast, the rugged Gower Peninsula, and the imposing cliffs and sandy bays of Pembrokeshire. Cardigan Bay's great west-facing curve runs north to the seabird cliffs of Anglesey, set against a mountainous backdrop.

Key

— Motorway

— Principal A road

(See 'Finding your way', page 7)

Holyhead

Anglesey

Llandudno

Rhyl

Bangor

Queensferry to Rhoscolyn p266-275

Mold

Caernarfon

A55

A470

Betws-y-coed

Rhosneigr to Penmaenpool p276-283

A5

A494

Wrexham

Whitchurch

Llangollen

A499

Porthmadog

Snowdonia National Park

Bala

A470

A494

Dolgellau

A458

Welshpool

Machynlleth

A483

Newtown

Aberystwyth

A44

LLangurig

Knighton

Fairbourne to Abereiddy p284-291

A470

Cambrian Mountains

Llandrindod Wells

A44

Cardigan

A485

Builth Wells

A483

Fishguard

Pembrokeshire Coast National Park

Llandovery

Brecon

A470

A438

Black Mountains

St David's Head to Llansteffan p294-301

Carmarthen

A40

A48

Llandeilo

Brecon Beacons National Park

A40

Abergavenny

Monmouth

Haverfordwest

A4076

A477

Milford Haven

Tenby

Llanelli

A465

Merthyr Tydfil

A449

A40342

Chepstow

Neath

Swansea

Port Talbot

Pembrey to Severn Bridge p302-309

A470

Newport

Bridgend

M4

Cardiff

QUEENSFERRY TO RHOSCOLYN

Separated from mainland Wales by the turbulent waters of the narrow Menai Strait, spanned by two great bridges, Anglesey is the largest island in England and Wales

❶ Queensferry
Until 1897, when the first bridge was built there, Queensferry was the last ferry crossing on the Dee before the river widened into its estuary. Today the modern town boasts a large leisure centre.

❷ Connah's Quay
The silting of the River Dee over the centuries resulted in port facilities being moved ever closer to the sea. The river was converted to a canal in the 18th century and a port was founded at Connah's Quay, but nothing stemmed the inexorable march of the sands, and these docks also fell into disuse.

To the south is Wepre Country Park, containing the ruins of ancient Ewloe Castle (Cadw), built by Welsh princes and extended in the 13th century by Llywelyn ap Gruffudd. To the east, a ruined Norman fortress stands near 18th-century Hawarden Castle. For many years the home of the Victorian prime minister William Gladstone, the castle is still the Gladstone family seat and is not open to visitors.

Gladstone founded St Deiniol's Library, in Hawarden village, in 1896 and endowed it with his books and papers.

❸ Flint
Flint Castle was the first of the string of fortifications designed by Edward I to subdue and hold Wales. Begun in 1277, it was once the centrepiece of the town, it is now in ruins but the great keep with its circular gallery is still impressive.

❹ Holywell
The name of the small inland town is derived from St Winefride and her well.
According to legend, a local chieftain cut off the 7th-century saint's head after she had spurned

his advances, and where her blood fell a well sprang up, which was known for its healing properties. St Beuno, Winefride's uncle, cursed the murderer, who was swallowed up by the earth, and miraculously brought his niece back to life.

The well is just north of the town, in the Greenfield Valley Heritage Park; it is in the ornate 15th-century St Winefride's Chapel, the second chapel to have been built on the site. At the northern end of the park, near the coast, are the ruins of Basingwerk Abbey, thought to have been founded in 1132 by the Savigny order of monks but transferred to the Cistercians soon afterwards. In the 15th century, guests attracted by Winefride's shrine were so numerous that there were two sittings at meal times.

Between these two ecclesiastical sites is an area that once resounded to the hammers and wheels of industry; there are remains of old copper works and a cotton mill, and a farming museum.

❺ Talacre
The area around the Point of Ayr is a lonely area of salt marshes, with wide views across the broad Dee estuary to the Wirral.
A footpath along the top of the sea wall leads south towards the site of what was the last deep coal mine in North Wales, with excavations that stretched far out beneath the estuary.

To the southeast, the coast all the way to Flint is lined by large industrial units, and high sea walls separate the shore from inland areas.

❻ Prestatyn
Rhyl's quieter neighbour relies for its popularity on its three sandy beaches. At Ffrith Beach, to the west, steep dunes overlook the low stone sea wall and the groynes that help

to stabilise the broad sweep of sand, while at Central Beach there is an indoor swimming pool complex. Barkby Beach, to the east, is dominated by a large holiday camp.

Prestatyn marks the northern end of the 177 mile Offa's Dyke Path, which heads south to Chepstow on the Severn estuary. The path follows in part the great bank and ditch built as a boundary between England and Wales by Offa, King of Mercia, in the 8th century; you can find out more from the Offa's Dyke Interpretative Centre in Prestatyn. Other walks in the surrounding hills include one to Gop Hill, about 3 miles inland, with a large Bronze Age cairn.

7 Rhyl

The slender 73m (240ft) Sky Tower on the waterfront offers sweeping views down the coast and inland towards the distant hills of Snowdonia, while the promenade and sea wall provide a 5 mile walk eastwards to Prestatyn.

Pleasure craft and a scattering of fishing boats moor at Foryd Harbour, the oldest part of this busy holiday resort. A wide range of attractions line Rhyl's 3 miles of sand, including a marine boating lake, SeaQuarium and the Moments in Time exhibition. Strong currents by the mouth of the River Clwyd, at the west of the beach, make swimming dangerous, though.

8 Kinmel Bay

A wide expanse of sand ends where the River Clwyd meets the sea. The beach there is popular with bathers, but strong currents make it dangerous to swim near the estuary.

9 Towyn

In 1990 high seas broke through the coastal defences and flooded the town. The damage has been repaired and the resort with its sand and pebble beach has been restored to its former popularity. Trotting races are held on the Tir Prince Raceway.

10 Pensarn

Captain Matthew Webb trained here before going on to become, in 1875, the first person to swim the English Channel. The village, and its inland neighbour Abergele, sit at the centre of a 7 mile beach of shingle and low-tide sand.

11 Llanddulas

The elevated coast road sweeps over Llanddulas, where a long beach of sand and shingle is punctuated by groynes. The town has been beset by railway disasters. In 1868, several wagons loaded with paraffin came loose and rolled downhill into a mail train, engulfing it in flames and killing more than 30 people; in

August 1879 floods swept away the stone viaduct carrying the railway; and in 1950 a mail train collided with an engine, killing six people.

Inland, narrow lanes follow the course of the River Dulas, and you can get fine views of the coast from the cave-pitted limestone hill of Cefn yr Ogof.

12 Colwyn Bay

Three miles of sand backed by a promenade stretch from Rhos-on-Sea to the town of Old Colwyn. Residential areas are largely separated from the beach by the busy A55 and the main-line railway. Nonetheless, the area remains an excellent centre for watersports from sailing to jet skiing, and there is a wide range of seaside attractions, such as the Eirias Park amusement park.

On a hillside overlooking the bay is the Welsh Mountain Zoo, which has a large section devoted to chimpanzees.

13 Rhos-on-Sea

At low tide, the remains of an old fish trap created by the monks of an ancient monastery can be seen in the sand. The fish trap consisted of a rough triangle of stone walls in which fish were caught as the tide went out, as if in a giant rock pool. To the west of the resort's promenade, where the monastery once stood, is a tiny chapel, just 4m x 2m (12ft x 6ft), built in the 16th century and dedicated to 6th-century St Trillo.

14 Penryhn Bay

Impressive sea defences consisting of immense boulders line the shingle beach here, which has rock pools to explore. The beach is backed by rows of mostly 1930s seaside villas.

15 Little Ormes Head

Peace, solitude and superb views greet those who make the trek to the top of this 141m (464ft) headland, which marks the eastern end of Llandudno Bay. Unlike visitors to Great Ormes Head, you have no option but to use your feet to make this ascent. Several paths climb to the summit, most of them starting on the Penryhn Bay side of the headland.

16 Llandudno

The bustling resort is a child of the railway age. In 1850 the population was around 1000, but by the time the branch line opened in 1858 a new town was being developed with wide streets, large houses and a promenade along the North Shore. The completion of the pier with its ornate pavilions brought still more visitors by paddle steamer.

Llandudno has never lost its elegance, and today's pavement cafes give it an almost Continental air. Its major attractions remain the beaches, with such traditional amusements as donkey rides and Punch and Judy shows.

West Shore's sand and shingle beach faces south over Conwy Bay, where the sea recedes a long way at low tide and walkers must take care not to get trapped. North Shore is a 2 mile crescent of sand stretching east to Little Ormes Head.

Llandudno's local history museum covers the area's history from the Bronze Age to Roman times, while the Alice in Wonderland Visitor Centre explains the town's connection with the writer Lewis Carroll.

⑰ Great Ormes Head
The headland rises as a great rocky pile to a 207m (679ft) summit, at the western end of Llandudno Bay. If you want to reach the top without walking, you have three alternatives: to go by car along the Marine Drive toll road; to take the cable car; or to use Britain's last cable-hauled street tramway, opened in 1902.

Copper was mined at Great Ormes Head in the 18th and 19th centuries, but recent excavations have uncovered mines that were first worked around 1800 BC, during the Bronze Age. The tramway stops at the mines, where you can explore the old workings.

At the summit is a country park with a visitor centre offering tremendous views over Snowdonia to the south and, on clear days, to the mountains of Cumbria some 60 miles north. On the sheltered eastern slopes are the public gardens of Haulfre, with good views of the sands of both Llandudno and West Shore, and on the exposed northern face is the little 7th-century church and well of St Tudno, after whom Llandudno was named.

The strip of land and rock around the base of the headland is a local nature reserve.

CONWY CASTLE

⑱ Deganwy

The ruins of a fortress built 600 years before Conwy Castle crown the hill above the estuary at Deganwy. To save it falling into English hands, the Welsh prince Llywelyn ap Gruffudd had it destroyed in 1260, as part of his campaign against Edward I. The castle was fought over, destroyed and rebuilt over the centuries.

Towards the end of the 19th century, Deganwy developed as a slate-shipping port, but it is now a popular seaside resort; facing south-west, it enjoys maximum sunshine and protection from the winds. Strong estuary currents can make swimming from the shingle beach hazardous, though.

⑲ Conwy

Immense, well-preserved walls enclose the town and castle (Cadw) of Conwy, making it Britain's finest medieval fortified town. The walls run for nearly a mile, broken up by 21 jutting bastions every 46m (50yd).

Between 1283 and 1289, around 1500 craftsmen constructed the massive Conwy Castle for Edward I, with a barbican at either end and eight tall towers. From the ramparts of the castle you can get good views down to the crowded streets below and out over the Conwy estuary.

A wealth of old buildings located within the walls includes the 14th-century timber-framed Aberconwy House (NT) and 16th-century Plas Mawr (Cadw), which is distinctive for its ornate plasterwork.

On the quayside, overlooking a collection of fishing boats, is what is said to be the smallest house in Britain, with a frontage just 2.5m (8ft 4in) in height and 1.8m (6ft) across. Pleasure cruises and sea-fishing trips leave from the quay.

Four crossings link the two banks of the river: Thomas Telford's 1820s suspension bridge, now used by pedestrians only; a tubular rail bridge designed by Robert Stephenson in the 1840s; a road bridge; and a road tunnel carrying the Conwy bypass.

North of the town is a marina with a residential development, and the wide sands of Morfa Beach. On the north bank of the Conwy estuary at Llandudno Junction is an RSPB reserve, accessed from the A55.

⑳ Penmaenmawr

The little resort is squeezed into a gap between the mountains and the sea. The coast road dives through tunnels at either side of the town, while a relief road swings right across the end of the promenade on tall concrete legs. South of the town, the tall hills have been worked for their granite since prehistoric times.

When Robert Stephenson built the railway line along this stretch of coast in the mid 19th century he had to protect it with avalanche shelters and a strong sea wall; a later sea wall lines the promenade along the pebbly beach.

Parc Plas Mawr, an industrial heritage park, combines art and history, and to the south is the impressive Maenie Hirion Bronze Age stone circle, also known as the Druid's Circle.

㉑ Llanfairfechan

A good centre for exploring the foothills of Snowdonia, the unassuming town sits between the hills and the sea, in a narrow gap that also accommodates the railway and the main coast road. There is a substantial sea wall, and groynes reach out into the Lavan Sands.

㉒ Penrhyn Castle

An extravagant example of the early 19th-century taste for neo-Norman architecture, the castle (NT) was designed for the Pennant family in 1820 by Thomas Hopper. Inside are elaborate stone carvings and an exhibition of paintings by old masters such as

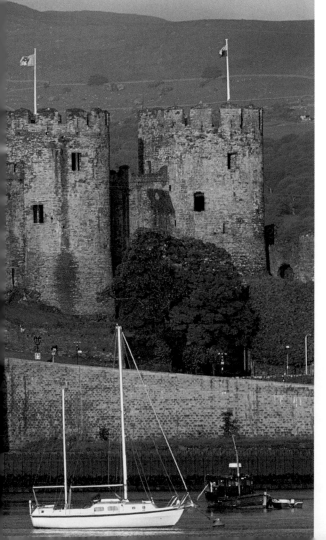

Rembrandt and Canaletto. The stables house a doll museum and a collection of industrial locomotives, and the lush grounds include a ruined medieval chapel and pet cemetery.

You can see kingfishers, peregrine falcons and firecrests at the Spinnies Nature Reserve, to the east of the castle.

㉓ Bangor
The university city dates from the foundation of the cathedral by St Deiniol in AD 548. Near the cathedral is the Bible Garden, so called because it was created to show plants mentioned in the Bible.

Gwynedd Museum and Art Gallery covers the development of north Wales from prehistoric times to the present day, while north of the town an ornate pier reaches out more than halfway into the Menai Strait. Pleasure boats moor at nearby Porth Penrhyn, developed in the 19th century for the export of slate from local quarries.

㉔ Plas Newydd
The imposing mansion of Plas Newydd (NT) was built in the 1790s, in a mixture of classical and Gothic styles, by James Wyatt and Joseph Potter for the Paget family, later the Marquesses of Anglesey. Among the relics on display is the artificial leg of the first Marquess of Anglesey, Wellington's second-in-command at Waterloo. In the dining room is an immense mural painted by Rex Whistler in the 1930s.

㉕ Llanfairpwllgwyngyll
The Victorian equivalent of today's tourist board invented the name Llanfairpwllgwyngyllgogery-chwyrndrobwllllantysiliogogogoch, which is

MENAI BRIDGE

literally translated as 'St Mary's Church in the hollow of white hazel near a rapid whirlpool and the Church of St Tysilio near the red cave'. The name has attracted visitors ever since, though it is commonly shortened to Llanfair P.G. When British Rail closed the station in 1966 there was an uproar, and it was officially reopened in 1973. The platform ticket with the town's name in full is an attraction in itself. Near the station is an old road tollhouse with its original list of charges, starting at three halfpennies for a horse carrying a load of lime.

Llanfair P.G. is linked to the mainland by the Britannia Bridge, built by Robert Stephenson in 1850 to carry the Holyhead Railway The bridge was damaged by fire in 1970 and was reconstructed as a double-decker, with a road on the upper level and the railway underneath this.

On the shoreline is a statue of Admiral Nelson, erected in 1873 as a navigation aid, and in the village is a 27m (88ft) column that serves as a monument to the first Marquess of Anglesey; inside the column is a spiral staircase that you can climb for stupendous views of Snowdonia and the strait.

26 Menai Bridge

For centuries, many lost their lives crossing the treacherous Menai Strait until Thomas Telford's bridge was built. Parliament approved the building of a bridge in 1819, and the engineer Thomas Telford opted for a suspension bridge – a new concept in his day. The village on the strait's northern bank, which at the time was called Porthaethwy, was renamed in honour of the bridge, and is now a small town.

The bridge is best seen from the north bank shoreline promenade, at the western end of which is Church Island and the 14th-century church of St Tysilio. The island can be reached by a causeway exposed at low tide.

Northwest of the town is the Pili Palas butterfly and bird house, which also includes many reptiles and insects.

㉗ Beaumaris
Built by Edward I, Beaumaris Castle (Cadw), is one of Britain's most sophisticated examples of medieval military architecture and dominates the fine little town. The 13th-century castle's moat was originally linked to the sea, and two rings of walls are punctuated by defensive towers.

Other buildings of note in the town include the Grammar School of 1603, the Courthouse of 1614, still in use and open for visits in summer, and the nearby early 19th-century jail.

㉘ Penmon
Elaborately carved Celtic crosses and a 1000-year-old font are some of the treasures to be seen in the ruins of an old priory. According to tradition, a priory was founded here in the 6th century by Cynlas, St Seiriol's brother, though the original building was destroyed by Viking raiders, and rebuilt in the 12th century. A good deal of Norman architecture survives. Nearby are the spring of St Seiriol's Well, a cell said to have been used by the hermit saint, and a 17th-century dovecote.

A toll road leads past some disused quarries to the point of Trwyn Du and spectacular views across Conwy Bay.

㉙ Puffin Island
Puffins, shags, cormorants and seals are regular visitors to this uninhabited island, which lies half a mile out to sea from the Trwyn Du lighthouse on Anglesey's eastern tip. St Seiriol founded a settlement here in the 6th century. Remains can be seen of the monastery, which was abandoned in the 13th century, and of a 19th-century telegraph station. Access is restricted to naturalists with permits, but there are boat trips around the island from Beaumaris.

㉚ Red Wharf Bay
Low tide exposes some 10 square miles of sand, backed by dunes and low grassland and enclosed by rounded headlands. There is ample scope for beachcombing, but walkers should beware of the incoming tide, which rushes along a multitude of small channels to flood the beach. From the little harbour of Red Wharf Bay, a path leads north to the earthen ramparts of the Celtic fort of Castell-mawr.

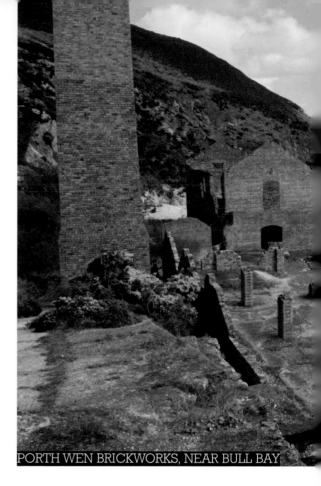

PORTH WEN BRICKWORKS, NEAR BULL BAY

㉛ Benllech
Backing the beach are cliffs studded with fossils, including corals – evidence that this was once a subtropical seabed. A popular holiday resort, Benllech has a long, sandy beach lined by a row of shops and cafes, and offering traditional seaside amusements.

㉜ Moelfre
The small holiday resort and its sheltered pebbly beach are popular with bathers, sailors and other watersports enthusiasts. To the north is a Seawatch Centre with displays on marine life, ships and shipwrecks; it is open in summer and at other times by arrangement.

The headland that shelters the harbour presents a dangerous obstacle to shipping in stormy weather. In October 1859 the steam clipper *Royal Charter*, bound for Liverpool from the Australian goldfields with a cargo of gold, ran aground on the rocks, and all but a dozen of the 450 passengers were lost. About two-thirds of the gold was later recovered. Charles Dickens visited Moelfre two months after the disaster and adapted the story for a tale in *The Uncommercial Traveller*. There is a memorial to the victims in Carmel Church, and another on the cliffs above.

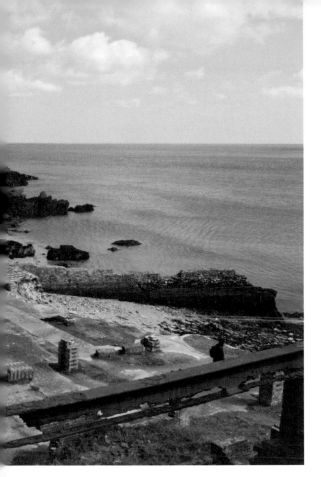

From the church, a lane leads down to a sand and shingle beach sheltered by lichen-covered cliffs. The path continues to a lighthouse on the narrow rocky headland of Point Lynas; in 1766 the Liverpool Pilotage Service was established on the point, to send out six-oared gigs to meet ships heading for the Merseyside docks.

36 Parys Mountain

A rocky and unstable wilderness surrounded by orc-stained pools, the eerie landscape of these old copper mines is a reminder of the late 18th century when this was the world's leading copper-producing area.

There had been mining in the area as far back as Roman times, but the great boom began in the late 18th century; by 1780 the Parys Mountain Copper Company employed 1500 men, women and children from the nearby port of Amlwch. It endowed the town's Church of St Eleth, built in 1800, and even minted its own coins for local use. Examples of the coins, which had the company's initials on one side and a druid's head on the other, can be seen at the National Museum in Cardiff.

By 1815 Welsh copper mining was in decline, and the industry was destroyed by competition from African and American mines in the 1900s.

A 2 mile path explores the ravaged landscape of the mines and on the hill above are the stump of an old windmill and a ruined engine house.

37 Bull Bay

The holiday village, built around a rocky cove, was in the 19th century a busy little fishing port and shipbuilding centre. The falling tide leaves a multitude of pools on the rocky beach, and there are caves to explore at the foot of the cliffs to the west, as well as sea fishing from the rocks round about.

A 1½ mile clifftop walk to the west leads to Porth Wen, with its secluded sandy beach. Structures resembling huge beehives on the western side of the bay are the remains of an old brickworks.

38 Cemaes Bay

The village of Cemaes was once a centre for fishing, shipbuilding, and a good deal of smuggling. It was Northern Anglesey's main harbour until the development of Amlwch in the 18th century. Today pleasure craft outnumber the few fishing boats sheltering behind the harbour breakwater.

Cemaes sits at the centre of the bay's five sheltered beaches; the biggest and sandiest of these, to the east of the harbour, is separated from the village by the small Afon Wygyr river.

To the southeast of Cemaes is a set of electricity-generating wind turbines, and the clifftop footpath north of the village leads past

33 Traeth Lligwy

Wide flat sands make the large beach a popular spot for holidaymakers. A path heads north to the more secluded sandy bay of Traeth yr Ora, while to the east it follows the line of the cliffs to Moelfre. The lane leading southeast from Traeth Lligwy to the hamlet of Llanallgo passes two archaeological sites, both managed by Cadw. The older is Lligwy Chambered Barrow, a Bronze Age tomb consisting of eight upright stones supporting a massive capstone. Nearby is Din Lligwy, a native settlement dating from between the 1st and the 4th centuries AD.

34 Dulas

Gulls wheel over pleasure boats moored on the mudflats, where traces remain of brickworks and limekilns that once lined the shore. North of the bay is the rocky island of Ynys Dulas, where a tower serves as a landmark for sailors. Grey seals can often be seen basking against its walls.

35 Llaneilian

In the hilltop village is the largely 15th-century Church of St Eilian, which was built on the site of a 5th-century hermitage. Inside are some fine woodcarvings.

14th-century St Padrig's Church, dedicated to St Patrick, who is said to have been shipwrecked nearby. It continues on to the cove of Porth Llanlleiana. Dotted around the cove are the ruins of a former china-clay works, and nearby are the remains of the Celtic hill fort of Dinas Gynfor and the dramatically named inlet of Hell's Mouth.

39 Wylfa Head
The twin reactors of the Wylfa nuclear power station stand out on the western shore of a low headland, and the visitor centre has interactive exhibits about the plant. From the nearby car park, paths lead north to Wylfa Head and to the east a nature trail runs through woodland to the coast.

40 Cemlyn Bay
Grassy headlands overlook a rocky bay, in which a shingle ridge shelters a saltwater lagoon. The ridge and lagoon form the Cemlyn Nature Reserve, home to a wide variety of sea birds and waterfowl, including red-breasted mergansers and several species of tern. On the western edge of the bay, a memorial stone records the launch in 1828 of Anglesey's first lifeboat. A path heads west to a sand and shingle beach at the secluded cove of Hen Borth.

41 Carmel Head
Anglesey's remote northwestern corner drops away to the sea in steep cliffs. Two navigation beacons stand on the headland, and a third is set on the rocky islet of West Mouse.

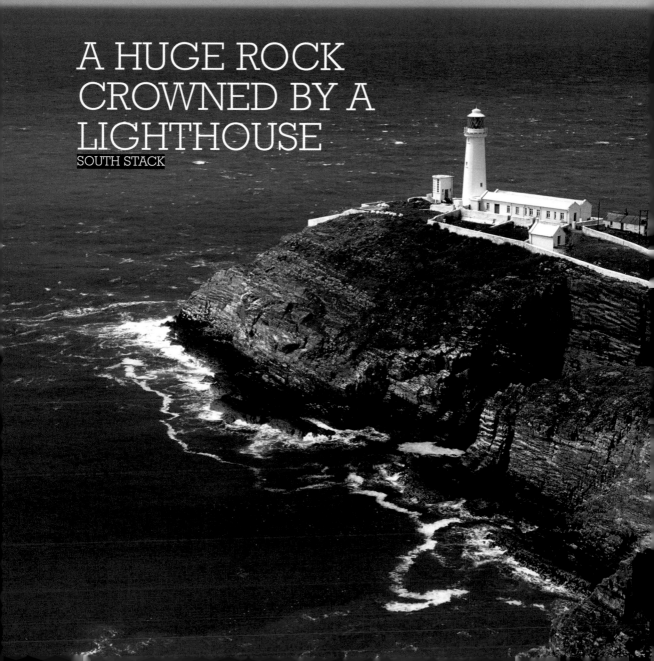

A HUGE ROCK CROWNED BY A LIGHTHOUSE
SOUTH STACK

Farther out are The Skerries with their lighthouse; it was built in 1841 to replace a fire in a brazier that was kept burning by a man and wife who lived out on the rocks to maintain this lonely duty.

Carmel Head (NT) is reached by a footpath sited by a sharp bend in the road north of Llanfairynghornwy. The cliffs here are popular with birdwatchers, who may spot choughs and peregrine falcons. On the head is a pine forest where pheasants are reared by a local landowner; the coast path is closed during the shooting season, from mid September to early February.

42 Penrhos Coastal Park
Woodland and coastal paths crisscross the estate of Penrhos, whose woods contain some 15,000 broad-leaved trees. Created in the early 1900s, most of the original trees were replaced in the 1960s with commercial forestry species, and the park is today a refuge for birds such as kestrels, reed buntings, linnets, terns and shelducks. Freshwater lakes flooded by seawater during exceptionally strong storms in 1990 are slowly recovering.

The 19th-century toll house built at the start of Thomas Telford's new road from Holyhead to London has been moved from its original position, and re-erected in the park as a tea room.

43 Holyhead
A Roman fortress was built here in the 4th century AD and much of the original walls that once surrounded it remain, encircling the 13th-century Church of St Cybi (Cadw). In the southwest corner of the churchyard is the small chapel of Eglwys-y-Bedd, marking the grave of Seregri, leader of a band of Irish raiders in the 6th century.

A large port from the 16th century, Holyhead acquired a direct link with London on the completion in 1821 of a new toll road from the capital; it was engineered by Thomas Telford and is now the A5. Its opening in the presence of George IV is commemorated by a triumphal arch, situated on the harbour. The road was soon joined by the railway, and a 1½ mile breakwater was built; there are good views of harbour activity from the lighthouse at the tip of the breakwater, reached by a promenade.

A ferry service to and from Dun Laoghaire and Dublin in the Republic of Ireland operates from Holyhead.

44 Holyhead Mountain
Rough tracks lead through gorse and heather to the stony grandeur and stupendous views of Holyhead Mountain, at 219m (720ft) the highest hill in Anglesey. On the summit are the remains of the Iron Age fort of Caer y Twr (Cadw), which houses the ruins of a 4th-century Roman watchtower or beacon. On the lower slopes to the west is the settlement of Cytiau'r Gwyddelod (Cadw), inhabited during the 3rd and 4th centuries. The low stone walls of 20 huts survive, some showing where the inhabitants placed their fires, seats and beds.

On the northeastern slopes of Holyhead Mountain is the small Breakwater Country Park, a former quarry used for the building of Holyhead's breakwater and now the home of choughs and peregrine falcons.

45 South Stack
Holy Island's northwestern tip consists of a huge rock crowned by a 27m (90ft) lighthouse and overlooked by 61m (200ft) cliffs. You can cross to the island by descending some 400 stone steps then crossing over an aluminium footbridge.

The cliffs above South Stack, part of an RSPB nature reserve, are noted for their vast numbers of sea birds, including a large colony of puffins. Standing on the rockface to the south of the lighthouse, crenellated Twr Elin, or Ellen's Tower, built in the 18th century as a summerhouse by the Stanleys of Alderley, is now the reserve's visitor centre. There are spectacular clifftop walks northeast around Gogarth Bay to the promontory and islet of North Stack.

46 Trearddur Bay
The bay cuts deeply into the narrow neck of Holy Island, an area of rocky coves and small sandy beaches. Watersports at the main beach, a long stretch of sand with rocky outcrops, include surfing, canoeing and wind-surfing.

Porth Diana Nature Reserve, at the southern end of the bay, is based on a rocky escarpment, which in late spring is covered in the blossoms of rock roses. To the northwest of Trearddur Bay is the sandy, cliff-girt cove of Porth Dafarch, also a popular spot for watersports.

47 Rhoscolyn
A narrow lane leads from the village of Rhoscolyn to sandy Borthwen Bay, from where footpaths follow the rocky coast. To the east are the sands of Silver Bay, and to the west is the ancient St Gwenfaen's Well, whose waters were once thought to have curative powers.

Visitor information
Bangor ☎ (01248) 352786
Conwy ☎ (01492) 592248
Holyhead ☎ (01407) 762622
Llandudno ☎ (01492) 876413
Llanfair P.G. ☎ (01248) 713177
Rhyl & Prestatyn ☎ (01745) 344515

RHOSNEIGR TO PENMAENPOOL

The thin finger of the windy Lleyn Peninsula is one of the most unspoiled parts of Wales; its north coast, the site of prehistoric remains, was once an ancient pilgrims' route

① Rhosneigr

The little town with its narrow streets of whitewashed cottages, once a base for shipbuilding and for shipwrecking gangs, developed as a resort towards the end of the 19th century. To the north are the broad sands of Crigyll Beach and Cymyran Beach, and holiday activities include wind-surfing, horseriding in the gorse and dunes, golf and sea fishing.

② Porth Trecastell

Also known as Cable Bay, after the transatlantic telegraph cable that comes ashore there, the bay's small sandy beach often has ideal conditions for surfing.

On the headland is the burial chamber of Barclodiad y Gawres (Cadw), built around 2500 BC. Its top was destroyed by quarrying, but the passage and side chambers have been recovered, and the abstract patterns carved on the walls are similar to those found in Irish tombs of the same period. The chambers are not open to the public.

③ St Cwyfan's Church

On an islet set between two tiny coves sits the disused Church of St Cwyfan, reached on foot by a causeway at low tide. The first church dedicated to the Irish saint was built in the 7th century, but the present building was begun some 500 years later. The islet can be approached by road as well as by a 2 mile clifftop walk from Aberffraw.

④ Aberffraw

The quiet little village was once the capital of Gwynedd, the kingdom of North Wales. Its period of greatness began in AD 870 under Rhodri the Great, and continued until Llywelyn ap Gruffudd was killed by the forces of Edward I in 1282. Some of the stonework in the 12th-century Church of St Beuno is said to be

remains from the royal palace, thought to have been located nearby. There are exhibitions on the area's history and wildlife in the Llys Llywelyn Coastal Heritage Centre.

The swift-flowing Afon Ffraw passes under the village's 18th-century stone bridge before skirting the western edge of a large area of sand dunes; it reaches the sea by sandy Traeth Mawr.

⑤ Malltraeth

The great sweep of marsh and dunes that stretches along the eastern side of the Cefni estuary are part of the Newborough Warren National Nature Reserve. Redshanks, godwits, ruffs and shelducks are frequent visitors to the area, and these you can observe from hides by the small Parc Mawr lake, at the northern tip of Newborough Forest.

The long inlet of the Cefni estuary gave the village its name, which means 'salt marsh' in Welsh. Flooding was a regular occurrence until 1818, when Thomas Telford built the great embankment known as Malltraeth Cob, and the river was canalised.

⑥ Llanddwyn Bay

The 4 mile stretch of sand in the bay gives spectacular views across the Menai Strait to the mountains of Snowdonia. The sands are bordered by a vast area of dunes to the east and Newborough Forest to the west, which offers a number of forest walks.

Llanddwyn Island, technically a peninsula rather than an island, forms part of the Newborough Warren National Nature Reserve. The island is named after St Dwynwen, patron saint of Welsh lovers, who founded a convent there in the 5th century. Crosses commemorate the saint and her followers, and ruins survive of a Tudor church built on the site of her chapel. At the tip of the island is a disused 19th-century lighthouse, standing beside the cottages that once belonged to pilots who guided vessels over the sandbars at the entrance to the Menai Strait. One of the houses has been restored to show how it would have been around 1900, and another has exhibitions on wildlife and the environment. You can visit both in summer.

❼ Newborough Warren
Thyme and marsh orchids thrive in the unforrested dunes and wet hollows of the warren, which is now a national nature reserve. The small lake of Llyn Rhos Ddu on the reserve attracts ducks, grebes, coots and moorhens.

Violent storms in the Middle Ages covered what was once a huge area of farmland in southern Anglesey with sand. In Tudor times the dunes were stabilised by planting marram grass; more recently, Newborough Warren, as the area became known, was home to a huge colony of rabbits, until the animals were almost wiped out by myxomatosis in 1954.

❽ Caernarfon
Begun by Edward I in 1283, Caernarfon Castle (Cadw) was one of the most powerful fortresses in the chain built to keep the Welsh under English domination. In 1969 it was the scene of the investiture of Prince Charles as Prince of Wales; and the Queen's Tower houses the regimental museum of the Royal Welch Fusiliers. The oldest part of Caernarfon town is enclosed by the medieval town walls that extend from the castle and surround a maze of narrow streets lined with 18th and 19th-century houses.

The quayside next to the castle is the departure point for pleasure boat excursions and fishing trips on the Menai Strait; there are walks along the foreshore westwards towards Foryd Bay. At Victoria Dock, outside the city walls, a small maritime museum opens in summer.

Twthill, east of Caernarfon, was the site of a pre-Roman Celtic fortress; and in AD 78 the

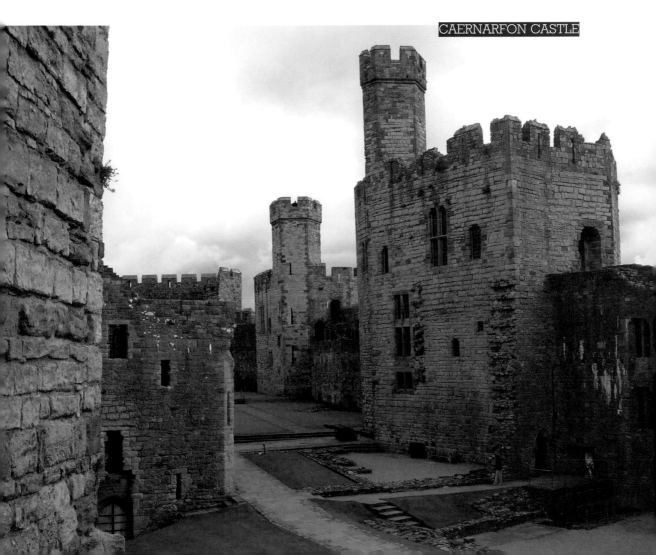
CAERNARFON CASTLE

Romans built the fort of Segontium (Cadw). You can still see the foundations of the barracks where 1000 troops were housed; the museum houses coins and pottery found there.

⑨ Dinas Dinlle

An Iron Age hill fort on the crest of the 30m (100ft) hill dominates this flat stretch of coast. Erosion makes the summit dangerous for walkers, and there is no public right of way to the fort. To the north is a 3 mile sandy beach, backed by a shingle bank constructed to protect the low-lying land from floods.

The road skirting the beach ends by Caernarfon Airport, a former RAF airfield now used for pleasure flights along the Menai Strait and over the Snowdonia mountains. The airport's Air World Museum includes a collection of old RAF aircraft and a 'hands-on' flight simulator.

East of the airfield, a path borders Foryd Bay, a wide expanse of sand, mud and shingle, teeming with wildfowl and wading birds. Quicksand and fast currents make walking on the flats and swimming in the estuary dangerous.

⑩ Clynnog Fawr

The village of small whitewashed cottages has one of Wales's best-known churches, a stopping place for pilgrims on the road to Bardsey Island since its foundation by St Beuno in the 7th century, although the present building is 16th century. Inside is St Beuno's Chest, a medieval wooden trunk that held money paid to the church by the owners of lambs or calves born with 'Beuno's Mark' – a split in the ear.

At the foot of the hills by the roadside south of the village is St Beuno's Well, whose waters were thought to have curative powers. Sufferers from various ailments drank its water, and completed the remedy by spending the night on the saint's tomb in the church.

⑪ Yr Eifl

Granite quarried from the flanks of the three peaks of Yr Eifl has left giant terraces, especially on the seaward side. There are paths around the peaks, the tallest of which rises to 564m (1849ft).

From the village of Llithfaen, to the south, a lane winds steeply down to the valley of Nant Gwrtheyrn. At its end a woodland track leads to the former quarrymen's village of Porth y Nant, abandoned in 1959, and whose buildings have been restored as a centre for the teaching of Welsh. A nature trail follows the stream that flows behind the centre.

⑫ Pistyll

Set in a grove of trees overlooking the sea, is the small 7th-century Church of St Beuno; Pistyll, like its neighbour Nefyn, was a stopping place for Bardsey Island pilgrims. A stream flows noisily past the church leading to a long shingle beach.

⑬ Nefyn

The long beach has firm sand backed by shingle, with low-tide rock pools. Boat trips and shore fishing are available; and when the waves roll in from the north there is surfing in the bay.

In 1284 the former fishing village was chosen by Edward I as the site of a tournament held to celebrate the downfall of Llywelyn ap Gruffudd and the conquest of North Wales. Throughout the Middle Ages, Nefyn was a stopping place for pilgrims travelling along the coast to Bardsey Island. Its medieval Church of St Mary houses the Lleyn Historical and Maritime Museum, a record of life in the local community from the 19th century.

⑭ Traeth Penllech

The winding road from Penllech Bach to Pen-y-graig dives into a valley where a stream flows through a wooded ravine. From the bottom of the hill, a 5 minute walk beside the stream leads to a sandy beach backed by low cliffs. To the south is the sandy cove of Porth Colmon, and a clifftop walk leads north to the tiny rocky bay of Porth Ychain.

⑮ Porth Iago

The deep cleft in the shoreline, containing a small crescent of sand backed by grassy slopes, is signposted from the road between Pen-y-graig and Carreg, though the descent from the car park to the beach is difficult in wet weather. The bay offers good surfing, and diving from the rocks round its edge.

⑯ Porth Oer

This sandy cove is also known in English as Whistling Sands, because footsteps cause dry sand grains to make a squeaking or whistling noise as they rub against each other. A steep track near a picnic area by the cliffs leads down to the long sandy beach, protected by rocky promontories. At low tide, rock pools form by the cliffs at the southern end of the beach.

⑰ Mynydd Mawr

The Lleyn Peninsula's southwestern tip is crowned by the 160m (524ft) Mynydd Mawr. The narrow winding road up the hill has two car parks; from the lower of the two, a rough track leads down to a tiny cove, from where medieval pilgrims used to embark on the crossing to Bardsey Island. Nearby St Mary's Well has fresh water, though it is covered at high tide.

18 Bardsey Island National Nature Reserve

The remote mass of rock, dominated by a 167m (548ft) hill, is 2 miles from the mainland across a sound seething with strong currents. In Welsh, Bardsey is called Ynys Enlli, or 'Island of the Eddies'. It became a refuge for early Christians after the Romans left Britain, and later was an important pilgrimage site. So many pilgrims were buried there that it became known as the Isle of Twenty Thousand Saints.

The island is now a national nature reserve, and farmhouses have been converted into holiday accommodation. Day visits can be made from Aberdaron by booking a place on the boat a few days ahead.

19 Aberdaron

A fishing village of whitewashed cottages stands snugly in a fold of rugged coastline. The twin-naved Church of St Hywyn was built at a safe distance from the sea 1400 years ago, but erosion has taken its toll, and the church now has its own sea wall to protect it. The long sand and shingle beach is sheltered from winds except those from the south and southwest.

The bay is popular with surfers and divers, and offshore fishing trips can be arranged.

20 Porth Ysgo

A path to the sheltered little bay follows a valley of ferns, gorse and foxgloves, down which a stream cascades to the sea in a series of small waterfalls. The path starts from a small car park by a deserted farmhouse on the road heading east from Aberdaron.

Wooden steps lead to the sand and shingle beach, which is covered at high tide; at low water, it is studded with blue-black rocks from a disused manganese mine on the hills behind the bay.

21 Plas yn Rhiw

A small 17th-century manor house set in a large woodland garden crammed with fuchsias, roses and hydrangeas, Plas yn Rhiw (NT) stands on a steep slope overlooking the vast expanse of Porth Neigwl bay. Inside are furnishings, books and paintings collected by the former owners, who refurbished the house in the late 1930s.

22 Porth Neigwl

A 4 mile sweep of sand and low cliffs, Porth Neigwl frequently has rolling waves that provide perfect conditions for surfing. The English name for the bay is Hell's Mouth, because of the threat it posed to sailing ships blown inshore. The sands are most easily reached from a car park west of Llanengan, at the southern end of the bay.

Inland is a flat stretch of farmland, and a 3 mile circular walk starting from the northern end of the bay takes in the disused Church of St Gwyninin, standing in the fields by Llandegwning farmhouse.

23 St Tudwal's Islands

A 5th-century Breton saint founded a priory on the more easterly of these two offshore islands as a refuge after the collapse of the Roman Empire. You can still see the ruins of a later, medieval chapel from boats that cruise round the islands from Abersoch; the islands are privately owned, and landing is not allowed.

24 Abersoch

The once-quiet fishing village is now a centre for powerboat and sailing enthusiasts, and Abersoch's two sandy beaches are separated by a headland crowned with houses. The southern beach is backed by high dunes and a golf course; to the north the sands run for 2 miles to Trwyn Llanbedrog headland.

Two nearby villages have interesting churches. The twin-naved Church of St Engan at Llanengan, to the southwest, was founded in the 6th century and has a beautifully carved rood screen. The Church of St Cian at Llangian, to the northwest, has a small triangular stone pillar on its south side with a Latin inscription, now illegible, dating from the 5th century. It commemorates 'Melus the doctor, son of Martinus', providing the earliest surviving mention of a doctor anywhere in Wales.

25 Llanbedrog

A curving beach of sand and shingle is sheltered by the wooded headland of Trwyn Llanbedrog to the south. From the hill's 131m (430ft) summit, known as Mynydd Tir-y-cwmwd, there are fine views out to sea to St Tudwal's Islands, and along the coast east to Pwllheli. South of the village is the restored Victorian Gothic manor house of Plas Glyn-y-weddw, now an arts gallery and residential centre.

26 Pwllheli

A promenade lined by small hotels and boarding houses runs along South Beach, a long strip of sand that is backed by shingle. The port and market town is the biggest and busiest settlement on the Lleyn Peninsula. Pwllheli's inner and outer harbours have both been developed, and a marina is situated in the inner harbour.

East of the harbour, sandy Glan-y-don beach extends for almost 4 miles towards the headland of Pen-ychain.

㉗ Llanystumdwy

Set on the banks of the turbulent little Afon Dwyfor, the village of Llanystumdwy is where the Liberal prime minister David Lloyd George grew up. His simple and dignified grave, marked by a single massive boulder inscribed 'DLG 1863–1945', lies within a stone enclosure in a glade beside the river. On the main village street is the Lloyd George Museum, which displays photographs, personal effects and political cartoons, and also contains a reconstruction of a Victorian schoolroom. Nearby is Highgate, the small stone cottage where he lived until 1880.

Southeast of the village, the Afon Dwyfach joins the Dwyfor to form a long estuary. A riverside walk of about a mile leads to a pebbly shore where rock pools form at low tide. You can walk along the shore to Criccieth.

㉘ Criccieth

The ruins of Criccieth Castle (Cadw) stand high on a towering headland, overlooking the Victorian terraces of the little town of Criccieth on one side and the open sea on the other. Constructed by the Welsh prince Llewelyn ap Gruffudd in the middle of the 13th century, the fortress passed into English hands when Edward I captured it in 1283, but it was retaken by Owain Glyndwr during his rebellion in 1404. Some of the cracks and splits in the stonework probably date from the final siege, when the castle was sacked and burnt by the Welsh. The castle's visitor centre has an exhibition on castles built by the Welsh princes, and another on Giraldus Cambrensis, or Gerald of Wales, the 12th-century churchman and Welsh historian.

West of the headland is a pebbly beach protected by groynes, and a high sea wall shelters a line of hotels. To the east, beyond a short breakwater, a curving sweep of sand and pebble stretches towards Morfa Bychan.

㉙ Morfa Bychan

The village's huge sandy beach, Black Rock Sands, is backed by dunes stretching east to the Glaslyn estuary, and there are caves among the rocks on the headland at the western end. The bay provides good surfing, but strong currents make swimming dangerous at the estuary end of the beach.

Small Morfa Bychan Nature Reserve, set in dunes beside a golf course east of the village, is a nesting site for moorhens, larks and partridges.

㉚ Borth-y-Gest

Trim cottages, many of them colourwashed, fringe a small sheltered bay on the bank of the Glaslyn, reached by a road from Porthmadog to the northeast. To the northwest are the towering crags of Moel-y-Gest, from where there are splendid views across the estuary towards Harlech and the mountains inland. According to Welsh legend, Prince Madog, son of the king Owain Gwynedd, set sail from Borth-y-Gest in 1170 and reached America more than 300 years before Columbus.

㉛ Porthmadog

The restored narrow-gauge Ffestiniog Railway provides a 13 mile scenic trip through the mountains. The railway was originally built to bring stone from the quarries of Blaenau Ffestiniog to the harbour in Porthmadog, where the stones were loaded onto ships. The harbour town was created early in the 19th century, with the building of the mile-long embankment called The Cob across the Glaslyn estuary, which reclaimed 7000 acres of land from the river's mudflats. Porthmadog grew prosperous from the slate trade and an old slate warehouse is now the Maritime Museum.

The town is also a centre for rock climbing, hill walking, riding and fishing. Porthmadog is also a terminus for the narrow-gauge Welsh Highland Railway.

㉜ Portmeirion

Buildings in extravagant Italianate style rub shoulders with architectural oddments brought from all over Britain in this fantasy folly on the grandest scale. Inspired by a visit to the Italian resort of Portofino in the 1920s, the architect Clough Williams-Ellis returned home determined to create a 'dream village'. Portmeirion was built in stages between 1925 and 1972, consisting of 50 buildings arranged around a central plaza, and a tiny harbour. It includes a tall bell tower, built by Williams-Ellis, and an 18th-century colonnade salvaged from Bristol. In the 1960s Portmeirion was used as the setting for the television series *The Prisoner*.

The village sits on a hillside overlooking the Dwyryd estuary, and footpaths lead through gardens of subtropical plants and trees to a wide sandy beach. Strong currents and swift tides make swimming dangerous.

㉝ Morfa Harlech

An expanse of dunes and salt marshes, a nature reserve with colonies of wading birds stretches south and east of Harlech Point. To the south of the broad sandy estuary of the Glaslyn and the Dwyryd is a wide stretch of flatland reclaimed from the sea, now mainly grazing land, while along the northern edge of the Morfa are the sands of Traeth Bach.

㉞ Harlech

One of Edward I's string of fortresses, Harlech Castle (Cadw) stands dramatically on a 61m (200ft) rocky bluff. In 1404 it was captured by Owain Glyndwr, who based his court there until it was retaken by the English five years later. During the Wars of the Roses it was held by the Lancastrians and withstood a seven-year siege by the Yorkists before falling in 1468. The song 'Men of Harlech' is said to have been inspired by the Lancastrians' resistance.

The small town of Harlech is built along a ridge behind the castle bluff, and to the west paths cross high dunes to a large sandy beach. Nearby is Royal St David's golf course.

35 Llandanwg
Part of this village, including the church of St Tanwg, has been half-buried by the Artro estuary's shifting sands. Strong currents round the sandy beach, on the seaward side, make bathing dangerous on the falling tide.

36 Llanbedr
The village sits on the southern bank of the Artro, and lanes head east towards the rugged peaks of Snowdonia. In the 16th-century Church of St Peter is a stone found in the nearby hills, marked with a spiral design that is thought to date from the Bronze Age.

From Llanbedr, a road heads west to Shell Island, known in Welsh as Mochras. A peninsula rather than an island, it is covered in more than 200 different kinds of shell carried there by peculiarities of the offshore currents. You can reach the 'island' across a causeway at low tide; a noticeboard indicates when it is safe to cross.

37 Dyffryn Ardudwy
Seven miles of sandy beach, backed by grass-covered dunes, stretch from Shell Island to Barmouth passing this village. To

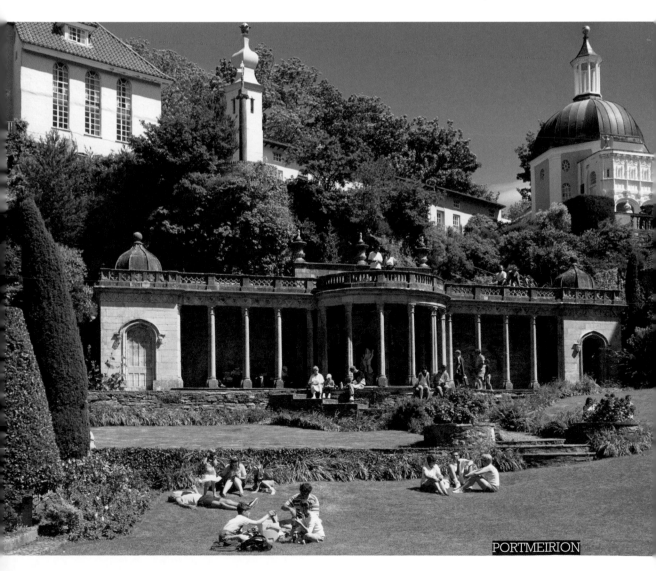

PORTMEIRION

the northwest is the unspoilt wilderness of Morfa Dyffryn National Nature Reserve.

On the southern outskirts of the village are the remains of a prehistoric burial chamber, managed by Cadw, and many other sites lie in the nearby hills. Pony-trekking is available.

38 Llanaber

A narrow village squeezed between the mountains and the sea, Llanaber has a superb example of early Gothic architecture in its Church of St Mary and St Bodfan, which dates from the early 13th century. In the church is an inscribed monolith known as the Caelixtus Stone, dating from the 5th century AD, while old slate tombs in the churchyard are said to have been used by smugglers as hiding places for their contraband.

39 Barmouth

Clinging to the hillside above the harbour, the old town is a maze of cottages and slate-stepped alleyways while the seafront of this popular holiday resort has sandy beaches, donkey rides and bright arcades.

On the quayside is Ty Gwyn, a small museum containing artefacts from a local Tudor shipwreck, housed in a 15th-century building, while nearby Ty Crwn is a circular lock-up house built in 1834.

A trail leads from the old town to the viewpoint of Dinas Olau, which in 1885 was the first piece of land to be acquired by the National Trust. A 4 mile track dubbed the Panorama Walk skirts the hills overlooking the estuary and leads to the hamlet of Cutiau.

The railway bridge across the estuary has a pedestrian walkway, and a ferry service connects with the Fairbourne and Barmouth Steam Railway.

40 Penmaenpool

Water, woods and mountains surround the hamlet of Penmaenpool on the south bank of the upper Mawddach estuary. A signal box beside a disused railway, offering a good vantage point for birdwatchers, houses a Wildlife Centre, and from here 7 miles of level track-bed provide a peaceful walk along the estuary to the Morfa Mawddach station.

Visitor information

Caernarfon ☎ (01286) 672232
Harlech ☎ (01766) 780658
Holyhead ☎ (01407) 762622
Porthmadog ☎ (01766) 512981
Pwllheli ☎ (01758) 613000

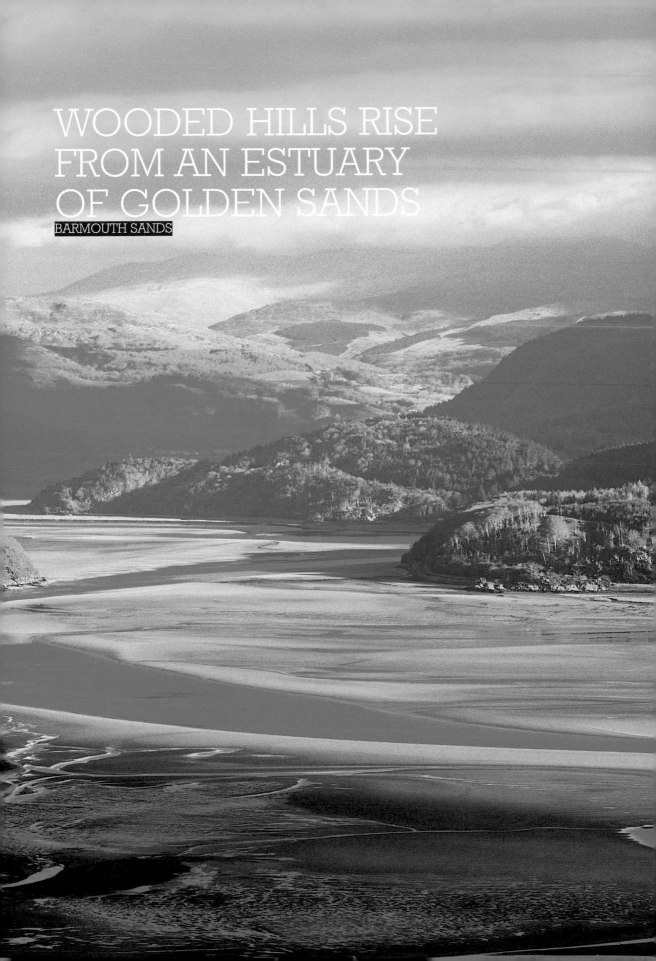

WOODED HILLS RISE FROM AN ESTUARY OF GOLDEN SANDS

BARMOUTH SANDS

FAIRBOURNE TO ABEREIDDY

A striking section of coastline, the northern section of the Pembrokeshire coast stretches round Cardigan Bay, with its constantly changing sand dunes, secluded coves and high cliffs

❶ Fairbourne

Half-scale replicas of vintage engines power the steam locomotives which run along the Fairbourne and Barmouth Steam Railway. Originally built in 1890 as a horse-drawn tramway, the line was equipped with steam trains to run on its 12¼in tracks in 1916.

Today, the trains run along the shore of this small but sprawling resort in summer to connect with a ferry across the estuary to Barmouth.

❷ Llwyngwril

Steep mountains loom above this busy village, from whose sand and shingle beach there are fine views northwards to the Lleyn Peninsula. At Llangelynnin to the south is the clifftop Church of St Celynnin, dating from the 11th century, which retains traces of medieval frescoes on the chancel wall.

❸ Llanegryn

Colonies of cormorants populate the gaunt cliffs of Craig-yr-Aderyn, or Birds' Rock, a few miles upstream from the small village. The village overlooks the fertile Dysynni valley, known for its ancient Welsh Black cattle. On a hill just north of the village is the 13th-century parish Church of St Mary and St Egryn; it contains an intricately carved oak rood screen, one of the finest in Wales.

Nearby are the melancholy ruins of Castell y Bere (Cadw), a small fortress built on a precipitous crag by the 13th-century Prince Llywelyn ab Iorwerth.

❹ Tywyn

The busy little town is a terminus of the narrow-gauge Talyllyn Railway, which runs through 7 miles of spectacular mountain scenery to Abergynolwyn and the former quarries at Nant Gwernol, the starting point for several woodland walks. Tywyn station houses a museum with vintage steam locomotives.

'Tywyn' is the Welsh word for sand dune, reflecting the nature of the coast around this town, from where 4 miles of sand stretch south to Aberdyfi.

❺ Aberdyfi

Miles of sandy, dune-backed beach line the seashore to the north of the attractive little resort, also known as Aberdovey. Located at the mouth of the Dyfi, the resort is a popular centre for sailing and watersports.

An exhibition in the Snowdonia National Park Visitor Centre explains the town's shipping and shipbuilding activities in the 19th century, and tells the legend of a land lost beneath the sea, remembered in the Victorian song 'The Bells of Aberdovey'.

There are fishing expeditions and boat trips from the harbour, and an 18-hole championship golf course occupies a magnificent position on the dunes.

❻ Ynys-hir RSPB Reserve

A variety of habitats, including woodland, salt marsh, peat bog and reed beds, means you can see a wide range of birds in the reserve. Spring is the best time for spotting woodland birds, including pied flycatchers and redstarts, while in May, and from October to December, Ynys-hir is host to great numbers of estuary birds such as whimbrels, dunlins, wigeons and curlews. Winter

CORS FOCHNO, NEAR YNYSLAS

birds of prey include red kites and peregrines. The reserve is one of only a handful of places in England and Wales to be visited in winter by the Greenland white-fronted goose.

❼ Dyfi Furnace
The charcoal-burning blast furnace that stands by a gushing waterfall on the River Einion, in the village of Furnace, is probably the best preserved in Britain.
Dyfi Furnace (Cadw) was built about 1755 for smelting iron ore, and operated for about half a century. The huge water wheel attached to the outside of the building is similar to the one that originally powered the furnace's giant bellows. Visitors may look inside the blast furnace and bellows room.

❽ Ynyslas
The tip of the peninsula that extends into the flat, watery expanses of the Dyfi estuary is made up of sand dunes that are constantly changing and moving, as well as of extensive areas of salt marsh. A visitor centre at Ynyslas explains how dunes are formed, and describes their plants and wildlife.

The centre is the starting point for guided nature walks in summer, and polecats and weasels are among the animals resident in the vicinity. Orchids grow in the damp, low-lying areas between the dunes, and ringed plovers lay their well-camouflaged eggs on a shingle ridge along the west side of the dunes.

Ynyslas is part of the Dyfi National Nature Reserve, which includes the estuary of the River Dyfi, and Cors Fochno, a raised bog to the south dotted with numerous pools. Cors Fochno was dug for peat for many centuries until the 1950s.

Low tide on the beach between Ynyslas and Borth reveals the remains of a forest that grew after the end of the Ice Ages, 10,000 years ago, and was gradually submerged as the sea level rose.

❾ Borth
A mile-long line of houses straggles behind Borth's sea wall and its long sand and pebble beach, popular with bathers and surfers. A visit to the Animalarium, located towards the southern end of the village, will let you see a variety of creatures, including lemurs, wallabies, snakes and tarantulas.

To the south of Borth, a coastal path passes a war memorial and follows exhilarating clifftops for some 5 miles; halfway to Aberystwyth, the path descends to a remote sand and shingle beach at Wallog. You can return from Aberystwyth to Borth by train.

❿ Clarach Bay
At low tide the bay has a pleasant sandy beach which is popular with holiday-makers but visitors seeking solitude can head in either direction along steeply rising clifftop paths. Chalets and caravan parks are spread along the seafront in the bay and inland.

285

⑪ Aberystwyth

Bay-windowed guest houses and hotels stretch round the curved promenade of the Victorian seaside resort and university town, whose name means 'mouth of the River Ystwyth'. There are panoramic views of Aberystwyth and its sand and shingle beach from the top of Constitution Hill, which you can reach by a stiff climb from the north of the bay or by Britain's longest electrically powered cliff railway. At the top of the hill is a camera obscura with a bird's-eye view of the surrounding landscape on a white concave surface.

Substantial castle ruins stand on a headland at the southern end of the bay. Begun in 1277 by Edward I, the castle was captured in 1404 by Owain Glyndwr, and suffered a pounding by Oliver Cromwell's cannons in the Civil War in 1649; much of the rubble was removed by local residents to build houses.

Aberystwyth's old harbour, at the mouth of the River Rheidol, offers fishing trips and boat tours for wildlife enthusiasts, while a marina has berths for visiting small-boat sailors.

The Ceredigion Museum, housed in an Edwardian theatre, contains relics of the area's lead-mining and seafaring days, as well as domestic items and a reconstruction of a traditional cottage. Nearby, the narrow-gauge Vale of Rheidol Railway leaves from next to the main railway station and runs for almost 12 miles to Devil's Bridge.

The main campus of the University of Wales is on Penglais Hill, not far from the National Library of Wales, with a changing programme of exhibitions. Close by, the Arts Centre includes galleries with exhibitions of ceramics, photography, paintings and crafts. The university's first constituent college was housed within a prominent Gothic-revival Victorian building, designed as a grand hotel, on the seafront.

Llanbadarn Fawr, a mile southeast of Aberystwyth, has a long history as a religious settlement. In the 6th century, Padarn, a Celtic saint, arrived there from Brittany with 847 monks and founded a religious order. The early 13th-century Llanbadarn Church contains several carved Celtic crosses, some dating from the 10th century.

⑫ Morfa Bychan

High cliffs stretch southwards from Aberystwyth, and the only access to the sea for more than 7 miles is at Morfa Bychan. The road to the coast ends at a holiday park, and a short walk to the north leads to steps that descend to a stony beach. A hilly coastal path leads northwards before dropping down to Aberystwyth.

⑬ Llanrhystud

Hills rising to more than 122m (400ft) shelter the compact village. North and south of the mouth of a broad stream flowing into the sea are shingle and sand beaches, while the southern beach, near the Morfa site, is the easier to reach, with a road ending behind the shore.

VALE OF RHEIDOL RAILWAY, ABERYSTWYTH

⑭ Llansantffraed

The coast road between Aberarth and Llannon gives fine views towards Aberystwyth. A lane from Llannon leads to Llansantffraed, a neighbouring village on the coast. You can drive your car as far as St Bride's Church, from where it is a few minutes' walk to a shingle beach.

⑮ Aberarth

A tight knot of lanes lined with 19th-century terraced cottages recalls the busier days of Aberarth, once a port at the mouth of the Arth. You can reach a shingle beach from the east side of the river.

At the Derwen Welsh Cob Centre, east of Aberarth, you can see these versatile horses at close quarters; a museum explains their agricultural role.

⑯ Aberaeron

Terraces of pastel-shaded early 19th-century houses give Aberaeron's streets something of a Mediterranean flavour. Pleasure craft and fishing boats use the harbour, and there are shingle beaches near its mouth.

Clôs Pencarreg is a major craft workshop that has been established in a former farm; crafts demonstrated there include pottery, glass-blowing, etching and watercolour painting.

⑰ New Quay

Streets wind down to a harbour filled with fishing boats and other craft in this former port and shipbuilding centre. A quayside building displays a list of tolls dating from the days when there was also a busy coastal trade at New Quay. The quay after which the village was named was built in the early 19th century, providing the only safe harbour along this whole stretch of coast. Mackerel can be caught from the shore, and boat trips to watch dolphins leave from the harbour in summer.

To the southeast, the Bird Hospital treats oiled and injured sea birds and seals. Check with the tourist information centre for opening times.

The poet Dylan Thomas lived in New Quay in the 1940s.

⑱ Cwmtydu

The layers of rock in the grey shale cliffs near Cwmtydu are strikingly buckled and tilted. The secluded shingle beach, reached by a long drive along narrow lanes, is overlooked by the remains of an old limekiln.

To the east of the cove, a path climbs steeply onto a grassy slope and passes the site of Castell Bach, a promontory fort occupied by a small Celtic community about 2000 years ago. The path continues along the coast to New Quay.

⑲ Llangrannog

A 165m (541ft) hill, crowned by the site of a prehistoric fort overlooks the headland of Ynys-Lochtyn. It is reached by a path from the sand and pebble beach in Llangrannog, a small but bustling resort. In the evening the dry ski slope at the Urdd Centre, a youth centre a mile east of Llangranog, is open to the public.

⑳ Traeth-Penbryn

This small sandy beach, tucked between low cliffs at the end of a wooded combe, is owned by the National Trust. A narrow road leads to the sea, but you must park your car in the hamlet of Penbryn, a 10 minute walk away.

㉑ Tresaith

The stone-built hamlet lies at the foot of a hill by a beach of firm sand below a strip of shingle. Walkers can head west along the cliffs to Aberporth or, when the tide is out, east along the sands for a mile to the beach at Penbryn.

㉒ Aberporth

The quiet resort of Aberporth clusters round two sandy beaches. Until the beginning of the 20th century, Aberporth was a herring-fishing centre. Huge shoals spawned round Cardigan Island; during one night in 1808 some nine million fish were caught.

A short distance west of Aberporth is a Ministry of Defence missile testing centre, while Felinwynt Rainforest Centre, 3 miles west of the village, has exotic butterflies in a simulated tropical environment.

㉓ Mwnt

A drive along a narrow, tortuous lane ends at a spectacular sandy cove, enclosed by high cliffs. Near the clifftop car park is the 14th-century Church of the Holy Cross, formerly used by pilgrims on their way to Bardsey Island, off the Lleyn Peninsula.

㉔ Gwbert

Sand dunes, which support some 160 plant species, give way just north of the village of Gwbert to rocky cliffs that stretch as far as New Quay. The beach at Gwbert is shingle, with muddy sand exposed at low tide; river currents make swimming dangerous.

At the Coastal Farm Park and Waterfowl Centre, on the headland almost a mile north of Gwbert, visitors can see rare breeds from many parts of the world. The headland also provides good views of Cardigan Island, a nature reserve inhabited by Soay sheep; it is not open to the public, though you can see bottle-nosed dolphins, Atlantic grey seals, shags, black-backed gulls and herring gulls round the island.

When a steamer was shipwrecked off Cardigan Island in 1934, a number of brown rats came ashore and destroyed the island's colonies of puffins and Manx shearwaters. Lures to tempt these species to return to the island include dummy puffins and a machine that imitates the call of the shearwaters.

25 Cardigan
Pleasure craft and small fishing boats moor at the quays of Cardigan. The busy town stands on gentle slopes above the east bank of the River Teifi, which is crossed by two road bridges. In the 18th and 19th centuries Cardigan was a thriving port serving the valley.

26 Cilgerran
The impregnable-looking Cilgerran Castle (Cadw/NT) perches above a wooded gorge on the winding River Teifi. The castle, founded by the Normans, dates mostly from the 13th century; in 1387 it withstood a siege by the Flemish.

There is a fine view of the castle from the river, which is popular with canoeists. Cilgerran hosts a Coracle Regatta in August.

27 St Dogmaels
The sloping village above the River Teifi grew up round St Dogmaels Abbey (Cadw), established by the Welsh, probably in the 7th century. The ruins date from the 12th century. Next to the abbey is the Church of St Thomas, which has a stone whose inscriptions provided the key to an early alphabet.

On the River Teifi, a few fishermen use seine nets to catch salmon. One end is held on shore, and the other by a boat; the seine is then cast in a semicircle, and the ends are pulled together.

28 Poppit Sands
Dunes flank the wide, popular sandy beach at the mouth of the Teifi estuary. Swimmers should beware of currents at mid-tide and avoid the deep-water channel farther out at all times. There is a testing uphill walk from the beach to Cemaes Head, and southwest of the headland cliffs rise to more than 152m (500ft).

The beach lies at the northern end of the 186 mile Pembrokeshire Coast Path, which follows the coast to Amroth, north of Tenby.

29 Moylgrove
Lanes dip down steeply into this peaceful one-street village. To the northwest, at the narrow inlet of Ceibwr Bay, low tide reveals a shingle beach beneath imposing cliffs; it is the only point you can reach by road on the 11 miles of coast from Newport Bay to Poppit Sands.

A mile's walk southwest along the coast from the bay passes a dramatic blowhole called Pwll-

Ancient craft on the Teifi

Coracles are still used for salmon fishing on the River Teifi, mainly between Cilgerran and Cenarth; the latter is home to the National Coracle Centre, which has a collection of coracles from around the world. Today, however, this ancient method is used mainly for enjoyment and as a way of keeping an ancient art alive.

Easily carried, the boats are made of intertwined laths of willow and hazel covered with fabric and pitch. The bowl-shaped design is unchanged since the Iron Age, though ancient Britons used animal hide to cover the craft.

▶ Cilgerran 26, left

y-wrach (the Witches' Cauldron). Beyond the blowhole, the coast path can be treacherous in places as it follows high cliffs.

30 Nevern
The tranquil village sits in the valley of the Nyfer, whose birdlife includes the scarce avocet. A stone cross carved in the 10th or 11th century stands in the churchyard of ancient St Brynach's Church here, and in an avenue of yews leading to the church porch is the tree known as the 'bleeding yew', from which sticky red sap oozes. Little remains of a nearby Norman castle.

31 Newport
St Mary's Church overlooks the small town's most attractive corners, including its castle, dating from Norman times and now a private house. Carreg Coetan Arthur burial chamber, erected round 3500 BC, stands among modern houses.

The sandy Parrog Beach, on the south side of the Nyfer estuary, retains a small quay, a vestige of Newport's days as a port, while a mile-long walk beside the north side of the estuary, or a 3 mile drive, leads to Newport Sands, backed by dunes. The town has an information centre on the Pembrokeshire Coast National Park.

32 Dinas Head
Jutting out between Fishguard Bay and Newport Bay, the stubby peninsula of Dinas Head provides a 3 mile circular walk along cliffs and through Cwm Dewi, the sheltered valley that divides it from the mainland. Cwm-yr-Eglwys, the village at the eastern end of Cwm

Dewi, has a sandy beach and is a good starting point for walks. The village's ruined St Brynach's Church was a victim of a great storm of 1859, which in a single night wrecked more than 100 ships off the Welsh coast.

Pwllgwaelod, to the west of Cwm Dewi, is a beach of sand and rocks.

㉝ Fishguard

The French surrender of 1797 was signed in the Royal Oak inn, which stands in The Square in a hilly area of narrow streets that forms the hub of the town. The pub contains battle memorabilia.

Lower Town, set round the mouth of the River Gwaun, preserves the character of a fishing village; just to the north, a short path leads to the ruins of Old Fort, constructed in 1781.

Southeast of Fishguard, lanes lead along the unspoilt Gwaun valley.

㉞ Goodwick

Sited at the western end of Fishguard Bay, the village retains a distinctly Victorian character. A creation of the Great Western Railway, it was intended to be a terminal for liners sailing to and from New York, but the transatlantic trade later shifted to Southampton. Today ferries leave for Rosslare, in Ireland, and day trips run to Dublin, Waterford and Cork.

㉟ Carregwastad Point

An inscribed stone at Carregwastad Point commemorates the most recent invasion of Britain, which took place in 1797 during the Napoleonic Wars. A ragged, drunken force of some 1200 men, made up of Frenchmen and convicts, came ashore, led by an elderly American; they surrendered only a few days later. The invaders seized Tre-Howel, a farmhouse still standing a mile inland, as their headquarters.

Carregwastad Point can be reached only on foot, by paths from Tre-Howel and Llanwnda.

㊱ Strumble Head

The remote headland gives splendid views of the nearby cliffs and of the lighthouse on Ynys Meicel, an island just offshore. In very clear conditions you can see the Irish coast. Strumble Head's car park is a popular starting point for walks along the coast path.

㊲ Pwllderi

A memorial to Dewi Emrys, an early 20th-century poet of the Pembroke stands on the clifftop near a viewpoint above the rocky cove of Pwllderi. On a clear day you can see St David's Head 21 miles to the southwest.

A dramatic stretch of the coast path winds northeast to Strumble Head, while a steeper route ascends to the Iron Age fortress of Garn Fawr. In clear conditions you can see the coast of Ireland from ramparts on the summit.

㊳ Aber Mawr

Low tide exposes tree stumps lying in the sand and shingle of this isolated beach. Perfectly preserved by the saltwater, they are the remnants of a forest drowned by a sudden flood 8000 years ago as the European ice sheets melted. Melin Tregwynt, a mile to the east, is a working 18th-century woollen mill.

㊴ Abercastle

Only limekilns, an old granary and a few cottages now line the quiet creek which from Tudor times until the 1930s was a thriving port and boat yard. Half a mile to the west, at Longhouse Farm, Carreg Sampson is a magnificent 5000-year-old cromlech, an open-sided tomb of massive stones.

㊵ Porthgain

Immense brick walls tower over the harbour of Porthgain. Constructed in the 19th century, the walls once formed storage bins for granite roadstone, 40,000 tons of which were loaded into coastal steamers every year. The crushing plant and quarries closed in 1932, but the village remains a thriving community.

㊶ Abereiddy

In a former slate quarry, a deep sheer-sided pool called the Blue Lagoon now provides a sheltered and romantic anchorage for small boats. It is reached by a short path from Abereiddy past ruined cottages.

Slate-grey sands create an unusual beach on the fine west-facing bay of Abereiddy. To the north are isolated sandy beaches beneath the cliffs at Traethllyfn.

Visitor information

Aberaeron ☎ (01545) 570602
Aberdyfi ☎ (01654) 767321
Aberystwyth ☎ (01970) 612125
Barmouth ☎ (01341) 280787
Borth ☎ (01970) 871174
Cardigan ☎ (01239) 613230
Dolgellau ☎ (01341) 422888
Fishguard Harbour ☎ (01348) 872037
Fishguard Town ☎ (01437) 776636
Machynlleth ☎ (01654) 702401
New Quay ☎ (01545) 560865
Tywyn ☎ (01654) 710070

A SHELTERED ANCHORAGE FOR SMALL BOATS

BLUE LAGOON, ABEREIDDY

There's scrumptious

On the mudflats and in the rock pools along the coasts
of Wales lies a bountiful larder of edible delights

HARDY COCKLE
PICKERS TOIL ON
THE MUDFLATS
AS THEY HAVE FOR
GENERATIONS
GOWER PENINSULA, WALES

Nature is pretty good at providing food for
the animal kingdom, and nowhere more
so than round the magnificent coastline of Wales.
These 750 miles of sand and mud flats, dunes,
estuaries and rock pools are teeming with life:
monkfish, bass, mackerel and hake along with
their flatfish cousins the sole, turbot and skate
under the sea; cockles and winkles, mussels and
oysters in the tidal streams; lobsters and crabs,
shrimps and prawns among the seabed rocks
and in the pools.

All these can be a gourmet treat if prepared
in the right way. An Anglesey oyster swallowed
straight from the half-shell or steamed in its own
juices; a Cardigan Bay sea bass caught on a line
and baked in salt; a plate of Penclawdd cockles

wrapped in streaky bacon: such sea-borne
delights are the very essence of natural Welsh
cuisine. But fish and shellfish are only half
the larder.

All's fair game for the pot

When it came to getting a full stomach,
our Welsh ancestors were not squeamish.
Anything that could be fished, caught, shot,
scraped, picked, dredged or dug from the
coasts of Wales went straight into the pot.
That included the eggs and young of puffin,
gannet and other seabirds on the cliffs, rabbits
from islands off the Welsh coast such as
Ramsey, Skokholm and Skomer, shellfish from
limpets to mussels and winkles to oysters,

a particular hot-spot being the Gower peninsula west of Swansea. You have to wash it and boil it for a long time, and looking at the greeny-black sludge that results you might wonder what all the fuss is about. But roll it in oatmeal flour and fry it in a nice bit of bacon fat, and you've got laverbread, a spinach-flavoured and subtle accompaniment to mashed potatoes or Welsh lamb – especially if that lamb was raised on a Welsh saltmarsh, flavouring its own meat as it grazed samphire, salt grass and sea lavender.

Samphire itself is another great delicacy of the Welsh coast, either the rock samphire with its delicate citrus flavour to accompany a nice piece of hake, or a dish of pickled marsh samphire – often likened to asparagus – to sharpen up the rich taste of crabmeat. And sea beet, blanched for a little while to retain the flavour and texture, possesses an extraordinarily intense minerality, part iron and part acid, which makes it a fine side-dish with Welsh black beef or mixed with Penclawdd cockles or Anglesey mussels.

A sharp bite to eat

In Gower the rock pools of the Worm's Head causeway, refreshed by every tide, are celebrated hunting grounds for shrimps. Big crabs and lobsters occasionally get stranded there, too. Under the sand of many Welsh beaches live the seldom-seen razorfish, their presence betrayed by the long, fragile empty shells like old-fashioned barbers' razors left strewn on the tideline.

Patient fishers watch for the spouts of water the razorfish ejects while feeding, or walk backwards over the sand looking for the telltale dimple as the creature buries itself deeper in reaction to a heavy footfall. A quick flick of a stick, a dig of a knife blade or a sprinkle of salt around the hole, and the razorfish is yours to take home, steam for a very short time in a pan, and savour with plenty of parsley butter.

There are plenty of food fairs and festivals featuring specialities of the Welsh coast, including the Llyn Seafood Festival at Pwllheli and the Cardigan Bay Seafood Festival at Aberaeron (both in July), and the autumn Conwy Food Festival in October. Our forebears would have been amazed at our delight in rediscovering the fillip that everyday items such as seaweed and rock plants can provide for modern tastebuds. To them it was all just food, a bit nicer or a bit nastier according to taste, provided by nature, to be gathered however and wherever they could. Yet there is something fine about the fact that the natural bounty of the Welsh coasts is no longer lying forgotten, but is once more being shared and appreciated by the descendants of those hardy old pickers of samphire and gatherers of gannet eggs.

seaweed from the rocks at low tide, rock samphire and scurvy grass, sea beet and marsh samphire.

For the past hundred years or so, such humble fare has been out of favour, associated as it has been with poverty and hardship. Yet contemporary palates have proved to be not quite so fastidious. With the help of celebrity chefs and a fashion for turning back to the wild for fresh ideas and inspiration, the coasts of Wales are providing some major culinary pleasures for discerning diners.

The humble laver, a thin sheet of reddish weed that turns black when dried, is the most famous edible seaweed of the Welsh coast. It's harvested all round the south and west edges of Wales, with

ST DAVID'S HEAD TO LLANSTEFFAN

From St Brides Bay, home to Britain's smallest city, round past the port of Milford Haven, and east to sheltered Carmarthen Bay, the western side of the Pembroke peninsula is an area of contrasts

❶ St David's Head
Stone outcrops rise above wild but beautiful moorland on this peninsula. An ancient route that once linked Pembrokeshire with Salisbury Plain and Ireland leads down to the shore, and there is a Neolithic cromlech on the skyline. An Iron Age fort on the headland stands near a stone rampart known as The Warrior's Dyke.

❷ Whitesands Bay
One of the most popular beaches in Pembrokeshire, Whitesands Bay is divided into different areas for surfing, canoeing and swimming. There is a fine expanse of sand, and the views across to Ramsey Island from the beach, particularly at sunset, are spectacular.

❸ St Justinian
This appealing but rockbound cove is named after a 6th-century Breton saint. A ruined chapel stands on the spot where he was buried, overlooking St Justinian's lifeboat station, which was used as the location for the 1990s television drama series *Lifeboat*.

❹ Ramsey Island RSPB Reserve
Boats to this superb bird sanctuary of cliffs and mountain heath depart in summer from St Justinian. Guillemots, razorbills and kittiwakes nest on 122m (400ft) precipices above isolated coves where grey seals breed, while fields grazed by sheep and deer provide a perfect habitat for birds such as lapwings.

❺ St David's
The cathedral has a superb setting in a valley by the massive and ornate ruins of Bishop's Palace (Cadw), which date mainly from the 14th century. The smallest of all cathedral cities, St David's was the birthplace of the patron saint of Wales. St David founded a monastery there during the 6th century, and the city became a place of pilgrimage in the Middle Ages. The present cathedral dates largely from the late 12th century, but incorporates later features such as the carved Renaissance ceiling in the nave.

There is an attractively sited golf course on the road to Whitesands Bay, and a new Art Gallery celebrates local history and culture.

St Non's Chapel (Cadw), south of the city, is traditionally identified as the birthplace of St David's mother, and has a healing well that still attracts visitors.

⑥ Caerfai Bay
Low tide reveals extensive sands beneath the cliffs of red, mauve and green stone. A lane from St David's leads to a clifftop with sweeping views across St Brides Bay. The climb down to the beach at Caerfai is steep. The purple sandstone used for St David's Cathedral came from nearby quarries at Caer Bwdy.

⑦ Solva
Set on a narrow, sheltered inlet that winds inland beneath steep hills, Solva has a history of sea trade, piracy and smuggling dating back to the 7th century. By the early 19th century the village had a population of 1200 and a fleet of 30 ships, and there were even scheduled crossings to America. Its last steamship was torpedoed by a U-boat in the harbour mouth in 1915. Today, pleasure craft abound.

⑧ Newgale
Two miles of sand attract surfers and swimmers to Newgale, and at high tide waves break against a shingle bank thrown up by violent storms. Brandy Brook, at the northern end of the beach, is said to mark the divide between English-speaking Pembrokeshire and the Welsh-speaking country to the north.

⑨ Nolton Haven
Remnants of a landing quay overlook a sandy cove backed by grassy slopes. Few traces remain of the coal industry that once brought prosperity to the pretty village of Nolton Haven, but tunnels from abandoned workings run out deep beneath the sea.

⑩ Druidston Haven
A pebble bank at high tide, low water reveals a mile of sand on this isolated beach. Narrow lanes and a steep climb down a cliff path ensure that the beach is seldom crowded.

⑪ Broad Haven
A wide expanse of sand has ensured the popularity of this lively resort. Shops and hotels overlook the little esplanade that runs behind the attractive beach, while natural arches and other interesting rock formations can be seen in the cliffs to the north and south.

⑫ Little Haven
Narrow lanes wind past charming old cottages, and engaging pubs overlook the quay in this pretty fishing village, where steep hills backing a small harbour have restricted development. At low tide you can walk along the shore across the sandy beaches at The Settlands to Broad Haven.

⑬ St Brides Haven
This remote sandy cove has a gentle beauty that contrasts with the wilder seascapes of the surrounding area. There are rock pools to explore and the evening tide attracts sea anglers.

The ancient Church of St Bride, with its churchyard of old stone monuments, overlooks the beach, while remains of early Christian graves can be seen in cliffs beyond the ruined limekiln on the headland.

The Gothic mansion to the west, known as St Bride's Castle, was built in 1800 by Lord Kensington, a former local MP; it is now divided into flats.

⑭ Martin's Haven
Walks across uncultivated grassland take in clifftop scenery with superb views of the coast in an area of wilderness known as the Deer Park (NT). The area, enclosed by an old stone wall which cuts off the headland from the rest of the peninsula, offers the chance to glimpse rare birds such as the chough, a member of the crow family. The deer, if there were ever any there, have long escaped.

Martin's Haven is the departure point for summer trips to the islands of Skokholm and Skomer, Martin's Haven today consists of little more than a few houses and a car park.

⑮ Skomer Island National Nature Reserve
An estimated 165,000 pairs of Manx shearwaters nest in clifftop burrows on this island, the breeding ground of almost half the world's population of these birds. Puffins, guillemots and razorbills are also common, while grey seals breed in shoreline caves and dolphins fish the tidal races. Wild flowers such as sea pinks and yellow samphires are spectacular in spring and early summer. The island is reached by boat from Martin's Haven.

The seas, seabed and shore around Skomer form a marine nature reserve, whose range of habitats supports a great number of creatures and plants, including corals, sponges, sea firs, sea slugs and dogfish.

⑯ Skokholm Island
Smaller and more remote than Skomer, Skokholm was the site of Britain's first bird observatory in 1933, and the observatory and other converted farm buildings provide accommodation for staff and visitors. Manx shearwaters, puffins and storm petrels are abundant, and the island is a resting place for many migrant species.

⓱ Marloes Sands

You can reach one of Britain's finest beaches, with golden sands and colourful, dramatic cliffs, by a 10 minute walk from the car park west of Marloes village.

Marloes Mere, to the west of the beach, was once famous for its leeches, which were gathered for sale to London doctors in the 18th century.

⓲ St Ann's Head

A lighthouse, a coastguard station and a scattering of whitewashed cottages stand isolated on this windswept headland, whose cliffs provide splendid views of Skokholm Island and Milford Haven. In 1485 Henry Tudor, having previously fled from Wales to Brittany, landed at Mill Bay and within a fortnight won the English crown at Bosworth Field.

⓳ Dale

Yachting gear and wet suits are the summer fashions in this village on a sheltered bay, which gives distant views of Milford Haven's oil refineries. The shingle and sand beach is not for bathers or surfers, but it is ideal for every other form of watersport.

To the west of the Church of St James the Great, a short path descends to Westdale Bay, an isolated, sandy cove beneath a huge Iron Age fort. Visitors should beware of strong currents and unstable cliffs.

⓴ St Ishmael's

The Norman Church of St Ishmael, tucked away in a wooded valley to the south, is the village's secret gem. From the fascinating, overgrown churchyard, a short path winds through romantically abandoned gardens to a tiny cove at Monk Haven; here low tide exposes a thin strip of sand below the pebble beach.

A rugged clifftop route continues farther on, leading to an Iron Age fort located on Little Castle Head.

㉑ Sandy Haven

The blend of subtly coloured muddy sand and abstract shapes of driftwood along a beautiful tidal creek provided the inspiration for many scenes painted by the 20th-century artist Graham Sutherland.

MARLOES SANDS

22 Milford Haven

Huge tankers berth in Milford Haven's deep-water harbour, one of Europe's biggest oil ports until the early 1980s. During a brief visit in 1802, Lord Nelson pronounced Milford Haven to be the finest natural harbour in the Northern Hemisphere. His enthusiasm may well have been encouraged by his mistress, Emma Hamilton, however, whose husband Sir William was involved in building a new town that was given the same name as the waterway it borders.

Together with Charles Greville, Hamilton developed Milford Haven as a whaling station and a naval dockyard, but the venture failed to prosper and the town faced a decline until the 1880s, when large new docks became the centre of a thriving fishing industry. In the 1960s, Milford Haven entered its third age, developing and prospering from the oil industry until the end of the oil boom in the early 1980s.

The docks have been renovated to provide a variety of entertainments and attractions for visitors. The Heritage and Maritime Museum has displays of local history, and the Waterfront Art Gallery features the work of local artists.

23 Picton Castle

For the past 500 years, the castle has been the home of the Philipps family, who transformed it from a fortress to a country house. Built late in the 13th century on the site of an earlier fortification, Picton Castle can be visited by guided tour in summer. The castle's extensive grounds include landscaped gardens and woodland walks.

A gallery behind the house is devoted to the works of Graham Sutherland, who painted many pictures of the lonely tidal creeks along the Daugleddau and its tributaries.

The Eastern Cleddau can be reached along the lane that runs south from the castle gates.

24 Landshipping Quay

It is hard to imagine the industry and hardship that once characterised life on this peaceful stretch of river, where wading birds feed off the mudflats and you can occasionally see otters. Early in the 19th century, 6000 tons of coal were loaded at Landshipping Quay each year, but mining ceased in 1844 after floods swept through a local pit, costing some 40 lives.

25 Lawrenny

Pleasure boats congregate around the moorings at Lawrenny Quay, 12 miles from the open sea. On high ground above the quay, bordering National Trust woodland, the terrace of a long-demolished country house provides a picnic site with good views.

26 Carew

The ruined shell of Carew Castle, part medieval fortress, part Elizabethan mansion, overlooks the river crossing. The castle was besieged and slighted in the Civil War, but remains a fascinating and romantic place.

Next to the bridge by the castle is an intricately decorated 4m (14ft) Celtic Cross, one of the finest early Christian monuments in Wales. Downstream, opposite one of Britain's few remaining working tidal mills, a stone causeway serves as a footbridge to the north bank of the Carew. To the south, in Carew Cheriton, the early 14th-century church of St Mary includes medieval tiles from the castle.

27 Upton Castle Gardens

Formal terraces and woodland walks lead to a tree-lined riverside path in the large grounds of this privately owned 19th-century Gothic mansion. A small medieval chapel within the grounds contains some fine carved effigies dating from the 13th to the 15th centuries.

28 Pembroke Dock

The dockyard was established in 1814 by the Admiralty with defensive Martello towers and barracks, and rows of terraced houses for workers. It was built in response to the increasingly high prices being charged by the entrepreneur Charles Greville for building warships in his dockyard at Milford Haven during the Napoleonic Wars. The Gun Tower Museum is on the dockside.

Shipbuilding ceased here in 1926, but during the Second World War the town was an important base for flying boats and the starting point for Atlantic convoys, and consequently suffered many air raids. The docks are today used by both military and commercial ships, and a vehicle ferry runs to Rosslare in the Irish Republic.

29 Pembroke

The town is dominated by its massive castle, which stands on a butt of rock surrounded on three sides by water. The castle was badly damaged during the Civil War before being captured by Cromwell's forces – the first time it had fallen during a long and bloody history. The rounded keep is almost 24m (80ft) in height and battlemented walkways link the many towers.

Beneath the Northern Hall is the Wogan Cavern, an enormous natural cave overlooking the river. The small town itself includes a pleasing hotchpotch of old buildings.

30 Angle

The peaceful, end-of-the-road village keeps its greatest treasures hidden from view. Behind St Mary's Church is a fortified tower, probably Norman, of a type common in the Scottish borders but rare in Wales. And nearby is the tiny 15th-century Seamen's Chapel, with a painted vault and stained-glass windows depicting scriptural sea scenes.

A rough track leads down from the church to an inlet of Angle Bay, where a few boats are laid up on mud and shingle, and there is a good view over the Milford Haven waterway.

About a mile to the west of the village is West Angle Bay, where a large beach of soft sand and gently rolling surf offers views of the fortifications that once protected Milford Haven. The original Elizabethan East Blockhouse totters

on the edge of a cliff at the southern extremity of the bay; its 19th-century replacement is close by. West Blockhouse can be glimpsed across the Milford Haven estuary.

The fort on Thorn Island, to the north of West Angle Bay, is now a hotel.

31 Freshwater West

High dunes, a vast expanse of flat, sandy beach and crashing surf combine to make this a spectacular bay. It is also a dangerous one, with a strong undertow on the ebb tide and low-water quicksands at the north of the beach.

Halfway along the beach, at Little Furzenip, a small thatched hut dates from the time when seaweed was brought here for storing and making into laver bread, a South Wales delicacy.

32 Castlemartin

The most conspicuous feature of this village is what appears to be a walled traffic island, but is in fact an 18th-century cattle pound. The stone enclosure now contains a small public garden. Another curiosity is the Church of St Michael and All Angels, which stands in isolation at the bottom of the hill. Its immense castellated tower may have been built as a defensible strong-point against local pirates, a tradition throughout the southwest.

An army training range occupies the southwest of the peninsula, sending the Pembrokeshire Coast Path inland through Castlemartin. The eastern side of the range is accessible most weekends, when you can walk the coast path between Elegug Stacks and St Govan's Chapel.

33 Elegug Stacks

Two great limestone pillars rear up out of the waves beside high cliffs. In the summer-breeding season guillemots arrive in great flocks, perching on the ledges and jostling for space with an array of auks, razorbills, fulmars and kittiwakes.

Just to the west, a natural rock arch, known as the Green Bridge of Wales, thrusts out from the cliffs, while the headland immediately to the east shows traces of the defensive ditches and ramparts of an Iron Age fort. When Castlemartin Range is not in use, visitors can enjoy an exhilarating walk along the dramatic cliff path east from Elegug Stacks to St Govan's Head.

34 St Govan's Chapel

A flight of steep, well-worn stone steps leads down to a tiny church squeezed into a cleft in the rocks. According to tradition, St Govan was being pursued by pirates when the rocks split open to provide a hiding place, and he stayed here preaching and praying until his death in AD 586. The present chapel, however, dates

ST GOVAN'S CHAPEL

from the 11th century. Outside is a small well, now dry, whose waters were thought to have healing powers.

Legend is also behind the naming of nearby Bell Rock. The church bell, stolen by pirates, was said to have been saved by angels, who set it in the rock; when St Govan struck the boulder, it sounded as loud as a mighty cathedral bell.

Just to the west is a great gash in the cliffs known as Huntsman's Leap; a huntsman is said to have jumped his horse over this 55m (180ft) cleft – then, on looking back, to have died of fright.

35 Stackpole Estate

The estate, parts of which are a nature reserve, is centred on a vast area of lily ponds created in the 18th century to enhance the now-demolished Stackpole Court. From Stackpole and Bosherston, tree-shaded walks at the water's edge and over footbridges enable visitors to watch the waders and waterfowl that congregate on the ponds. There is also a walk out across the dunes to sandy Broad Haven, a sheltered south-facing bay almost enclosed by a horseshoe of rocks and dunes.

Stackpole Estate is owned by the National Trust, as is the stretch of coast to Freshwater East to the northeast.

36 Stackpole Quay

The quay, now disused, was built to ship local limestone and to bring in fuel for the Stackpole Estate and the dunes and grassland to the west of the bay form part of the estate's nature reserve. A clifftop walk leads southwest past an area of grey limestone stacks and arches to the fine sandy beach of Barafundle Bay.

To the south is Stackpole Head, where several caves have collapsed into blowholes. Northeast of Stackpole Quay, the limestone cliffs give way to rich orange sandstone.

37 Freshwater East

Wide sands backed by dunes make the crescent-shaped beach popular with families. Facing east, the beach is sheltered from prevailing winds and has good road access.

38 Manorbier

The Norman castle is sternly impressive, with its solid towers and gatehouse and high curtain walls. When the traveller and writer Giraldus Cambrensis, or Gerald of Wales, was born there in 1146, the new stone castle built by his family, the powerful de Barris, was noted for its sumptuous baronial hall and living quarters. The stout ruins look out over a popular sandy beach, noted for its good surf, though bathers should beware of powerful undertows in rough weather.

On the headland south of the beach are the remains of a 5000-year-old burial chamber, known as King's Quoit, which consists of a massive capstone supported on two uprights. Farther along the coast, past a firing range on Old Castle Head, a steep flight of steps leads down to the sandy beach of Skrinkle Haven and its high rock arch striding out into the sea.

39 Tenby

In the town's narrow streets, Georgian villas with intricate iron balconies jostle with fishermen's cottages. The resort's great appeal for holidaymakers lies in its beaches, which together offer over a mile of fine sand and sheltered bathing, and in its beautiful little harbour crowded with boats.

Much of Tenby's present character comes from its development in the 19th century as a watering place by Sir William Paxton, but its origins are much older. Little remains of the Norman castle, however; most of it was destroyed by Cromwell's forces during the Civil

War. But much does survive of the 13th-century town wall, including the old west gate, now known as Five Arches.

The medieval St Mary's Church is enlivened by carved figures looking down from the nave roof, and by ornate chancel vaulting, while the town's past prosperity is reflected in the refurbished Tudor Merchant's House (NT) and in displays at the museum and art gallery, which also has a section devoted to the work of the Tenby-born artist Augustus John. Other attractions include the Silent World aquarium.

On St Catherine's Island, which you can reach on foot at low tide, is a 19th-century fortress, an outpost of the protective ring that once defended the military dockyards of Milford Haven.

40 Caldey Island

A cross with an inscription in the Celtic ogham alphabet is a reminder that the island was first inhabited by monks in the 6th century. The Benedictines arrived in the 12th century and remained on the island until the dissolution of the monasteries by Henry VIII. Surviving buildings that date from this time include the gatehouse and the Prior's Lodging.

TENBY

42 Pendine Sands

Firm, flat sands stretch for 6 miles from the holiday village of Pendine to the Taf estuary. At low tide the sea can be a mile or more away from the foreshore, while the long expanse of shallow water at high tide makes it very popular with young families. The beach was used in the 1920s in several attempts to break the land-speed record, and was the site of Parry Thomas's fatal crash in 1927.

East of Pendine is a Ministry of Defence firing range, but the sands are usually open to the public most weekends and from 5pm on weekdays.

43 Laugharne

A generous sprinkling of handsome 18th-century houses gives the neat and quiet town of Laugharne, pronounced 'Larne', an air of solid respectability. The old castle, home in the 12th century to the Welsh prince Rhys ap Gruffud, stands guard over the saltflats of the Taf estuary. Two towers are all that remain of the original structure; the rest was rebuilt as a fortified mansion in the 16th century. The castle (Cadw) is open to the public.

Laugharne is best known for its association with the writer Dylan Thomas, and it is said to have been the model for the fictional village of Llareggub in his classic work *Under Milk Wood*.

A walk northwards out of the town passes Sea View, where Thomas lived before the Second World War, and continues to the Boathouse, where he spent the last years of his life and which now contains memorabilia. Nearby is the poet's 'writing shed', with superb views over the estuary. In addition, Thomas and his wife Caitlin are buried in St Martin's churchyard, and a likeness of the poet appears on the sign outside Brown's Hotel.

44 Llansteffan

Castle ruins, with massive walls that rise above the old earthworks, date from early in the 13th century although the site was probably fortified by the Normans. The castle's gatehouse remains impressive.

The peaceful little village stands at the mouth of the Tywi, where the river's muddy banks give way to soft sands. Upriver is a sandy beach, where strong currents make bathing hazardous except at high tide.

Monastic life resumed in 1929, and the rebuilt monastery is now home to Cistercian monks.

You can visit wooded Caldey Island by boat from Tenby during summer, and can see the churches, buy the perfume and chocolate made by the monks, or simply enjoy the calm, but only male visitors may enter the monastery itself.

There are splendid views of colonies of seals and sea birds from the top of the hill that crowns the island.

41 Amroth

The little village overlooks a vast sandy beach backed by shingle and rocks, and protected by wooden groynes. Exceptionally low tides reveal the stumps of trees belonging to an ancient forest, long since drowned.

A tiny stream meandering down to the beach marks both the old county boundary between Pembrokeshire and Carmarthenshire, and the southern end of the Pembrokeshire Coast Path, which starts near Cardigan some 180 miles away.

In a secluded valley just to the north is Colby Woodland Garden (NT), where a stream cascades down a hillside through pools and ponds. In spring bluebells and daffodils cover the grounds.

> **Visitor information**
> **Milford Haven** ☎ (01646) 690866
> **Pembroke** ☎ (01646) 622388
> **Pembroke Dock** ☎ (01646) 622753
> **St David's** ☎ (01437) 720392
> **Tenby** ☎ (01834) 842402

PEMBREY TO SEVERN BRIDGES

Pushing out into the sea, the Gower peninsula was the first place in Britain to be designated an Area of Outstanding Natural Beauty, thanks to its breathtaking valleys, high cliffs and rolling sands

❶ Pembrey

The area of dunes, woodland and sandy beach between the estuaries of the Tywi and the Loughor was not always as peaceful as it is now. In 1881 works were set up at Pembrey to produce explosives, and the site eventually became a Royal Ordnance factory. The factory closed in the 1960s, and in its place is the Pembrey Country Park, offering family attractions such as a miniature railway and an adventure playground. Also in the park are an equestrian centre and a dry-skiing slope.

Paths through the park lead to 7 miles of sandy beach, and to the north are walks in Pembrey Forest and a motorsports centre.

❷ Pen-clawdd

Little creeks meander through salt marshes to the mudflats of the Loughor estuary, overlooked by the cockling village of Pen-clawdd. This is a dangerous area of cloying mud and swift river currents, but each day the cocklers go out as they have done since the 16th century. Donkeys and carts were traditionally used, but tractors are today being introduced.

❸ Whiteford Sands

A glorious sandy beach stretches south from Whiteford Point. You can reach Whiteford Burrows National Nature Reserve on foot along a track near St Madog's Church in Llanmadoc village.

❹ Broughton Burrows

Immense sand dunes heave up at the southern end of Broughton Bay, and sandy paths snake through and over the dunes to the offshore island of Burry Holms, which you can reach at low water. The island has remains of an Iron Age fort, a ruined chapel associated with the 6th-century hermit St Cenydd, and a beacon that has replaced the old lighthouse on Whiteford Point.

❺ Rhossili Bay

A magnificent crescent of flat sand, with a creamy edge of curling surf, is set against a background of imposing cliffs, though the steep climb down to the shore from Rhossili village ensures that the beach is never as crowded as some of the more easily reached beaches on the Gower. It provides good surfing conditions, and the surrounding cliffs are popular with paragliders and hang-gliders.

Heather and bracken-covered Rhossili Down (NT), rising up behind the cliffs, is an excellent area for walks.

❻ Worms Head

The line of rocks snaking out from a headland forms part of the Gower Coast National Nature Reserve, which stretches east as far as Port-Eynon. Worms Head can be reached with care during the four hours either side of low tide.

The best starting point for a walk is the National Trust visitor centre just outside Rhossili village. From there a path leads for 3 miles over the cliffs, with superb views across Rhossili Bay. The two islands at the seaward end of the head are joined by a rock arch called the Devil's Bridge, where in high winds an eerie booming noise can be heard. This is caused by air rushing through the hole.

❼ Mewslade Bay

Backed by dramatic cliffs, the secluded, sandy bay can be reached by a short walk from Pitton village. The lack of a road makes this and adjoining Fall Bay peaceful havens.

❽ Port-Eynon

The abandoned cottages of Salthouse fishing hamlet and the fortified 16th-century Salt House stand on Port-Eynon Point, whose cliff caves were inhabited in prehistoric times. You can reach one, Longhole Cave, from a path overlooking Overton Cliff. The great cleft of Culver Hole, walled up with medieval masonry, may have been a dovecote for a now-vanished castle.

St Cadoc's churchyard, in Port-Eynon village, has a memorial to three local lifeboatmen who died in 1916 trying to save the survivors from the SS *Dunvegan*, which foundered in heavy seas at Oxwich Bay.

❾ Oxwich

Standing at the western end of broad Oxwich Bay, this charming village of stone cottages and thatched roofs has a popular sandy beach offering watersports, while Oxwich National Nature Reserve, an area of dunes, marshes and woodland, provides habitats for a variety of plants, such as the carnivorous lesser bladderwort, and lizards, dragonflies and birds.

Oxwich Castle (Cadw) dates from the 14th century, but has been much altered since. Its impressive gateway is emblazoned with the crest of the Mansel family, the original owners.

❿ Threecliff Bay

Flanked by limestone cliffs, the bay is one of the most beautiful on the South Wales Coast. The name comes from the three crags that rear up above the beach, one of which has

THREECLIFF BAY, GOWER PENINSULA

been pierced by the sea to form a rock arch. Like several of the most scenic bays along the Gower peninsula, Threecliff can be reached only on foot from either Parkmill or Southgate. The motte of a medieval castle can be seen on the western side of the valley.

⑪ Southgate
The residential village is a good starting point for exploring the southern Gower. To the west there is a gentle walk along the cliffs to the ruins of 13th-century Pennard Castle, while a more rugged clifftop path leads east for 2½ miles to Pwlldu Head and a sandy cove at Pwlldu Bay.

A mile northwest of Southgate, at the village of Parkmill, is the Gower Heritage Centre, a restored water-powered corn and sawmill, dating from the 17th century, with a craft centre.

⑫ Caswell Bay
Rocky headlands shelter the sandy bay, which has good surfing. Bishop's Wood Nature Reserve is an area of grassland scrub and woodland that stretches up a valley from the coast. A car park gives access to a visitor centre and to paths round the reserve, where you may see many species of birds and butterflies.

⑬ Langland Bay
The sand that characterises Gower beaches gives way to sand and shingle at Langland, and the bay here is popular with surfers. Houses and hotels line the cliffs that back the bay.

⑭ The Mumbles
The headland pokes out in a triple hump, like a serpent's back, to the lighthouse on the point, and to the east is the immense sweep of Swansea Bay. The Mumbles town is a cheerful resort, which developed after the building of the Swansea and Mumbles Railway in 1804. The railway has gone, but the pier along which it ran remains, with its pavilions and lifeboat station.

Overlooking the town are the substantial ruins of Oystermouth Castle, built by the Normans to control the Gower peninsula. The castle was rebuilt in stone around 1280 after the original timber castle burnt down.

⑮ Swansea
Once a major industrial centre, Swansea has undergone a complete transformation in recent years. The copper smelters have gone, and the old dock area on which Swansea's prosperity was founded has become the Maritime Quarter, where a waterfront village has grown up around a marina.

The quarter includes the National Waterfront Museum landmark building, while Ty Llyn, the Dylan Thomas Centre, is the national literature centre for Wales; it holds literary readings, performances and interpretative exhibitions. Swansea is a popular seaside town, whose other attractions include sandy beaches, the city museum, a leisure centre and Plantasia, a glass pyramid with more than 5000 plants of 1000 different varieties.

About a mile to the east of Swansea is Crymlyn Bog National Nature Reserve, an unspoilt area supporting a wealth of plants, insects, and birds such as reed buntings, water rails and marsh tits.

⑯ Aberavon and Port Talbot
Established in the early 1900s, the steelworks remain a dominant feature of Port Talbot, although their operations were scaled down in the early 1980s. As the works developed, they outgrew the old dock and a new deep-water harbour was built. Other industries, notably a large chemical business, were attracted to the town. But between the chemical works to the north and the steel mills to the south an area of sand dunes was levelled to create a wide, flat beach, and along the sands the resort of Aberavon developed.

Holiday activities in Aberavon are focused on the 2 miles of beach, which is pounded by rolling surf. Seaside amusements line the promenade, and on the seafront is Afon Lido.

⑰ Margam Sands
The ruins of 12th century Margam Abbey stand away from the quiet stretch of sandy beach, which is best reached by foot from Kenfig Sands to the south. All that remains of the Norman building is the monastery nave, now a parish church.

Earlier Christian memories are evoked by the intricately carved Celtic crosses in the nearby Stones Museum, which stands just outside Margam Country Park, a large estate featuring an Iron Age hill fort, a 19th-century Gothic-style mansion house and an elegant orangery built in 1789. Other attractions in the grounds, where deer roam, include a putting green, a boating lake and a sculpture park.

⑱ Kenfig Sands
The scant remains of a castle can be seen rising out of the high dunes. The area was once occupied by a medieval town, complete with castle, church, guildhall and markets. By the 17th century the settlement had been abandoned to the rising sands, blown in from the seaward side by the wind.

The sands now form a national nature reserve noted for its orchids, butterflies and moths; its large pool, fed by springs, attracts a variety of birds, including coots and swans.

The archaeology and natural history of the area are explained at a visitor centre, from where footpaths lead through dunes to the sea.

⑲ Rest Bay
This stretch of sand is one of the best surfing beaches in South Wales, backed by wide, smooth rock ledges. Easy access and a large car park also make it very popular with holidaymakers.

⑳ Porthcawl
The long esplanade is lined with viewing galleries and kiosks and the 1932 Grand Pavilion overlook the sea in this bright, cheerful seaside resort. The town started life as a 19th-century coal port, before new docks at Barry to the southeast and Port Talbot to the north killed the trade. The slides and rides of the Coney Beach funfair stand on the old ballast tip. There are good beaches, such as the rock-fringed Sandy Bay and Trecco Bay east of the town, though swimmers should avoid the waters near the headlands, where there are dangerous currents. Newton Point is the start of an 18 mile Heritage Coast Walk south to Gileston.

㉑ Merthyr Mawr
A delightful hamlet of thatched stone-built cottages scattered along tree-shaded lanes by the banks of the River Ogmore, Merthyr Mawr lies hidden away from the sea by immense sand dunes known as the Merthyr-mawr Warren.

A narrow lane leads down through the village to Candleston Castle. This 15th-century fortified manor house is now largely ruined, but interesting details survive, such as the elaborately carved fireplace of the great hall. There are paths through the desert-like dunes to the sandy beach of Traeth yr Afon, though currents near the mouth of the Ogmore make swimming dangerous.

Just south of Merthyr Mawr are the lonely ruins of Ogmore Castle, reached by stepping stones across the river. The castle was built by the Norman invader William de Londres in the 12th century; the keep, built of massive boulders, is slightly later.

In Ewenny, a riverside village about a mile to the east, are the remains of a fortified priory founded in the 12th century, and the workshops of the Ewenny Pottery, one of Wales's oldest.

㉒ Ogmore-by-Sea
The village perches on the towering clifftops at the mouth of the Ogmore river, with wide views across the Bristol Channel entrance. A short walk from the southern edge of the town leads down to a sandy beach backed by flat rock ledges, where there are clearly marked bathing areas away from estuary currents.

㉓ Southerndown
The clifftop village of modest stone houses has developed into a popular little holiday centre. You can follow footpaths from here north towards Ogmore-by-Sea, and south to Dunraven Bay.

㉔ Dunraven Bay
Extraordinary 'candy-striped' cliffs of alternating horizontal layers of limestone and shale back the popular holiday beach of wide stone ledges and firm sand. You are advised to keep well clear of the unstable rockface, and to confine any swimming to inshore waters at high tide, clear of the strong currents that swirl around the Trwyn y Witch headland.

The Heritage Coast Walk passes Dunraven Bay, and a heritage centre explains the wildlife and history of the area, notorious for its tales of smuggling and shipwrecking.

㉕ Monknash
The coast of high crumbling cliffs and flat stones resembling a manmade pavement can be reached by a pleasant stroll from this tiny village set back from the coast. A lane meanders down to the deep, wooded valley of Cwm Nash. North of the valley are two remote and lovely beaches, Traeth Mawr and Traeth Bach, Welsh for 'big beach' and 'little beach'; they are tide traps at high water, and bathing can be dangerous.

㉖ Nash Point
A grassy headland above a small sand and shingle bay with low-water rock pools is reached by a lane from Marcross. Two lighthouses on the point, only one of which is in use, were built in the 1830s after the wreck of a passenger ship. A clifftop saunter offers splendid views across the Bristol Channel.

㉗ St Donat's Castle
What appears to be a mock-Norman fantasy castle overlooking a bay is in fact a 14th-century fortress, turned into a more comfortable residence during the Elizabethan era with the addition of an inner courtyard and great hall. The castle became neglected in the 18th century, but in 1925 the US newspaper magnate William Randolph Hearst took it over and restored it, installing such features as a magnificent dining-room ceiling rescued from a Lincolnshire church.

St Donat's Castle is now an international sixth-form college, but you can take a guided tour in late August and September. The castle shares grounds with a refurbished 14th-century tithe barn housing an art gallery and a theatre, and a public footpath leads down past the church to a small bay and a stony beach.

㉘ Llantwit Major

The ancient town of narrow crooked streets was the site of Britain's first Christian college. St David, St Gildas and, according to legend, St Patrick were all educated there. The town was founded around AD 500 as Caer Wogan. The parish church of St Illtud, to the west of the town, was founded by a Celtic scholar in the 6th century and contains a 1000-year-old font as well as examples of intricately carved crosses from the 8th and 9th centuries.

From Llantwit Major, a road leads through a wooded valley to a sand and shingle beach at Col-huw Point, where there are extensive rock pools. The Heritage Coast Walk passes along the top of wave-battered coastline of dramatic cliffs and sea caves.

㉙ Summerhouse Point

The rocky headland is a good place for bracing clifftop walks, offering excellent views over the Bristol Channel. You come to it by a short walk down an unsurfaced track, reached by a lane from Boverton village, on the eastern edge of Llantwit Major, and passing the privately owned Boverton Mill Farm.

The Seawatch Centre, housed in a former coastguard station, has displays of weather-forecasting instruments and radar.

㉚ Limpert Bay

The attractive shoreline has rock ledges descending to a sand and shingle beach and is dominated by the tall chimneys of Aberthaw power station. The bay marks the end of the Heritage Coast Walk, which starts just outside Porthcawl, 18 miles to the northwest.

㉛ Sully Bay

A small offshore island, accessible by a causeway at low tide, lies off a south-facing pebbly beach. The bay is popular with holidaymakers seeking to avoid the more crowded beaches of Barry Island, though currents that swirl in between the island and the mainland make bathing hazardous at the eastern end of the beach.

㉜ Lavernock Point

In 1897 the first radio message across the sea was received at Lavernock point, sent by Guglielmo Marconi and Post Office engineers from the island of Flat Holm in the Bristol Channel, whose lighthouse is visible in the distance.

Approached by a narrow lane near Cosmeston Lakes Country Park, the Point stands at the eastern end of the wild and inaccessible St Mary's Well Bay and its crumbling cliffs.

WAVE-BATTERED CLIFFS AND SEA CAVES
LLANTWIT MAJOR

PENARTH PIER

33 Penarth

A great sweep of promenade, with a fine pier and quirky 1930s pavilion, overlooks a shingle beach, and in the old docks area is a thriving marina. Like Barry, Penarth developed from a dock area created in the 19th century, and it too has adopted a new identity as a seaside resort. Clifftop walks north from the town to Penarth Head and south to Lavernock Point give superb views of the bay, thronged in summer with watersports enthusiasts, and across the Bristol Channel to the Somerset coast.

South of Penarth is Cosmeston Lakes Country Park, whose centrepiece is a reconstruction of a medieval village, built on its original site.

34 Cardiff

Roman legions built the first fortress on the site of what is now the Welsh capital in the 1st century AD; 1000 years later the Normans incorporated these defences into their own castle. Cardiff Castle grew and developed over the centuries, but owes its present form to the Marquess of Bute who in the 1870s, with the architect William Burges, restored the building in an extravagant mock-Gothic style.

Cardiff's prosperity was founded on the export of coal. In 1830 the Bute family obtained permission to build what was to become Bute West Dock on Cardiff Bay. As at Barry and Penarth, the decline of the coal trade has brought new developments. The barrage that lies across Cardiff Bay has created a vast freshwater lake by sealing off the estuary of the Taff and Ely rivers, and the concentration of buildings around the waterfront has rejuvenated the area. In addition to The Senedd, the home of the National Assembly for Wales, there is 'The Tube' visitor centre, Techniquest (a science discovery centre) and the Millennium Centre for the performing arts. Older buildings include the restored Norwegian Church, now an arts centre.

Near the castle are the lawns and gardens of riverside Bute Park, and to the north is the Civic Centre, whose complex of dazzling white neoclassical buildings, begun in 1897, include the splendid City Hall and the National Museum Cardiff. The museum has a large archaeological section, an industrial gallery, and a fine collection of French impressionist paintings.

On the western side of Cardiff is Llandaff Cathedral, built on a site first occupied by a religious community in the 6th century. Restored after extensive bomb damage in the Second World War, it is the home of Sir Jacob Epstein's giant sculpture *Christ in Majesty*.

35 Peterstone Wentlooge

Although the village is set half a mile from the sea, a plaque on the wall of St Peter's Church recalls the day in 1606 when flood waters rose up its walls to a height of 6ft. A walk down the path beside the churchyard reveals the measures taken to prevent a recurrence of such flooding: a chequerboard of fields divided by drainage channels. The path reaches a high sea wall that stretches right along the coast as far as Newport.

Beyond the wall is Peterstone Wentlooge Marshes nature reserve; visitors include locally rare species such as avocets and spotted crakes.

36 Newport

Prosperity came to Newport with the opening of the Monmouthshire Canal in 1796, which brought iron and coal from the valleys, and grew with the expansion of the docks in the 19th century. Parts of the docks are now being transformed into an area for leisure and the arts. A visitor centre stands beside the flight of 14 locks, which raise the canal 51m (168ft) up a watery staircase, and the Transporter Bridge, built in 1906, has been restored to carry cars and pedestrians on a platform across the River Usk.

The ruins of 13th-century Newport Castle (Cadw) can be seen in the city centre, while Newport's role in the Chartist uprising of 1839 is the subject of a display in the Museum and Art Gallery, whose other exhibits include a collection of 500 teapots.

To the southwest is 17th-century Tredegar House, set in magnificent parkland.

37 Caerleon

The most spectacular relic at the Roman legionary fortress at Caerleon (Cadw) is the amphitheatre, where gladiatorial contests took place. It was large enough to seat the fortress's entire garrison. The modern town's streets still follow the grid pattern laid down when Caerleon was Isca Silurum, home to around 6000 Roman soldiers. The old town's history is told in the Roman Legionary Museum; alongside it is the Capricorn education centre.

38 Magor

The delightful village is centred on a square of elegant houses and the fine old Church of St Mary the Virgin, known as the 'Cathedral of the Moors'. Dating from the 13th century, with 15th-century additions, it stands at the edge of Caldicot Level, an area of grassland running down to the coast. Magor Marsh Nature Reserve has been established in the last vestige of what was once all undrained farmland.

39 Caerwent

The best preserved Roman town walls in Britain can be seen in this village on the site of the old market town of Venta Silurum (Cadw) which was established in the 1st century AD. Modern roads pass through what were once chariot gateways and foundations of some of the original Roman houses, shops and forges have been found, but the most impressive building is the octagonal temple outside the walls.

40 Chepstow

Of all the great Norman castles that line the frontier between England and Wales, few can claim a more dramatic location than Chepstow Castle (Cadw), which glowers down from its clifftop perch. Begun in 1067, the castle saw its last military action in the Civil War, almost 600 years later.

Chepstow was once a port and shipbuilding centre, and its development is recalled in the Chepstow Museum. The River Wye, which flows through the town centre, is spanned by three bridges: a high-arched cast-iron span of 1814, the railway bridge of 1962 and the modern road bridge. Chepstow is also the gateway to the Wye valley, with its towering limestone cliffs.

Offa's Dyke begins near Beachley, to the southeast of the town, and a long-distance footpath follows part of its course for 177 miles to the north coast of Wales.

41 Severn Bridges

With a main span of 988m (3240ft), and towers that reach 136m (445ft) in height, the first Severn Bridge was completed in 1966. Before the bridge was built, the only way to cross the river with a vehicle was by a long road detour or by ferry. The newer bridge opened in 1996 and carries the M4.

> **Visitor information**
>
> **Barry Island** ☎ (01446) 747171
> **Caerleon** ☎ (01633) 422656
> **Cardiff** ☎ 08701 211258
> **Chepstow** ☎ (01291) 623772
> **Kilgetty** ☎ (01834) 814161
> **Llanelli** ☎ (01554) 777744
> **Newport** ☎ (01633) 842962
> **Penarth** ☎ 029 2070 8849
> **Porthcawl** ☎ (01656) 786639
> **Swansea** ☎ (01792) 468321

INDEX

Front Cover britainonview.com/Lee Pengelly (Durdle Door, Dorset) **Back Cover** Corbis/Lee Frost/ Robert Harding World Imagery (Brighton Pier, East Sussex) **1** naturepl.com/David Noton (Gewnnap Head, Land's End) **2-3** The National Trust/Joe Cornish (Strangles Beach, Cornwall) **6-7** Getty Images Ltd/Peter Adams (Southwold, Suffolk) **8-9** The National Trust/Claire Takacs (South West Coastal path near Tintagel, Cornwall) **11** Alamy Images/© Colin Palmer Photography **12-13** britainonview.com **14** Alamy Images/CJ Imagery **18** Axiom/© Chris Parker **20-21** www.lastrefuge.co.uk **23** Alamy Images/Colin Shepherd **25 T** www.bridgeman.co.uk/Fitzwilliam Museum, University of Cambridge **B** Cornish Picture Library/Paul Watts **28-29** Beachfeature.com/Sam Morgan Moore **30-31** Alamy Images/AA World Travel Library **35** Photolibrary.com/Ron Sutherland **36-37** The National Trust/David Noton **39** The National Trust/David Sellman **40** naturepl.com/Colin Seddon **43** britainonview.com/Philip Fenton **46-47** Collections/Robert Estall **48 49** ardea.com/Dae Sasitorn **51** Guy Edwards **54-55** Atmosphere Picture Library/Bob Croxford **56** Guy Edwards **58-59** Alamy Images/Shoosmith Jersey Collection **61** Atmosphere Picture Library/Bob Croxford **62-63** ardea.com **64-65** britainonview.com/David Noton **66** Frank Lane Picture Agency/Martin B Withers **69** Alamy Images/Michael Dutton **72-73** Getty Images Ltd/ Ian Sanderson (White Cliffs of Dover) **75** Lucy Griffiths Photography **76-77** britainonview.com **81** English Heritage Picture Library **84-85** britainonview.com/Dave Porter **86-87** Axiom/Chris Parker **88-89** Heritage Image Partnership/English Heritage, National Monuments Record **91** britainonview.com/David Sellman **92** Alamy Images/Headline Photo Agency **94** Alamy Images/Stephen Bond **100-101** britainonview.com/David Sellman **102-103** Frank Lane Picture Agency/Robert Canis **104-105** britainonview.com/Rod Edwards (Hunstanton, Norfolk) **107** britainonview.com **108** britainonview.com/Rod Edwards **110-111** Alamy Images/Worldwide Picture Library **115** britainonview.com/ Roz Gordon **116-117** Frank Lane Picture Agency/David Hoskings **118** Neil Holmes **120-121** Alamy Images/Tom Mackie **123** britainonview.com/Rod Edwards **124** Alamy Images/David Moore **126-127** The National Trust/Joe Cornish **130-131** britainonview.com/Marc Bedingfield **132-133** Alamy Images/Steven Allen Travel Photography (Lindisfarne Castle, Holy Island) **136-137** Alamy Images/Totolincs/Alamy **138** Construction Photography.com/Chris Henderson **141** britainonview.com/Joe Cornish **144-145** David Tarn **146-147** britainonview.com/Joe Cornish **150-151** Axiom/Ian Cumming **152** iStockphoto.com/Liz Leyden **154-155** Scottish Viewpoint/Iain Mclean (Ailsa Craig, Arran) **157** Alamy Images/Angus McComiskey **158** Getty Images Ltd/Jason Hawkes **160-161** Getty Images Ltd/Paul Harris **163** Scottish Viewpoint/John Pringle **165** Scottish Viewpoint/Colin McPherson **166** Scottish Viewpoint/John Pringle **170-171** Scottish Viewpoint **172-173** Scottish Viewpoint/Allan Coutts **176-179** Scottish Viewpoint/P Tomkins **180-181** Scottish Viewpoint/VisitScotland **184** Alamy Images/John Peter Photography **186-187** David Lyons **190-191** Alamy Images/Doug Houghton **193** Scottish Viewpoint/Richard Clarkson **199** Alamy Images/David Lyons **201** Alamy Images/DGB **202-203** britainonview.com/Joe Cornish **204-205** Getty Images Ltd/Panoramic Images **210-211** Scottish Viewpoint/Doug Houghton **213** Alamy Images/Michael Jenner **214-215** Getty Images Ltd/Macdutt Everton **216-217** Alamy Images/David Lyon **218-219** Photolibrary.com/Anthony Blake **222-223** Alamy Images/David Robertson **224-225** Alamy Images/John La Gette **227** Keith Hunter Photography **230** britainonview.com **232-233** Alamy Images/Dimitri **236-237** Alamy Images/Doug Houghton **238-239** Scottish Viewpoint/Allan Devlin **240-241** Alamy Images/David Pledger (North Pier, Blackpool) **244-245** Alamy Images/David Lyons **248-249** The National Trust/Joe Cornish **250-251** Alamy Images/Michael Sayles **252-253** ShutterStock, Inc/Ant Clausen **255** britainonview.com/Derek Croucher **259** Axiom/© Chris Parker **260-261** The National Trust/Joe Cornish **264-265** Getty Images Ltd/Jim Richardson (Whitesands Beach near St David's Head, Wales) **268-269** Jupiter Images/Steve Vidler **270-271** Alamy Images/Robert Harding Picture Library **272-273** Alamy Images/Realimage **274-275** iStockphoto.com/Maciej Noskowski **277** iStockphoto.com/John Tarrant **281** Jupiter Images/Steve Vidler **282-283** Alamy Images/Nigel Hicks **285** Alamy Images/Frank Naylor **286** Alamy Images/David Martyn Hughes **290-291** The National Trust/David Sellman **292-293** Photolibrary.com/Anthony Blake **296-297** The Photolibrary Wales/Billy Stock **299** The Photolibrary Wales/Dave Newbould **300-301** iStockphoto.com **302-303** Jupiter Images/Ed Collacott **306-307** The Photolibrary Wales/Glyn Evans **308** Alamy Images/Neil McAllister

Contributors

Editor Caroline Boucher
Art Editor Louise Turpin
Editorial Consultant Alison Ewington
Sub-editor Ali Moore
Assistant Editor Rachel Weaver
Picture Researcher Rosie Taylor
Proofreaders Barry Gage, Rosemary Wighton
Indexer Marie Lorimer
Maps European Map Graphics Limited

READER'S DIGEST GENERAL BOOKS

Editorial Director Julian Browne
Art Director Anne-Marie Bulat
Managing Editor Nina Hathway
Head of Book Development Sarah Bloxham
Picture Resource Manager Christine Hinze
Pre-press Account Manager Dean Russell
Product Production Manager Claudette Bramble
Senior Production Controller Katherine Tibbals

Origination Colour Systems Limited, London

Printed and bound in China

The Most Amazing Places on Britain's Coast is published by The Reader's Digest Association Limited, London

First edition copyright © 2008
The Reader's Digest Association Limited,
11 Westferry Circus, Canary Wharf,
London E14 4HE
www.readersdigest.co.uk

Second reprint 2009

The Most Amazing Places on Britain's Coast is based on material previously published in Reader's Digest Illustrated Guide to Britain's Coast (1996)

We are committed both to the quality of our products and the service we provide to our customers. We value your comments, so please do contact us on 08705 113366 or via our website at www.readersdigest.co.uk

If you have any comments or suggestions about the content of our books, email us at gbeditiorial@readersdigest.co.uk

Front cover Durdle Door, Dorset
Back cover Brighton Pier, East Sussex

ISBN 978 0 276 44337 4
Book Code 400-376 UP0000-4
Oracle Code 250011774H.00.24